THE SOCIAL ORGANIZATION OF LAW

Contributors

Paul Bohannan

Donald Black

William Chambliss

Elliott P. Currie

Stanley Diamond

Peter Garnsey

James L. Gibbs, Jr.

Irving Kaplan

Takeyoshi Kawashima

Friedrich Kessler

Robert H. Lowie

Stewart Macaulay

Gregory Massell

Leon Mayhew

Duane Metzger

Maureen Mileski

James C. Miller

Laura Nader

Robert Nisbet

Albert J. Reiss, Jr.

Richard D. Schwartz

Philip Selznick

THE SOCIAL
ORGANIZATION
OF LAW

Edited by

Donald Black
YALE UNIVERSITY

Maureen Mileski
UNIVERSITY OF CALIFORNIA
AT BERKELEY

SEMINAR PRESS   *New York   San Francisco   London*

A Subsidiary of Harcourt Brace Jovanovich, Publishers

SEMINAR PRESS, INC.
111 Fifth Avenue, New York, New York 10003

United Kingdom Edition published by
SEMINAR PRESS LIMITED
24/28 Oval Road, London NW1

K
376
.B4

Library of Congress Cataloging in Publication Data

Black, Donald   comp.
    The social organization of law.

    Includes bibliographies.
    CONTENTS: Selznick, P.   Sociology and natural law.—
Black, D.   The boundaries of legal sociology.—
Kawashima, T.   Dispute settlement in Japan.—[Etc.]
    1.   Sociological jurisprudence—Addresses, essays,
lectures.   I.   Mileski, Maureen, joint comp.
II.   Title.
LAW   340.1'15   72—9998
ISBN 0–12–808350–6

CONTENTS

v

PREFACE

L AW IS a social activity. It is possible to discover the principles and mechanisms of its operation and to predict when and how it comes into play in society. In this sense, it has social organization. Nevertheless, law, like art or love, is often granted an immunity, exempted from the jurisdiction of science and abandoned to the heavens. But ethereal though it may seem, law, like all behavior, is a natural phenomenon. As such it is subject to science, even if it also may be known in other ways.

This book organizes and illustrates theoretical discourse about the social nature of law. Our introduction isolates several components into which law may be divided for study; it identifies a number of social properties intimately involved with legal behavior; and it suggests various formulations which order otherwise unconnected findings and render them predictable. Always our discussion looks beyond the detailed case, beyond the single society, time, and species of legal life. But it provides nothing more than beginnings, and these are often rustic if not altogether shapeless.

The two of us have worked closely together for a number of years, and this book expresses a long-standing interest that we share: a general theory of social life free of metaphysics and independent of psychology. But Black is primarily responsible for the particular theoretical strategy outlined here; he developed it while preparing a graduate seminar in the sociology of law which he presented at Yale Law School in the fall of 1970. As a graduate student at the time, Mileski became actively involved in refining the approach, and the following year taught a similar seminar at the University of California at Berkeley. A number of doctoral dissertations influenced by the strategy, both as it applies to law and to other forms of social control, are now in the making.

ACKNOWLEDGMENTS

IN RECENT years, each of us has enjoyed a Russell Sage Fellowship in Law and Social Science at the Yale Law School. The Russell Sage Program allowed us to devote full time to the study of law, facilitating a crucial period of development for both of us. For making this possible, and for tolerating our refusal to be practical, we thank Abraham S. Goldstein, now Dean, and Stanton Wheeler, Director of the Program. Black has also benefited from an intermittent association with the Law and Modernization Program at Yale Law School, under the direction of David M. Trubek.

Others at Seminar Press have made this book possible and have improved its quality. And for many kinds of help, we thank M. P. Baumgartner.

INTRODUCTION

Donald Black
Maureen Mileski

T HIS BOOK outlines a theoretical orientation for the sociology of law. Specifically, it presents a way to approach law as a system of behavior. The great diversity of opinion about the requirements, achievements, and potential of legal sociology prevents any one book of readings from representing the field while still retaining an intellectual integrity of its own. Thus, we do not attempt to survey the many activities that today are known as legal sociology. Sociology has never enjoyed much scholarly consensus as to its proper goals and strategies, and this has been particularly apparent in the sociological study of law. In this collection of writings we ignore some of the better known works, instead drawing attention to some lesser known materials that better illustrate our theoretical orientation. In this introduction, after a review of earlier work in the field, we sketch our approach to the study of law and then comment upon the book's selections from the standpoint of this theory.

I

For our purposes, the sociology of law had its beginnings in sociology's classic era, a period that began in the late nineteenth century in Europe and continued until World War I. For historical purposes, the starting point could be placed much earlier with such work as Baron de Montesquieu's *The Spirit of the Laws* in 1748, or Sir Henry Maine's *Ancient*

Law in 1861. But it was not until the turn of the century that Emile Durkheim (1933), Max Weber (1954), and Eugen Ehrlich (1936) began a self-conscious application of sociological method to legal systems. The great ambitions of classical sociology in its approach to politics, economic life, religion, and social structure characterized the study of law as well. The method was comparative, in the sense that it ranged across societies, historical periods, and even civilizations; it also moved deftly in an inner comparison from one dimension of a legal system to the next—from the sanctioning process to legislation, from judicial reasoning to the emergence of a legal profession, and so on—always feeling for the larger patterns of which these arrangements are only so many expressions. Put another way, the classical scholars tried to develop general theories of law, with master propositions that would apply to any legal system. We should add that for them theory pertained to fact rather than value, to the "is" and not the "ought." For just a beginning, the classical work carried us quite far. Yet for years it stood unattended. When sociological interest in the law came alive again recently, this heritage had been nearly forgotten.

During its almost half-century of neglect by sociologists, however, the social character of law attracted some attention from academic lawyers and anthropologists. Among academic lawyers in the United States, two movements of thought deserve special comment: "sociological jurisprudence" and "legal realism." These movements are still in evidence in some law schools. Sociological jurisprudence, which is usually associated with the name of Roscoe Pound, attempts to inform legal policy making with an understanding of law's social environment, in hopes of thereby enhancing the efficiency of law (see Pound, 1943). Further, its goal is to develop legal policy in the interests of society as a whole, making it a version of what moral philosophers call social eudaemonism—the ethic of group happiness. Legal realism, on the other hand, is concerned less with explicit policy making and more with detached contemplation of the empirical world of law in action as it compares to the law in theory (for example, Frank, 1949; Llewellyn, 1962). Pointing to the gap between legal theory and practice, the legal realists seek to expose the myth of law's perfection and thus show its human nature. Law is what actually happens in courtrooms; it is not what we read in law books. Legal realism has failed to develop very far in the direction of either social theory or empirical research, but it has been an important rebellion against traditional legal thought, helping to make room for a more systematic behavioral approach to law.

For a sociology of law, however, legal scholarship has probably been less significant than a number of anthropological studies of the nature and place of law in tribal societies. Much of the early effort in the anthropology of law aimed to establish the mere existence of law among what Westerners often viewed as "savage" and hence "lawless" peoples. As this came to be taken for granted, the anthropological contributions reached much further. Bronislaw Malinowski (1962) was the first professional anthropologist ever to live among tribal people, having been stranded as an enemy alien in Oceania during World War I. Venturing among the people of the Trobriand Islands, he was fascinated with how similar their system of law was to our own, and he studied it by direct observation. Another major landmark in legal anthropology was a study of law among the Cheyenne Indians of North America, a collaborative work by Karl Llewellyn, a realist lawyer, and E. Adamson Hoebel, an anthropologist (1941). Equally significant was Max Gluckman's *The Judicial Process among the Barotse of Northern Rhodesia* (1955). Llewellyn and Hoebel provided the first collection of legal cases or disputes from among a tribal people, though the descriptions are based on interviews with old men and may not be entirely representative. Gluckman, by contrast, directly observed the cases on which his impressive study was based. Many other anthropological investigations of the legal process among preliterate peoples have since been made, and the literature is now rich in empirical detail, though somewhat lacking in theoretical direction and systematization.

When sociologists finally returned to the study of law in the early 1960s, their work expressed major sociological concerns of the time, notably the study of occupations and professions on the one hand, and criminology on the other. No claim was made for a theoretical mission distinctive to the study of law; in this sense, there was research on law but no sociology of law. From occupational sociology came a flurry of studies of the daily routines of lawyers including, for example, individual practitioners (Carlin, 1962), matrimonial lawyers (O'Gorman, 1963), and Wall Street lawyers (Smigel, 1964). Works also appeared on the ethics of lawyers (Carlin, 1966), their education, and their social mobility (Ladinsky, 1963). Since these studies approach the legal profession largely as sociologists would study other professionals— whether medical doctors, clergymen, teachers, or whatever—little is learned about the character of law as a system of social control. We learn what kinds of people enter law, where they receive their education, and where they take their jobs, and we learn about differences in legal practices, but the occupational approach typically does not inquire into the implications of these patterns for the behavior of law as a normative system.

Another stream in the recent study of law originates in the older and more practical criminological tradition in sociology. For years, students of crime and other forms of deviant behavior assumed that the central problem of their field was why people violate rules, and they concentrated their energies and imagination on that question. By mid-century, however, sociologists slowly began to approach the problem from the other side; they came to recognize that whether a person becomes, for example, a criminal may have as much to do with what is defined in the larger society as criminal as it has with the person's motivation to be antisocial (see, for example, Becker, 1963). They also noted that the labeling of a person as "deviant" may go far toward closing off the possibility of his return to conformity, owing to how the deviant label changes social responses to him. Sociologists had thus turned to the study of social control. Seeing the importance of the social label in the making of deviants, their attention shifted to some of the systems that apply these labels to specific individuals. Unlike the occupational approach, this was a study of normative life, a study of the regulation of human conduct.

Sociological interest in the normative aspects of law produced for the first time a large body of empirical research on legal control. Much of this research describes the routine processing of deviants by the police and the criminal courts in the United States (for example, Piliavin and Briar, 1964; Skolnick, 1966; Blumberg, 1967). Like the legal realists, these sociologists repeatedly claim that the lofty ideals of law are reflected only dimly in the everyday world. We hear that the ideal of "due process" is nudged aside by organizational demands to process people, that full-fledged trials are replaced by mass processing and backstage plea bargaining (Mileski, 1971), that "innocent until proven guilty" is a slogan, not a rule. Sociologists find cooperation in the courtroom where they expect justice to arise from adversariness (Skolnick, 1967; Blumberg, 1967), and they note bureaucratic and career pressures dominating the police where law and order with fairness are expected (Skolnick, 1966).

This recent work on law as a normative system has been historically valuable in the rebirth of legal sociology, but it has serious limitations, two of which should be emphasized here. First, because it has continually referred legal practices to legal ideals, the sociology of law has been, at its core, evaluative. It has failed to treat law as an entirely empirical phenomenon, since the legal ideals it discusses are not observable in the world of human action. Of course, people continually appeal to legal ideals in the world of action, but the interpretation of these ideals is inherently partisan. Like any values, legal ideals have no objective meaning shared by everyone. The interpretation of legal ideals takes us outside of sociology, strictly speaking, and into the realm of legal criticism and advocacy. Contemporary legal sociology thus is more like conventional legal thought than it claims. This issue is discussed in our first two selections: Selznick takes the view that sociology can provide an objective basis for legal criticism—a natural law approach—whereas Black argues that science by its nature is unable to criticize anything—a positivist approach. A second major limitation of recent legal sociology is its grounding in American law. This means that its theoretical aspirations can go no further than America and, hence, keeps the field culture bound. Rarely has theory even ventured beyond criminal justice in the United States, since research has long ignored contracts, torts, domestic law, and administrative law, to mention a few large and legitimate contenders for sociological attention. A simple way to put all of this is that legal sociology has not been building a general theory of law. It has offered little more than a history and critique of the present.

II

In this book we emphasize the comparative aspects of the sociology of law. Our aim is to thread together patterns from legal systems of different times and cultures, looking for what they share beneath superficial variation. We look for principles and mechanisms according to which they operate, hoping to understand their differences as well as their similarities. To this end, we have collected a diverse set of materials on legal behavior, most describing law in countries and periods other than our own.

In general, these selections lend themselves to a positivist conception of law. According to this conception, law is as susceptible to the scientific method as any other phenomenon. By contrast, some consider legal study a unique intellectual challenge where fact and value come together (see Selznick, Chapter 2 of this volume). In the popular mind, too, law is often seen as peculiarly difficult to understand, or even mysterious. But as a science, sociology is not intimidated by the mystique of law. From our standpoint, law is governmental social control, and nothing more pretentious (see Black, Chapter 3). Besides demystifying and objectifying law, this concept is intended to refer only to legal action, not to people's legal sentiments. Our approach does not deny the influence of these sentiments but merely bypasses them en route to truly social theory about law. Moreover, it does not claim to know what is just about justice. It is limited to the world of fact, to what is observable and identifiable by anyone.

Even when sheared of its intangibles, law remains an affair of extreme complexity. Analysis becomes easier when law is broken down into its component parts. Accordingly, we can divide law as a process of social control into three distinct components: prescription, mobilization, and disposition (Black, 1971: 1104, 1110). The prescriptions of law define its jurisdiction, the range of conduct subject to its control. They generally arise from legislation and judicial decisions, outlining boundaries for the population at large with substantive law and setting limits upon legal agents themselves with procedural law. When lawyers speak of "the law," they usually mean prescription.

The second component, mobilization, is the process by which a legal system acquires its cases (see Black, 1973). The state may gather its cases, as in narcotics or traffic control, or citizens may bring their own cases, as in breaches of contract or negligence suits. Mobilization is a relatively invisible component of law; we tend to take it for granted when it occurs, and we are none the wiser when it does not. Without mobilization of the law, however, potential legal cases are left to nonlegal means of control, or they are neglected entirely. It should be clear that without mobilization the prescriptions of law are but hollow commands.

The third component of law is disposition. This is the official handling of the case, which may involve settlement of a dispute, routine application of a sanction, or dismissal. Dispositions often take place in a court or courtlike setting, but they also occur in more informal settings such as encounters with police or other government officials. At his disposition the common man meets justice face to face. His sentence is pronounced, fine levied, damages awarded or demanded, alimony set. Some of our selections describe aspects of legal disposition, others the prescription or mobilization of law.

Indeed, the selections might have been arranged according to these three components of law. Instead, the book is divided into six parts corresponding to major aspects of social life, each of which relates to all three. After the programmatic statements by Selznick and Black, to which we return at the close of this introduction, these sections highlight several dimensions of social life: social control other than law, social stratification, social morphology, collective action, culture, and legal organization. Each combines with law to define a topic of theoretical interest. How does the behavior of law vary with each of these configurations? What do these social properties predict about law? Each aspect of our scheme is highly general and problematic in social systems of all kinds. By studying how these features of society intertwine with law, law's social existence becomes understandable.

III

Law and Other Social Control

In the first of our topics, we examine the role of law in the machinery of social control at large. How does law combine with social control found in bureaucratic organizations, the family, church, and informal groupings such as neighborhoods, friendship circles, and ethnic enclaves? Does it supplement these other control systems? Can it substitute for them? Much empirical evidence is now available to support at least one relevant theoretical claim: law comes into play when other forms of social control are weak or unavailable.

Kawashima discusses this pattern in modern Japan, where traditional authority norms still have a strong hold on interpersonal relations. He finds that disputes are unlikely to be brought to court except where these norms are flimsy or absent, as in conflicts between people living in different communities or in the tense relations between usurers and debtors. As the modernization of Japan proceeds, moreover, traditional authority weakens. Kawashima observes that with this weakening of traditional authority the mobilization of law will become ever more frequent in Japan. But tradition is only one among many alternatives to law. Macaulay, in our second example, shows how informal pressures inherent in continuing business relationships can take the place of law in resolving contract disputes. We may infer that in more distant business relationships, such as those involving only a single transaction, the mobilization of law would be more likely. Nader and Metzger, with findings from two Mexican villages, describe how family authority may have a similar impact. In one village the head of the family has relatively uncontested authority; there family disputes rarely go to court. By contrast, such disputes are more often litigated in the village where no one has enough authority to settle them within the family itself. Finally, Schwartz investigates two small communities—*kibbutzim* in Israel— and finds that a lawlike system of control arises only in the community where there are comparatively few informal mechanisms of social control. Schwartz makes much of the psychological aspects of law, but we can also understand his findings with a social theory. In sum, law seems to pour into gaps where social life offers no other form of control. Examples could easily be multiplied, but here we only point to uniformities in scattered empirical materials as a starting place for theory.

Law and Social Stratification

At least since Karl Marx, the relation of law to social stratification has been prominent in social theory. Marx saw law as an offshoot of the underlying class struggle. Social stratification, however, extends beyond social classes to include the sexes, racial and ethnic groups, generations, business, religious, and governmental organizations, and even nation-states with differential status and power. Unfortunately, most research treats only the stratification of social classes; but law reflects and reinforces many kinds of social stratification, and this process should be studied in all of its manifestations.

A historical study by Chambliss traces the changing uses of vagrancy law as a weapon for regulating the laboring classes in the interests of economic elites. As feudalism declined in England, large landowners used an anti-vagrancy statute in their efforts to combat the social forces draining their cheap labor supplies. With the emergence of a commercial class, social elites found new but analogous uses for vagrancy law. Garnsey, too, details legal mechanisms operating to the advantage of elites, in this case the aristocracy of ancient Rome. He shows how the formal standing of people before the law varied with their social positions, both in their ability to mobilize the law and in the dispositions they met. In modern society, social elites sometimes enjoy more subtle legal advantages. For instance, Kessler explains how standard form contracts, such as insurance policies, leases, and transportation tickets, benefit the large and powerful organizations for which these transactions are routine, whereas ordinary citizens have no choice but to accept them. In the Anglo-American system, contract law ignores differences in bargaining power, though they profoundly affect the character of economic exchange. The law assumes that people freely choose the contracts they make, and yet the common man often has no choice when his basic needs are at stake. Law's relation to social ranking becomes more complicated when we consider the findings of Mayhew and Reiss. They show that the upper and lower strata in the United States use the law in different patterns; this cannot be explained with differing opportunities alone, however, since they lead different lives and do not have the same legal needs. Even so, their findings describe another way that the legal process is geared largely to serve the requirements of the upper strata.

Law and Social Morphology

Viewing social stratification as the vertical dimension of social life, we might consider social morphology the horizontal dimension. It includes the size and density of population, the communications structure, technology, and other mechanisms binding people into integrated systems; it also includes the networks and links between individuals and groups, specifying whether their relationships are broad and have multiple functions or narrow with only one specialized function. Although the concept of social morphology is not widely used today, it has a history going back as far as Durkheim in the late nineteenth century. In fact, in *The Division of Labor* (1933), his first evolutionary study, Durkheim explained the emergence of modern legal systems as an outcome of increasing population density and social differentiation.

It is not coincidence that the selections in this section are the work of anthropologists, since other social scientists have largely neglected law's morphological context. Nader, in her comparison of Lebanese and Mexican villages, presents evidence that dispute settlement through law is workable only if there is a social linkage of some kind, however remote, between the disputants. She found no local law bridging the disparate social worlds of the Lebanese village, whereas law was strong and vibrant in the Mexican village with its crosslinked membership. In other words, law does not seem to arise to settle disputes where the parties are not somehow interdependent. It is therefore predictable that at present international disputes often are resolved without law. But the settlement of a dispute has implications beyond the immediate dispute itself; it also prescribes conduct for an entire citizenry. From his study of the Chagga of East Africa, Kaplan concludes that such factors as population size, social differentiation, and communications technology, as well as features of social stratification, may profoundly affect the impact of law courts in modernizing nations. Legal actions radiate into a network of social relations, and how this network is woven together determines the speed and distance of law's movements. However strong the social base underlying a dispute-settlement process might be, then, other aspects of social morphology may undermine law's penetration into the larger society.

Law and Collective Action

A social system is engaged in collective action when it is wrested away from its loosely integrated everyday activities and draws together to engage in a corporate project. Warfare is a prime example of collective action, but it may also involve less dramatic activities such as annual harvesting or a religious festival. A society does not always return to its earlier state after a period of collective activity. Aspects of planned modernization in new nations, for example, may be seen as collective action, and in some respects this process is irreversible. Totalitarian and other government-sponsored movements display collective action, and so does a small community in the face of natural calamity or civil strife.

The problem of law and collective action brings together a variety of research findings, though no tradition of systematic inquiry has been established in this area. There is ample evidence that under conditions of collective action the intensity of law increases along all three fronts—prescription, mobilization, and disposition. The scale of collective action may range from the corporate behavior of a whole nation-state or set of nation-states on the one hand to that of a small group, neighborhood, or village on the other. It may embrace a day, a year, a decade, or an epoch. Whatever its scale or duration, however, collective action seems to make legal activity more likely and more intrusive.

Massell details the Soviets' attempt to pry loose the traditional bonds of an Islamic society in order to bring it within the communist movement. He uncovers points of resilience in traditional custom that blocked these legal efforts, suggesting that in some cases law alone is not enough to catapult a community into collective action. In our second selection, Nisbet describes the destruction of kinship authority, *patria potestas*, in ancient Rome as the government began building an empire. He reasons that family authority was assaulted because it was in competition with a polity organizing for near-permanent warfare. In the third selection, Lowie surveys the political life of American Indians, noting a cyclical fluctuation between collective action and decentralization. During such activities as warfare or the buffalo hunt, a lawlike order emerged, but once again dissolved during periods of quiescence. In sum, when aggregates of people strain to become single actors law, too, is likely to come to life. In these times law may face a struggle for power, only to wither and disappear when the collective mission is won or forgotten.

Law and Culture

Legal scholars have long speculated about the subject of law and culture. This may be the broadest topic covered in our scheme, and yet, perhaps because it is so broad, it has stimulated little empirical research. If we define culture as the symbolic sphere of social life, this topic includes the relation of law to belief systems, such as ideology, science, and religion, and to other normative systems, such as values, custom, and morality.

Legal philosophers and policy-makers sometimes ask about the proper relation of law and culture. Should the law be used mainly to enforce custom? Should it ever conflict with custom? In the sociology of law, by contrast, we ignore what the law and custom relationship should be, asking instead what it is in fact.

In the first reading, Bohannan advances the view that law reinforces the norms of major social institutions such as the family, religion, and economic life. He calls this "double institutionalization." Nevertheless, Bohannan recognizes that his conception of the law–custom relationship is inadequate where there is more than one culture, as in colonial societies, or where there is more than one center of power, as in international relations and so-called "stateless" societies. In the second selection, Diamond takes issue with Bohannan's view, arguing that law, far from buttressing custom, weakens and even "cannibalizes" custom. Diamond draws particular attention to the repressive process by which governments have gained sovereignty over populations in Africa. It seems that there is truth in both views and that neither Bohannan nor Diamond has recognized sufficiently how intricate the relationship between law and culture can be.

Legal Organization

Our final section features the social arrangement of the legal process itself. Legal processes vary in many ways, such as in their decision-making roles, their degree of specialization, and in the dispute-settlement mechanisms they use. We inquire into the social basis of these arrangements and their implications for social control. Our readings examine legal organization in comparative perspective, revealing important differences across disposition and mobilization systems, as well as findings on the broader process of legal evolution.

Drawing on his observations of the Kpelle of Liberia, Gibbs distinguishes between two forms of dispute settlement: therapeutic and coercive. Therapeutic dispute settlement is a conciliatory process in which an effort is made to restore relationships torn by conflict. Dispositions of this kind are especially common in tribal societies, where most social ties are intimate and permanent. On the other hand, coercive dispute settlement is adversarial, pitting one party against the other, declaring a winner and a loser, and thus is likely to harden the conflict and destroy any future relationship between the parties. Such adversarial dispositions are most frequent where disputants are strangers to each other in an impersonal context; this type of disposition is characteristic of modern courts of law. In the second selection, Currie compares witchcraft prosecutions in England with those on the European continent and finds strikingly different systems of mobilization. On the Continent, government officials often prosecuted wealthy and influential people as witches, confiscating property and money as they advanced their own careers. In England, however, witch cases were brought to the government by ordinary citizens who did not materially gain from the enterprise. This placed a different class of persons under suspicion as witches, namely, those who were seen as peculiar or bothersome in the community and who, as a rule, had little in the way of wealth and status.

Last, with findings from 51 societies, Schwartz and Miller investigate the process of legal differentiation. They find that clusters of legal roles emerge as the larger society becomes more complex, whereas the most simple societies have no such roles at all. They add that their data conflict with Durkheim's evolutionary theory of law. In his *Division of Labor* (1933), Durkheim argues that in the movement from primitive to modern society, legal sanctions change from predominantly repressive to predominantly restitutive in nature, a distinction corresponding roughly to a movement from criminal to civil law. Schwartz and Miller reason that since policelike roles emerge late on their evolutionary scale, repressive law, too, must be late. But Durkheim was interested less in agents of disposition than in the form and style of disposition. He claimed that in primitive societies moral feeling is strong and severe, and deviant behavior outrages the community as a whole. By examining only legal roles, then, Schwartz and Miller may interpret Durkheim a bit narrowly. The police may arrive late in social evolution, but law as a whole may nevertheless grow less repressive in the long term. Primitive societies, however, appear far less punitive than Durkheim imagined. The evolution of law seems to follow more than a single unbending path.

The readings begin with essays by Selznick and Black, each presenting a unique starting place for the sociological study of law. Selznick suggests that law, like friendship or love, has an ideal nature not entirely grounded in concrete institutions. Though neither tangible nor observable, this aspect of law nonetheless plays an important role in legal development. Selznick emphasizes that legal life gravitates toward its own ideals as it evolves over time. Man creates society, and its advance involves an increasingly finer tuning of the legal instruments he designs—instruments now only roughly fashioned and sometimes even in conflict with man's aspirations. Selznick contends that we can build a model of objective morality, that with a pragmatic science the difference between fact and value blurs. Legality is a value by which the law actually operates; as appeals are made to it, legality becomes increasingly specific and secure and increasingly harmonious with human nature. Ultimately we can objectively assess whether law has fulfilled its own promise.

Black's view, by contrast, is that legal sociology has suffered from its involvement with legal ideals. He argues that only concrete legal institutions can be studied sociologically, and that whether they are true to their own ideals is a question beyond the reach of science. Under the heading of "legal-effectiveness research," Black addresses a wide range of work comparing legal reality to legal ideals. It is often impossible to define legal ideals objectively, since ideals such as "legality" and "due process" are by their nature ambiguous and open to various interpretations. These ideals form a retreating horizon, subject to continual negotiation and redefinition, and are far too elusive for a scientific model. Black asserts that strategies like Selznick's natural law approach lend themselves easily to misuse, since the investigator may unwittingly mistake his own values for those of society and advance as a scientific conclusion what is in fact a political evaluation. Even when legal practice is measured against a seemingly unambiguous standard, such as an explicit legal doctrine, the scientific significance is unclear. Such work is at best applied sociology, but even its practical significance is unclear as well. Nearly all legal practice arguably departs from legal theory to some extent, so the "policy implications" of a single study cannot be obvious. With these reservations, among others, Black advocates a radically positivist approach to law, understanding law as observable behavior alone and seeking a general theory of its relation to other aspects of social life. Consistent with Black's views, this book articulates one alternative to natural law. It offers a pure sociology of law.

REFERENCES

Becker, H. S.
  1963   *Outsiders: Studies in the sociology of deviance.* New York: Free Press.
Black, D.
  1971   The social organization of arrest. *Stanford Law Review* **23** (June): 1087–1111.
  1973   The mobilization of law. *Journal of Legal Studies* **2** (January): 125–149.
Blumberg, A.
  1967   The practice of law as a confidence game: Organizational cooptation of a profession. *Law and Society Review* **1** (June): 15–39.
Carlin, J. E.
  1962   *Lawyers on their own: A study of individual practitioners in Chicago.* New Brunswick: Rutgers Univ. Press.
  1966   *Lawyers' ethics.* New York: Russell Sage Foundation.
Durkheim, E.
  1933   *The division of labor in society.* New York: Free Press. (Orig. pub. 1893.)
Ehrlich, E.
  1936   *Fundamental principles of the sociology of law.* Cambridge: Harvard Univ. Press. (Orig. pub. 1913.)
Frank, J.
  1949   *Courts on trial.* Princeton: Princeton Univ. Press.
Gluckman, M.
  1955   *The judicial process among the Barotse of Northern Rhodesia.* Manchester, England: Manchester Univ. Press.
Ladinsky, J.
  1963   Careers of lawyers, law practice, and legal institutions. *American Sociological Review* **38** (1963): 47–53.
Llewellyn. K. N.
  1962   *Jurisprudence: Realism in theory and practice.* Chicago: Univ. of Chicago Press.
Llewellyn, K. N., and E. A. Hoebel
  1941   *The Cheyenne way: Conflict and case law in primitive jurisprudence.* Norman: Univ. of Oklahoma Press.
Malinowski, B.
  1962   *Crime and custom in savage society.* Paterson: Littlefield, Adams. (Orig. pub. 1926.)
Mileski, M.
  1971   Courtroom encounters: An observation study of a lower criminal court. *Law and Society Review* **5** (May): 473–538.
O'Gorman, H. J.
  1963   *Lawyers and matrimonial cases.* New York: Free Press.
Piliavin, I., and S. Briar
  1964   Police encounters with juveniles. *American Journal of Sociology* **70** (September): 206–214.
Pound, R.
  1943   A survey of social interests. *Harvard Law Review* **57** (1943): 1–39.

Skolnick, J. H.
  1966   *Justice without trial: Law enforcement in democratic society.* New York: Wiley.
  1967   Social control in the adversary system. *Journal of Conflict Resolution* **11** (March): 52–70.
Smigel, E. O.
  1964   *The Wall Street lawyer.* New York: Free Press.
Weber, M.
  1954   *Law in economy and society.* Cambridge: Harvard Univ. Press. (Orig. pub. 1922.)

Part I

DEPARTURE

SOCIOLOGY AND NATURAL LAW*

Philip Selznick

AMONG MODERN sociologists, the reputation of natural law is not high. The phrase conjures up a world of absolutisms, of theological fiat, of fuzzy, unoperational "mystical" ideas, of thinking uninformed by history and by the variety of human situations. This is sad, because sociology should have a ready affinity for the philosophy of natural law. Both are anti-formalist in spirit. Each looks beyond what is given and immediate to what is latent and inchoate; each is committed to the study of "nature" as yielding something more permanent and more universal than the transitory judgments of the hour or the epoch.

One of the chief writers on the sociology of law, Eugen Ehrlich (1936), made a cardinal point of questing for law, not in formal institutions alone, but in the "inner order" of human associations, in the natural settings and adaptive outcomes of group life. "At the present as well as at any other time," Ehrlich wrote, "the center of gravity of legal development lies not in legislation, nor in juristic science, nor in judicial decision, but in society itself" (p. xiv).[1] This is not in itself a natural law viewpoint. It does, however, reflect the general emphasis in sociology that education, politics, religion, and other social activities, are found outside of the specialized institutions established to deal with them. Sociology has located these phenomena "in

---

*Author's note: For a revised formulation, distinguishing the *concept* of law, which embraces legal ideals, from a weaker *definition* of law, see Selznick, (1969: 4–11).

[1] In his Foreword, Ehrlich offers this as a one sentence summary of his book.

Reprinted from "Sociology and Natural Law" by Philip Selznick, *Natural Law Forum*, Vol. 6 (1961); pp. 84–108. This is a slightly revised version of the original paper.

society," that is, in more informal and spontaneous groupings and processes. A corollary view, not usually made explicit, is that sociologists, in looking beyond formal arrangements, are identifying something closer to a "natural" order.

Most sociologists today, addressing themselves to the legal order, would still agree with Ehrlich that "the center of gravity of legal development" lies in altered ways of life and in the changing organization of society. They would argue, however, that it is bootless and sterile to call every kind of order "law" and that the study of legal development, including probable future changes in law, entails no commitment to a theory of justice. There would be a fairly ready acceptance of the distinction between law as commonly understood and the *sources* of law as the whole range of influences on legal development and stability. In this way, they would hope to avoid seemingly endless terminological discussions and vexing philosophical issues.

There is much that is appealing and wholesome in this way of thinking. It does indeed apply to broad areas in the study of law and society. But in some very important respects it is a superficial and profoundly mistaken view. In this essay I shall attempt to state why I think this is so and why I believe that a modern version of natural law philosophy is needed for a proper understanding of the law as well as for the fulfillment of sociology's promise. I speak here of natural law as a legal philosophy and not as a general system of ethics.

In approaching this task, I accept two basic commitments. First is a commitment to naturalism. My approach purports to be in all respects consistent with the spirit and logic of scientific inquiry. I offer only the caveat that it is John Dewey's philosophical pragmatism, and not a narrower positivism, which frames my view of naturalism. A second commitment is to a demanding concept of natural law. We are speaking of something more than a name for the sources of law, or for the moral foundations of law. Natural law is more than "the law that ought to be." If it is to mean anything significant, natural law must be itself legally efficacious, in some sense legally authoritative.

First I shall consider two obstacles to natural law thinking in sociology —the separation of fact and value and the doctrine of moral relativism. Then I shall analyze the meaning of legality and of positive law, finally turning to some attributes of natural law as they bear on sociological inquiry.

I.   MASTER IDEALS IN SOCIOLOGY

The main drift of contemporary sociology has been toward positivism, especially toward an ever-greater emphasis on empirical observation and techniques of measurement. A striving for objectivity, for clarity of thought, and for scientific respectability has produced a strong feeling against speculative inquiry and especially against moral philosophy. At least, these ancient preoccupations are thought to have no place in modern sociology, whatever other value they might have as literature. This movement of thought has much to commend it. At the same time, just because it is a "movement," it harbors many illusions and often serves to close minds rather than to open them. It is a procedural canon of inquiry that the study of fact must be assiduously protected from contamination by the value preference of the observer. From this methodological requirement has been derived a quasi-metaphysical dogma, namely, that fact and value belong to alien spheres.

It is easy to understand why this separation of fact and value should arise. Surely one of the first necessities of education is to impress upon unsophisticated minds the necessity of distinguishing what the world is really like from what they would like it to be. As educators, we certainly have the obligation to lead the student toward realistic understandings. This very often requires that harsh truths be faced and that old habits of thought, so largely influenced by private needs and wishes, be set aside. Furthermore, the advance of science seems to require that we respect the autonomy of nature and recognize that there are structures in being and forces at work whose existence depends not at all on human awareness or contrivance. For these and similar reasons it makes good sense to segregate preference from observation and to stress the logical distinction between normative statements and fact statements.

But the needs of the unsophisticated cannot forever dominate the minds of scholars and teachers. Education also means unlearning, if need be, the easy and reassuring formulae of our intellectual youth. So it must be with the separation of fact and value. It is not that this principle lacks all merit but that too much is claimed for it. We must limit those claims if social science is to deal effectively with some of the most important dimensions of social life.

The entire issue of fact and value is too large to be set forth here, but I shall try to contribute to the discussion, and at the same time advance the argument of this paper, by analyzing briefly one area in which a significant intersection of fact and value occurs. I have in mind those phenomena in the social world whose very nature encompasses the realization of values.

Social scientists are not troubled by the idea of a "norm" or standard of behavior. A great deal of anthropological and sociological writing is devoted to the description and analysis of norms and systems of norms. That a cultural prescription exists, that it changes, that it is related to other prescriptions in determinate ways—these matters of fact can be handled by the social scientist quite blandly, without an uneasy conscience. From the standpoint of the observer, norms are factual data and that is that.

But suppose we are interested in the following: friendship, scholarship, statesmanship, love, fatherhood, citizenship, consensus, reason, public opinion, culture (in its common sense and value-laden meaning), democracy. These and a great many other similar phenomena are "normative systems," in a special and "strong" sense of that term. I have in mind more than a set of related norms. A democracy is a normative system in that much complex behavior, as well as many specific norms, is governed by a master ideal. Behavior, feeling, thought, and organization are all bound together by a commitment to the realization of democratic values. It is impossible to understand any of these phenomena without also understanding what ideal states are to be approximated. In addition we must understand what forces are produced within the system, and what pressures exerted on it which inhibit or facilitate fulfilling the ideal.[2]

In a normative system, the relation between the master ideal and discrete norms may be quite complex. For example, it might be concluded that under certain circumstances maximizing the number of people who vote, irrespective of competence or interest, would undermine rather than further the democratic ideal. This is one reason for stressing the difference between a normative system and a set of related norms. A normative system is a living reality, a cluster of problem-solving individuals and groups, and its elements are subject to change as new circumstances and new opportunities alter the relation between the system and its master ideal. Put another way, the norms applicable to friendship or democracy are derived, not directly from the master ideal, but also from knowledge of what men and institutions are like. Only thus can we know what specific norms are required to fulfill the ideal.

The study of friendship cannot long avoid an evaluation of the extent to which particular social bonds approximate the ideal. Nor can it properly escape specifying the elements of friendship—what modes of response and obligation are called for by the ideal. None of this is inconsistent with detachment on the part of the observer. The observer need not have any personal commitment to the value in question, at least at the time and in the circumstances at hand. He may assess, quite objectively and impersonally, such connections and discrepancies as may exist between the ideal and its fulfillment.

Though this may be true, there is an odd reluctance on the part of social scientists to deal with normative systems. The disposition is to reduce such phenomena to arrangements that can be studied without assessment by the investigator, even when that assessment would entail nothing more than applying a culturally defined standard as to how far an implicit ideal has been realized. Thus, in the name of objectivity and rigor, the idea of friendship is left largely unanalyzed, and sociometric studies of reciprocal choice

[2] Compare the criticism of Max Weber in Strauss (1953: 49 ff).

or differential association become the major line of inquiry. These measures, of course, say little about the quality of the relationship, not so much because they are incapable of doing so as because the studies do not begin with the normative perspective that would be appropriate. Similarly, the study of public opinion, where it is not mere polling, looks for stable patterns of response and for underlying attitudes and values, without much concern for public opinion as a normative idea. Again, social scientists have been much happier with the word "culture" since they have been able to strip it of normative significance and to bar the view that the idea of culture has something to do with excellence.

There is another side to this story, however. In theory, as opposed to the main trend of empirical research, some recognition of normative systems does exist. There is not much of a theory of friendship, or of love, in social science, but we do have the concept of the "primary relation," of which love and friendship are characteristic illustrations. What is a primary relation? It is a social bond marked by the free and spontaneous interaction of whole persons, as distinguished from the constrained and guarded arm's length contact of individuals who commit only a part of themselves to the social situation. In the primary relation, there is deep and extensive communication; individuals enter this experience as a way of directly attaining personal security and well-being, not as a means to other ends. This rough and elliptical statement is very close to what most sociologists would accept. Yet clearly it states an ideal only incompletely realized in the actual experience of living persons.

This illustration permits us to clarify the role of assessment in the observation and analysis of normative systems. The normative concept or model tells us what are the attributes of a primary relation. Only with this in mind can we properly classify our observations or identify the significant forces at work. To formulate the ideal primary relation is part of what theory is about in social psychology. This formulation, to be sure, will avoid the language of morality. It will specify social and psychological states, such as the quality of communication. Still, the intellectual function of the model is to provide a framework for diagnosis, including standards against which to assess the experience being studied. The small nuclear family is largely based on primary relations, but where communication between generations is weakened, and where authority requires impersonal judgment and discipline, the fulfillment of the primary-relations ideal is limited.

Whatever the assessment, it is always *from the standpoint of the normative system being studied.* The student of a normative system need not have any personal commitment to the desirability of that system. We may all agree that primary relations are a good thing, and the values they realize "genuine" values, but it is precisely the role of the social scientists to avoid the moralistic fallacy that primary relations are always a good thing. Where impersonality and objectivity are needed, the intimacy and commitment associated with primary relations may well be inappropriate. A different ideal, that of "official" behavior, may be called for. This ideal, too, is a demanding one and it is likely to be fulfilled in practice only partially. The investigator, in making his assessments from the standpoint of some purportedly operating normative system, can be quite detached about whether that system's ideals should be striven for in the circumstances. Indeed, the social scientist should be able to say whether the context is appropriate for the institution and support of a particular normative system. It might well be concluded that in the circumstances the attempt to create a friendship, to sustain a university, or to establish a democracy could only result in a distortion of the ideals these phenomena embody.

These remarks about detachment are made without prejudice to the view that certain ideals may be elements of an objective moral order. Whatever we may think of the appropriateness of friendship or love in a *given* context, we may still conclude that the values inherent in primary relations are of vital importance to man's well-being, and sometimes to his survival. This is only to say that he must find them somewhere, not that they are always appropriate. It may also be argued that no normative system is possible, or at least viable, unless it contains some ideals that all men can recognize as having a general moral validity. This position has much merit, but it is not necessary to the argument I am developing here.

Another illustration of support in sociological theory for the relevance of normative systems is the concept of "public opinion." Again, the trend of empirical research is to neutralize the term, to reduce it to the mere distribution of attitudes in a population. But conceptually a "public" is usually distinguished from a "crowd" or "mass" in that the behavior of a public, including the formation of public opinion, has a greater rational component and a greater self-consciousness. The member of a public acts rationally, usually in his own immediate self-interest, but also potentially in the light of a larger sense of public interest. The formation of public opinion involves rational debate and is not merely the result of suggestibility or emotional rapport.

Clearly this view of public opinion presumes a normatively oriented system of organization and interaction. Given such a concept, which specifies standards, we can critically analyze opinion-making, not out of our own subjective preferences, but on the basis of a theory stating the conditions under which public opinion as a distinctive phenomenon is created. It follows that the state of opinion we actually observe will only approximate the theoretical ideal.

Concepts that specify ideal states are familiar enough in social science, and elsewhere as well. Any typology must designate, at least implicitly, a "pure" or "ideal" state with which purported instances of the type may be compared. The term "model" suggests a similar logic. However, not all types or models are normative; they do not necessarily have to do with the realization of values. When the realization of values is involved, social scientists seem to lose their zest for model building. This probably has much to do with anxieties provoked by the epistemological dogma that values are "subjective."

The study of normative systems is one way of bridging the gap between fact and value. At the same time, the objectivity and detachment of the investigator can remain unsullied. The great gain is that we can more readily perceive latent values in the world of fact. This we do when we recognize, for example, that fatherhood, sexuality, leadership, and many other phenomena have a natural potential for "envaluation." Biological parenthood is readily transferred into a relationship guided by ideals. This occurs, not because of arbitrary social convention, but because the satisfactions associated with parenthood—satisfactions which are biologically functional—are not fully realized unless a guiding ideal emerges. The same holds true for the dialectic of sex and satisfaction. On a different plane, but according to the same logic, if leadership is to be effective and satisfying, it must go beyond simple domination to encompass a sense of responsibility.

This perception of latent values in behavior and organization is no mere sop to the moralizer. It enriches the thought and refines the observations of the student of society. Taken seriously, it may also serve to clear up some difficulties in contemporary sociological theory. Thus much attention is devoted these days to "functionalism." This is the view that items of behavior and of social structure should be examined for the work they do in sustaining or undermining some going concern or system. What is apparently or manifestly propaganda may be interpreted as latently a way of contributing to group cohesion by keeping members busy; a mode of punishment sustains the common conscience; selective recruitment of administrative personnel undermines an established policy or bolsters a shaky elite. Functional analysis is most familiar in the study of personality where a great many items of perception and behavior become meaningful only when their contribution to the maintenance of personal adjustment, including neurotic adjustment, is understood.

In all such interpretations, a system must be posited, whether it be at the level of personality or of group structure. The system is known insofar as a theory can be elaborated stating what the system "needs" to sustain itself. These needs are sometimes called "functional requisites." But here a persistent difficulty arises. There is a strong and understandable tendency to identify what is required for the maintenance of a system with what is required for the *bare survival* of a group or individual. The very term "survival" suggests that what is at stake is the biological extinction of the individual or the complete dissolution of the group. In fact, however, systems may decay despite the continuity of individual or group life. If a man extricates himself from neurotic dependence on another person, then a system has changed. If an organization maintains its personnel and budget, and even its formal identity, but transforms its effective goals, capabilities, commitments, and role in the community, then too a system has changed. To be sure, *some* systems are indispensable if life is to exist at all; but other systems are required if a certain *kind* of life is to survive. And it is fair to say that in social science the most important analyses have to do not with the bare continuity of life but with certain kinds and levels of organization.

A great many such systems are normative in the sense that their organization and development are governed by certain master ideals. A familiar and widespread illustration is the governing ideal of rationality in economic and administrative systems. In normative systems, it should be noted, terms like "maintenance" and "survival" are relevant but not adequate. They do not prepare us for observing, when it occurs, the evolutionary development of the system toward increased realization of its implicit ideals.

Sociology has studied normative systems, and even the self-realization of systems, for a long time (as witness the monumental work of Max Weber on the unfolding of rationality in modern institutions), but we have not thought through the implications of this intellectual concern. When we do, it will be a matter of course to recognize that a system may be known precisely by its distinctive competence or excellence, as well as by its special inner strains and vulnerabilities.

I have offered these remarks with malice prepense. They are meant to suggest that sociological inquiry has ample warrant for the study of law as a normative order. And this is the first, indispensable step toward a rapprochement between sociology and natural law.

II.   RELATIVISM AND HUMAN NATURE

A second barrier to the acceptance of natural law among social scientists is the widespread commitment to moral relativism. But whatever else it may or may not be, the natural law philosophy is not relativist. At least, it is committed to the view that universal characteristics of man, and concomitant principles of justice, are discoverable. It does not necessarily hold that such generalizations are *known*, only that they are *knowable*.

What should a reading of modern sociology, and related subjects, tell us on this issue? Here we must remember the polemical context within which sociology developed. We must also keep in mind the moral impulses, and the high-minded educational aspirations, that have guided writing and teaching in this field. Sociology was nurtured by the revolt against an atomist, individualist image of man and the corollary view of society as the product of human will, albeit an imperfect will. Society was the dependent variable, created by beings endowed *ab initio* with mind and self. Sociological theory countered by stressing the *creative* role of society, especially in making possible just those attributes of self-awareness, reason, and symbolic imagination that are distinctively human. This approach proved seminal indeed, and a great deal of very valuable work, in many special areas, has resulted from it. At the same time, it lent powerful support to the notion that there really is no such thing as "human nature," that, in familiar accents, man may have a history, but not a nature.

The moral and educational aims of sociologists, social psychologists, and anthropologists helped relativism considerably. These social scientists accepted a liberalizing mission, and many pursued this mission with admirable zeal. They sought more tolerance, more sympathetic understanding, a deeper sense of human community. This breadth of vision and generosity of spirit was to be gained by stressing the fateful dependency of man on his social environment. If we realize that what men can achieve and what they strive for, what they respect and what they fear, are deeply and decisively affected by the conditions under which they grow up, then surely sympathetic understanding will be encouraged. If we recognize the great diversity of cultures, with what variety and ingenuity communities have solved the problems of survival and designed valued ways of life, then our parochial views will be modified and the richness of human experience appreciated. Above all, the easy tendency to treat our own ways as natural and to see them as stemming from "human nature" will be rejected. This understanding would contribute to freedom and enlightenment. It would yield benign doctrines encouraging the transformation of social conditions in order to correct moral ills, shifting the locus of responsibility from the individual to organized society.

A critical scrutiny of this intellectual movement suggests, however, that radical conclusions regarding human nature and moral relativism are neither well grounded in theory nor truly supported by the empirical evidence. In particular, the argument from cultural diversity is at best inconclusive. To be sure, the diversity of cultures is impressive. It is especially impressive to undergraduates and is a very valuable antidote for any tendency to guffaw at strange practices and call other people "gooks." No doubt, many older efforts to identify essential traits of human nature, for example that men are naturally acquisitive or pugnacious, have been discredited. But if older generalizations have been wrong, new and more sophisticated ones may yet be valid.

That there is unity in this diversity—what some anthropologists have called the "psychic unity of mankind"—is often acknowledged. This acknowledgment comes easily if we are speaking of drives, such as hunger or sex, and potentialities, such as the capacity to learn and use language. But there are other features of man's psychic unity (not much studied, to be sure) more directly relevant to what is universal in social organization and pervasive in human values. I have in mind such motivating forces as the search for respect, including self-respect, for affection, and for surcease of anxiety; such potentialities as the union of sex and love, the enlargement of social insight and understanding, reason, and esthetic creativity. That man has morally relevant needs, weaknesses, and potentialities is supported, not contradicted, by the anthropological evidence. Moreover, if there are many different ways in which self-respect can be won, it does not follow that a study of those ways would not reveal certain common attributes. Human dignity, and the conditions for sustaining it, would be a proper subject for sustained inquiry. But there has been little interest in it.

There is an odd paradox in the teachings of cultural relativism. The very impulse which moves these teachings presumes that there is a morally relevant common humanity. *The whole point of the doctrine has been to encourage respect for others as human.* The underlying assumption is that all men need and deserve respect despite their diverse ways of life. What is this if not a theory of human nature? Moreover, the doctrine assumes that there are general principles for showing respect effectively, despite the fact that for each culture there may be variations in detail. The paradox is that a moral impulse, a bid for humility and sympathetic understanding, has become an obstacle to moral judgment. But that need not be so. A more careful consideration of the conclusions regarding man's nature implicit in the doctrine of cultural relativism, and derivable from comparative studies, can remove the paradox and free inquiry from some formidable roadblocks.

I conclude that the findings of modern social science do not refute the view that generalizations about human nature are possible, despite the effects of social environment and the diversity of cultures. Nothing we know today precludes an effort to define "ends proper to man's nature" and to discover objective standards of moral judgment. This does not mean that proper ends and objective standards are knowable apart from scientific inquiry. It does mean that psychic health and well-being are, in principle, amenable to definition; and that the conditions weakening or supporting psychic health can be discovered scientifically. It also means that all such conclusions are subject to revision as our work proceeds.

Whether we are able now to say what human nature consists of, is not important. We are not completely at a loss, but any current formulation would still be very crude. The essential point is that *we must avoid any dogma that blocks inquiry*. Relativism is pernicious when it insists, on woefully inadequate theoretical and empirical grounds, that the study of human nature is a chimera, a foolish fancy. To say we "know" there is no sure thing, and that there is no use looking for it, is to abandon the self-corrective method of science. It is also to ignore much evidence regarding the psychic unity of mankind.

III. POSITIVE LAW AND THE LEGAL ORDER

Most definitions of law—and they are not really so various as is sometimes suggested—remind us that we are dealing with a normative system and a master ideal, in the sense discussed above. Aquinas is perhaps more explicit, calling law "an ordinance of reason for the common good, made and promulgated by him who has care of the community." But even the efforts of Gray and Holmes to avoid a normative definition surely fail when they emphasize "the rules which the courts, that is, the judicial organs of that body, lay down for the determination of legal rights and duties" or, in the Holmesian formula "the prophecies of what the courts will do in fact, and nothing more pretentious, are what I mean by the law." For the meaning of "court" or "judicial organ" is plentifully supplied with normative connotations, such as the idea of being duly constituted, independent rather than servile, and offering grounded decisions.

In framing a general concept of law it is indeed difficult to avoid terms that suggest normative standards. This is so because the phenomenon itself is defined by—it does not exist apart from—values to be realized. The name for these values is "legality." Sometimes this is spoken of as "the rule of law" or, simply "the legal order." Legality is a complex ideal embracing standards for assessing and criticizing decisions that purport to be legal, whether made by a legislature or a court, whether elaborating a rule or applying it to specific cases.

The essential element in legality, or the rule of law, is the governance of official power by rational principles of civic order. Official action, even at the highest levels of authority, is enmeshed in and restrained by a web of accepted general rules. Where this ideal exists, no power is immune from criticism nor completely free to follow its own bent, however well intentioned it may be. Legality imposes an objective environment of constraint, of tests to be met, of standards to be observed, and, not less important, of ideals to be fulfilled.

This concept of legality is broad enough, but it is not so broad as the idea of justice. Justice extends beyond the legal order as such. It may have to do with the distribution of wealth, the allocation of responsibility for private harms, the definition of crimes or parental rights. Such issues may be decided politically, and law may be used to implement whatever decision is made. But the decision is not a peculiarly legal one, and many alternative arrangements are possible within the framework of the rule of law. How far government should intervene to direct social and economic life is a question of political prudence, in the light of justice, but how the government behaves if it does exercise broader controls or enter new spheres of life quickly raises questions of legality.

The ideal of legality has to do with the way rules are made and with how they are applied, but for the most part it does not prescribe the content of legal rules and doctrines. The vast majority of rules, including judge-made rules, spell out policy choices, choices not uniquely determined by the requirements of legality. Whether contracts must be supported by consideration; whether a defendant in an accident case should be spared liability because of the plaintiff's contributory negligence; whether minors should be relieved of legal consequences that might otherwise apply to their actions —these and a host of other issues treated in the common law are basically matters of general public policy. For practical purposes, and especially because they arise in the course of controversies to be adjudicated, a great many of these policy matters are decided by the courts in the absence of, or as a supplement to, legislative determination. In making these decisions, and in devising substantive rules, the courts are concerned with dimensions of justice that go beyond the ideal of legality. Legality is a part of justice, but only a part. It is indeed the special province of jurists, but it is not their only concern. On the other hand, when they act outside the province where the ideal of legality is at issue, the courts share with other agencies of government the responsibility for doing justice. It is not legality alone which determines what the rule should be or how the case should be decided. That depends also on the nature of the subject matter and on the claims and interests at stake. Whether the outcome is just or unjust depends on more than legality.

However, there are times when the ideal of legality does determine the content of a legal rule or doctrine. This occurs when the purpose of the rules is precisely to implement that ideal, the most obvious illustration being the elaboration of procedural rules of pleading and evidence. In addition, principles of statutory interpretation, including much of constitutional law, directly serve the aim of creating and sustaining the "legal state." Some of these rules are "merely" procedural in the sense that they are arbitrary conveniences, chosen because some device was necessary, for which some other procedure might readily be substituted. Others are vital to just those substantial rights which the ideal of legality is meant to protect. These include all that we term civil rights, the rights of members of a polity to act as full citizens and to be free of oppressive and arbitrary official power.

Again, it is not the aim of this ideal to protect the individual against all power, but only against the misuse of power by those whose actions have the color of authority. Of course, in our society we may have to extend our notions of who it is that acts "officially."

Perhaps the most difficult area governed by the ideal of legality is the process of judicial reasoning itself. Fundamentally, of course, this is part of the law of procedure, but it has a special obscurity as well as a special significance. The crucial problem here is to justify *as legal* the exercise of judicial creativity. That there is and must be creativity, whatever the name we give to it, is no longer seriously disputed. The question remains, however, whether there is something beyond the bare authority of the court, or reliance on a vague "sense of justice," to support the idea that judge-made policy has the stamp of legality.

One approach to this problem gives special weight to the legal tradition, to the received body of concepts, principles, doctrines, and rules. By working with theses preexistent legal materials, the law is in some weak sense "discovered," at the same time that creativity is permitted. Using familiar concepts establishes a link with the past and tends to create (though it does not guarantee) a smooth, gradual transition from one accepted policy to another. In this way legal craftsmanship, defined by its familiarity with the limits and potentialities of a certain body of materials and certain modes of decision, can ease social change by extending the mantle of legitimacy. A new policy, if it can be blanketed into contract doctrine or fitted into the law of torts, can have a peculiarly "legal" quality simply because of the ideas with which it is associated. It seems fair to say that this peculiar function of the law is weakening because it has become less attractive to the legal profession. This is so in part because of the modern interest in avoiding arcane language, in making policy objectives explicit, and in criticizing conventional legal categories. One may wonder, however, whether enough attention has been given to the role of legal concepts in defining an implicit delegation of power to the courts. This might be thought of as a working arrangement by which society allows the courts to make policy within areas marked out by the received body of legal ideas. It is assumed that these ideas are bounded, not limitless; the legal reasoning and judicial behavior contain some built-in restraints; and there is no contrary action by a legislature.

Another approach is to emphasize, not the "artificial reason" of the law, but the role of natural reason in the ideal of legality. Among the attributes of legality is a commitment to the search for truth, to consistency of thought, and to logical analysis of evidence as relevant, of classifications as inclusive, of analogies as persuasive. In this sense, there is no special legal reasoning; there is only the universal logic of rational assessment and scientific inquiry.

The ideals of science and of legality are not the same, but they do overlap. Judicial conclusions gain in *legal* authority as they are based on good reasoning, including sound knowledge of human personality, human groups, human institutions.

The *meaning* of law includes the ideal of legality. That ideal, even though not yet completely clarified or specified, is the source of critical judgment concerning constituent parts of the legal order, especially particular rules and decisions. When a part of the law fails to meet the standards set by that ideal, it is to that extent wanting in legality. It does not necessarily cease to be law, however. It may be inferior law and yet properly command the respect and obligation of all who are committed to the legal order as a whole. At the same time, a mature legal system will develop ways of spreading the ideals of legality and of expunging offending elements.

The subtlety and scope of legal ideas, and the variety of legal materials, should give pause to any effort to define law within some simple formula. The attempt to find such a formula often leads to a disregard for more elusive parts of the law and excessive attention to specific rules. But even a cursory look at the law will remind us that a great deal more is included than rules. Legal ideas, variously and unclearly labeled "concepts," "doctrines," and "principles," have a vital place in authoritative decision. "Detrimental reliance," "attractive nuisance," "reasonable doubt," "exhaustion of remedies," "agency," and "interstate commerce" are among the many familiar concepts which purport to grasp some truth and provide a foundation for the elaboration of specific rules. In addition, of course, there are even more general ideas or principles stating, for example, the necessary conditions of "ordered liberty" or that guilt is individual rather than collective. It would be pointless to speak of these as merely a "source" of law; they are too closely woven into the fabric of legal thought and have too direct a role in decision-making.

Variety in law is manifest in other ways, too. We may speak, for example, of variety in function: Law is called upon to organize public enterprises; to establish enforceable moral standards; to mediate differences while maintaining going concerns; to arrange contractual or marital divorces; to make public grants; to investigate; to regulate some private associations; to destroy others. These and other functions have yet to be adequately classified or systematically studied. It seems obvious that such study is a precondition for formulating a valid theory of law.

There are also well-known qualitative differences in the authority of legal pronouncements. If opinions are divided; if there is manifest confusion of concepts, monitored by legal scholarship; if rules or concepts are based on received tradition alone; if a particular rule is inconsistent with the general principles of a particular branch of law—then the authority of opinion or judgment is weakened. If all laws are authoritative, some are more authoritative than others.

These considerations support Lon Fuller's view (1958) that the legal order has an implicit or internal morality, a morality defined by distinctive ideals and purposes. To say this, of course, is not to end inquiry but virtually to begin it. We must learn to distinguish more sharply between "bad law" that is merely bad public policy and law that is bad because it violates or incompletely realizes the ideals of legality. And we must attain a better understanding of how public purpose affects legal principle, as when we recognize that society binds itself especially tightly in the administration of criminal justice, generally requiring evidence of intent and barring retroactive legislation.

If the legal order includes a set of standards, an internal basis for criticism and reconstruction, then an essential foundation is laid for a viable theory of justice. In his sympathetic treatment of the natural law position, Morris Cohen (1953) was almost right in arguing that we must be able to appeal from the law that is to the law that ought to be, from positive law to principles of justice. But he did not quite see that at least some principles of justice are ingredients of the ideal of legality and are therefore part of "the law that is." In many cases, we appeal from specific rules or concepts in the law to other concepts and to more general principles that are also part of the law. This is sometimes put as an appeal from "laws" to "the law,"[3] and there is merit in that approach. But it has the disadvantage of suggesting that "the law" is something disembodied and unspecifiable, when in fact all we mean is that general principles of legality are counterposed to more specific legal materials. Both belong to a normative system whose' "existence" embraces principles of criticism and potentialities for evolution.

With this approach in mind, we can give to positive law its proper place and meaning. "Positive law" refers to those public obligations *that have been defined by* duly constituted authorities. This is not the whole of law, and it may be bad law. Law is "positive" when a particular conclusion has been reached by some authorized body—a conclusion expressed as an unambiguous rule or as a judgment duly rendered. This definition differs from the suggestion made by Holmes that law is what the courts *will* do, assuming that he meant to define positive law. I am emphasizing what the courts *have done*, because what they will do may depend on the whole body of legal materials.

Positive law is the product of legal problem solving. The legal order has

[3]See Pound (1959: 106, 107): "Law in the sense we are considering is made up of precepts, technique, and ideals: A body of *authoritative* precepts, developed and applied by an *authoritative* technique in the light or on the background of *authoritative* traditional ideals" (emphasis supplied).

the job of producing positive law as society's best effort to regulate conduct and settle disputes. What is done may be only imperfectly guided by legal principles, perhaps because those principles themselves are inadequate, but it remains law for the time being. As such, it has a claim on obedience. Positive law invokes a suspension of personal preference and judgment with regard to the *specific issue*. To suspend judgment, of course, is not necessarily to fail to have a judgment, but someone else's judgment is taken as an authoritative guide to behavior. Suspension in this sense is rightfully invoked because obedience to positive law is essential to the survival and integrity of the system as a whole. For the system to function, it is necessary that only specially appointed individuals may disregard a positive law, by changing or reinterpreting it, or by modifying its effect in a particular case when other rules can be brought to bear.

Obedience to positive law, irrespective of private judgment, is not an abandonment of reason. On the contrary, as has been well understood for a long time, it is a natural outcome of reasoned assent to the system as a whole. It in no way precludes criticism or testing of positive law, including the assertion that it is void and without effect. But criticism, testing, and change proceed within the broader framework of the legal order, appealing to its own ideals and purposes when they are relevant. Of special importance is the duty of legal officers, including private counsel, to respond critically to the positive law.

Plainly, positive law includes an arbitrary element. For him who must obey it, it is to some extent brute fact and brute command. But this arbitrary element, while necessary and inevitable, is repugnant to the ideal of legality. Therefore the proper aim of the legal order, and the special contribution of legal scholarship, is *progressively to reduce the degree of arbitrariness in the positive law*. This rule is comparable to that in science where the aim is to reduce the degree of empiricism, that is, the number of theoretically ungrounded factual generalizations within the corpus of scientific knowledge.

If reducing the degree of arbitrariness is accepted as the central task of jurisprudence, a long step is taken toward natural law philosophy. For whatever its variations, or its special errors, the concept of natural law has survived, and flourished periodically, precisely because of the need to minimize the role of arbitrary will in the legal order. The basic aim of this philosophy is to ground law in reason. The question then is, What shall we understand as the meaning of "reason"? I shall take it to mean what John Dewey meant by "intelligence" and, following his basic teachings, suggest that scientific inquiry, including inquiry about proper ends and values, is the road to a science of justice or natural law.

IV. NATURAL LAW

As a doctrine or perspective, the chief tenet of natural law is that arbitrary will is not legally final. It holds that an appeal to principle's of legality and justice is always available. This appeal assumes that every legal order, to the extent that it is one, has an implicit constitution. Thus understood, natural law is more than a "method." It is that surely, because it offers a rule, a guide to inquiry. But it also has content in that it looks to the ultimate formulation of principles stating the conditions of just governance. Science also combines method and content. Even when we emphasize method, there are conclusions to be drawn about the requirements of science as an intellectual enterprise. Similarly, liberalism and conservatism are methods of political thought and action, but they presume some general truths about man and society.

Method and content come together when the conclusions of natural law inquiry become *principles of criticism* to be applied to existing positive law. These conclusions are not more sacrosanct or eternal than any scientific generalization. On the other hand, a conclusion subject to correction is not necessarily precarious. It may be firmly grounded in theory and effectively supported by evidence. Therefore it does not lack the authority of reason as a guide to human action.

By its very name, "natural law" connotes a concern for drawing conclusions about nature. In other words, natural law *presumes inquiry*. And this entails a commitment to the ideals and canons of responsible thought. This does not mean, of course, that legal rules or doctrines are the same as scientific generalizations. The latter are "laws" in a quite different sense. Legal norms or principles are "natural law" to the extent that they are *based upon* scientific generalizations, *grounded in* warranted assertions about men, about groups, about the effects of law itself.

To put the matter this way may seem all too innocent. Among those who seek to improve legal doctrine and the administration of justice, few would question the importance of having more knowledge about how people behave in legal settings. Studies of deterrence and criminal law, of jury behavior, of arbitration, and of legally relevant changes in industrial organization, would all be welcome. Such studies are safe enough when they do not address themselves to the basic ideals of legality and therefore to the constitution of the legal order. In principle, however, there is no reason why the most general concepts of law—equality, reasonableness, fairness, and the like—should not be as subject to criticism, on the basis of scientific investigation, as are narrower legal concerns. When that occurs all innocence is lost and the quest for law is uneasily resumed.

Whatever the scope of our concern, natural law inquiry *presumes a set of ideals or values*. Most broadly, this is the welfare of man in society; law is examined for its potential contribution to that welfare. A more specific objective of natural law inquiry is to study the structure of the legal order as a normative system and to discover how the system can be brought closer to its own inherent ideals. Thus law is tested in two ways: first, against conclusions regarding the needs of man, including his need for a functioning society; second, against tested generalizations as to the requirements of a legal order. To some extent, the latter really includes the former, because among the requirements of a legal order is the capacity to serve human well-being by protecting and facilitating at least some vital aspects of social life.

On one vital point it seems wise to limit our intellectual commitments. It is not necessary for natural law supporters to prove or maintain that man *qua* man has any inherent duties, including the duty to live at all or to choose the good and avoid evil. This may be so on other grounds, but it is not essential to the natural law perspective. To be sure, the duties of man as father or as citizen are subject to social and legal definition, but that is a mere limited assertion. Moreover, I should like to shift the emphasis. From the standpoint of natural law, *the duty lies in the legal order*. If there is to be a legal order, it must serve the proper ends of man. It must not debase him or corrupt him. It must not deprive him of what is essential to the dignity and status of a human being. Whether or not any particular human being accepts a commitment to life, or to the good life, the law has no such freedom. It exists, on any theory, precisely to insure that at least the minimum conditions for the protection of life are established. The master ideals of justice and legality broaden that commitment considerably. But broad or narrow, it is the *system* that has the commitment.

As I have suggested earlier, there is nothing strange about this viewpoint to the sociologist acquainted with "functional" analysis. Functionalism, in stating "the requirements of a going concern," must identify what is essential to the system it is studying and then work out what is needed to sustain it at some specified level of activity or achievement. The level specified is not necessarily an arbitrary preference; it is at least partly set by the theory of what "is" a nuclear family or a trade union or an industrial society. To study a type of society is to learn what its distinctive structure is and what it is capable of, as well as what forces are generated within it tending to break it down or transform it. At no point in that analysis is it necessary to show that all participants desire the system or have a duty to uphold it. But if the system is to be maintained, then certain requirements taking account of natural processes must be met.

Thus far I have argued:

a. Natural law presumes scientific inquiry;
b. Natural law presumes an end in view, a master ideal which guides inquiry;
c. Natural law searches for and incorporates enduring truths regarding the morally relevant nature of man, e.g., his need for self-respect;
d. Natural law searches for and incorporates enduring truths regarding the morally relevant nature of society, e.g., the distribution and use of social power;
e. Natural law searches for and incorporates enduring truths regarding the nature and requirements of a legal order.

It is obvious that the authority of natural law and its development must depend on progress in the social sciences. Where social knowledge is weak, as in the formulation of theoretically well-grounded and empirically tested generalizations about universal psychic or political phenomena, natural law must also be limited in its authority. Just because this is so, the natural law school has the right and the obligation to criticize social science and help make it more fruitful and more sophisticated.

One response to the difficulty of discovering general truths about man and society is to emphasize the "flexibility" or "variable content" of natural law. (This may also be a defensive reaction to the criticism of natural law philosophy as absolutist and dogmatic.) There is an important insight here, but it must be placed in proper perspective. It is true that natural law *presumes changing legal norms*, but this does not require abandoning the quest for universals or the assertion of them when they are warranted. A grasp of this point is essential if the relation between sociology and natural law is to be rightly understood.

Why does natural law presume changing norms? The reason is that its basic commitment is to a governing ideal, not to a specific set of injunctions. This ideal is to be realized in history and not outside of it. But history makes its own demands. Even when we know the meaning of legality we must still work out the relation between general principles and the changing structure of society. New circumstances do not necessarily alter principles, but they may and do require that new rules of law be formulated and old ones changed.

In a system governed by a master ideal, many specific norms, for a time part of that system, may be expendable. The test is whether they contribute to the realization of the ideal. Many norms evolve or are devised to take account of quite specific circumstances; and when those circumstances change, the norm may lose its value for the system. Thus the governing ideal of the system may be administrative rationality, but specific norms will vary depending on the purpose of the enterprise and upon its stage of development. For example, the norm of decentralization does not always serve the end of administrative rationality. Yet that end continues to have a vital influence on the selection of appropriate norms.

There are two valid interpretations of the idea that natural law has a changing content.

(1) As inquiry proceeds, it is always possible that basic premises about legality, including underlying assumptions regarding human nature and social life, will be revised.

(2) As society changes, new rules and doctrines are needed in order to give effect to natural law principles by adapting them to new demands, new circumstances, new opportunities.

These perspectives demand that we detach natural law from illusions of eternal stability. They also require us to reject the notion that natural law must be a directly applicable code or it is nothing. A set of principles is not a code, any more than the principle of the conservation of energy is specific physical theory. Natural law provides the authoritative material for devising codes and for criticizing them, in precisely the same way as constitutional principles affect legislation and judge-made rules.

It may be helpful to illustrate briefly the dialectic of continuity and change in natural law. At the same time, we can see something of the relevance of sociological inquiry. Let us consider the idea of "fiduciary responsibility." This is a legal concept containing the implicit principle that where power is exercised under the color of benefit to another, then the one who holds power must comport himself in ways consistent with the fiduciary basis of his authority.[4] A fiduciary cannot treat his beneficiary as if he were merely his obligee in a contractual arrangement. He owes duties of loyalty and good faith appropriate to the status assumed. Different fiduciary relations call for different duties, but they have some attributes in common.

After much more analysis and testing, the general principle stated here may emerge as part of the corpus of natural law. It is based both on ideals of justice and on empirical theories regarding the temptations that beset men under certain conditions. These conclusions are subject to inquiry and to correction as may be necessary. But even as the principle remains, there is still the problem of giving it effect by embodying it in specific rules and doctrines.

Traditionally, the principle of fiduciary responsibility has been applied primarily in the law of property. In effect, a "trustee" is a kind of fiduciary who holds title to property and has a legal obligation to keep or use that property for someone else's benefit. There are fairly elaborate rules, and

---

[4] This statement does not necessarily include all the obligations, or embrace all the relations, that may be included in the legal concept of fiduciary duty.

associated concepts and doctrines, stating how various kinds of trusts may be created and specifying the powers and responsibilities of trustees. This application of the broader principle reflects, of course, the needs of economic and social life in a particular historical epoch, as for pooling of investment funds, for the protection of family interests, of the interests of minors, and of those for the benefit of whom a public trust may be created. Social needs have joined with concepts of fairness to determine what specific rights will be protected, what norms embodied in positive law, and what legal ideas accepted to guide and justify the formulation of new rules. At the same time, legal development is constrained by a more or less conscious awareness of the limitations of positive law as an instrument of social control.

There are good reasons why at any given time the general principle of fiduciary responsibility is not universally or automatically applied wherever fiduciary authority exists. The situations to which it could be applied might not be sufficiently important to justify the social cost of exercising formal control; such control might be ineffective because the resources and techniques of the law are inadequate; there might be other values, such as the autonomy of group life, which overweigh the need for justice based upon this principle. Yet the principle remains latent in the law and can be applied when needed as part of authoritative legal materials.

New historical developments, especially the rise of large bureaucratic enterprises, may well give the principle of fiduciary responsibility a fuller role in the law. The principle has already been applied for some time in regulating the conduct of corporation directors. The director is not technically a trustee, but that he is in some sense a fiduciary is not seriously questioned. Difficulties arise as to whether the fiduciary relation extends from the director to the corporation as an institution, to the stockholders, or perhaps to other classes of beneficiaries, including creditors, employees, customers, and the general public. Some voices are heard to say that all of these interests partake of the *beneficium*, though it is hard to formulate workable norms of responsibility to so heterogeneous a constituency. The important point is, however, that the principle of fiduciary responsibility is no longer clearly tied to a definite *res* or property interest, as that is understood in the law of trusts. The responsibility of the corporate director is more diffuse, both as to subject matter and as to beneficiary.

Some steps have been taken to apply the principle of fiduciary responsibility to trade union leaders (Cox, 1960: 827–829). It is becoming increasingly clear that at least the trade union "international" has been evolving in a bureaucratic direction, with self-perpetuating leaders and with an essentially passive membership which "buys" a service with its dues. This is not the whole truth, of course, but it is sufficiently true to justify the development of new legal safeguards against overreaching and potentially tyrannical union directorates. The sociological truth is that the modern large trade union, like the modern large corporation, cannot be adequately controlled by internal democratic processes. This is so because of a fundamental change in social organization and not because leaders are venal or members morally debilitated. The nature of membership has been profoundly altered. The trade union member does not see the need for effective participation beyond the payment of dues to support the power of the organization and the professional services of the union staff. To be sure, this change is probably not as radical as the shift in the meaning of shareholding, but the direction is the same.

The outcome is that members or owners of large enterprises, abdicating effective control, are in need of outside support for the protection of their interests. Such support can come by invoking the principle of fiduciary responsibility. This will not necessarily be effective in the courts, or in legislation, depending on whether the application of it in these circumstances can meet other demands, including consistency with related legal rules and with the effective administration of justice. But the natural law principle can be a starting point for legal craftsmanship.

The application of such a principle often depends on what may be called "institutional assessment." I have in mind the study of a complex enterprise, or type of enterprise, such as a school, church, political party, business firm, or government agency. The aim of institutional assessment is to determine what goals or objectives can be attributed to the enterprise, the capabilities it has, the strategies it lives by, its characteristic weaknesses, the distinctive significance it has for the life of the member, and what its probable line of evolution may be. Institutional assessment is one of the great practical and theoretical aims of social science, to which the sociology of large-scale organizations can make very important contributions. The development of this line of inquiry is still very primitive, but the needs of the legal order may require us to do the best we can with the intellectual tools now available. This is just what is being done in current discussions of the responsibilities of corporation directors and trade union leaders.

As a legal approach to the creation of responsible leadership, the fiduciary principle may have a "competitor." This is the concept of private government. In the assessment of modern industrial institutions, one conclusion taking shape today is that large, stable business enterprises and trade unions are performing significant governmental functions (see Eels, 1960: Chapter 3; compare Wolin, 1960: Chapter 10).[5] If this is more than a vaguely suggestive idea, the question is raised whether general principles of just governance should be applied to the exercise of authority in industry. Should

[5] Also see the writings of A. A. Berle and Peter Drucker.

the concepts and norms of "due process" be carried over? This would not necessarily depend on a doctrine of implied delegation of powers from the "official" government to the "private" government. It might mean simply that wherever the functions of governance are exercised there should be corresponding restraints on the exercise of authority. If such a view is ultimately clarified and adopted, the principle of fiduciary responsibility may drop out as a direct source of guidance. It is arguable, however, that the fiduciary principle underlies the responsibility of governors and therefore would still make its contribution to the legal result.

A general theory of responsibility and authority would be part of natural law. The theory rests on both logic and experience, on the clarification of meanings as well as on propositions about anxiety, aspiration, and group structure. Insofar as its elements withstand the test of inquiry, the theory remains a permanent part of the legal order. But how and where principles of responsible authority are applied depends on social needs and opportunities, as well as on circumstances that determine whether a particular rule will have the desired effect.

The significance of historical opportunity may merit a special word. When we consider the problems of large organization, it is tempting to take the view that the growth of private power has created vast new possibilities of oppression, and to make this the ground for seeking the extension of legal protection. I doubt that this accords with reality, and I think it reflects a mistaken view of legal development. Our problem is not so much the resistance of oppression as it is the fulfillment of opportunities. This is not to say that oppression is absent, or that new forms of it have not developed. But far more important is the fact that we now have opportunities not available before to build the ethic of legality into large segments of the economic order. Extending the ideals of due process to private associations might at any time have been a worthy objective. But the development of an inner order within bureaucratic enterprises brings that objective into close accord with a naturally evolving social reality. Legal ideals cannot always be completely realized, principles of justice cannot always be effectively applied, but they remain as living potentialities, awaiting the appearance of historical developments that will permit their application.

A legal principle, including a principle of natural law, belongs to an intricate, interdependent whole. It is not applied mechanically, in isolation from other legal materials. For this reason, among others, *natural law is applied with caution*. This is not an unfamiliar idea, as students of judicial review well know. Natural law, like constitutional interpretation, presumes a conservative posture. Excesses of logical extrapolation, overconfidence in the power and authority of an abstract idea, will thereby be minimized. This means also that the effects of a change in rule or doctrine on the legal system as a whole, or on some especially integrated parts of it, will be weighed.

The principle of caution recognizes a rebuttable presumption in favor of positive law. This is so for two reasons. First, it helps sustain the authority of the machinery for making positive law, and this is necessary to the integrity and effectiveness of the entire legal order. Second, the presumption recognizes that the funded experience of the political community has a special merit, although not absolute merit. Positive law is always partly a reflection of arbitrary will and naked power politics, but it also registers the problem-solving experience of the community. Above all, it can be a vehicle for the emergence of rational consensus. Therefore positive law makes its own vital contribution to the development of natural law. As a road to natural law, the evolution of positive law has a special claim to respect, because it is a kind of funded experience and because it can bring with it an added dimension of legal authority. This is a corollary of the statement made earlier about "reducing the degree of arbitrariness" in positive law. As that is done, the competence of positive law to aid the development of general legal principles will be enhanced.

In this essay I have outlined some of the foundations for a fruitful collaboration between sociology and natural law philosophy. This has required a critical discussion of both the sociological and the natural law perspectives. I have argued that sociological analysis is quite compatible with the study of social systems, such as the legal order, that are governed by master ideals; and that the relativity of moral judgment is not essential to the sociological view of man and society. I have also offered an interpretation of positive law and of natural law that is consistent with the premises of scientific inquiry. Yet I suggest that this interpretation captures the essential truth in the natural law approach.

I have no doubt that the sociology of law can gain immensely valuable guidance from the study of problems posed by the quest for natural law. I also believe that natural law philosophy would benefit from a greater effort to increase the scientific component of its discourse. A vigorous research program, devoted to the formulation and testing of natural law principles, might do much to advance both the cause of justice and sociological truth.

ACKNOWLEDGMENTS

I should like to record my thanks to the Center for Advanced Study in the Behavioral Sciences, where this paper was written. For intellectual assistance and encouragement I am especially indebted to Gertrude J. Selznick, Yosal A. Rogat, and to Robert M. Hutchins and his colleagues at the Center for the Study of Democratic Institutions.

REFERENCES

Cohen, M. R.
  1953 *Reason and nature.* New York: Free Press.
Cox, A.
  1960 Internal affairs of labor unions under the labor reform act of 1959. *Michigan Law Review* **58** (1960): 819–854.
Eels, R.
  1960 *The meaning of modern business.* New York: Columbia Univ. Press.
Ehrlich, E.
  1936 *Fundamental principles of the sociology of law.* Cambridge: Harvard Univ. Press. (Orig. pub. 1913.)
Fuller, L. L.
  1958 Positivism and fidelity to law—A reply to Professor Hart. *Harvard Law Review* **71** (1958): 630–672.
Pound, R.
  1959 *Jurisprudence.* Volume 2. St. Paul: West Publ.
Selznick, P.
  1969 *Law, society, and industrial justice.* New York: Russell Sage Foundation.
Strauss, L.
  1953 *Natural right and history.* Chicago: Univ. of Chicago Press.
Wolin, S.
  1960 *Politics and vision.* Boston: Little, Brown.

THE BOUNDARIES OF LEGAL SOCIOLOGY

Donald Black

I

CONTEMPORARY SOCIOLOGY of law is characterized by a confusion of science and policy. Its analysis proceeds in the disembodied tongue of science, in the language of "system," "structure," "pattern," and "organization," or in the vocabulary of technique, of "needs," "functions," and "viability." Rarely does the language impart emotion, indignation, or even personal involvement on the part of the investigator. But while legal sociology is presented in this scientific language and scientific tone, normative considerations—the "ought" and the "just"— become subtly implicated.

Legal sociologists[1] typically criticize one another according to the usual scientific standards of methodological precision and theoretical validity; however, they frequently become preoccupied with the "policy implications" of their research. In assessing one another, they occasionally shed the mantle of science and become unabashedly political. Recently, for instance, a sociologist characterized the literature of legal sociology as

---

[1] In what follows I shall use the term "sociologists" as a matter of convention, though I intend to refer not only to Ph.D.s in sociology but also to lawyers and political scientists and anyone else claiming to contribute to the scientific study of law as a social phenomenon. Most of my examples, however, derive from the scholarly literature explicitly labeled "sociology of law" and authored by academic sociologists.

Reprinted by permission of The Yale Law Journal Company and Fred B. Rothman & Company from "The Boundaries of Legal Sociology" by Donald Black, *The Yale Law Journal*, Vol. 81 (May, 1972): pp. 1086–1100. This is a slightly revised version of the original paper.

bourgeois, liberal, pluralist, and meliorist (Currie, 1971).[2] He went on to argue that a more radical sociology is required, one that is "more critical in its premises and farther-reaching in its proposals" (p. 145).[3] But whether liberal or radical, legal sociologists tend to share a single style of discourse that deserves attention and comment.

It is my contention that a purely sociological approach to law should involve not an assessment of legal policy, but rather, a scientific analysis of legal life *as a system of behavior*. The ultimate contribution of this enterprise would be a general theory of law, a theory that would predict and explain every instance of legal behavior. While such a general theory may never be attained, efforts to achieve it should be central to the sociology of law. By contrast, the core problems of legal policy-making are problems of value. Such value considerations are as irrelevant to a sociology of law as they are to any other scientific theory of the empirical world.

Invoking the language of science and relying upon its aura of respectability, sociologists move, in a special and almost imperceptible way, beyond science and deal with questions of legal evaluation. Because they confuse scientific questions with policy questions, they severely retard the development of their field. At best, they offer an applied sociology of law, at worst, sheer ideology.

After examining the type of discourse that passes for a sociology of law and noting its apparent shortcomings, I shall discuss more directly the nature and aims of a pure sociology of law.

II

With one phrase, *legal effectiveness*, we capture the major thematic concern of contemporary sociology of law. The wide range of work that revolves around the legal-effectiveness theme displays a common strategy of problem formulation, namely a comparison of legal reality to a legal ideal of some kind. Typically a gap is claimed between "law in action" and "law in theory." Often the sociologist then goes on to explain this gap and to suggest how the reality might be brought closer to the ideal. Law is

---

[2] Currie's discussion is a review of Friedman and Macaulay (1969) and Schwartz and Skolnick (1970). These two collections of the legal sociology literature not only present representative materials but also attempt to explain the relevance of the materials, thereby providing excellent examples of the style of discourse now dominating the field.

[3] A striking feature of Currie's review is that he pays little attention to the scientific adequacy of the work he criticizes. Instead, he focuses more upon the reform implications of the existing work and condemns it on political rather than methodological or theoretical grounds. Thus, while he suggests that the work could greatly benefit from the perspectives of Marxian scholars, he fails to show that the Marxian approach to law has a superior explanatory power.

regarded as ineffective and in need of reform owing to the disparity between the legal reality and the ideal.[4]

Legal-effectiveness studies differ from one another, however, in the kinds of legal ideals against which their findings are measured. At one extreme are "impact studies" that compare reality to legal ideals with a very plain and specific operational meaning. Here the legal measuring rod is likely to be a statute whose purpose is rather clearly discernible or a judicial decision unambiguously declarative of a specific policy. The *Miranda* decision, for example, requiring the police to apprise suspects of their legal rights before conducting an in-custody interrogation, has a core meaning about which consensus is quite high.[5] Soon after *Miranda* was handed down by the Supreme Court, research was initiated to evaluate the degree of police compliance with the decision (e.g., Yale Law Journal, 1967). When the core meaning of a decision thus is clear, this type of research can be expected to show whether or not a decision has, in fact, been implemented.

Sociologists, however, may launch these implementation studies where legislation or judicial opinion is considerably more ambiguous than in *Miranda*. In such instances, the "impact" may be difficult to measure. What must be done, for example, to implement *In re Gault*?[6] Though it is generally recognized that *Gault* guarantees to juvenile suspects constitutional rights previously accorded only to adults, the extent of these juvenile rights is not at all clear (see Foster, 1968).[7] Hence it becomes difficult, perhaps

---

[4] Because research in legal sociology consistently shows these disparities, the field has become identified with debunkery and the unmasking of law. In legal scholarship this debunking spirit goes back to the legal realism movement which has haunted American law schools since it emerged around the turn of the century. Much legal sociology, then, is a new legal realism, appearing in the prudent garb of social science, armed with sophisticated research methods, new language, and abstract theoretical constructs.

[5] Miranda v. Arizona, 384 U.S. 436 (1966). Although there may be some disagreement as to the peripheral meanings of "custody" and "interrogation" [see, e.g., Mathis v. United States, 391 U.S. 1 (1968); Orozco v. Texas, 394 U.S. 324 (1969)], there is little doubt that a suspect under arrest in a police station who is probingly questioned about his involvement in a crime is both in custody and under interrogation as these concepts are used by the Court. Moreover, no question remains as to the required *content* of an apprising of rights. 384 U.S. at 478–479. Yet, there may even be disagreement as to what constitutes an "adequate" and "effective" apprising of rights (p. 467). Compare United States v. Fox, 403 F.2d 97 (2d Cir. 1968) with State v. Renfrew, 280 Minn. 276, 159 N.W.2d 111 (1968). For example, would a police procedure of giving the suspect a preprinted card listing his rights meet the requirement of an adequate and effective apprisal? Would that procedure meet the *Miranda* test if the suspect were illiterate?

[6] 387 U.S. 1 (1967).

[7] For examples of judicial conflict in the applicability of specific rights, compare: (1) Stanley v Peyton, 292 F.Supp. 213 (W.D. Va. 1968), *cert. denied*, 400 U.S. 828 (1970) (dictum) *and* State v. Acuna, 78 N.M. 119, 428 P. 2d 658 (1967), *with* Steinhauer v. State, 206 So.2d 25 (Fla. Dist. Ct. App. 1967), *quashed and remanded on other grounds*, 216 So.2d 214 (1968), *cert. denied*, 398 U.S. 914 (1970) (Douglas, J., dissenting on denial of cert.) (right to counsel at waiver of juvenile court jurisdiction hearing); (2) *In re* Fletcher, 251 Md. 520, 248 A.2d 364 (1968), *cert. denied*, 396 U.S. 852 (1969), *with In re* D., 30 App. Div. 2d 183, 290 N.Y.S.2d 935 (1968) (necessity of giving *Miranda* warnings to *both* juvenile and parents at pretrial custodial interrogation); (3) *In re* Wylie, 231 A.2d 81 (D.C.Ct. App. 1967), *with In re* Urbasek, 38 Ill.2d 535, 232 N.E.2d 716 (1967) (right to standard of proof beyond a reasonable doubt).

impossible, to identify the degree to which *Gault* has been implemented.[8]

Finally, the sociologist may attempt to compare legal reality to an ideal grounded in neither statutory nor case law. Here the investigator assesses his empirical materials against standards of justice such as "the rule of law," "arbitrariness," "legality," or a concept of "due process" not ex-plicitly anchored in the due process clause of the Constitution. Jerome Skolnick, for instance, asserts that the police employ the informer system in narcotics enforcement "irrespective of the constraints embodied in principles of due process" (1966: 138). But there is no indication of where Skolnick locates these principles. Presumably he realizes that no court in the United States has declared the practice illegal, and there is no reason to think such a decision is likely in the near future.[9] In another study, Skolnick investigates plea bargaining in the courtroom, concluding that the co-operation underlying this practice "deviates" from some unarticulated adversarial ideal (1967). Similarly, Leon Mayhew (1968), in arguing that the Massachusetts Commission Against Discrimination failed to define discrim-ination adequately and thereby ignored much illegal conduct, provides neither a legal argument nor an empirical referent for his interpretation of the Commission's proper mission (see Black, 1970; Mayhew, 1970). In short, then, some studies in legal sociology seem to move beyond the law when they measure legal reality against an ideal.

At its most useful, legal-effectiveness research may be valuable to people in a position to reform the legal order. In this sense it consists of studies in *applied* sociology of law. This would appear to be particularly true of those investigations that relate empirical findings to legal ideals which are clearly expressed in the written law. Such research might provide legal reformers with a kind of leverage for change, though the mere evidence of a gap be-tween "law in action" and "law in theory" would not in itself overwhelm all resistance to change. Who can imagine a study, after all, that could not dis-cover such a gap? Little is more predictable about the law than that these gaps can be located.

However, legal-effectiveness research sometimes moves beyond applied

---

[8]See, e.g., Lefstein, Stapleton, and Teitelbaum (1969), in which these problems of operationalization are evident.

[9]Much less than viewing the use of informers as a violation of constitutional safeguards, the Supreme Court has refused even to require that an informer's identity be revealed. Specifically, police reliance upon anonymous informants to provide the requisite information for probable cause to sustain an arrest or search warrant has been held not to violate either the Fourth Amendment or due process clause. See McCray v. Illinois, 386 U.S. 300 (1967); Draper v. United States, 358 U.S. 307 (1959). But if the police utilize an informant as a participant in an illegal narcotics transaction, even where there is no question of entrapment, the government will be required to disclose the identity of the informant at trial when such disclosure may be "relevant and helpful to the accused's defense." The failure to disclose in this context would violate due process. Roviaro v. United States, 353 U.S. 53 (1957).

sociology. When legal reality is compared to an ideal with no identifiable empirical referent, such as "the rule of law" or "due process," the investigator may inadvertently implant his personal ideals as the society's legal ideals. At this point social science ceases and advocacy begins. The value of legal-effectiveness research of this kind is bound to be precarious, for it involves, perhaps unwittingly, moral judgment at the very point where it promises scientific analysis.

III

As I have described it, the sociology of law significantly resembles a broader style of thought that has come to be known as *technocratic* thought,[10] or, to use an earlier term, scientism. In the technocratic world view, every problem—factual, moral, political, or legal—reduces to a question of technique. A good technique is one that works, and what works can be learned through science. Any problem that cannot be solved in this way is no problem at all, hardly worthy of our attention. In theory, moreover, every problem can be solved if only the appropriate expertise is applied to it. Among the key words in the technocratic vocabulary are efficiency and, one I noted earlier, effectiveness. It is a style of thought in some respects akin to pragmatism, but it is a pragmatism with unstated goals, a search for the most rational way to go somewhere that is never clearly specified. Rather, we must infer what these goals are, and that is how some technocratic approaches come to be known as liberal and bourgeois, others as radical and critical. Technocrats do not make political arguments in the usual sense; they do not moralize. They simply want to get the job done.

The technocratic style dominates much discussion of social controversy at the higher reaches of American life. We are given to understand that scientific research will reveal whether marijuana should be legalized, that the Vietnam War was a miscalculation, and that economic analysis will determine the most "rational" tax program. The new nations of Africa and Asia are studied to determine what their modernization "requires." Riots, violence, and pornography give rise to government study commissions and research grants for the universities. Moral problems of every sort are translated into problems of knowledge and science, of know-how. To discuss the criminal in the moral terms of right and wrong comes to be seen as primitive and unschooled; medical terminology is introduced into the discussion of the treatment of criminal offenders. In the name of science and progress, what was once seen as evil is studied and treated, not condemned.

---

[10] For a recent discussion of technocratic thought, see Roszak (1969: 5–22).

The logic of this technocratic mentality has helped to catapult sociology to a position of some prominence in these times of rapid social change and conflict. Sociology, it is thought, will point the way to solutions to the many problems before us. The sociologists themselves have shown little reluctance to accept this responsibility. The typical sociologist knows almost nothing about moral or social philosophy, but if public policy is no more than a matter of scientific technique, why should he? In a technocratic era, moral philosophy is an oddity in the real world of action, a quaint remnant of the nineteenth century, something for the undergraduates.

IV

Law can be seen as a thing like any other in the empirical world. It is crucial to be clear that from a sociological standpoint, law consists in observable acts, not in rules as the concept of rule or norm is employed in the literature of jurisprudence and in everyday legal language.[11] From a sociological point of view, law is not what lawyers regard as binding or obligatory precepts, but rather, for example, the observable dispositions of judges, policemen, prosecutors, or administrative officials. Law is like any other thing in the sense that it is as amenable to the scientific method as any other aspect of reality. No intellectual apparatus peculiar to the study of law is required. At the same time, a social science of law true to positivism, the conventional theory of science, cannot escape the limitations inherent in scientific thought itself.[12] Perhaps a word should be said about these limitations.

Within the tradition of positivist philosophy, three basic principles of scientific knowledge can be noted. First, science can know only phenomena and never essences.[13] The quest for the one correct concept of law or for anything else "distinctively legal" is therefore inherently unscientific.[14] The essence of law is a problem for jurisprudence, not science. Second, every scientific idea requires a concrete empirical referent of some kind.[15] A

---

[11] Hence, this sociological conception of law is very different from but not logically incompatible with the legal positivism of Hans Kelsen and his "pure theory of law." See, e.g., Kelsen (1961). Similarly, to take another well-known example, a sociological approach does not conflict with the rule-oriented jurisprudence of Hart (1961).

At the level of social life in its narrow sense, law is behavior and nothing more. If the concept of rule or norm is used in a sociological analysis, it should always refer to a behavioral pattern of some kind. See, e.g., Durkheim (1953).

[12] A good introduction to positivism is Kolakowski (1968).

[13] This has been called the principle of phenomenalism. See Kolakowski (1968: 3–4).

[14] Philip Selznick, one of the most ambitious and influential students of legal effectiveness, considers the "cardinal weakness" of the sociological approach to law to be its "failure to offer a theory of the distinctively legal" (1969: 51).

[15] This is the principle of nominalism (see Kolakowski, 1968: 5–7).

science can only order experience, and has no way of gaining access to non-empirical domains of knowledge. Accordingly, insofar as such ideals as justice, the rule of law, and due process are without a grounding in experience, they have no place in the sociology of law. Third, value judgments cannot be discovered in the empirical world and for that reason are without cognitive meaning in science (see Kolakowski, 1968: 7–8).[16]

It is for this last reason that science knows nothing and can know nothing about the effectiveness of law. Science is incapable of an evaluation of the reality it confronts. To measure the effectiveness of law, or of anything else for that matter, we must import standards of value that are foreign to science.[17] What is disturbing about the contemporary literature on legal effectiveness then is not that it evaluates law,[18] but rather, that its evaluations and proposals are presented as scientific findings. Far from denying this confusion, Philip Selznick has gone so far in the opposite direction as to claim that "nothing we know today precludes an effort to define 'ends proper to a man's nature' and to discover objective standards of moral judgment" (1961: 93–94).

Legal sociologists involved in the study of effectiveness have thus come to advance a conception of scientific criticism of law. This is illogical; it is a contradiction in terms.

It is apparent by now that my critique of contemporary legal sociology is premised on the notion that sociology is a scientific enterprise and, as such, can be distinguished from moral philosophy, jurisprudence, or any other normatively oriented study—in other words, that the study of fact can be distinguished from the study of value. This is not to say that I would disregard the criticisms that are often levied against a purely value-free social

---

[16]Some legal sociologists are willing to tolerate an obfuscation of factual and normative discourse. Selznick, for instance, while conceding that the separation of fact and value has some merit, nevertheless suggests that this distinction is meant for "unsophisticated minds." We must, he continues, unlearn this "easy and reassuring" formula from our "intellectual youth." Selznick finds a natural law approach more appropriate for the mature thinker (1961: 86).

[17]This does not say that scientific studies of legal effectiveness are impossible. As long as a social goal is introduced into the analysis and is adequately defined for purposes of the investigation, the study of effectiveness is perfectly feasible. Such applied science can be as rigorously conducted as any other research.

[18]As a rule I do not personally find the policy criticisms and proposals of legal sociologists to be particularly objectionable, the exception being those proposals that increase the power of the government to intervene in citizens' lives. Thus, for instance, I find the therapeutic approach to criminal offenders a frightening advance of an already too powerful criminal justice system. In fact, I align myself more broadly and precisely in the philosophical tradition of anarchism. For me, the validity of law is at all times contingent upon my own assessment of its moral validity, and thus I recognize no a priori legitimacy in the rule of law. For a brief introduction to this political ethic, see Wolff (1970).

I would add that the students of legal effectiveness I am discussing are, politically speaking, the elite of our society, however critical of the legal process they may seem. Often the government even finances their research on its own effectiveness. It is my view that the confusion of fact and value operates as a form of mystification that helps to keep the established order intact. Nevertheless, I do not wish to promote my political philosophy in this context (see Weber, 1958).

science. But while accepting these criticisms, I am unable to reach the conclusion that the effort to develop an objective science of man should be abandoned.

It is important to understand precisely how values become involved in social science. One widely recognized intrusion of values occurs at the first stage of scientific inquiry: the choice of the problem for study. The values of the investigator may determine, for example, whether he selects a problem with great relevance for public policy or one of wholly academic interest. This intrusion of values was noted long ago by Max Weber, perhaps the most illustrious proponent of value-free sociology. Weber contended that the role of values in the choice of a problem is unavoidable and should be faced squarely, but he insisted that the problem, once selected, could and should be pursued "nonevaluatively" (1949: 21–22).[19]

But I would go further than Weber and grant that these value orientations may bias the analysis of the problem as well as its selection. Though various methodological techniques have been developed to minimize the effects of these biases, good social science still requires a disciplined disengagement on the part of the investigator—so disciplined, in fact, that it may rarely be achieved. Various arguments can be made to the effect that bias is built into social science at its very foundations. For example, the claim has been made that every social science study necessarily implicates the investigator in the perspective of an actual hierarchical position, seeing social life from either the social top or the bottom, and is therefore inherently biased (Becker, 1967). For purposes of discussion I grant even this. Similarly it is arguable that all social science is, beyond science, a form of ideology, if only because it is by its nature an instance of social behavior subject to the scrutiny of the very discipline of which it is a part. Sociology, that is, can be analyzed sociologically. Sociology does not occur in a vacuum and is undoubtedly influenced by social forces. Accordingly, sociology may be viewed as ideology supporting either the defenders of the status quo or their opponents.[20]

Finally, because much social science can be interpreted in an ideological framework, its theories and findings can be used as weapons in the arena of public policy-making. The polemical impact of social science may be particularly great at this historical moment, given the enormous prestige of science in modern society. Not only do these theories and findings feed into existing policy debates, but they also can stimulate controversy and change by drawing attention to empirical situations that might otherwise be unknown or ignored by policy-makers and social critics. Thus social science performs—

---

[19] For a direct attack on Weber's approach to these questions, see Gouldner (1962).
[20] This is a major theme of a recent critique of sociological theory (Gouldner, 1970).

willingly or not—an intelligence function in the political process.[21] Because of such political ramifications, the argument has been put forward that the sociologist remains responsible for the consequences of his work: Only by making an explicit moral commitment can the social scientist hope to protect himself and others from the unintended consequences of his work (Dahrendorf, 1968: 17). It is apparent that social science resonates into the realm of ideology, thereby raising serious questions about the scholar's responsibilities to his fellow man.

In several senses, then, values enter into the activity of social science. While values may play a similar role in science of all kinds, it can at least be admitted that their role is especially visible and dramatic when man is studying himself. Values may be all the more prominent in the study of man's moral life, of which legal sociology is one branch. The major arguments against the possibility of a pure science of man, in short, seem to have some merit.[22] But the crucial question is what all of this implies for the traditional distinction between fact and value. I say it implies nothing. Indeed, much of the criticism of value-free sociology itself rests upon observable patterns of value impact upon social science and for that reason relies upon the fact–value distinction for its own validity.

[21] It should be clear that the policy impact of science is never direct but is always mediated by normative analysis, whether explicit or implicit. Policy cannot be deduced from scientific propositions alone. All of this is dramatically illustrated by the relation between the Marxian theory and public policy. Surely no theory of social science has had more impact upon the world. It has been an important weapon in ideological debate, and it has alerted policy-makers and the public to the situation of the working class and the role of class conflict in social change. Yet as a scientific theory the Marxian analysis of society and history has no logical implications for political action. Without passing judgment upon the exploitation and growing misery of the proletariat, one could just as well sit back passively and watch history unfold as join the revolution. Both responses are logically independent of the theory.

[22] Of course in this brief discussion I cannot begin to review the sizable literature on the subject. Perhaps I should note, however, one criticism of the value-neutral strategy that bears directly on the study of law—one, moreover, that seems to me to be wholly without merit. This criticism asserts that the study of normative life, because it is normative, requires a partially normative approach on the part of the investigator if he is to comprehend its empirical character. The investigator must take the normative view of the participants if he is to understand their normative behavior. Selznick, for instance, suggests that the sociologist should make an "assessment" of the degree to which a normative system reaches an ideal "from the standpoint of the normative system being studied" though "the student of a normative system need not have any personal commitment to the desireability of that system" (Selznick, 1961: 88). In the study of law, therefore, it seems we must include an assessment of legal reality in terms of the ideals of the legal system we study.

In my view this argument incorrectly assumes that such normative ideals can be identified at a wholly empirical level. I do not believe, for example, that the degree of conformity of law with, let us say, a constitutional ideal is a wholly empirical question. The nature of the ideal is itself a normative question, a question of normative interpretation. In the study of law such interpretation is the heart of legal scholarship, and from a positivist standpoint that activity is, at its core, normative rather than scientific. It advances an "ought" as the proper measure of reality, and it does not matter whether or not the interpreter himself subscribes to the "ought." It remains an unavoidably normative judgment. In effect, then, Selznick's view is that in order to understand normative life we must be normative. This view, I believe, is seriously mistaken.

We have seen that a social scientist may be affected by values in the choice of his problem and may be biased in his approach to it. Critics of a value-free social science assert that these psychological effects, along with the ideological character of social science when viewed as the object of analysis itself, undermine the validity of social science. But this is to confuse the origins and uses of a scientific statement with its validity (Dahrendorf, 1968: 9–10). *The fact that scientific statements are influenced by values does not make them value statements.* The psychological and social influence of values on scientific inquiry has no logical implications for the validity of a scientific proposition. Its validity is determined only by empirical verification. A value statement, by contrast, is not subject to such a test.[23] How, for example, is the following statement to be empirically verified? "Democratic process is an ultimate good." The fact that we can distinguish between scientific propositions and such value statements is all we need to assert the possibility of social science. In short, values may affect social science profoundly, but that is no reason to abandon the enterprise.[24]

V

The proper concern of legal sociology should be the development of a general theory of law. A general theory involves several key elements that may not at first be obvious. To say that a theory of law is general means that it seeks to order law wherever it is found. It seeks to discover the principles and mechanisms that predict empirical patterns of law, whether these patterns occur in this day or the past, regardless of the substantive area of law involved and regardless of the society. By contrast, the contemporary study of law is ideographic, very concrete and historical. Legal scholars tend to rebel at the suggestion of a general theory of their subject matter. Nevertheless, unless we seek generality in our study of law, we abandon hope for a serious sociology of law.

If the sweep of legal sociology is to be this broad, a correspondingly broad concept of law is required. I like to define law simply as *governmental social*

---

[23] Although not subject to empirical verification, a value statement may be subject to other criteria such as its logical status in relation to a more general axiological principle.

[24] My critique of contemporary legal sociology arises from a very conventional conception of scientific method, a conception associated with the broader tradition of positivist thought. I have not made and do not intend to make a philosophical defense of this tradition. I wish only to advocate a sociology of law true to basic positivist principles as they have come to be understood in the history of the philosophy of science.

control.[25] This is one possibility among many consistent with a positivist strategy. It is a concept easily employed in cross-societal analysis, encompassing any act by a political body that concerns the definition of social order or its defense. At the same time it excludes such forms of social control as popular morality and bureaucratic rules in private organizations. It is more inclusive than an American lawyer might deem proper, but more selective than anthropological concepts which treat law as synonymous with normative life and dispute settlement of every description, governmental or otherwise. If we are to have a manageable subject matter, our concept must construe law as one among a larger array of social control systems. And if we are to have a strategically detached approach, our concept must be value neutral. We need a theoretical structure applicable to the law of the Nazis as well as American law, to revolutionary law and colonial law as well as the cumbersome law of traditional China. What do these systems share, and how can we explain the differences among them?

Ultimately a theory is known and judged by its statements about the world. These statements both guide and follow empirical research. They propose uniformities in the relation between one part of reality and another. Thus a general theory of law is addressed to the relation between law and other aspects of social life, including, for instance, other forms of social control, social stratification, the division of labor, social integration, group size, and the structure and substance of social networks. At the moment we have only a small inventory of theoretical statements, or propositions, of this kind. The relevant literature is sparse, and many of our leads must come from the classic works of Maine (1871, 1963), Durkheim (1933, 1958, 1973), Weber (1954), Ehrlich (1936), Pound (1917, 1942, 1943), and the like. Marx,

---

[25] I mention this only as a means of delineating the subject matter of legal sociology. A definition of the subject matter is a prerequisite to any scientific inquiry. Just as a physicist must first define motion before he can describe its characteristics, a sociologist of religion, for example, must first define the pattern of social behavior that constitutes religion before he can proceed with his research. This does not mean that there is only one proper definition. Law itself has been defined nonnormatively in a variety of ways. Weber's approach is one example:

An order will be called *law* when conformity with it is upheld by the probability that deviant action will be met by physical or psychic sanctions aimed to compel conformity or to punish disobedience, and applied by a group of men especially empowered to carry out this function (1964: 127).

I have chosen "governmental social control" as a definition of law for the reasons that follow in the text. I should add, however, that for me the choice of a particular sociological concept of law is not at all critical to my larger aim, since my ultimate interest goes beyond law *per se* to all forms of social control. For me, the study of law is preliminary and subordinate to the more general study of social control systems of all kinds. Therefore, if my concept of law is too narrow or too broad it does not matter *theoretically*, since it will in any case be relevant to a sociology of social control.

too, should not be forgotten, though he gave law only passing attention.[26] Apart from classical sociology and comparative jurisprudence, anthropological literature, notably the work of such scholars as Malinowski (1962),[27] Hoebel (1954; Llewellyn and Hoebel, 1941), Gluckman (1955, 1965), Bohannan (1957, 1965), and Nader (1964, 1965), has contributed more than sociology to a general theory of law. Contemporary sociologists tend to limit their attention to the American legal system, and even there disproportionate emphasis is given the criminal justice system. Rarely do they compare American law to governmental social control in other societies, yet if legal sociology is not comparative its conclusions will inevitably be time-bound and ethnocentric.

This is not to suggest that American criminal justice is unworthy of study. But one must address problems at a higher level of generality, thereby contributing to and benefiting from scholarship in other realms of law. If we investigate the police, for example, our fundamental interest as sociologists must be in what police work can teach us about law, generically understood, and we must bring to a study of the police whatever we know about other forms of legal life. From my standpoint, in other words, the major shortcoming of most sociological literature on the police is that it concerns the police alone, instead of treating police behavior as an instance of law. Often sociologists occupy themselves with the unique world of the policeman, his attitudes, hopes and fears, his relations with his fellow officers, his social isolation in the wider community—in brief, with the "human" dimensions of police work (e.g., Skolnick, 1966; Bittner, 1967; Werthman and Piliavin, 1967; Westley, 1970). Insofar as such studies rise above descriptive journalism or ethnography, then, they tend to focus upon the psychology of the policeman on his day-to-day round. Yet from a purely sociological point of view it is not important to know that policemen are, after all, "human," or to know how their minds work. A pure sociology of law does not study humans in the usual sense. It studies law as a system of behavior. Taken in this sense, law feels nothing. It has no joy or sorrow or wonderment. Scientifically conceived as a social reality in its own right, law is no more human than a molecular structure. It has no nationality, no mind, and no ends proper to its nature.

I do not mean to criticize categorically the rather impressive body of police research that has accumulated in recent years, but only to suggest that its contribution to the sociology of law is limited. We must give up the notion that the sociology of law embraces any and all forms of empirical research relating to the legal system. A scientific discipline is defined by its

---

[26]Marx did, however, inspire some interesting sociological work on law (see, e.g., Renner, 1949; Pashukanis, 1951).

[27]This study is considered the first ethnography of law.

theoretical mission, by what it tries to explain, not by its sources of data. Thus, research on the human body may contribute to any of a variety of disciplines—biochemistry, genetics, endocrinology, physiological psychology, or whatever. The same is true of research on law or the police. Accordingly, a study of the police contributes to legal sociology only if it provides insights into legal behavior, its empirical profile, the social conditions under which it occurs, and its social implications. I am not saying that every sociologist must be a theorist, but only that any sociologist who does research on a legal topic without knowing, roughly, its theoretical relevance does so at his peril.

Police research should tell us something about the social control function of the police: What legal matters do they handle? How do they come to deal with those matters? What are the principles according to which they process their cases? Ideally a study would also tell us how police behavior resembles other known patterns of legal behavior and how it differs. We know, for example, that the police make arrests relatively infrequently when some other form of social control is available in the situation. Thus, they rarely make an arrest when one family member criminally offends another, a situation where other means of social pressure typically are at hand, whereas the same offense committed by one stranger against another is very apt to result in arrest (Black, 1971: 1107). This pattern of legal behavior is known to have analogues in a wide variety of legal settings, in civil as well as criminal cases, in the invocation of law as well as its application, in many countries and historical periods, and even in the evolution of law itself (Black, 1971: notes 30–34, 1107–1108). We may state the pattern as a theoretical proposition: Law tends to become implicated in social life to the degree that other forms of social control are weak or unavailable (Black, 1971: 1108). Hence, what we discover in the behavior of policemen turns out to be simply an instance of a much more general pattern in the conditions under which the law acts upon social life. We thereby add systematically to existing knowledge of this pattern, and, what is more, we can *explain* the behavior of the police, since it can be predicted and deduced from a more general proposition about law (see Braithwaite, 1959). If the likelihood of legal control is greater where other forms of social control are absent, it follows that the police are more likely to arrest a stranger who, let us say, assaults a stranger than a son who assaults his father. To be able to explain something so mundane and microscopic as behavior in a police encounter with the same proposition that we use to explain the historical emergence of law itself is exciting and encouraging. It provides a glimpse of general theory in action. This kind of theoretical structure is built up and elaborated over time through a process of give-and-take between data and tentative propositions stated at a high level of abstraction. It is the classical pattern of scientific advance, and I cannot see why the sociology of law should be any less ambitious or any less rigorous.

VI

We should be clear about the relation between sociological and legal scholarship. There is, properly speaking, no conflict of professional jurisdiction between the two. A legal problem is a problem of value and is forever beyond the reach of sociology. Jurisdictional conflict arises only when the sociologist makes policy recommendations in the name of science: In matters of legal policy, the lawyer must rely on his own wits.

But a more significant matter than jurisdictional clarity is the relation between pure and applied sociology of law. My view, hardly novel, is that the quality of applied science depends upon the quality of pure science. Just as major advances in mechanical and chemical engineering have been made possible by theoretical formulations in pure physics and chemistry, so legal engineering ultimately requires a general theory of how legal systems behave as natural phenomena. The case for a pure sociology of law does not rest solely on its social usefulness, but if utility is at issue, then in the long run the type of work I advocate is crucial. At present, applied sociology of law has little to apply. What more serious claim could be brought against it?

ACKNOWLEDGMENTS

This paper has benefited from the reactions of several readers: Leon Lipson, Maureen Mileski, David Trubek, and Stanton Wheeler. In March, 1972, an early draft occasioned an informal seminar at the Center for the Study of Law and Society of the University of California at Berkeley. I thank the following participants in that seminar for helping me to sharpen my ideas: David Matza, Sheldon Messinger, Philippe Nonet, Jerome Skolnick, and Philip Selznick. Finally, I want to express appreciation to Henry M. Fields, a law student who first suggested that I write this paper and then went on to contribute his considerable scholarly and editorial abilities to its preparation.

REFERENCES

Becker, H. S.
    1967   Whose side are we on? *Social Problems* 14 (Winter): 239–247.
Bittner, E.
    1967   The police on skid row: A study of peace-keeping. *American Sociological Review* 32 (October): 699–715.
Black, D.
    1970   On law and institutionalization. Review of *Law and equal opportunity*, by L. H. Mayhew. *Sociological Inquiry* 40 (Winter): 179–182.
    1971   The social organization of arrest. *Stanford Law Review* 23 (June): 1087–1111.
Bohannan, P.
    1957   *Justice and judgment among the Tiv.* London: Oxford Univ. Press.
    1965   The differing realms of the law. In *The Ethnography of Law*, supplement to *American Anthropologist* 67 (1965): 33–42.
Braithwaite, R. B.
    1959   *Scientific explanation: A study of the function of theory, probability and law in science.* London: Cambridge Univ. Press.

Currie, E.
1971 Sociology of law: The unasked questions. Review of *Law and the behavioral sciences*, edited by L. M. Friedman and S. Macaulay; *Society and the legal order*, edited by R. D. Schwartz and J. H. Skolnick, *Yale Law Journal* **81** (November): 134–147.
Dahrendorf, R.
1968 Values and social science: The value dispute in perspective. In *Essays in the theory of society*, pp. 1–18. Stanford: Stanford Univ. Press. (Orig. pub. 1961.)
Durkheim, E.
1933 *The division of labor in society*. New York: Free Press. (Orig. pub. 1893.)
1953 The determination of moral facts. In *Sociology and philosophy*, pp. 35–62. New York: Free Press. (Orig. pub. 1924.)
1958 *Professional ethics and civic morals*. New York: Free Press. (Orig. pub. 1950.)
1973 Two laws of penal evolution. Working paper No. 7, Working Papers of the Russell Sage Program in Law and Social Science, Yale Law School.
Ehrlich, E.
1936 *Fundamental principles of the sociology of law*. Cambridge: Harvard Univ. Press. (Orig. pub. 1913.)
Foster, H., Jr.
1968 Notice and 'fair procedure': Revolution or simple revision? In *Gault, What now for the juvenile court?* edited by V. D. Nordin, pp. 51–69. Ann Arbor: Institute of Continuing Legal Education.
Friedman, L. M., and S. Macaulay (Eds.)
1969 *Law and the behavioral sciences*. Indianapolis: Bobbs-Merrill.
Gluckman, M.
1955 *The judicial process among the Barotse of Northern Rhodesia*. Manchester, England: Manchester Univ. Press.
1965 *Politics, law and ritual in tribal society*. New York: Mentor Books.
Gouldner, A.
1962 Anti-Minotaur: The myth of a value-free sociology. *Social Problems* **9** (Winter): 199–213.
1970 *The coming crisis of western sociology*. New York: Basic Books.
Hart, H. L. A.
1961 *The concept of law*. London: Oxford Univ. Press.
Hoebel, E. A.
1954 *The law of primitive man: a study in comparative legal dynamics*. Cambridge: Harvard Univ. Press.
Kelsen, H.
1961 *General theory of law and state*. New York: Russell and Russell. (Orig. pub. 1945.)
Kolakowski, L.
1968 *The alienation of reason: A history of positivist thought*. Garden City, New York: Anchor. (Orig. pub. 1966.)
Lefstein, N., V. Stapleton, and L. Teitelbaum
1969 In search of juvenile justice: *Gault* and its implementation. *Law and Society Review* **3** (1969): 491–562.
Llewellyn, K., and E. A. Hoebel
1941 *The Cheyenne way: Conflict and case law in primitive jurisprudence*. Norman: Univ. of Oklahoma Press.
Maine, H. S.
1871 *Village communities in the East and West*. London: Murray.
1963 *Ancient Law*. Boston: Beacon Press. (Orig. pub. 1861.)
Malinowski, B.
1962 *Crime and custom in savage society*. Paterson: Littlefield, Adam. (Orig. pub. 1926.)

Mayhew, L. H.
  1968 *Law and equal opportunity: A study of the Massachusetts commission against discrimination.* Cambridge: Harvard Univ. Press.
  1970 Teleology and values in the social system: A reply to Donald J. Black. *Sociological Inquiry* **40** (Winter): 182–184.
Nader, L.
  1964 An analysis of Zapotec law cases. *Ethnology* **3** (1964): 404–419.
  1965 Choices in legal procedure: Shia Moslem and Mexican Zapotec. *American Anthropologist* **67** (1965): 394–399.
Pashukanis, E. B.
  1951 The general theory of law and marxism. In *Soviet legal philosophy*, edited by H. W. Babb, pp. 111–225. Cambridge: Harvard Univ. Press.
Pound, R.
  1917 The limits of effective legal action. *International Journal of Ethics* **27** (1917): 150–167.
  1942 *Social control through law.* New Haven: Yale Univ. Press.
  1943 A survey of social interests. *Harvard Law Review* **57** (1943): 1–39.
Renner, K.
  1949 *The institutions of private law and their social functions.* London: Routledge & Kegan Paul.
Roszak, T.
  1969 *The making of a counter culture: Reflections on the technocratic society and its youthful opposition.* Garden City, New York: Anchor Press.
Schwartz, R. D., and J. H. Skolnick (Eds.)
  1970 *Society and the legal order: Cases and materials in the sociology of law.* New York: Basic Books.
Selznick, P.
  1961 Sociology and natural law. *Natural Law Forum* **6** (1961): 84–108.
  1968 The sociology of law. In *International encyclopedia of the social sciences*, Vol. 9, edited by D. L. Sills, pp. 50–59. New York: Macmillan and Free Press.
Skolnick, J. H.
  1966 *Justice without trial: Law enforcement in democratic society.* New York: Wiley.
  1967 Social control in the adversary system. *Journal of Conflict Resolution* **11** (March): 52–70.
Weber, M.
  1949 *The methodology of the social sciences.* New York: Free Press. (Orig. pub. 1904–1917.)
  1954 *Max Weber on law in economy and society.* Cambridge: Harvard Univ. Press. (Orig. pub. 1922.)
  1958 Science as a vocation. In *From Max Weber: Essays in sociology*, pp. 129–156. London and New York: Oxford Univ. Press. (Orig. pub. 1919.)
  1964 *The theory of social and economic organization.* New York: Free Press. (Orig. pub. 1922.)
Werthman, C., and I. Piliavin
  1967 Gang members and the police. In *The police: Six sociological essays*, edited by D. J. Bordua, pp. 56–98. New York: Wiley.
Westley, W.
  1970 *Violence and the police: A sociological study of law, custom, and morality.* Cambridge: M.I.T. Press.
Wolff, R. P.
  1970 *In defense of anarchism.* New York: Harper.
Yale Law Journal
  1967 Interrogations in New Haven: The impact of *Miranda*. *Yale Law Journal* **76** (1967): 1519–1648.

Part II

LAW
AND OTHER
SOCIAL CONTROL

DISPUTE SETTLEMENT IN JAPAN

Takeyoshi
Kawashima

THERE IS probably no society in which litigation is the normal means of resolving disputes. Rarely will both parties press their claims so far as to require resort to a court; instead, one of the disputants will probably offer a satisfactory settlement or propose the use of some extrajudicial, informal procedure. Although direct evidence of this tendency is difficult to obtain, the phenomena described offer indirect support for the existence of these attitudes among the Japanese people.

FORMAL MEANS OF DISPUTE RESOLUTION: LAWSUITS

During the last years of World War I, when the housing shortage became critical, active speculation in real estate existed and there arose a large number of disputes regarding land and leases, both residential and farm. Because of the patriarchal nature of the traditional lease in Japan, tenants had not previously dared to dispute the terms of meaning of a lease. Thus when tenants began to press these disagreements, the choice of a

Reprinted by permission of the publishers from "Dispute Resolution in Contemporary Japan" by Takeyoshi Kawashima, in *Law in Japan: The legal order in a changing society*, Arthur T. von Mehren, editor, pp. 41–72. Cambridge: Harvard University Press. Copyright © 1963 by the President and Fellows of Harvard College. This is a shortened version of the original paper.

method for resolution was influenced almost entirely by the advantages and disadvantages of the alternatives. Although the increase of litigation regarding these contracts threatened the government so seriously that the instiution of *chōtei* (mediation) was hastily legalized,[1] in the following years the volume of litigation was relatively small when we take into account the seriousness of the housing shortage and the social unrest caused by it. This suggests that only a small portion of the disputes were brought to the courts. Furthermore, if we compare the number of mediation cases regarding leases and farm tenancies after mediation was legalized with the lawsuits of the same type, the latter figure is considerably smaller, showing the extent to which mediation was preferred to litigation.

Similarly, a comparison of the number of lawsuits and mediation cases regarding leases during the years immediately after the Japanese surrender in 1945, when the complete destruction of housing by air raids in most of the cities had produced a serious housing shortage, suggests that litigation was resorted to in only a relatively small number of cases. Mediation was vastly preferred.

It is also indicative in this connection that during the years of economic depression after the panic of 1927—in Japan the depression started two years earlier than in the United States—the statistics do not show any significant increase in the number of lawsuits, although a large number of debtors became insolvent. The judicial statistics of the same period of some states in the United States, on the other hand, show a remarkable increase in the number of lawsuits. The fairly small number of lawyers in Japan relative to the population and the degree of industrialization suggests that people do not go to court so frequently as in Western countries and that the demand for lawyers' services is not great (Hattori, 1963).

Finally, it is of significance that, according to a survey conducted by this writer, extremely few claims arising from traffic accidents involving railroads and taxis were brought to court, and almost all of the cases were settled by extrajudicial agreements. A railroad was involved in a total of 145 traffic accidents which caused physical injury during the period from April, 1960 to September, 1960; but not a single case was brought to court, and only two cases were handled by attorneys. Of all the accidents of the same company which caused physical injury during the past seven years, only three cases were brought to court, and all three were settled during the course of the litigation. Of the total of 372 accidents which caused physical injury and involved another railroad in 1960, not a single case was brought to court, and only one case was handled by an attorney.

[1] By the Leased Land and Leased House Mediation Law, Law No. 41 of 1922.

The volume of litigation arising in 1960 from traffic accidents caused by taxis is reported in Table 1.[2]

TABLE 1
ACCIDENT LITIGATION INVOLVING TAXIS

Company	Personal injury	Property damage	Total	Litigation
A	221	2041	2262	1
B	10	195	205	1
C	4	54	58	0
D	0	appr. 42	appr. 42	0

There are several possible explanations of this relative lack of litigation. On the one hand, litigation takes time and is expensive, but this seems to be true in almost all countries having modern judicial systems and can hardly account for the specifically strong inclination of the Japanese public to avoid judicial procedures. Or one might point out that monetary compensation awarded by the courts for damage due to personal injury or death in traffic accidents is usually extremely small. In a large number of cases, the damages awarded by the courts for a death caused by a traffic accident were said to be less than 300,000 yen (approximately 833 dollars); thus the Automobile Damage Compensation Security Law[3] when originally enacted provided that the compulsory insurance for a death need cover only 300,000 yen.[4] A more decisive factor is to be found in the social-cultural background of the problem. Traditionally, the Japanese people prefer extrajudicial, informal means of settling a controversy. Litigation presupposes and admits the existence of a dispute and leads to a decision which makes clear who is right or wrong in accordance with standards that are independent of the wills of the disputants. Furthermore, judicial decisions emphasize the conflict

[2] The following figures from a study by Franklin *et al.* (1961) suggest the significance of these Japanese figures. "Each year in New York City some 193,000 accident victims seek to recover damages for injuries ascribed to someone else's fault. For about 154,000 of these claimants the first step is retaining an attorney, while 39,000 proceed without aid of counsel. Theoretically, a claim is but the first step on the road to the courthouse, but in fact very few of the 193,000 claims ever get that far. Approximately 116,000 are closed without suit, leaving 77,000 that are actually sued. Almost all claimants who have been unable to recover without suit, and who wish to continue, retain an attorney" (p. 10).

[3] Law No. 97 of 1955.

[4] Automobile Damage Compensation Security Law, art. 13; Automobile Damage Compensation Security Law Enforcement Order, Cabinet Order No. 86 of 1955, art. 2. An amendment to the Enforcement Order by Cabinet Order No. 227 of 1960 subsequently increased the amount to 500,000 yen. For a full discussion, see Kato (1963).

between the parties, deprive them of participation in the settlement, and assign a moral fault which can be avoided in a compromise solution.

This attitude is presumably related to the nature of the traditional social groups in Japan, which may be epitomized by two characteristics. First, they are hierarchical in the sense that social status is differentiated in terms of deference and authority. Not only the village community and the family, but even contractual relationships have customarily been hierarchical. From the construction contract arises a relationship in which the contractor defers to the owner as his patron; from the contract of lease a relationship in which the lessee defers to the lessor; from the contract of employment a relationship in which the servant or employee defers to the master or employer; from the contract of apprenticeship a relationship in which the apprentice defers to the master; and from the contract of sale a relationship in which the seller defers to the buyer (the former being expected in each case to yield to the direction or desire of the latter). At the same time, however, the status of the master or employer is patriarchal and not despotic; in other words, he is supposed not only to dominate but also to patronize and therefore partially to consent to the requests of his servant or employee. Consequently, even though their social roles are defined in one way or other, the role definition is precarious and each man's role is contingent on that of the other. Obviously this characteristic is incompatible with judicial decisions based on fixed universalistic standards.[5]

Second, in traditional social groups relationships between people of equal status have also been to a great extent "particularistic" and at the same time "functionally diffuse." For instance, the relationship between members of the same village community who are equal in social status is supposed to be "intimate;" their social roles are defined in general and very flexible terms so that they can be modified whenever circumstances dictate. In direct proportion with the degree to which they are dependent on or intimate with each other, the role definition of each is contingent upon that of the other. Once again, role definition with fixed universalistic standards does not fit such a relationship.[6]

In short, this definition of social roles can be, and commonly is, characterized by the term "harmony." There is a strong expectation that a dispute should not and will not arise; even when one does occur, it is to be solved

---

[5] The terms "universalistic," "particularistic," and "functionally diffuse" are used here in the sense of the "pattern variables" scheme of Parsons (1951: 62–65; Parsons and Shils, 1951: 82–84).

[6] One of the clues to understanding the social-cultural background of divorce by agreement, which is so characteristic of Japanese culture, is found in this point. Whenever a conflict or a dispute arises between husband and wife, it is most appropriate to attempt to reach agreement through mutual understanding in the context of the complicated and subtle circumstances of the families of both husband and wife, instead of resorting to court for a decision in accordance with universalistic standards.

by mutual understanding. Thus there is no *raison d'être* for the majority rule that is so widespread in other modern societies; instead the principle of rule by consensus prevails.[7]

It is obvious that a judicial decision does not fit and even endangers relationships. When people are socially organized in small groups and when subordination of individual desires in favor of group agreement is idealized, the group's stability and the security of individual members are threatened by attempts to regulate conduct by universalistic standards. The impact is greater when such an effort is reinforced by an organized political power. Furthermore, the litigious process, in which both parties seek to justify their position by objective standards, and the emergence of a judicial decision based thereon tend to convert situational interests into firmly consolidated and independent ones. Because of the resulting disorganization of traditional social groups, resort to litigation has been condemned as morally wrong, subversive, and rebellious.[8]

On the other hand, there were, even in the traditional culture, disputes in which no such social relationship was involved. First, disputes arising outside of harmonious social groups, namely *between* such social groups,[9] have a completely different background. Such disputes arise, so to speak, in a social vacuum. Since amicable behavior from the other party is not to be expected in such a context, both parties to the dispute tend to become emotionally involved to a great extent, and the traditional culture contains no fixed rules of behavior to indicate the acceptable course of action. Yet, even in the absence of a specific tradition of harmony and in spite of strong emotional antagonism, disputes of this type are often settled by reconciliation. If one disputant apologizes, it is postulated by traditional culture that the other party must be lenient enough to forgive him, and, as a matter of fact, emotional involvement is usually quite easily released by the apology of an enemy. Occasionally disputes, usually antagonisms of long standing, are settled because the disadvantage of continuing disagreement outweighs the price of concession. These agreements are usually achieved through the mediation of third parties and are similar in nature to peace treaties. Until

[7] This principle is still observed today in village communities with regard to a "right of common" in land. To bring about any alteration of rights respecting "common," the mores require unanimous consent of the villagers, and majority rule is not admitted. This traditional principle is recognized as customary law by art. 2 of the Law for the Application of Laws, Law No. 19 of 1898. Legal recognition of the unanimity rule makes it extremely difficult for villagers to introduce innovations in the use of common, so that vast areas of common lands are left uncultivated despite a serious shortage of agricultural land.

[8] The writer personally knows a farmer in a village near Tokyo whose whole family has been socially ostracized by all the villagers because his deceased father had sued another farmer in a dispute about the boundaries of his farm.

[9] E.g., disputes concerning irrigation rights among various villages, disputes between a village community alleging the existence of customary rights of common or of collective use of land, on the one hand, and an electric-power company denying such rights, on the other.

and unless such a peaceful settlement is made, sheer antagonism and the rule of power, very often of violence, prevail. Disputes of this kind are also settled when one party can impose a *fait accompli* by force. In other words, superiority in power establishes a new social order. The only way in which the weaker party can escape from this rule of power is through the lawsuit. For this reason, a large number of suits relating to the "right of common" (*iriaiken*) in land recorded in the law reports of the prewar period were disputes between village communities.

A second class of disputes, those between a usurer and his debtor, lacks from the very beginning a harmonious relationship comparable to that normally found between lessor and lessee or master and servant. Usurers never fail to be armed not only with nonlegal means with which to enforce the factual power situation but also with means founded upon law that enable them to resort to the courts. Since the Meiji era (1867–1912), long before industrialization was under way, official statistics have shown a surprisingly large number of cases involving claims of this sort.

In short, a wide discrepancy has existed between state law and the judicial system, on the one hand, and operative social behavior, on the other. Bearing this in mind, we can understand the popularity and function of mediation procedure as an extrajudicial informal means of dispute resolution in Japan.

This attitude is also reflected in the customary characteristics of contracts. Parties to a contractual agreement are not expected to become involved in any serious differences in the future. Whenever they enter such a relationship, they are supposed to be friendly enough not to consider eventual disputes, much less preparation for a lawsuit. Parties do not, or at least pretend that they do not, care about an instrument or other kinds of written evidence and rather hesitate to ask for any kind of written document, fearing that such a request might impair the amicable inclination of the other party. Even when written documents are drawn up, they do not provide machinery for settling disputes.[10] The contracting parties occasionally insert clauses providing that in case of dispute the parties "may" (instead of "must") negotiate with each other. . . .

The contractual relationship in Japan is by nature quite precarious and cannot be sustained by legal sanctions. If the disputants seek to continue their relationship, some agreement is worked out, even if this means, in rare cases, that one party accepts the status quo imposed by the other. This rarely happens, however, because business and social custom forbid one to terminate a harmonious social tie by selfishly insisting on one's own interests.

---

[10] Von Mehren (1958: 1494) points out "there are still very large areas of Japanese life in which it is difficult to predict whether a dispute will be settled by reference to legal standards (applied either in court or in an out-of-court settlement) or in terms of quite different conceptions. It is often impossible to know in advance whether a party will seek to enforce his legal rights."

Usually it is clear that the unilaterally imposed solution is totally inadmissible when no agreement can be reached, and the wronged party is then supported by the moral opinion of the community, leaving the contract breaker in an untenable position. Thus what seems at first glance to be an absurd and serious deficiency in the contractual concept is in actuality only a reflection of the normal way of conducting business transactions.[11] A similar reliance on custom may be seen in the American practice of buying and selling comporate stock through verbal orders.

This emphasis on compromise has produced its own abuses. A special profession, the *jidan-ya*, or makers of compromises, has arisen, particularly in the large cities. Hired by people having difficulty collecting debts, these bill collectors compel payment by intimidation, frequently by violence. This is of course a criminal offense,[12] and prosecution of the *jidan-ya* is reported from time to time in the newspapers. But their occupation is apparently flourishing. Furthermore, public opinion seems to be favorable or at least neutral concerning this practice; even intimidated debtors thus compelled to pay seem to acquiesce easily and do not indicate strong opposition. This attitude is doubtlessly due to some extent to the delay and expense of litigation, but at the same time the traditional frame of mind regarding extrajudicial means of dispute resolution undoubtedly has had some influence on public opinion toward the *jidan-ya*. The common use of the term *jidan-ya* seems to suggest that extrajudicial coercion and compromise are not distinctly differentiated in the minds of people.

Finally, the specific social attitudes toward disputes are reflected in the judicial process. Japanese not only hesitate to resort to a lawsuit but are also quite ready to settle an action already instituted through conciliatory processes during the course of litigation. With this inclination in the background, judges also are likely to hesitate, or at least not seek, to expedite judicial decision, preferring instead to reconcile the litigant parties. Complaint about delay in reaching judicial decisions is almost universal, particularly in recent years, and the reasons for the delay are diverse. But one reason may be this judicial hesitancy to attribute clear-cut victory and defeat to the respective parties.[13] It is, though, interesting to note that the percentage of judicial decisions has tended to rise since 1952, while the

---

[11] It seems that here we have another clue to an understanding of the social-cultural background of divorce by agreement.

[12] Penal Code arts. 249–50.

[13] In this connection another aspect of this judicial attitude should be pointed out: because of the inclination to avoid attributing to one party clear-cut victory or defeat, judges are apt to attribute some fault to both parties. For instance, in case of a suit for damages based on tort, in which a truck driver, ignoring the right of way of another car, crossed a street and collided with the latter, the court declared that the victim was also negligent in not slowing down his speed, and reduced the amount of damages for personal injury and property damage to 30,000 yen (approximately 83 dollars). Yanaki v. Yūgen Kaisha Kubota Shōji (Kubota Commercial Limited Liability Co.), Tokyo District Court, March 24, 1959, 19 *Kakyū Saibonsho Minji Saiban Reishū* (A Collection of Civil Cases in the Inferior Courts) 545.

percentage of judicial proceedings terminated by compromise and successful mediation has tended to fall. It would be incautious to conclude hastily
that these figures indicate a popular shift from the traditional attitude to a
more individualistic one, but the beginning of such a tendency may be
suggested.

Furthermore, it seems that judges are rather commonly inclined to attach
importance to the status quo or to a *fait accompli*. The legal adage, *pereat
mundus, fiat justitia*, is apparently alien to the Japanese public as a whole
and to Japanese lawyers in particular. Once a certain situation is set, especially when it has been in existence for some time, people are inclined to
accept it even if it is not legally permissible. The courts reflect this attitude
of the people and then attempt to rationalize the result. Such a tendency also
seems to be related to the traditional popular conception of social relationships, which sees them not as something controlled by objective fixed standards but as something precarious depending on and changing with actual
situations. . . .

Considering these facts, parties in dispute usually find that resort to a
lawsuit is less profitable than resort to other means of settlement. A lawsuit
takes more time and more expense, terminates the harmonious relationship
between the parties, and gives the plaintiff just as little as, quite often less
than, what he would obtain through extrajudicial means. Who would resort
to a lawsuit in view of these disadvantages except pugnacious, litigious
fellows?

Jerome Frank (1950: 33) has noted that an overwhelmingly large number
of lawsuits in the United States are not appealed to a higher court and that
nearly 95% of the cases come to an end in the trial court. Such finality is in
striking contrast to the comparatively large number of cases appealed to a
higher court in Japan. Presumably this reflects the reluctance of litigants to
accept a court decision rendered and imposed upon them without being
convinced of the righteousness of its content; in the traditional ways of
settling a dispute the solution was, in principle, reached through agreement
by both parties. The notion that a justice measured by universal standards
can exist independent of the wills of the disputants is apparently alien to
the traditional habit of the Japanese people. Consequently, distrust of judges
and a lack of respect for the authority of judicial decisions is widespread
throughout the nation.

INFORMAL MEANS OF DISPUTE RESOLUTION: RECONCILEMENT AND CONCILIATION

The prevailing forms of settling disputes in Japan are the extrajudicial means of reconcilement and conciliation. By *reconcilement* is meant
the process by which parties in the dispute confer with each other and reach

a point at which they can come to terms and restore or create harmonious relationships. As stated above, social groups or contractual relationships of the traditional nature presuppose situational changes depending on their members' needs and demands and on the existing power balance; the process of conferring with each other permits this adjustment. Particularly in a patriarchal relationship the superior (*oyabun*) who has the status of a patriarch is expected to exercise his power for the best interests of his inferior (*kobun*), and consequently his decision is, in principle, more or less accepted as the basis for reconcilement even though the decision might in reality be imposed on the inferior. Reconcilement is the basic form of dispute resolution in the traditional culture of Japan. *Conciliation*, a modified form of reconcilement, is reconcilement through a third person.

In the legal systems of Western countries as well as of Japan, dispute resolution through a third person as intermediary includes two categories: mediation and arbitration. In mediation a third party offers his good offices to help the others reach an agreement; the mediator offers suggestions which have no binding force. In contrast, a third party acting as arbitrator renders a decision on the merits of the dispute. In the traditional culture of Japan, however, mediation and arbitration have not been differentiated; in principle the third person who intervenes to settle a dispute, the go-between, is supposed to be a man of higher status than the disputants. When such a person suggests conditions for reconcilement, his prestige and authority ordinarily are sufficient to persuade the two parties to accept the settlement. Consequently, in the case of mediation also, the conditions for reconcilement which he suggests are in a sense imposed, and the difference between mediation and arbitration is nothing but a question of the degree of the go-between's power. Generally speaking, the higher the prestige and the authority of the go-between, the stronger is the actual influence on the parties in dispute, and in the same proportion conciliation takes on the coloration of arbitration or of mediation. The settlement of a dispute aims to maintain, restore, or create a harmonious "particularistic" relationship, and for that purpose not only mediation but also arbitration must avoid the principles implicit in a judicial settlement: the go-between should not make any clear-cut decision on who is right or wrong or inquire into the existence and scope of the rights of the parties. Consequently the principle of *kenka ryō-seibai* (both disputants are to be punished) is applied in both mediation and arbitration.

If a dispute is very likely to arise and the parties thereto are more or less equal in their status (in other words, the power balance is not sufficient to settle an eventual dispute), they normally agree in advance on a third person as mediator or arbitrator. For example, when marriage takes place, it is a common custom in Japan to have a go-between (sometimes each of the marrying families appoints its respective go-between) witness the marriage and play the role of mediator or arbitrator if serious troubles arise later. Or, when a man is employed (not only as a domestic servant or apprentice of a carpenter, painter, or merchant, but also as a clerk in such business enterprises as steel mills, chemical plants, and banks), it is still common practice for the employer to demand from the employee an instrument of surety signed by a *mimoto hikiukenin* or *minoto hoshōnin* (literally translated, a person who ensures the antecedents of the employee). Originally this man had to undertake the role of mediator or arbitrator in case of sickness, breach of trust of the employee, or other eventual troubles; in recent years he simply undertakes the obligation as a surety. The reason that a very small portion of disputes are brought to court is to be found, as stated above, in the fact that most of the disputes are settled through these informal means.

Kankai

Very soon after the Meiji Restoration, the government was forced to make concessions to this centuries-old practice (Henderson, 1952) and accordingly legalized conciliation; in 1876 the government initiated *kankai* (literally, invitation to reconcilement) as a legal court procedure and provided for its preferred usage prior to a regular judicial proceeding.[14] In 1883 the Ministry of Justice issued a directive that *kankai* should be a compulsory procedure prior to regular judicial process in all except commercial cases.[15]

Kankai—the Japanese word gives the impression that it is a recommendation favoring reconcilement—was actually the imposition of a settlement under authority of the court with the litigants often being in no position to refuse the proposal. A scene of a famous Kabuki drama, *Suitengū Megumi no Fukagawa* (first performance in 1885), by Mokuami presents a very realistic description of the image of *kankai* then held by the people.[16] The usurer Kimbei comes, accompanied by Yasuzo, a pettifogger, to the home of his debtor Kobei, an indigent former samurai. In front of the debtor's home Yasuzo says to his client: "If the debtor is not likely to pay the debt, let's intimidate him by saying that we well resort to *kankai* in case he does not deliver a pledge." They enter the house and demand that Kobei deliver them pledges as a substitute for the payment of his debt: "If you are delayed

---

[14] Ministry of Justice Pronouncement A (*Kō*) No. 17 of 1876.

[15] Ministry of Justice Directive of Oct. 23, 1883 in response to an inquiry from Ibaragi Prefecture.

[16] Mokuami Kawatake is known as a dramatist whose plays give a very realistic description of the Japanese society of his time (the late Tokugawa and early Meiji periods).

in delivering them, I will bring the case to *kankai*, have them arrest you, and let you enjoy a cool breeze."

Table 2 shows how frequently *kankai* was resorted to and what an important function it had. Probably this was due to the fact that, in the social chaos of the early Meiji era, the traditional extrajudicial means such as reconcilement and conciliation were insufficient for settling disputes. In 1890 the institution of *kankai* was abolished by the Code of Civil Procedure. This was but one of the codes promulgated during the 1890s as preparatory measures to bring to an end the privileges of extraterritoriality for alien residents in Japan; and it was with this aim in mind that the government strove to follow the pattern of Western nations in its recognition of judicial institutions. The reactions to the reform can be inferred from the comments on it given thirty years later by members of the House of Representatives when the reinstitution of mediation was under debate.

TABLE 2
NUMBER OF *KANKAI* AND LAWSUITS

Year	Kankai filed	Lawsuits filed
1879	651,604	135,009
1880	675,218	131,813
1881	732,217	130,426
1882	908,932	181,639
1883	1,094,216	238,071
1884	760,106[a]	138,250
1885	592,311	51,873
1886	509,915	49,920
1887	388,215	51,008
1888	327,600	50,707

[a]The reason for this abrupt decrease is not clear.
Source: *Shihō-shō* (Ministry of Justice), *Dai 5–14 Minji Tōkei Nempō* (5th–14th Annual Reports of Civil Statistics) (1879–1888).

Shōtoku Taishi, who drafted the "Constitution of Japan," write in Article 17 that harmony is to be honored. Japan, unlike other countries where rights and duties prevail, must strive to solve interpersonal cases by harmony and compromise. Since Japan does not settle everything by law as in the West but rather must determine matters, for the most part, in accordance with morality and human sentiment (*ninjō*), the doctrine of mediation is a doctrine indigenous to Japan. . . . The great three hundred year peace of the Tokugawa was preserved because disputes between citizens were resolved harmoniously through their own autonomous administration, avoiding, so far as possible, resort to court procedure.... However, later the justice bureaucrats, assuming upon the appearance of the Code of Civil Procedure that the bureaucracy should attempt to settle all problems in dispute, extremely perverted the thought of the people.[17]

Even after 1945, a leading lawyer, Yoshikata Mizoguchi, now Chief Judge of the Tokyo Family Court, declared in the preface to *Chōtei Tokuhon*, (Mediation Reader; published by the Japanese Federation of Mediation Associations in 1954): "Needless to say, the basic idea of *chōtei* [mediation] is harmony and since, as Crown Prince Shotoku revealed to us in Article I of his Constitution of Seventeen Articles enacted 1350 years ago which stated that 'harmony is to be honored,' respect for harmony is a national trait, the development of the *chōtei* institution in our country seems natural." We can imagine, then, the popular reaction which followed the abolition of *kankai*.

Chōtei

During World War I the industrialization and urbanization of Japan developed rapidly and upset the traditional social structure. In such a time of social unrest, the trust in those traditionally in positions of authority, such as employers or landlords, was weakened; and those who had been in an inferior position began to assert their legal rights. The traditional authority and prestige of superiors was no longer effecive to prevent, much less to solve, disputes with inferiors. Lawsuits by landlords or lessors against their tenants or lessees, which had been quite rare in the past, were becoming frequent, thus sharpening the antagonism between parties who were supposed to be friendly toward each other. What the government attempted, facing this dissolution of the social structure upon which the political regime had been based since the Meiji Restoration, is interesting from our point of view. Instead of coordinating the conflicting vested interests by legislation, the government reinstituted *chōtei*, with which the disputes themselves were to be "washed away" (*mizu ni nagasu*) by reconcilement; the emerging individualistic interests of lessees, tenants, and employees were to be kept from being converted into firmly established vested interests independent of the will of their superiors.

A member of the House of Representatives urged, when the Leased Land and Leased House Mediation Law was under deabte: "By endeavoring to be

---

[17] *Dai* 51 *Kai Teikoku Gikai Shugi In Iinkai Sokkiroku* (Stenographic Record of House of Representatives' Committees in the 51st Session of the Imperial Diet), category 5, no. 18, 3rd session, at 2 (1926).

sympathetic and by expressing harmony, we amicably reap rights which are not actually rights in themselves."[18] Another member argued:

> Handling this matter as merely a determination of the problem of the rights of a lessee of land or a tenant of a house so that the owner may assert his own rights even to the point of rapacity, in a period such as that of today when a shift in society in the harmony of supply and demand brings only shortages, with anyone being able to assert his own rights exclusively, makes it quite difficult, in the final analysis, to obtain true stability of rights. Therefore, the establishment of the Mediation Law is not so that someone by sticking to the law can determine the relationship of rights among the parties. That is, the relationship between a tenant and a house owner, a land lessee and a landowner differs from that between complete strangers. Therein is the personal expression of sympathy; therein is morality. And in the sense that it attempts to base settlement on these things exists the *raison d'être* of mediation.[19]

The institution of *chōtei* was to replace the informal mediators of the past who had been mostly men of "face"—for instance, village elders and sometimes even policemen—by mediation committees (consisting of laymen and a judge) and to have parties reach agreement under the psychological pressure derived from the "halo" of a state court. This attempt was quite successful. A large number of disputes arising out of leases were brought to *chōtei* procedure and not to regular judicial proceedings.

The number of mediation cases concerning land and house leases, farm tenancies, pecuniary debts, and domestic relations increased surprisingly after the institution of mediation,[20] but, remarkably enough, the number of regular judicial cases underwent no significant decrease. In other words, a large number of disputes which had been solved outside of the court or left unsolved were now brought to *chōtei*, which meant that (1) *chōtei* was much preferred to regular judicial proceedings, (2) traditional informal means of dispute resolution already had lost their function in this sector of personal relations, and (3) society needed control by a governmental agency of some kind during a period of social disorganization.

The tendency to settle disputes by compromise is also illustrated by the many suits withdrawn or formally compromised and the number of mediation cases withdrawn. Such a termination takes place when the need for a judicial decision or *chōtei* disappears; in most such instances, this occurs because the parties have settled the dispute themselves. The court takes an active role in encouraging settlement at stages short of a final decision.

---

[18]*Dai* 4S *Kai Teikoku Gikai Shūgi in Iinkai Sokkiroku* (Stenographic Record of House of Representatives' Committees in the 45th Session of the Imperial Diet), category 5, no. 5, 2nd session, at 4 (1922).

[19]*Ibid.*, 3rd session, at 1 (1922).

[20]That is under the following statutes: Leased Land and Leased House Mediation Law, Law No. 41 of 1922; Tenant Farming Mediation Law, Law 18 of 1924; Monetary Obligation Temporary Mediation Law, No. 26 of 1932; Personal Affairs Mediation Law, Law No. 11 of 1939.

In Summary Courts the number of cases settled by judicial compromise entered in the official record is approximately equal to the number settled without the formal aid of the court and withdrawn. In District Courts, the ratio is lower, but the number of judicial compromises is only a little less than half that of the cases settled privately. Practicing attorneys report that, in a large number of cases, the judge urges the parties to compromise at least once during the course of the trial. Both the tendency of parties to settle and the court's practice of encouraging compromise reflect the general attitude of the people.

In addition to *chōtei*, there is a long tradition of police intervention in disputes between citizens. Officers act as mediators on the basis of their authority, particularly when another man with sufficient prestige and authority is not available. *Chōtei*, as legalized by the series of mediation statutes, may in a sense be a modified, perhaps rationalized, form of the type of mediation performed by police officers. But even after *chōtei* was legalized, mediation by the police did not lessen. With their authority and psychological dominance, particularly under the authoritarian regime of the old Constitution, police mediators were by and large effective and efficient. The total number of cases brought to police officers for mediation is presumed to be still very great, though the exact figures are kept secret. Reports show a considerable quantity of cases brought to the Tokyo police for consultation and a large percentage of them solved through this informal procedure. A certain portion of the cases in which solutions were not reported presumably were resolved by party agreement based on the recommendations made. If these are taken into account, the number of cases solved by the police is quite sizable. In my own investigations, I have found that a rather large number of cases in the Family Courts were first brought to police officers for mediation and came to court only after mediation proved futile. Presumably the same may be true for *chōtei* cases in other courts.

RECENT CHANGES

I have tried to show the main features of various forms of dispute resolution, with particular emphasis on their specifically Japanese aspects. However, there are indications of gradual change. Some of these have been touched on. Since the Meiji Restoration, Japan has been in the process of rapid transition from a premodern, collectivistic, and non-industrial society. The traditional forms of dispute resolution were appropriate to the old society, whereas judicial decision and arbitration as contemplated in the provisions of the Code of Civil Procedure are alien to it.[21] But all modern societies, including Japanese society, are characterized by citizens with equal status and, consequently, by a kind óf check and balance of individual power. It is against this background that traditional relationships serving to make a proposed settlement acceptable have been disrupted and that the need for decisions in accordance with universalistic standards has arisen.

Furthermore, there is another aspect specific to the modern industrialized society: the economic value of calculability (Berechenbarkeit, as Max Weber [1947: 94] calls it) or foreseeability of rights and duties, without which the rational operation of capital enterprise would be seriously endangered.[22] As industrialization proceeds, the need for perfection of the judicial system and of legal precepts becomes both more extensive and more intensive, and the traditional informal means of dispute resolution are found to be disruptive to capital enterprises. In the latter years of World War I, the outward signs of this change were the increase in collective transactions, the growing number of lawsuits involving immovable property, and the development of a new form of labor relations. Though further changes were not apparent under the strong control of the totalitarian regime during the 1930s and 1940s, the large-scale industrialization necessitated by the war in China and later with the Allied powers undoubtedly accelerated the transition. During the whole period of the war, Japanese family life was gradually disorganized, accompanied by dissolution of the social controls exercised by the family. The result was a large number of serious conflicts within families and kinship groups which the traditional means of social control (patriarchal power and the family council) could no longer effectively resolve. The traditional family system being the very basis of the official ideology (shūshin) and the power structure of the state, the government adopted chōtei to settle disputes arising from the disorganization of the family. Rather than adjustment through a system of legal rights, disputes were to be "washed away" in order that the family might be strengthened and preserved.

With the collapse of government through the Emperor, the authority of the traditional social institutions as a vehicle of social control was lost or at least greatly weakened. Although various "superiors" still survive to some degree, they are no longer so influential as to be able to solve all controversies arising out of their relationships with their "inferiors." The most conspicuous of these changes is in the area of family disputes. Today neither the authority of the head of the family, the family council, nor the marriage go-between is capable of settling all family disputes. The large number of

---

[21] For example, Code of Civil Procedure art. 786–805.

[22] A prerequisite for such operations is "full calculability in the functioning of the administrative system and the legal order and dependable strictly formal guarantees of all agreements by the political authority (formal rationale Verwaltung und formal rationales Recht)."

such disputes brought to the Family Courts in the postwar era suggests this fact.

In 1950 the Ministry of Labor made a very interesting nationwide survey of social attitudes.[23] Among questions on family solidarity, parental authority, selection of a marriage partner, primogeniture, equality of the sexes, and the like, there was this one: "If you checked the weight of rationed sugar [in those days sugar was tightly rationed] and found a shortage, would you notify the merchant or not?" This question was designed allegedly to determine the extent to which people would uphold their rights. From a sample of 2808 (randomly selected), 90% of the men and 82% of the women replied "I would notify him," 9% of the men and 16% of the women replied "I would not," and 1% of the men and 2% of the women replied "I don't know." Perhaps this particular question was not entirely appropriate to probe the attitude sought because a deficit in the weight of rationed sugar was of vital importance to everyone in those days of food shortages; thus, while important, one should not overgeneralize from this response.

In 1952, the National Public Opinion Institute conducted a nationwide survey, a part of which bears upon our problem.[24] The institute investigated the reaction to the following question: "There is a saying, 'yield to a superior force' [*nagai mono ni wa makarerō*: literally, allow oneself to be enveloped by a long object]. Have you ever heard of this?" Those who replied affirmatively were then asked: "Do you think that the attitude expressed in that saying should be approved and that nothing else can be done?" Purportedly these questions were designed to measure the extent to which people yield to authority or power. Out of 3000 random samples, 51% of the men and 30% of the women replied that such an attitude should not be approved. Of course, this question simply pertained to the attitude toward authority and did not cover the exact problem under consideration, but it indirectly reveals the attitude of people toward informal means of dispute resolution in which the authority of the go-between plays a significant role.

Probably of greater significance is a change which seems to be taking place in *chōtei* cases, particularly in the Family Courts of large cities such as Tokyo or Osaka; it is not at all rare for parties to be aware of their legal rights and to insist upon them so strongly that reconcilement becomes at times quite difficult. Parties to *chōtei* cases have frequently complained that lay mediators did not pay sufficient attention to their rights under the law. From time to time various political leaders complain of the people's awareness of their

---

[23] *Fujin Shōnen Kyoku* (Women and Juvenile Bureau), *Rodo sho* (Ministry of Labor), *Hōkensei ni Tsuite no Chōsa* (A Survey Regarding Feudal Characteristics) 22 *Fujin Kankei Shiryō* Series (Materials Relating to Women Series) No. 7, 1951).

[24] *Kokuritsu Seron Chōsajo* (National Public Opinion Research Institute), *Shakai Kyōiku ni Tsuite no Yoron Chōsa* (A Public Opinion Survey Regarding Social Education) (1953).

rights and of the decay of harmony-minded traditions. Whatever their feelings about this may be, the legal institution of *chōtei* no longer functions to maintain the precarious nature of the interests involved in the traditional social and contractual relationships. The transition is irretrievably in process, and the outcome is clear.

REFERENCES

Frank, J.
   1950   *Courts on trial.* Princeton: Princeton Univ. Press.
Franklin, M. A., R. G. Chanin, and I. Mark
   1961   Accidents, money, and the law: A study of the economics of personal injury litigation. *Columbia Law Review* **61** (1961): 1–39.
Hattori, T.
   1963   The legal profession in Japan: Its historical development and present state. In *Law in Japan: The legal order in a changing society,* edited by A. T. von Mehren, pp. 111–152. Cambridge: Harvard Univ. Press.
Henderson, D. E.
   1952   Some aspects of Tokugawa law. *Washington Law Review* **27** (1952): 85–109.
Kato, I.
   1963   The treatment of motor vehicle accidents: A study of the impact of technological change on legal relations. In *Law in Japan: The legal order in a changing society,* edited by A. T. von Mehren, pp. 399–421. Cambridge: Harvard Univ. Press.
Parsons, T.
   1951   *The social system.* New York: Free Press.
Parsons, T., and E. Shils
   1951   Categories of the Orientation and Organization of Action. In *Toward a General theory of action.* Cambridge: Harvard Univ. Press.
von Mehren, A. T.
   1958   Some reflections on Japanese law. *Harvard Law Review* **71** (1958): 1486–1496.
Weber, M.
   1947   *Wirtschaft und Gesellschaft.* (3rd ed.) (Grundriss der Sozialökonomik, III Abteilung.) Tübingen: J. C. B. Mohr.

CONTRACT LAW AMONG AMERICAN BUSINESSMEN*

Stewart Macaulay

W HAT GOOD is contract law? Who uses it? When and how? Complete answers would require an investigation of almost every type of transaction between individuals and organizations. In this report, research has been confined to exchanges between businesses, and primarily to manufacturers.[1] Furthermore, this report will be limited to a presentation of the findings concerning when contract is and is not used and to a tentative explanation of these findings.[2]

---

*Revision of a paper read at the annual meeting of the American Sociological Association, August, 1962. An earlier vision of the paper was read at the annual meeting of the Midwest Sociological Society, April, 1962.

[1] The reasons for this limitation are that (a) these transactions are important from an economic standpoint, (b) they are frequently said in theoretical discussions to represent a high degree of rational planning, and (c) manufacturing personnel are sufficiently public-relations-minded to cooperate with a law professor who wants to ask a seemingly endless number of questions. Future research will deal with the building construction industry and other areas.

[2] For the present purposes, the what-difference-does-it-make issue is important primarily as it makes a case for an empirical study by a law teacher of the use and nonuse of contract by businessmen. First, law teachers have a professional concern with what the law ought to be. This involves evaluation of the consequences of the existing situation and of the possible alternatives. Thus, it is most relevant to examine business practices concerning contract if one is interested in what commercial law ought to be. Second, law teachers are supposed to teach law students something relevant to becoming lawyers. These business practices are facts that are relevant to the skills which law students will need when, as lawyers, they are called upon to create exchange relationships and to solve problems arising out of these relationships.

Reprinted from "Non-Contractual Relations in Business: A Preliminary Study" by Stewart Macaulay, *American Sociological Review*, Vol. 28 (1963): pp. 55–67.

This research is only the first phase in a scientific study.[3] The primary research technique involved interviewing 68 businessmen and lawyers representing 43 companies and six law firms. The interviews ranged from a 30-minute brush-off where not all questions could be asked of a busy and uninterested sales manager to a six-hour discussion with the general counsel of a large corporation. Detailed notes of the interviews were taken and a complete report of each interview was dictated, usually no later than the evening after the interview. All but two of the companies had plants in Wisconsin; 17 were manufacturers of machinery but none made such items as food products, scientific instruments, textiles or petroleum products. Thus the likelihood of error because of sampling bias may be considerable.[4] However, to a great extent, existing knowledge has been inadequate to permit more rigorous procedures—as yet one cannot formulate many precise questions to be asked a systematically selected sample of "right people." Much time has been spent fishing for relevant questions or answers, or both.

Reciprocity, exchange, or contract has long been of interest to sociologists, economists, and lawyers. Yet each discipline has an incomplete view of this kind of conduct. This study represents the effort of a law teacher to draw on sociological ideas and empirical investigation. It stresses, among other things, the functions and dysfunctions of using contract to solve exchange problems and the influence of occupational roles on how one assesses whether the benefits of using contract outweigh the costs.

To discuss when contract is and is not used, the term "contract" must be specified. This term will be used here to refer to devices for conducting exchanges. Contract is not treated as synonymous with an exchange itself, which may or may not be characterized as contractual. Nor is contract used to refer to a writing recording an agreement. Contract, as I use the term here, involves two distinct elements: (a) rational planning of the transaction with careful provision for as many future contingencies as can be foreseen, and

---

[3] The following things have been done. The literature in law, business, economics, psychology, and sociology has been surveyed. The formal systems related to exchange transactions have been examined. Standard form contracts and the standard terms and conditions that are found on such business documents as catalogues, quotation forms, purchase orders, and acknowledgment-of-order forms from 850 firms that are based in or do business in Wisconsin have been collected. The citations of all reported court cases during a period of 15 years involving the largest 500 manufacturing corporations in the United States have been obtained and are being analyzed to determine why the use of contract legal sanctions was thought necessary and whether or not any patterns of "problem situations" can be delineated. In addition, the informal systems related to exchange transactions have been examined. Letters of inquiry concerning practices in certain situations have been answered by approximately 125 businessmen. Interviews, as described in the text, have been conducted. Moreover, six of my students have interviewed 21 other businessmen, bankers, and lawyers. Their findings are consistent with those reported in the text.

[4] However, the cases have not been selected because they *did* use contract. There is as much interest in, and effort to obtain, cases of nonuse as of use of contract. Thus, one variety of bias has been minimized.

(b) the existence or use of actual or potential legal sanctions to induce performance of the exchange or to compensate for nonperformance.

These devices for conducting exchanges may be used or may exist in greater or lesser degree, so that transactions can be described relatively as involving a more contractual or a less contractual manner (a) of creating an exchange relationship, or (b) of solving problems arising during the course of such a relationship. For example, General Motors might agree to buy all of the Buick Division's requirements of aluminum for ten years from Reynolds Aluminum. Here the two large corporations probably would plan their relationship carefully. The plan probably would include a complex pricing formula designed to meet market fluctuations, an agreement on what would happen if either party suffered a strike or a fire, a definition of Reynolds' responsibility for quality control and for losses caused by defective quality, and many other provisions. As the term contract is used here, this is a more contractual method of creating an exchange relationship than is a home owner's casual agreement with a real estate broker giving the broker the exclusive right to sell the owner's house which fails to include provisions for the consequences of many easily foreseeable (and perhaps even highly probable) contingencies. In both instances, legally enforceable contracts may or may not have been created, but it must be recognized that the existence of a legal sanction has no necessary relationship to the degree of rational planning by the parties, beyond certain minimal legal requirements of certainty of obligation. General Motors and Reynolds might never sue or even refer to the written record of their agreement to answer questions which come up during their ten-year relationship, while the real estate broker might sue, or at least threaten to sue, the owner of the house. The broker's method of *dispute settlement* then would be more contractual than that of General Motors and Reynolds, thus reversing the relationship that existed in regard to the "contractualness" of the *creation* of the exchange relationships.

TENTATIVE FINDINGS

It is difficult to generalize about the use and nonuse of contract by manufacturing industry. However, a number of observations can be made with reasonable accuracy at this time. The use and nonuse of contract in creating exchange relations and in dispute settling will be taken up in turn.

The Creation of Exchange Relationships

In creating exchange relationships, businessmen may plan to a greater or lesser degree in relation to several types of issues. Before reporting the findings as to practices in creating such relationships, it is necessary to describe what one can plan about in a bargain and the degrees of planning which are possible.

People negotiating a contract can make plans concerning several types of issues:

(1) They can plan what each is to do or refrain from doing; e.g., S might agree to deliver ten 1963 Studebaker four-door sedan automobiles to B on a certain date in exchange for a specified amount of money.

(2) They can plan what effect certain contingencies are to have on their duties; e.g., what is to happen to S and B's obligations if S cannot deliver the cars because of a strike at the Studebaker factory?

(3) They can plan what is to happen if either of them fails to perform; e.g., what is to happen if S delivers nine of the cars two weeks late?

(4) They can plan their agreement so that it is a legally enforceable contract—that is, so that a legal sanction would be available to provide compensation for injury suffered by B as a result of S's failure to deliver the cars on time.

As to each of these issues, there may be a different degree of planning by the parties.

(1) They may carefully and explicitly plan; e.g., S may agree to deliver ten 1963 Studebaker four-door sedans which have six cylinder engines, automatic transmissions and other specified items of optional equipment and which will perform to a specified standard for a certain time.

(2) They may have a mutual but tacit understanding about an issue; e.g., although the subject was never mentioned in their negotiations, both S and B may assume that B may cancel his order for the cars before they are delivered if B's taxicab business is so curtailed that B can no longer use ten additional cabs.

(3) They may have two inconsistent unexpressed assumptions about an issue; e.g., S may assume that if any of the cabs fails to perform to the specified standard for a certain time, all S must do is repair or replace it. B may assume S must also compensate B for the profits B would have made if the cab had been in operation.

(4) They may never have thought of the issue; e.g., neither S nor B planned their agreement so that it would be a legally enforceable contract.

Of course, the first and fourth degrees of planning listed are the extreme cases and the second and third are intermediate points. Clearly other intermediate points are possible; e.g., S and B neglect to specify whether the cabs should have automatic or conventional transmissions. Their planning is not as careful and explicit as that in the example previously given.

The following diagram represents the dimensions of creating an exchange relationship just discussed with "X's" representing the example of S and B's contract for ten taxicabs.

	Definition of performances	Effect of contingencies	Effect of defective performances	Legal sanctions
Explicit and careful	X			
Tacit agreement		X		
Unilateral assumptions			X	
Unawareness of the issue				X

Most larger companies, and many smaller ones, attempt to plan carefully and completely. Important transactions not in the ordinary course of business are handled by a detailed contract. For example, recently the Empire State Building was sold for $65 million. More than 100 attorneys, representing 34 parties, produced a 400-page contract. Another example is found in the agreement of a major rubber company in the United States to give technical assistance to a Japanese firm. Several million dollars were involved and the contract consisted of 88 provisions on 17 pages. The 12 house counsel—lawyers who work for one corporation rather than many clients—interviewed said that all but the smallest businesses carefully planned most transactions of any significance. Corporations have procedures so that particular types of exchanges will be reviewed by their legal and financial departments.

More routine transactions commonly are handled by what can be called standardized planning. A firm will have a set of terms and conditions for purchases, sales, or both printed on the business documents used in these exchanges. Thus the things to be sold and the price may be planned particularly for each transaction, but standard provisions will further elaborate the performances and cover the other subjects of planning. Typically, these terms and conditions are lengthy and printed in small type on the back of the forms. For example, 24 paragraphs in eight-point type are printed on the back of the purchase order form used by the Allis Chalmers Manufacturing Company. The provisions: (1) describe, in part, the performance required, e.g., "DO NOT WELD CASTINGS WITHOUT OUR CONSENT"; (2) plan for the effect of contingencies, e.g., ". . . in the event the Seller suffers delay in performance due to an act of God, war, act of the Government, priorities or allocations, act of the Buyer, fire, flood, strike, sabotage, or other causes beyond Seller's control, the time of completion shall be extended a period of time equal to the period of such delay if the Seller gives the Buyer notice in writing of the cause of any such delay within a reasonable time after the beginning thereof"; (3) plan for the effect of defective performances, e.g., "The buyer, without waiving any other legal rights, reserves the right to cancel without charge or to postpone deliveries of any of the articles covered by this order which are not shipped in time reasonably to meet said agreed dates"; (4) plan for a legal sanction, e.g., the clause "without waiving any other legal rights," in the example just given.

In larger firms such "boiler plate" provisions are drafted by the house counsel or the firm's outside lawyer. In smaller firms such provisions may be drafted by the industry trade association, may be copied from a competitor, or may be found on forms purchased from a printer. In any event, salesmen and purchasing agents, the operating personnel, typically are unaware of what is said in the fine print on the back of the forms they use. Yet often the normal business patterns will give effect to this standardized planning. For example, purchasing agents may have to use a purchase order form so that all transactions receive a number under the firm's accounting system. Thus, the required accounting record will carry the necessary planning of the exchange relationship printed on its reverse side. If the seller does not object to this planning and accepts the order, the buyer's "fine print" will control. If the seller does object, differences can be settled by negotiation.

This type of standardized planning is very common. Requests for copies of the business documents used in buying and selling were sent to approximately 6000 manufacturing firms which do business in Wisconsin. Approximately 1200 replies were received and 850 companies used some type of standardized planning. With only a few exceptions, the firms that did not reply and the 350 that indicated they did not use standardized planning were very small manufacturers such as local bakeries, soft drink bottlers, and sausage makers.

While businessmen can and often do carefully and completely plan, it is clear that not all exchanges are neatly rationalized. Although most business-men think that a clear description of both the seller's and buyer's perfor-mances is obvious common sense, they do not always live up to this ideal. The house counsel and the purchasing agent of a medium-size manufacturer of automobile parts reported that several times their engineers had com-mitted the company to buy expensive machines without adequate specifica-tions. The engineers had drawn careful specifications as to the type of machine and how it was to be made but had neglected to require that the machine produce specified results. An attorney and an auditor both stated that most contract disputes arise because of ambiguity in the specifications.

Businessmen often prefer to rely on "a man's word" in a brief letter, a handshake, or "common honesty and decency"—even when the transaction involves exposure to serious risks. Seven lawyers from law firms with business practices were interviewed. Five thought that businessmen often entered contracts with only a minimal degree of advance planning. They complained that businessmen desire to "keep it simple and avoid red tape" even where large amounts of money and significant risks are involved. One stated that he was "sick of being told, 'We can trust old Max,' when the problem is not one of honesty but one of reaching an agreement that both sides understand." Another said that businessmen when bargaining often talk only in pleasant generalities, think they have a contract, but fail to reach agreement on any of the hard, unpleasant questions until forced to do so by a lawyer. Two outside lawyers had different views. One thought that large firms usually planned important exchanges, although he conceded that occasionally matters might be left in a fairly vague state. The other dissenter represents a large utility that commonly buys heavy equipment and buildings. The supplier's employees come on the utility's property to install the equipment or construct the buildings, and they may be injured while there. The utility has been sued by such employees so often that it carefully plans purchases with the assistance of a lawyer so that suppliers take this burden.

Moreover, standardized planning can break down. In the example of such planning previously given, it was assumed that the purchasing agent would use his company's form with its 24 paragraphs printed on the back and that the seller would accept this or object to any provisions he did not like. However, the seller may fail to read the buyer's 24 paragraphs of fine print and may accept the buyer's order on the seller's own acknowledgment-of-order form. Typically this form will have 10–50 paragraphs favoring the seller, and these provisions are likely to be different from or inconsistent with the buyer's provisions. The seller's acknowledgment form may be received by the buyer and checked by a clerk. She will read the *face* of the acknowledgment but not the fine print on the back of it because she has neither the time nor ability to analyze the small print on the 100–500 forms she must review each day. The face of the acknowledgment—where the goods and the price are specified—is likely to correspond with the face of the purchase order. If it does, the two forms are filed away. At this point, both buyer and seller are likely to assume they have planned an exchange and made a contract. Yet they have done neither, as they are in disagreement about all that appears on the back of their forms. This practice is common enough to have a name. Law teachers call it "the battle of the forms."

Ten of the 12 purchasing agents interviewed said that frequently the provisions on the back of their purchase order and those on the back of a supplier's acknowledgment would differ or be inconsistent. Yet they would assume that the purchase was complete without further action unless one of the supplier's provisions was really objectionable. Moreover, only occasionally would they bother to read the fine print on the back of suppliers' forms. On the other hand, one purchasing agent insists that agreement be reached on the fine print provisions, but he represents the utility whose lawyer reported that it exercises great care in planning. The other purchasing agent who said that his company did not face a battle of the forms problem works for a division of one of the largest manufacturing corporations in the United States. Yet the company may have such a problem without recognizing it. The purchasing agent regularly sends a supplier both a purchase order and another form which the supplier is asked to sign and return. The second form states that the supplier accepts the buyer's terms and conditions. The company has sufficient bargaining power to force suppliers to sign and return the form, and the purchasing agent must show one of his firm's auditors such a signed form for every purchase order issued. Yet suppliers frequently return this buyer's form *plus* their own acknowledgment form which has conflicting provisions. The purchasing agent throws away the supplier's form and files his own. Of course, in such a case the supplier has not acquiesced to the buyer's provisions. There is no agreement and no contract.

Sixteen sales managers were asked about the battle of the forms. Nine said that frequently no agreement was reached on which set of fine print was to govern, while seven said that there was no problem. Four of the seven worked for companies whose major customers are the large automobile companies or the large manufacturers of paper products. These customers demand that their terms and conditions govern any purchase, are careful generally to see that suppliers acquiesce, and have the bargaining power to have their way. The other three of the seven sales managers who have no battle of the forms problem, work for manufacturers of special industrial machines. Their firms are careful to reach complete agreement with their customers. Two of these men stressed that they could take no chances because such a large part of their firm's capital is tied up in making any one machine. The other sales manager had been influenced by a law suit against one of his competitors for over a half-million dollars. The suit was brought by a customer when the competitor had been unable to deliver a machine and put it in operation on time. The sales manager interviewed said his firm could not guarantee that its machines would work perfectly by a specified time because they are designed to fit the customer's requirements, which may present difficult engineering problems. As a result, contracts are carefully negotiated.

A large manufacturer of packaging materials audited its records to determine how often it had failed to agree on terms and conditions with its customers or had failed to create legally binding contracts. Such failures cause a risk of loss to this firm since the packaging is printed with the customer's design and cannot be salvaged once this is done. The orders for five days in four different years were reviewed. The percentages of orders where no agreement on terms and conditions was reached or no contract was formed were as follows:

$$
\begin{array}{ll}
1953 & \ldots\ldots\ldots 75.0\% \\
1954 & \ldots\ldots\ldots 69.4\% \\
1955 & \ldots\ldots\ldots 71.5\% \\
1956 & \ldots\ldots\ldots 59.5\%.
\end{array}
$$

It is likely that businessmen pay more attention to describing the performances in an exchange than to planning for contingencies or defective performances or to obtaining legal enforceability of their contracts. Even when a purchase order and acknowledgment have conflicting provisions printed on the back, almost always the buyer and seller will be in agreement on what is to be sold and how much is to be paid for it. The lawyers who said businessmen often commit their firms to significant exchanges too casually stated that the performances would be defined in the brief letter or telephone call; the lawyers objected that nothing else would be covered. Moreover, it is likely that businessmen are least concerned about planning their transactions so that they are legally enforceable contracts.[5] For example, in Wisconsin requirements contracts—contracts to supply a firm's requirements of an item rather than a definite quantity—probably are not legally enforceable. Seven people interviewed reported that their firms regularly used requirements contracts in dealings in Wisconsin. None thought that the lack of legal sanction made any difference. Three of these people were house counsel who knew the Wisconsin law before being interviewed. Another example of a lack of desire for legal sanctions is found in the relationship between automobile manufacturers and their suppliers of parts. The manufacturers draft a carefully planned agreement, but one which is so designed that the supplier will have only minimal, if any, legal rights against the manufacturers. The standard contract used by manufacturers of paper to sell to magazine publishers has a pricing clause which is probably sufficiently vague to make the contract legally unenforceable. The house counsel of one of the largest paper producers said that everyone in the industry is aware of this because of a leading New York case concerning the contract, but that no one cares. Finally, it seems likely that planning for contingencies and defective performances are in-between cases—more likely to occur than planning for a legal sanction, but less likely than a description of performance.

[5] Compare the findings of an empirical study of Connecticut business practices (Comment, 1957).

Thus one can conclude that (1) many business exchanges reflect a high degree of planning about the four categories—description, contingencies, defective performances, and legal sanction—but (2) many, if not most, exchanges reflect no planning, or only a minimal amount of it, especially concerning legal sanctions and the effect of defective performances. As a result, the opportunity for good faith disputes during the life of the exchange relationship often is present.

The Adjustment of Exchange Relationships and the Settling of Disputes

While a significant amount of creating business exchanges is done on a fairly noncontractual basis, the creation of exchanges usually is far more contractual than the adjustment of such relationships and the settlement of disputes. Exchanges are adjusted when the obligations of one or both parties are modified by agreement during the life of the relationship. For example, the buyer may be allowed to cancel all or part of the goods he has ordered because he no longer needs them; the seller may be paid more than the contract price by the buyer because of unusual changed circumstances. Dispute settlement involves determining whether or not a party has performed as agreed and, if he has not, doing something about it. For example, a court may have to interpret the meaning of a contract, determine what the alleged defaulting party has done and determine what, if any, remedy the aggrieved party is entitled to. Or one party may assert that the other is in default, refuse to proceed with performing the contract and refuse to deal ever again with the alleged defaulter. If the alleged defaulter, who in fact may not be in default, takes no action, the dispute is then "settled."

Business exchanges in nonspeculative areas are usually adjusted without dispute. Under the law of contracts, if B orders 1000 widgets from S at $1.00 each, B must take all 1000 widgets or be in breach of contract and liable to pay S his expenses up to the time of the breach plus his lost anticipated profit. Yet all ten of the purchasing agents asked about cancellation of orders once placed indicated that they expected to be able to cancel orders freely subject only to an obligation to pay for the seller's major expenses such as scrapped steel.[6] All 17 sales personnel asked reported that they often had to accept cancellation. One said, "You can't ask a man to eat paper [the firm's product] when he has no use for it." A lawyer with many large industrial clients said:

---

[6]See the case studies on cancellation of contracts in Harvard Business Review (1923–24: 238–40, 367–70, 496–502).

Often businessmen do not feel they have "a contract"—rather they have "an order." They speak of "cancelling the order" rather than "breaching our contract." When I began practice I referred to order cancellations as breaches of contract, but my clients objected since they do not think of cancellation as wrong. Most clients, in heavy industry at least, believe that there is a right to cancel as part of the buyer–seller relationship. There is a widespread attitude that one can back out of any deal within some very vague limits. Lawyers are often surprised by this attitude.

Disputes are frequently settled without reference to the contract or potential or actual legal sanctions. There is a hesitancy to speak of legal rights or to threaten to sue in these negotiations. Even where the parties have a detailed and carefully planned agreement which indicates what is to happen if, say, the seller fails to deliver on time, often they will never refer to the agreement but will negotiate a solution when the problem arises, apparently as if there had never been any original contract. One purchasing agent expressed a common business attitude when he said:

If something comes up, you get the other man on the telephone and deal with the problem. You don't read legalistic contract clauses at each other if you ever want to do business again. One doesn't run to lawyers if he wants to stay in business because one must behave decently.

Or as one businessman put it, "You can settle any dispute if you keep the lawyers and accountants out of it. They just do not understand the give-and-take needed in business." All of the house counsel interviewed indicated that they are called into the dispute-settlement process only after the businessmen have failed to settle matters in their own way. Two indicated that after being called in, house counsel at first will only advise the purchasing agent, sales manager, or other official involved; not even the house counsel's letterhead is used on communications with the other side until all hope for a peaceful resolution is gone.

Law suits for breach of contract appear to be rare. Only five of the 12 purchasing agents had ever been involved in even a negotiation concerning a contract dispute where both sides were represented by lawyers; only two of ten sales managers had ever gone this far. None had been involved in a case that went through trial. A law firm with more than 40 lawyers and a large commercial practice handles in a year only about six trials concerned with contract problems. Less than 10 percent of the time of this office is devoted to any type of work related to contracts disputes. Corporations big enough to do business in more than one state tend to sue and be sued in the federal courts. Yet only 2779 out of 58,293 civil actions filed in the United States District Courts in fiscal year 1961 involved private contracts (Director, 1961: 238). During the same period only 3447 of the 61,138 civil cases filed in the principal trial courts of New York State involved private contracts (State of New York, 1961: 209–211). The same picture emerges from a review of appellate cases.[7] Mentschikoff has suggested that commercial cases are not brought to the courts either in periods of business prosperity (because buyers unjustifiably reject goods only when prices drop and they can get similar goods elsewhere at less than the contract price) or in periods of deep depression (because people are unable to come to court or have insufficient assets to satisfy any judgment that might be obtained). Apparently, she adds, it is necessary to have "a kind of middle-sized depression" to bring large numbers of commercial cases to the courts. However, there is little evidence that in even "a kind of middle-sized depression" today's businessmen would use the courts to settle disputes (New York Law Revision Commission, 1954: 1391).

At times relatively contractual methods are used to make adjustments in ongoing transactions and to settle disputes. Demands of one side which are deemed unreasonable by the other occasionally are blocked by reference to the terms of the agreement between the parties. The legal position of the parties can influence negotiations even though legal rights or litigation are never mentioned in their discussions; it makes a difference if one is demanding what both concede to be a right or begging for a favor. Now and then a firm may threaten to turn matters over to its attorneys, threaten to sue, commence a suit, or even litigate and carry an appeal to the highest court which will hear the matter. Thus, legal sanctions, while not an everyday affair, are not unknown in business.

One can conclude that while detailed planning and legal sanctions play a significant role in some exchanges between businesses, in many business exchanges their role is small.

TENTATIVE EXPLANATIONS

Two questions need to be answered: (A) How can business successfully operate exchange relationships with relatively so little attention to detailed planning or to legal sanctions? and (B) Why does business ever use contract in light of its success without it?

---

[7] My colleague Lawrence M. Friedman has studied the work of the Supreme Court of Wisconsin in contracts cases. He has found that contracts cases reaching that court tend to involve economically marginal business and family economic disputes rather than important commercial transactions. This has been the situation since about the turn of the century. Only during the Civil War period did the court deal with significant numbers of important contracts cases, but this happened against the background of a much simpler and different economic system.

Why are relatively noncontractual practices so common?

In most situations contract is not needed.[8] Often its functions are served by other devices. Most problems are avoided without resort to detailed planning or legal sanctions because usually there is little room for honest misunderstandings or good faith differences of opinion about the nature and quality of a seller's performance. Although the parties fail to cover all foreseeable contingencies, they will exercise care to see that both understand the primary obligation on each side. Either products are standardized with an accepted description or specifications are written calling for production to certain tolerances or results. Those who write and read specifications are experienced professionals who will know the customs of their industry and those of the industries with which they deal. Consequently, these customs can fill gaps in the express agreements of the parties. Finally, most products can be tested to see if they are what was ordered; typically in manufacturing industry we are not dealing with questions of taste or judgment where people can differ in good faith.

When defaults occur they are not likely to be disastrous because of techniques of risk avoidance or risk spreading. One can deal with firms of good reputation or he may be able to get some form of security to guarantee performance. One can insure against many breaches of contract where the risks justify the costs. Sellers set up reserves for bad debts on their books and can sell some of their accounts receivable. Buyers can place orders with two or more suppliers of the same item so that a default by one will not stop the buyer's assembly lines.

Moreover, contract and contract law are often thought unnecessary because there are many effective nonlegal sanctions. Two norms are widely accepted: (1) Commitments are to be honored in almost all situations; one does not welsh on a deal. (2) One ought to produce a good product and stand behind it. Then, too, business units are organized to perform commitments, and internal sanctions will induce performance. For example, sales personnel must face angry customers when there has been a late or defective performance. The salesmen do not enjoy this and will put pressure on the production personnel responsible for the default. If the production personnel default too often, they will be fired. At all levels of the two business units personal relationships across the boundaries of the two organizations exert pressures for conformity to expectations. Salesmen often know

[8]The explanation that follows emphasizes a *considered* choice not to plan in detail for all contingencies. However, at times it is clear that businessmen fail to plan because of a lack of sophistication; they simply do not appreciate the risk they are running, or they merely follow patterns established in their firm years ago without reexamining these practices in light of current conditions.

purchasing agents well. The same two individuals occupying these roles may have dealt with each other from 5 to 25 years. Each has something to give the other. Salesmen have gossip about competitors, shortages, and price increases to give purchasing agents who treat them well. Salesmen take purchasing agents to dinner, and they give purchasing agents Christmas gifts hoping to improve the chances of making a sale. The buyer's engineering staff may work with the seller's engineering staff to solve problems jointly. The seller's engineers may render great assistance, and the buyer's engineers may desire to return the favor by drafting specifications which only the seller can meet. The top executives of the two firms may know each other. They may sit together on government or trade committees. They may know each other socially and even belong to the same country club. The interrelationships may be more formal. Sellers may hold stock in corporations which are important customers; buyers may hold stock in important suppliers. Both buyer and seller may share common directors on their boards. They may share a common financial institution which has financed both units.

The final type of nonlegal sanction is the most obvious. Both business units involved in the exchange desire to continue successfully in business and will avoid conduct which might interfere with attaining this goal. One is concerned with both the reaction of the other party in the particular exchange and with his own general business reputation. Obviously, the buyer gains sanctions insofar as the seller wants the particular exchange to be completed. Buyers can withhold part or all of their payments until sellers have performed to their satisfaction. If a seller has a great deal of money tied up in his performance which he must recover quickly, he will go a long way to please the buyer in order to be paid. Moreover, buyers who are dissatisfied may cancel and cause sellers to lose the cost of what they have done up to cancellation. Furthermore, sellers hope for repeat orders, and one gets few of these from unhappy customers. Some industrial buyers go so far as to formalize this sanction by issuing "report cards" rating the performance of each supplier. The supplier rating goes to the top management of the seller organization, and these men can apply internal sanctions to salesmen, production supervisors or product designers if there are too many "D's" or "F's" on the report card.

While it is generally assumed that the customer is always right, the seller may have some counterbalancing sanctions against the buyer. The seller may have obtained a large down payment from the buyer which he will want to protect. The seller may have an exclusive process which the buyer needs. The seller may be one of the few firms which has the skill to make the item to the tolerances set by the buyer's engineers and within the time available. There are costs and delays involved in turning from a supplier one has dealt with in the past to a new supplier. Then, too, market conditions can change so that a buyer is faced with shortages of critical items. The most extreme example is the post-World War II gray market conditions when sellers were rationing goods rather than selling them. Buyers must build up some reserve of good will with suppliers if they face the risk of such shortage and desire good treatment when they occur. Finally, there is reciprocity in buying and selling. A buyer cannot push a supplier too far if that supplier also buys significant quantities of the product made by the buyer.

Not only do the particular business units in a given exchange want to deal with each other again, they also want to deal with other business units in the future. And the way one behaves in a particular transaction, or a series of transactions, will color his general business reputation. Blacklisting can be formal or informal. Buyers who fail to pay their bills on time risk a bad report in credit rating services such as Dun and Bradstreet. Sellers who do not satisfy their customers become the subject of discussion in the gossip exchanged by purchasing agents and salesmen, at meetings of purchasing agents' associations and trade associations, or even at country clubs or social gatherings where members of top management meet. The American male's habit of debating the merits of new cars carries over to industrial items. Obviously, a poor reputation does not help a firm make sales and may force it to offer great price discounts or added services to remain in business. Furthermore, the habits of unusually demanding buyers become known, and they tend to get no more than they can coerce out of suppliers who choose to deal with them. Thus often contract is not needed as there are alternatives.

Not only are contract and contract law not needed in many situations, their use may have, or may be thought to have, undesirable consequences. Detailed negotiated contracts can get in the way of creating good exchange relationships between business units. If one side insists on a detailed plan, there will be delay while letters are exchanged as the parties try to agree on what should happen if a remote and unlikely contingency occurs. In some cases they may not be able to agree at all on such matters and as a result a sale may be lost to the seller and the buyer may have to search elsewhere for an acceptable supplier. Many businessmen would react by thinking that had no one raised the series of remote and unlikely contingencies all this wasted effort could have been avoided.

Even where agreement can be reached at the negotiation stage, carefully planned arrangements may create undesirable exchange relationships between business units. Some businessmen object that in such a carefully worked out relationship one gets performance only to the letter of the contract. Such planning indicates a lack of trust and blunts the demands of friendship, turning a cooperative venture into an antagonistic horse trade. Yet the greater danger perceived by some businessmen is that one would have to perform his side of the bargain to its letter and thus lose what is called "flexibility." Businessmen may welcome a measure of vagueness in the obligations they assume so that they may negotiate matters in light of the actual circumstances.

Adjustment of exchange relationships and dispute settlement by litigation or the threat of it also has many costs. The gain anticipated from using this form of coercion often fails to outweigh these costs, which are both monetary and nonmonetary. Threatening to turn matters over to an attorney may cost no more money than postage or a telephone call; yet few are so skilled in making such a threat that it will not cost some deterioration of the relationship between the firms. One businessman said that customers had better not rely on legal rights or threaten to bring a breach of contract law suit against him since he "would not be treated like a criminal" and would fight back with every means available. Clearly actual litigation is even more costly than making threats. Lawyers demand substantial fees from larger business units. A firm's executives often will have to be transported and maintained in another city during the proceedings if, as often is the case, the trial must be held away from the home office. Top management does not travel by Greyhound and stay at the YMCA. Moreover, there will be the cost of diverting top management, engineers, and others in the organization from their normal activities. The firm may lose many days of work from several key people. The nonmonetary costs may be large, too. A breach of contract law suit may settle a particular dispute, but such an action often results in a "divorce" ending the "marriage" between the two businesses, since a contract action is likely to carry charges with at least overtones of bad faith. Many executives, moreover, dislike the prospect of being cross-examined in public. Some executives may dislike losing control of a situation by turning the decision-making power over to lawyers. Finally, the law of contract damages may not provide an adequate remedy even if the firm wins the suit; one may get vindication but not much money.

Why do relatively contractual practices ever exist?

Although contract is not needed and actually may have negative consequences, businessmen do make some carefully planned contracts, negotiate settlements influenced by their legal rights and commence and defend some breach of contract law suits or arbitration proceedings. In view of the findings and explanation presented to this point, one may ask why. Exchanges are carefully planned when it is thought that planning and a potential legal sanction will have more advantages than disadvantages. Such a judgment may be reached when contract planning serves the internal needs of an organization involved in a business exchange. For example, a fairly detailed contract can serve as a communication device within a large corporation. While the corporation's sales manager and house counsel may work out all the provisions with the customer, its production manager will have to make the product. He must be told what to do and how to handle at least the most obvious contingencies. Moreover, the sales manager may want to remove certain issues from future negotiation by his subordinates. If he puts the matter in the written contract, he may be able to keep his salesmen from making concessions to the customer without first consulting the sales manager. Then the sales manager may be aided in his battles with his firm's financial or engineering departments if the contract calls for certain practices which the sales manager advocates but which the other departments resist. Now the corporation is obligated to a customer to do what the sales manager wants to do; how can the financial or engineering departments insist on anything else?

Also one tends to find a judgment that the gains of contract outweigh the costs where there is a likelihood that significant problems will arise.[9] One factor leading to this conclusion is complexity of the agreed performance over a long period. Another factor is whether or not the degree of injury in case of default is thought to be potentially great. This factor cuts two ways. First, a buyer may want to commit a seller to a detailed and legally binding contract, where the consequences of a default by the seller would seriously injure the buyer. For example, the airlines are subject to law suits from the survivors of passengers and to great adverse publicity as a result of crashes. One would expect the airlines to bargain for carefully defined and legally enforceable obligations on the part of the airframe manufacturers when they purchase aircraft. Second, a seller may want to limit his liability for a buyer's damages by a provision in their contract. For example, a manufacturer of air conditioning may deal with motels in the South and Southwest. If this equipment fails in the hot summer months, a motel may lose a great deal of business. The manufacturer may wish to avoid any liability for this type of injury to his customers and may want a contract with a clear disclaimer clause.

Similarly, one uses or threatens to use legal sanctions to settle disputes when other devices will not work and when the gains are thought to outweigh the costs. For example, perhaps the most common type of business contracts case fought all the way through to the appellate courts today is an action for an alleged wrongful termination of a dealer's franchise by a manufacturer. Since the franchise has been terminated, factors such as personal relationships and the desire for future business will have little effect; the

---

[9] Even where there is little chance that problems will arise, some businessmen insist that their lawyer review or draft an agreement as a delaying tactic. This gives the businessman time to think about making a commitment if he has doubts about the matter or to look elsewhere for a better deal while still keeping the particular negotiations alive.

cancellation of the franchise indicates they have already failed to maintain the relationship. Nor will a complaining dealer worry about creating a hostile relationship between himself and the manufacturer. Often the dealer has suffered a great financial loss both as to his investment in building and equipment and as to his anticipated future profits. A canceled automobile dealer's lease on his showroom and shop will continue to run, and his tools for servicing, say, Plymouths cannot be used to service other makes of cars. Moreoever, he will have no more new Plymouths to sell. Today there is some chance of winning a law suit for terminating a franchise in bad faith in many states and in the federal courts. Thus, often the dealer chooses to risk the cost of a lawyer's fee because of the chance that he may recover some compensation for his losses.

An "irrational" factor may exert some influence on the decision to use legal sanctions. The man who controls a firm may feel that he or his organization has been made to appear foolish or has been the victim of fraud or bad faith. The law suit may be seen as a vehicle "to get even" although the potential gains, as viewed by an objective observer, are outweighed by the potential costs.

The decision whether or not to use contract—whether the gain exceeds the costs—will be made by the person within the business unit with the power to make it, and it tends to make a difference who he is. People in a sales department oppose contract. Contractual negotiations are just one more hurdle in the way of a sale. Holding a customer to the letter of a contract is bad for "customer relations." Suing a customer who is not bankrupt and might order again is poor strategy. Purchasing agents and their buyers are less hostile to contracts but regard attention devoted to such matters as a waste of time. In contrast, the financial control department—the treasurer, controller, or auditor— leans toward more contractual dealings. Contract is viewed by these people as an organizing tool to control operations in a large organization. It tends to define precisely and to minimize the risks to which the firm is exposed. Outside lawyers—those with many clients—may share this enthusiasm for a more contractual method of dealing. These lawyers are concerned with preventive law—avoiding any possible legal difficulty. They see many unstable and unsuccessful exchange transactions, and so they are aware of, and perhaps overly concerned with, all of the things which can go wrong. Moreover, their job of settling disputes with legal sanctions is much easier if their client has not been overly casual about transaction planning. The inside lawyer, or house counsel, is harder to classify. He is likely to have some sympathy with a more contractual method of dealing. He shares the outside lawyer's "craft urge" to see exchange transactions neat and tidy from a legal standpoint. Since he is more concerned with avoiding and settling disputes than selling goods, he is likely to be less willing to rely on a man's word as the sole sanction than is a sales-man. Yet the house counsel is more a part of the organization and more aware of its goals and subject to its internal sanctions. If the potential risks are not too great, he may hesitate to suggest a more contractual procedure to the sales department. He must sell his services to the operating depart-ments, and he must hoard what power he has, expending it on only what he sees as significant issues.

The power to decide that a more contractual method of creating relation-ships and settling disputes shall be used will be held by different people at different times in different organizations. In most firms the sales department and the purchasing department have a great deal of power to resist contrac-tual procedures or to ignore them if they are formally adopted and to handle disputes their own way. Yet in larger organizations the treasurer and the controller have increasing power to demand both systems and compliance. Occasionally, the house counsel must arbitrate the conflicting positions of these departments; in giving "legal advice" he may make the business judg-ment necessary regarding the use of contract. At times he may ask for an opinion from an outside law firm to reinforce his own position with the out-side firm's prestige.

Obviously, there are other significant variables which influence the degree that contract is used. One is the relative bargaining power or skill of the two business units. Even if the controller of a small supplier succeeds within the firm and creates a contractual system of dealing, there will be no contract if the firm's large customer prefers not to be bound to anything. Firms that supply General Motors deal as General Motors wants to do business, for the most part. Yet bargaining power is not size or share of the market alone. Even a General Motors may need a particular supplier, at least temporarily. Furthermore, bargaining power may shift as an exchange relationship is first created and then continues. Even a giant firm can find itself bound to a small supplier once production of an essential item begins, for there may not be time to turn to another supplier. Also, all of the factors discussed in this paper can be viewed as *components* of bargaining power—for example, the personal relationship between the presidents of the buyer and the seller firms may give a sales manager great power over a purchasing agent who has been instructed to give the seller "every consideration." Another vari-able relevant to the use of contract is the influence of third parties. The federal government, or a lender of money, may insist that a contract be made in a particular transaction or may influence the decision to assert one's legal rights under a contract.

Contract, then, often plays an important role in business, but other factors are significant. To understand the functions of contract the whole system of conducting exchanges must be explored fully. More types of business communities must be studied, contract litigation must be analyzed to see why the nonlegal sanctions fail to prevent the use of legal sanctions, and all of the variables suggested in this paper must be clarified more systematically.

ACKNOWLEDGMENTS

This research has been supported by a Law and Policy Research Grant to the University of Wisconsin Law School from the Ford Foundation. I am grateful for the help generously given by a number of sociologists including Robert K. Merton, Harry V. Ball, Jerome Carlin, and William Evan.

REFERENCES

Comment
   1957   The statute of frauds and the business community: A re-appraisal in light of prevailing practices, *Yale Law Journal* **66** (June): 1038–1071.
Director of the Administrative Office of the United States Courts
   1961   Annual Report.
Harvard Business Review
   1923–1924   Vol. **2**: 238–240, 367–370, 496–502.
New York Law Revision Commission
   1954   Hearings on the Uniform Code: Commercial Code.
State of New York
   1961   The judicial conference. Sixth Annual Report.

CHAPTER

6

CONFLICT RESOLUTION IN
TWO MEXICAN COMMUNITIES*

Laura Nader
Duane Metzger

INTRODUCTION

I N DEALING with law, anthropologists have often limited themselves to an analysis of certain institutionalized forms of legal systems, such as councils, courts, duels, and go-betweens. Characteristically, such agents or agencies of conflict resolution claim our attention because they are most easily discernible as core portions of legal systems in a variety of societies. However, when anthropologists begin to concern themselves with the problem of explaining inter- or intrasocietal variation in the law, they necessarily include in their description of "a legal system" a broader range of social control forms than those mentioned, as well as certain variables that are crucial to a functional explanation of different forms of social control (Malinowski, 1932; Whiting, 1950; Schneider, 1957; Harper, 1957). The present paper discusses conflict resolution in two Mexican towns by exploring two central questions: (1) Are conflicts resolved differently in the two towns because authority is allocated differently? That is, to what extent does

*A portion of this paper was presented by Laura Nader at the 1961 meetings of the American Anthropological Association in Philadelphia, Pennsylvania.

Reprinted by permission of the American Anthropological Association from "Conflict Resolution in Two Mexican Communities" by Laura Nader and Duane Metzger, *American Anthropologist*, Vol. 65, No. 3, Pt. 1 (1963): pp. 584–592.

the distribution of authority coincide with the distribution of conflict resolution, and (2) what factors explain the differential distribution of authority in these towns? Our approach is to investigate alternative strategies employed by husbands and wives in resolving conflicts which occur between them. In addition, we discuss implications of these alternative strategies and offer a reconstruction of the development of authority patterns in these communities. We do this in order to understand the degree of correspondence between authority patterns and the role of remedy agent.

THE RANGE OF THE LAW

Before proceeding to the data, let us discuss the position that some anthropologists have taken regarding different levels of law and the implications their ideas have in this investigation.

At the turn of the century Durkheim (1933) and Mauss and Beuchat (1906) put forth the idea that within a single society there may be several legal systems complementing, supplementing, or conflicting with each other. Mauss and Beuchat described the presence of two legal systems among the Eskimos which were used alternatively during the summer and winter seasons. Malinowski (1932) later discussed a number of more or less independent systems of Trobriand Island law. Nadel (1942), in *A Black Byzantium*, discussed the tripartite division of legal labor among the British Colonial, the Moslem, and the Customary Law courts of the Nupe in Nigeria. Schneider (1957) explored the different agencies of punishment within a single society. And Pospisil (1958: 272) in his study of Kapauku law, states: "Every functioning subgroup of the society has its own legal system which is necessarily different in some respects from those of the other subgroups." All deny that there is a single unitary system within a given society; they argue instead that every subgroup in society has its own legal system. Furthermore, they suggest implicitly, and sometimes explicitly, that the distribution of power to settle conflicts is directly related to the distribution and specialization of authority in a society, and that the different levels of legal control act upon each other, i.e., are interdependent.

If we accept the idea of different legal levels in a society, then it becomes possible to compare these levels within a society or between two societies without necessarily comparing total legal systems. The comparison of legal levels within the same society illuminates relationships between various agencies of the law. The comparison of legal levels in two different societies illustrates how structurally similar legal agencies may function differently in contrasting settings. Such a comparison is the subject of this paper.

As we analyzed grievance resolution in two Mexican towns, the following patterns of action came to our attention. In both communities, an individual inextricably involved in a conflict has a wide range of remedy agents to whom he can appeal for resolution. These agents include people such as family heads, officials in the community court such as the president and/or judge, the priests, witches, ritual kinsmen, and even supernaturals such as the saints and the gods. However, we noticed that although there is a wide range of remedy agents, the choice of action is not random. We discovered that the legal level chosen by a plaintiff can be correlated with several factors, including the sex of the parties, their roles and ranks, the subgroups to which plaintiff and defendant belong, and the class of conflict. For example, usually females take slander complaints to the community court, whereas male plaintiffs ordinarily take similar complaints only to a local witch. In one and the same town conflicts between nonkin can be settled only at the community level, but kin conflicts can be settled by several remedy agencies. High-ranking families usually settle their squabbles out of court while low-ranking families utilize the town court more often. A husband will only reluctantly take a complaint against his spouse to the town court, whereas a wife will almost invariably take such a complaint to the court.

For purposes of comparative analysis we focus our discussion on the following variables: (1) specific classes of citizens in conflict: husbands and wives; (2) the two conflict resolving agencies to whom spouses may appeal—the family and the community court; (3) the distribution and strength of authority within the family and community court.

THE CONTRAST[1]

The two communities are several hundred miles from each other—one in the mountains of Oaxaca and the other in the mountains of Chiapas. They are characterized by certain similarities and differences. The Oaxacan community is a bilingual Zapotec–Spanish town of 2000 inhabitants. It is characterized by a relatively intricate development of social groups that crosslink prople who may not be related by blood or marriage. The Chiapas town has approximately a thousand inhabitants who speak a Mayan language. This town lacks the cross-linked groupings so typical of

[1]Fieldwork in the Oaxaca community was undertaken by Laura Nader during nine months between 1957 and 1959. The work was supported by grants from the Milton Fund at Harvard University, Radcliffe College, and the Mexican government. Fieldwork in the Chiapas community was carried out by Duane and Barbara Metzger during the years 1956–1959. Their work was done under the "Man in Nature Project" of the University of Chicago, supported by the National Science Foundation, and The Society of Junior Fellows at Harvard University. For a more detailed description of the data on which this study is based see Metzger (1960) and Nader (1961, 1964).

the Oaxacan town. The strongest links here are between an individual and his kinfolk or between individuals as members of a single community. Both towns are predominantly agricultural and have a system of bilateral inheritance. Both have strong leanings toward a patrilineal distribution of authority. From their Indian and Spanish pasts the two communities have inherited similar town government organizations. In each a body of co-opted officials, chosen from the community yearly and headed by a president and a judge, makes community decisions and tries or arbitrates cases brought before it by community members or interested parties from outside communities.

In both communities, legal decisions are formulated on several levels, two of which are the family and the community court. The loci of adjudication are the senior males in the family or families engaged in dispute and the senior males in the town court. Both communities provide alternative strategies, utilizing these two levels, for the resolution of conflict between husband and wife. The type of husband–wife conflict brought before each of these adjudicating bodies, however, is different in the two towns.

In the Chiapas community, when conflicts occur between spouses, the husband's usual response is to beat his wife; the wife's usual response is to leave the house and return to her parents' house. These responses call up an adjudicating process in which the families of the couple in conflict, and especially the males of senior generation, meet and debate the imperfections of husband and wife behavior. These families usually cooperate in reaching an acceptable outcome for the conflict. They may impose immediate penalties, such as whipping, and enjoin the spouses to improve their performances, or, alternatively, families may agree that the marriage should be terminated —in which case the spouses return to live with their respective parents. If one spouse has engaged in unacceptable behavior which involved other married or marriageable males or females—most commonly, adultery— the case may be taken to the community court, where this behavior is certified before senior males representing all the families in the community. Even in court, however, the immediate penalty (such as whipping) is imposed by senior males in lineal relation to the judged party. A general announcement is made that the relationship between the spouses is dissolved and that one (or both) of them should not marry again within the community.

This brief description of the Chiapas community illustrates the following points. When conflict occurs within role pairs whose interaction is predicated on relatively long exchange of scarce goods and resources (see further), we may distinguish at least three outcomes of the conflict. These three become increasingly radical, as follows: (1) one or both of the marriage partners is temporarily humiliated by a penalty in a setting which includes some highly significant alters—in this case, the families of the spouse; (2) in addition to (1) the marriage relationship is severed; (3) in addition to (1) and (2) the conflict is taken to court, and the role potential of one or both of the spouses is further impaired by restrictions placed on the ability to recruit a new partner. Inasmuch as senior male lineals impose the immediate penalty in all cases (even should the matter be taken to court), the impairment of role potential of the person suffering the penalty not only affects his role as spouse, but also has a serious effect on his roles vis-à-vis his household of orientation. Although it is not usual in condition (2), it is likely in condition (3) for the penalized individual to leave the community for an extended period rather than return to his household of orientation.

It is worth emphasizing that two legal levels are used, depending on the probable outcome. If the conflict between the spouses is reduced by joint family certification and administration of penalties, the case is not presented to the community court. If the conflict is not reduced but is thought not to result from the inability of one or the other of the individuals to engage in this type of role performance, the case is not taken to court. The case is carried to the community court *only* where the role relationship is terminated *and* the inability of one of the persons to engage in relevant role performances is established.

In the Oaxacan community the picture is somewhat different. Conflicts between spouses may be settled by self-help methods similar to those described for the Chiapas town. A husband may beat or abandon his wife. The wife may return to her family of orientation. But these actions may be preceded or they may be followed by mediation by senior family members— usually the wife's parents and the husband's parents. What happens after such adjudication or mediation depends on the sex of the spouse. If an appeal to her husband's parents and to her own parents and/or godparents fails to bring about a resolution, a wife will appeal to the community court to correct her husband's behavior by penalizing him. In contrast, a husband may appeal to his wife's parents; failing in this, he may consider the relationship severed, and either begin searching for a new wife (or lover) or leave town. Only rarely does a husband appeal to the town court; such cases usually involve the return of brideprice money. The important distinction is that wives are more likely to attempt correction of their husbands' conduct than to sever the relationship, while husbands are more likely to sever the relationship than to attempt correction of their wives' behavior by other than self-help or family remedies. In contrast to the Chiapas situation, if the relationship is severed in court, the senior lineals of the couple are not directly implicated. There are no cases in which a divorced spouse is forbidden, even by implication, to recruit a new partner.

Let us review the implications of these brief descriptive statements. Two classes of conflict outcome may be distinguished: (1) those conflicts which result in a continuation of relations (i.e., husband and wife continue to live together), and (2) those conflicts which result in the severing of relations (i.e., husband and wife are separated). Within class (2), (a) represents cases of simple severance of the relationship, and (b) represents cases in which the spouse(s)' freedom to seek another spouse is restricted. Two levels of adjudication are available to the spouses: (A) the family, and (B) the community court. Matching types of conflicts with levels of adjudication, we find the following distribution:

CLASSES OF CONFLICT OUTCOME

	(1a) Reconciled		(2a) Severed		(2b) Severed and penalized	
Adjudication level	Oax.	Chi.	Oax.	Chi.	Oax.	Chi.
(A) Family	x	x	—	x	—	—
(B) Community court	x	—	x	—	—	x

In the Chiapas town presentation of husband–wife conflicts to family members occurs when the desired decision may be either continuation or severance of the relationship. In contrast, when such conflicts are presented to the community court it is not in hope of reconciliation, but in a desire to make public the severance of the husband–wife tie and to impose spouse-recruiting restrictions. Senior male lineals participate in decisions in all classes of conflict. In the Oaxaca town, adjudication at the family level is sought primarily to continue this relationship. Appeal to the community court may be made when the aim is either to continue or to sever the relationship. The court does not attempt to restrict the freedom of spouses to recruit new partners. Senior male lineals are excluded from participating in court decisions, whereas the court may, at any of the three degrees of radical outcome, engage in participating in the outcome. In husband–wife cases before the Oaxaca community court there is a wide range of possible outcomes, while in the Chiapas town the range is indeed narrow.

DISCUSSION

What factors help explain these different patterns of legal process? One factor is demography. At the turn of the century, the Oaxaca town greatly increased in population. This increase was due primarily to the closing of a mine located two miles away. The mining families, originally recruited from some fifteen villages in the area, moved to town and took up farming. Many of these family groups were nuclear. The Oaxaca town still draws new members from nearby towns, and some of its own citizens leave the village for the state and national capitals. One might speculate that immigrating families could not use the extended family form of settling family conflicts because they did not live with or near their extended kinsmen. This isolation, and the consequent proliferation of secondary associations, may have contributed to the importance of the court in conflict resolution and to the development of specialized town officials. The president of the Oaxaca town has primary responsibility for settling conflicts. He is referred to as *el padre del pueblo* (the father of the town), and he resolves cases of husband–wife conflict as if he were a "father." He considers and decides the majority of cases. Those few cases bent on termination go on to the next court official, the judge.

The population of the Chiapas town, in contrast, has changed little in the past 60–75 years. The majority of citizens are born in the town and live near people who are closely related. The extended family is the only significant social group. Elders exert major authority over younger people. Specialization of the kind which occurs among the Oaxaca court officials is absent. The president and judge play the same role in adjudication, together or separately. In dealing with conflicts between husband and wife, they primarily lend solemn support to the senior male lineals who are involved in imposing the penalties upon the party or parties concerned. These cases are relatively few in number.

In the Oaxaca community the court has gained influence over husband–wife relations as marriage has become a matter of legal interest above and beyond the immediate interests of the two families concerned. To the traditional ceremony of exchanging goods and services between the families of bride and groom has been added the Catholic church wedding and, finally, civil marriage; these three ceremonies, celebrated separately or together, today constitute "legal" marriage. The court, as representative of the State, takes an official interest in the stability of marriage. In the Chiapas community, marriage is recognized as "legal" when certain formalities, gifts, and services have been exchanged between the families of the couple. Church weddings occur relatively infrequently, and civil marriage is actively discouraged by elders who see it as disruptive of the traditional relationship between spouses. Marriage here is still a monopoly of the extended family.

More important and more basic than either of these factors is the nature and distribution of authority, for patterns of authority seem to be central to an understanding of the distribution of conflict resolution in these towns. In both communities, husbands and wives in conflict recognize the authority of senior family males as well as the authority of the community court. However, in our judgment, the authority of senior family males is greater in the Chiapas town than in the Oaxaca community, and this contrast is mirrored in the use spouses make of the courts in the two towns. The crucial fact is that family heads assume exclusive rights to judge such conflicts in the Chiapas town and their judgments are nonappealable, while in the Oaxaca community spouses make further attempts to reduce their conflict by appeal to the community court. We suggest that such nonappealable outcomes occur when the tie between the couple in conflict and their senior family males holds great potential for the exchange of scarce goods and resources, and when there exists no substitute relationship which is nearly as productive. A father will be able to maintain his authority over his son only if the latter sees some payoff as a result; indeed, a father will be interested in maintaining strict authority over his son only if it benefits the father himself (Homans, 1961).

One specific indicator of the relationship between scarce goods and the authority of senior lineals over married offspring is found in the different modes of inheritance in the two communities. In the Chiapas town, inheritance begins at marriage for both spouses and continues intermittently until the senior lineals die. The aim is to provide all sons and daughters with equal parts of their parents' capital, equalizing the inheritance as the economic status of each child increases or decreases relative to that of the other children. In the Oaxaca community, the bulk of a child's inheritance is gained at the time of marriage. If he is to receive anything else, it will depend on how well he cares for his parents when they are old and sick. Thus, in the Oaxaca town, a father's ability to command or influence a married son or daughter is weakened by the fact that he has already distributed their share of inheritance at the time of marriage.

Another variable which may be associated with the nature of parental authority is residence. A father would seem to have greater control over his married children when they live near him, especially when he is their residence sponsor (Fischer, 1958; Goodenough, 1956). In the Chiapas community, the majority of couples live near, if not within, the house of the husband's father. Within the household, the father controls all scarce goods and resources and exercises considerable authority over his sons' behavior, both private and public. When sons live in separate but nearby households, the father continues to offer advice and impose sanctions, and he is regarded as spokesman for these sons in community decisions which involve heads of families. In the Oaxaca town, a shortage of land has led to the practice of fathers dividing their land among sons and, in such situations, leaving their houses to their daughters. Hence only about a third of the married men of the community live with or near their fathers. Where they live with their wives' families or separately, the influence of their fathers on their behavior may be relatively weak due to infrequency of interaction and absence of paternal control over economic activities.

Early inheritance and separate residence may have some bearing on the difference in legal strategies of men and women in the Oaxaca town. During one month twelve women brought charges against their husbands to the town court officials. During the same month only one man brought charges against his wife. It is possible that women take marital conflicts to the courts much more often than do men largely because they can find no other authority to which their husbands are accountable. The men are no longer responsible to their fathers and often live far from them; their wives' fathers, even when co-resident, have no claims on them. In contrast, a wife's behavior seems to be subject to several kinds of constraints. First, she is relatively likely to submit to the authority of her husband and his family, for if he abandons her, it is easier for him to get along than for her. While a man can buy his meals in town—and thus subsist without a wife—a woman finds it relatively difficult, though not impossible, to support herself without a husband. In the Chiapas town, neither men nor women can conveniently live alone without spouses; men cook in a rudimentary way only when far from home (cooked food is not for sale), and culturally acceptable ways for women to support themselves within the community are lacking. Both husbands and wives may be further constrained to accept parental authority due to their dependence on them for shelter and/or support in case the marriage is severed.

Some families in the Oaxaca town not only refuse shelter to their married children in case of a separation, but decline to use any influence at all toward resolving the conflict. This frequently occurs when a couple has married without or against the advise of their elders. Arrangement of marriage between families is the tradition, but independent choice of spouses is becoming more common as the age of marriage is now postponed to comply with the limits set by Mexican law. In the Chiapas community, in contrast, families assume responsibility for marriages even though independent choice of spouses is the rule.

It would appear, then, that the differences in the strategy of husband–wife conflict resolution in the two communities can be understood in terms of two sets of variables which affect the distribution, strength, and availability of authority among the two legal subsystems of family and court: (1) the differential availability of scarce goods such as food, sex, and family inheritance to married and single individuals, and (2) the degree to which institutionalized political organization concerns itself with the legal aspects of marriage.[2] In the Oaxaca town, limited authority of senior family males is associated with early inheritance, separate residence, readily available substitutes for both spouses and parents with respect to sex and subsistence, and the deliberate refusal of families to accept responsibility for marriages they have not arranged. The court assumes the responsibility lost or abandoned by the family and exercises authority over marriage vested in it as a representative of the State. In the Chiapas community, delayed inheritance, patrisponsored residence, and the absence of spouse- or parent-substitutes outside these relationships tend to support the authority of senior male lineals in the resolution of conflict between spouses. The role that the court plays is residual since marriage has not become an important concern of the court.

In these two towns we have the same number of legal levels available to husband–wife conflict, but they function differently. There are formal similarities in the adjudication process, but within this formally defined structure there are important structural differences. Investigation of these differences and the factors which mold them helps us to understand not only the variable functioning of similar formal structures but may also shed light on the corollary problem of the development of family law courts.

REFERENCES

Durkheim, E.
 1933   *The division of labor in society*. Glencoe: Free Press. (Orig. pub. 1893.)
Fischer, J. L.
 1958   The classification of residence in censuses. *American Anthropologist* **60** (1958): 508–517.
Goodenough, W.
 1956   Residence rules. *Southwestern Journal of Anthropology* **12** (1956): 23–37.
Harper, E. B.
 1957   Hoylu: A belief relating justice and the supernatural. *American Anthropologist* **59** (1957): 801–816.
Homans, G. C.
 1961   *Social behavior: Its elementary forms*. New York: Harcourt.

[2]David Schneider presents an interesting example from Yap which illustrates the degree to which community political organization concerns itself with family 'crimes.' "Fratricide is ... very different from patricide in terms of its effect on lineage structure in particular and the political system in general. When one brother kills another, the father-son relationship may still be maintained. When a son kills his father, or assaults him, the necessary link between the lineage and the community is broken. This offense is not merely against lineage solidarity, but is in addition an offense against the village.... The village is thus directly concerned with delicts against the head of the lineage; it has no concern with sons who are brothers" (1957:794). It would seem that in the Oaxaca town marital conflicts are not considered an offense against the extended family, but rather an offense which threatens public or town stability, as well as one which challenges the responsibility of town fathers.

Malinowski, B.
1932 *Crime and custom in savage society* London: Routledge and Kegan Paul. (Orig. pub. 1926.)
Mauss, M., and H. Beuchat
1906 Essai sur les variations saissonières des sociétés Eskimos: Étude de morphologie sociale. *L'Année Sociologique* 9 (1906): 39–132.
Metzger, D.
1960 Conflict in Chulsanto, a village in Chiapas. *Alpha Kappa Deltan* 30 (Winter): 35–48.
Nadel, S.
1942 *A black Byzantium*. London: Oxford Univ. Press.
Nader, L.
1961 Space and social organization in two Zapotec villages. Unpublished Ph. D. dissertation, Department of Anthropology, Radcliffe College.
1964 An analysis of Zapotec law cases. *Ethnology* 3 (1964): 404–419.
Pospisil, L.
1958 *Kapauku Papuans and their law.* New Haven: Yale Univ. Publ. in Anthropology.
Schneider, D.
1957 Political organization, supernatural sanctions and the punishment for incest on yap. *American Anthropologist* 59 (1957): 791–800.
Whiting, B.
1950 *Paiute sorcery.* New York: Viking Fund Publ. in Anthropology.

SOCIAL CONTROL IN TWO ISRAELI SETTLEMENTS

Richard D. Schwartz

> The substance of every attempt to state the fundamental principles of the sociology of law [is that] the center of gravity of legal development lies not in legislation, nor in juristic science, nor in judicial decisions, but in society itself.
>
> Eugen Ehrlich, *Fundamental Principles of the Sociology of Law XV* (1936)

L EGAL CONTROL is not exercised against all disturbing behavior. Sometimes, such behavior never reaches the courts.[1] At other times, it is not sanctioned by the courts because, we are told, it should be left to "the *interior* forum, as the tribunal of conscience has been aptly called."[2] The effects of nonlegal or informal control, whether or not ade-

---

[1] Professor Karl Llewellyn (1931) characterizes law as being concerned only with disputes "not otherwise settled."

[2] Mills v. Wyman, 20 Mass. 225, 3 Pick. 207 (1825).

"Without doubt there are great interests in society which justify withholding the coercive arm of the law from these duties of imperfect obligation, as they are called; imperfect, not because they are less binding upon the conscience than those which are called perfect, but because the wisdom of the social law does not impose sanctions upon them." *Id.* at 228, 3 Pick. at 210–211.

Reprinted by permission of The Yale Law Journal Company and Fred B. Rothman & Company from "Social Factors in the Development of Legal Control: A Case Study of Two Israeli Settlements" by Richard D. Schwartz, *The Yale Law Journal*, Vol. 63 (1964): pp. 471–491.

quately described in terms of "conscience," seem to be an important factor in a court's decision to withhold sanction.

The relationship between legal and informal controls can be theoretically stated and empirically described. The cultures of two Israeli communities were compared in an effort to determine the social effects of economic collectivism.[3] One of the differences noted was that the collective community, or *kvutza* (see Maletz, 1950; Baratz, 1943; Ben Yissakhar, 1949), had no distinctly legal institution, whereas the *moshav* (see Dayan, 1947; Messinger, 1949), a semiprivate property settlement, did. Speculation on the reasons for the difference led to the formulation of a theory of legal control. The theory cannot be presented in detail in this article,[4] but it will be used as a framework for the organization of the empirical data. While the data do not constitute empirical verification of the theory,[5] it is hoped that the theory will help to explain the data, and the data serve to illustrate the theory.

In attempting to ascertain whether or not a social group has legal controls and, if it does, why these controls are applied to some but not to other forms of behavior, this article rests upon several assumptions:

1. For a given individual at a given time, some states of affairs are more satisfying[6] than others.
2. A *gain* in satisfaction is defined as transition from a less to a more satisfying state of affairs; a *loss* of satisfaction as the reverse; an *indifferent* experience as no change in satisfaction.
3. The frequency, vigor, and speed with which an action is performed in a given situation is an *increasing function*[7] of the degree (frequency, magnitude, and immediacy) to which similar behavior has previously been followed by gain, and of the extent of similarity perceived by the present actor between the present behavior and behavior previously followed by gain. Conversely, the frequency, vigor, and speed with

---

[3] This work was carried out in 1949–50 with the aid of a Research Training Fellowship from the Social Science Research Council and a Sterling Predoctoral Fellowship from Yale University. A full ethnographic report is presented in Schwartz (1951).

[4] The detailed theory, on file in the Institute of Human Relations, Yale University, was developed in connection with the Institute's Postdoctoral Program in Behavior Science, under the directorship of Mark A. May. For the postulates which provided the starting point for this theory, see Hull (1951).

[5] For verification, this theory should be tested against data which did not contribute to its formulation, and which are more extensive than those presented here.

[6] Many methods have been proposed for the measurement of relative satisfaction, among them verbal reports, decisions of experts, and physiological indices. We would prefer to let the definition rest ultimately on choice behavior. When an individual is given the choice betwen two states of affairs after having fully experienced both, the one which he selects is defined as more satisfying for him. If verbal or other measures are found to be correlated with such choices under certain circumstances, they may be substituted for purposes of convenience.

[7] For "x is an increasing function of y," read, "Other factors equal, as y increases, x increases."

which an action is performed in a given situation is a *decreasing function* of the degree of gain following competing (alternative and incompatible) behavior, and of the extent of similarity perceived by the present actor between present competing behavior and similar behavior previously followed by gain.

These postulates are stated in general terms because it is purposed to apply them to the behavior of all participants in the process of social control. Social control involves *interaction*, i.e., behavior on the part of one actor which affects the behavior of another. Control is distinguished from other forms of interaction in that it includes *sanction*, i.e., the administration of gain or loss to an actor. Sanction is *positive* when it results in gain for the sanctionee, and *negative* when it results in loss.

From our assumptions it can be deduced that a sanctioner tends to employ positive sanctions following any behavior (x) which is typically gainful to him. If positive sanction occurs after x, the likelihood is increased that under similar circumstances x will be repeated vigorously and speedily. If x continues to be gainful to the sanctioner, his tendency to respond to it with positive sanction is reinforced.

In the same way it follows that negative sanction tends to be employed following behavior (y) which typically results in loss for the sanctioner. Imposition of negative sanction following the performance of y decreases the gain which its performer may have obtained by it and increases the likelihood that he will gain by switching from it to some incompatible behavior. If, as a result, the actor performs y less often and less vigorously, the sanctioner experiences a gain because there is a transition from a less to a more satisfying state of affairs. Therefore his tendency to respond to y with negative sanction is increased.

Other factors also affect the likelihood that a given sanction will recur. The impact of a sanction may be supplemented or reduced by collateral gains and losses experienced by the sanctionee. Even if, as a result of all these influences, sanctionee's behavior is modified in a way gainful to the sanctioner, the gainful effect need not reinforce the sanction; it can be offset by collateral losses experienced by the sanctioner. Important among these are any experiences which have strengthened the tendency of the potential sanctioner to respond in a competing way either by employing a different sanction or by exerting no sanction at all. The greater the tendency to perform such competing reactions, the less is the likelihood that the given sanction will be employed.

In the interactive aggregates of individuals which we call *social groups*, two main forms of control may be distinguished: that which is carried out by specialized functionaries who are socially delegated the task of intragroup control, and that which is not so delegated. These will be, respectively, designated *legal* and *informal* controls. When, as is often the case, these two forms of control are in competition, the likelihood of legal control arising at all in a given sphere is a decreasing function of the effectiveness of informal controls. It is the thesis of this article that the presence of legal controls in the moshav, the semiprivate property settlement, but not in the kvutza, the collective settlement, is to be understood primarily in terms of the fact that informal controls did not operate as effectively in the moshav as in the kvutza.

CONTROL SYSTEMS IN THE KVUTZA AND MOSHAV

In most of their superficial characteristics, the two settlements are essentially similar. Both were founded at the same time, 1921, by young settlers who had come from Eastern Europe "to build a new life." Though the kvutza was smaller at first, it has grown to a population (just under 500 persons) which is almost identical in size with that of the moshav. Both are located on a slope of the Jezreel Valley where they have to deal with the same climate and similar topography. Both have about 2000 acres of land, which supports a mixed farming economy. Both populations have rejected many of the East European Jewish customs, including traditional religious practices. Though many other Israeli collectives are left-wing socialist, the members of the kvutza under consideration resemble those of the moshav in adhering to the social-democratic political philosophy represented by the *Mapai* party.

Despite these similarities, the two communities have differed from the outset in their members' ideas about economic organization. In the kvutza, members felt they could implement the program "from each according to his abilities, to each according to his need," as the way to create a "just society." Moshav members, many of whom had spent a few years in collectives, decided that the family should be the unit of production and distribution, and that thus a class of small independent farmers could be developed in the moshav which would provide a strong agricultural base for the country.

As far as could be ascertained, there were no initial differences in specific ideas concerning legal control. Legal jurisdiction over crimes and civil wrongs is recognized by all to reside in the State of Israel, but very few cases involving members of these settlements have been brought before the State's courts or, earlier, before the courts of the British Mandate. The minimal role of these courts has resulted from an absence of serious crime; the shielding of fellow members from British (and now to a lesser extent even Israeli) "outsiders"; and internal controls which effectively handle existing disturbances. In both settlements, the power to exercise these internal controls stems from the General Assembly, a regularly held meeting of all members in which each one present casts a single vote. This form of government works effectively in both communities, perhaps because they are small enough for everyone to be heard and homogeneous enough so that there is basic agreement on means and ends. While the kvutza meetings are more frequent and cover a broader range of issues, moshav sessions are held at least biweekly and are generally well attended.

In both settlements, the General Assembly delegates responsibility for certain activities to committees whose membership it approves. Committees are, if anything, more active in the kvutza, which has separate permanent groups to deal with questions of economic coordination, work assignment, education, social affairs, ceremonies, housing, community planning, and health. The moshav also has its committees, but most of these deal with agricultural matters, particularly the dissemination to individual farmers of the kind of scientific information which is handled by managers in the kvutza.

The moshav's Judicial Committee, however, is a specialized agency for which no counterpart is found in the kvutza. This Committee consists of a panel of seven members elected annually by the General Assembly for the purpose of dealing with internal disputes. Complaints by members against members are brought before the Committee either directly or by referral from the General Assembly. A hearing of the complaint is then conducted by a panel of three drawn from the larger Committee. After investigating the circumstances and hearing the direct testimony of both sides, a panel decides whether and how the defendant should bear responsibility. Fines and damages, the major types of punishment, are usually paid upon imposition, but if not, they are enforceable by the secretary of the moshav. Though these panels follow simple procedures, there can be no doubt that they have acted as an agency of legal control in the moshav.

An example will illustrate the operation of this moshav system of legal control. A fifteen-year-old boy took a neighbor's jeep without permission, picked up some of his friends, and went for a joyride outside the village. During the ride, he crashed into a tree and damaged the fender and door of the vehicle. The owner brought a complaint against him which was heard by the panel. When the boy admitted his actions, he was charged for the full cost of repairs. The debt was subsequently discharged by the boy's parents, and the case was considered closed.

By contrast, the kvutza has not delegated sanctioning responsibility to any special unit. Even when administrative or legislative action results in gain or loss to an individual, this is not its primary purpose. In the event of a dispute between workers, for example, the Work Assignment Committee or the

Economic Council may decide that the interests of production would be better served if one or both of the workers were transferred. But the objective of such action is not punitive; rather it is to ensure the smooth functioning of the economy, and the decision is made in much the same manner as any decision relating to production.

In the course of its legislative work, the General Assembly of the kvutza also makes decisions which modify the gains and losses of members. Many of these are policy decisions which apply to classes of members, but sometimes an individual's behavior provides the occasion for a policy debate in the Assembly. One young member, for example, received an electric teakettle as a gift from his sister in the city. Though small gifts could be retained as personal property, the kettle represented a substantial item, and one which would draw upon the limited supply of electricity available to the entire settlement. Moreover, the kvutza had already decided against supplying each room with a kettle on the grounds that this would be expensive and would encourage socially divisive private get-togethers. By retaining the kettle, therefore, the young man was threatening the principles of material equality and social solidarity on which the kvutza is believed to rest. This at any rate was the decision of the Assembly majority following three meetings during which the issue was debated. Confronted with this decision, the owner bowed to the general will by turning his teakettle over to the infirmary where it would be used by those presumed to be in greatest need of it. No organized enforcement of the decision was threatened, but had he disregarded the expressed will of the community, his life in the kvutza would have been made intolerable by the antagonism of public opinion.

As will become apparent, it is the powerful force of public opinion which is the major sanction of the entire kvutza control system. It may be focused, as in the case of the electric teakettle, by an Assembly decision, or it may, as occurs more commonly, be aroused directly by the behavior it sanctions. In either case, it is an instrument of control which is employed not by any specialized functionaries but by the community as a whole. Since public opinion is the sanction for the entire kvutza control system, that system must be considered informal rather than legal. We turn now to a more detailed consideration of the factors which have made this system of control so much more effective in the kvutza than in the moshav.

SANCTION IMPACT

From our assumptions, we may deduce that the extent to which a sanction, legal or informal, modifies the tendency of given behavior is a function of the frequency, magnitude, and immediacy with which it follows the sanctioned behavior. Frequency of sanction depends on the number of times the behavior is performed, the proportion of times its performance is observed by potential sanctioners, the proportion of observations which evoke a reaction, and the proportion of reactions which actually have a sanctioning effect. For any given instance of sanction, magnitude of sanction depends on the vigor of reaction, the extent to which the reaction is implemented, and the average gain or loss to the sanctionee per unit of experienced sanction. For example, magnitude of sanction resulting from a fine would depend on how many dollars were demanded (vigor), how many of these were collected (implementation), and how great a loss each dollar constituted for the payer. Immediacy of sanction is a function of how soon after its performance the pertinent behavior is perceived by the sanctioner, how speedily he reacts to it, and how quickly the reaction is experienced by the sanctionee. It follows from all this that *sanction impact* is an increasing function of the numbers of potential sanctioners who perceive or are informed of the pertinent behavior, and of the accuracy, frequency, and speed with which this *information* is obtained; an increasing function of the capacity of informed would-be sanctioners to *implement* their reactions; an increasing function of the *magnitude* of gain or loss which that reaction, once implemented, imposes on the sanctionee; and an increasing function of the extent to which potential sanctionees perceive and therefore *vicariously* learn from the experience of sanctionees.

Information

For the control of any behavior which would, if known, be effectively sanctioned, it is important that potential sanctioners know accurately and quickly of its occurrence. Accuracy implies that the behavior comes to the attention of the reactors as often as possible and that they know who has done what, under which conditions. Each time such behavior is known to have occurred, reactors gain an opportunity to increase the frequency of sanction. The more quickly this information is obtained, the greater is the immediacy with which sanction can be administered.

Accuracy and speed of perception tend to be high in what Cooley has described as the "primary group," characterized by "intimate face-to-face association and cooperation" (see Cooley, 1909; Clow, 1919; Shils, 1951).[8] Though such groups are typically small in size, we shall see that under certain conditions a high frequency of face-to-face association or interaction can occur in groups as large as the kvutza. Cooley goes on to hypothesize

---

[8]Shils prefers to base his definition on characteristics of group culture rather than on more easily described characteristics such as size.

of primary groups that they are "fundamental in forming the social nature and ideals of the individual," which is close to saying that they are characterized by effective systems of control. Though there is little trustworthy evidence on this point,[9] it seems plausible in light of the propositions that accurate information is a prerequisite to control and that the face-to-face intimacy of the primary group makes such information possible.

The kvutza is in effect a large primary group whose members engage in continuous face-to-face interaction. Each able-bodied member works eight to ten hours a day, six days a week, at a job which is usually performed wholly or partially in the presence of others. The results of his efforts become known to his associates, the work manager, and the top officials who co-ordinate the economy. All three meals are eaten in a collective dining hall usually in the company of five other residents who happen to have arrived at the same time. Members of each sex share common washing and shower facilities, and these are used by most members at the same time, during the limited period when hot water is available. Housing is concentrated in one area of the kvutza and consists of rows of long houses, each partitioned to make six rooms, with a married couple or two roommates occupying each room. Because most rooms are surrounded by other dwellings, it is easily possible for neighbors to observe entrances and exits and even some behavior within. Child rearing is the primary responsibility of special nurses and teachers, but parents spend about two hours with their children on work days and usually more than this on their days of rest. Much of this relationship is subject to public view as parents and children stroll around the kvutza, eat together occasionally in the dining hall, or play in front of their rooms. Other leisure activities are also subject to public observation: participating in Assembly and Committee meetings, celebrating kvutza holidays, attending lectures and films, perusing newspapers and periodicals in the kvutza reading room, or taking a vacation tour of the country. Even sexual relations, particularly if they are illicit, can become the subject of general public knowledge, although this was the one type of activity excepted by a member when he said, "amongst us, all things except one are done together."

The same conditions of continuous interaction also make it possible to circulate information throughout the entire community. Mealtime and showering are two informal occasions when large numbers of people can gather and find opportunity for conversation. The shower in particular is a forum for the transmission of information where one can hear about anything from fractured ankles to broken hearts. Though "I heard it in the shower" is a kvutza equivalent for "take this with a grain of salt," much genuine news is disseminated there. Compared with these informal techniques, the weekly news bulletin and the Assembly meetings run slow supplementary seconds.

Moshav conditions do not permit as great a degree of public observation. Work is typically conducted alone, with other members of the family, or occasionally with the voluntary aid of a friend. As long as the moshav farmer maintains a solvent establishment and discharges such community obligations as payment of taxes and correct use of cooperative facilities, he is free to manage his farm as he sees fit. Meals consisting largely of produce from the farmstead are prepared by the housewife and eaten in a family dining room which occupies a central place in the home. Houses are small bungalows ranging from three to six rooms, separated from neighboring dwellings by a hundred yards or more, and screened by hedges and fruit trees. Many activities which are publicly performed in the kvutza can be, and usually are, carried out in the privacy of the moshav home, among them economic husbandry, care of clothing, showering, washing, child rearing, and such recreation as visiting, reading, and listening to the radio. There are, to be sure, places where members come into contact, such as the produce depots, cooperative store, Assembly and committee meetings, and cinema. Though such contacts provide some opportunities for the circulation of information, they are fewer and the information circulated is less complete than in the kvutza.

At least partially as a result of these differences, kvutza members do in fact learn more about the activities of more of their members than is known in the moshav. Less than a week of residence was necessary in the kvutza before virtually everyone knew the ostensible purpose of the writer's stay, whereas similar knowledge was not diffused as widely (or accurately) during two months in the moshav. Information thus transmitted is not confined to work performance and consumption, though these are of great interest, but range over such details as mail received, visitors contacted, time spent with children, and even style of underclothes worn. As a result, it becomes possible to control types of behavior in the kvutza which never become public knowledge in the moshav.

Since we are primarily interested in the effects of such factors as information status on the development of legal controls, it is unnecessary for our purposes to analyze in detail the reasons for these differences. It should be noted, however, that kvutza intimacy was not solely the result of conscious planning concerning social relations. Though the desire for intimacy was a factor, it was strongly supplemented by other pressures, such as those arising as unanticipated by-products of the need for economic efficiency in a collective economy.

Implementation

If it is important for effective control that the behavior in question be perceived by reactors, it is at least as necessary that their sanctions be perceived by sanctionees. Though a reactor may behave in a way which tends to exert sanction, this reaction cannot achieve maximum control over behavior unless it is experienced by someone who could be sanctioned by it. Uncollected damages and unserved jail sentences are presumably not as effective in controlling negligent or criminal behavior as are implemented judgments. Similarly, in the operation of informal control, the failure of sanction implementation constitutes a major reason for the apparently deviant behavior of such transient individuals as traveling salesmen, hoboes, railroad workers, and hotel guests (see, e.g., Burgess and Cottrell, 1939; Anderson, 1923, 1940; Cottrell, 1940; Hayner, 1928).

Conditions necessary for the implementation of a sanction depend on the nature of the sanction. The implementation of public opinion—major informal sanction in the Israeli settlements—requires that public approval or disapproval be accurately and speedily communicated to sanctionees. This is accomplished in the kvutza by essentially the same conditions as made the perception of behavior so readily possible, namely, the continuous interaction characteristic of the primary group. In the case of implementation, the interactive process is simply reversed, with sanctioners providing the action which is then perceived by sanctionees.

Public opinion can be manifested often, swiftly, subtly, and with varying degrees of intensity in the kvutza. In the course of a day's continual interaction, positive or negative opinion may be communicated by the ways in which members glance at an individual, speak to him, pass him a requested work implement or dish of food, assign him work, give him instructions, sit next to him, and listen to his comments. To an experienced member, these small signs serve to predict more intense reactions of public acclaim or social isolation. They therefore acquire sanctioning power in and of themselves and become able to control the behavior in question before extremes are reached. In the moshav, by contrast, there are fewer opportunities to convey public opinion quickly and accurately because there is so much less contact between members in the course of the daily regime. This is an important limitation in the use of public opinion as a means of control in the moshav.

Magnitude of Gain or Loss

In order for public opinion to be effective, it is important not only that changes in it be perceived but that these be capable of providing gain or loss to the sanctionee. If he is indifferent to public opinion, his behavior will not be directly changed by such sanction. If, on the other hand, he is "other-directed," so that modification in public attitude involves relatively greater loss or gain to him, we would expect him to be effectively sanctioned by public opinion.[10] As a whole, the population of the kvutza is far more concerned with public opinion than is that of the moshav. Several factors appear to have contributed to this characteristic, among them differences in immigration, emigration, child training, and adult experience.

Since these settlements were studied thirty years after they were founded, it is difficult to know whether immigrants were different at the outset. It is possible that people to whom public opinion was important may have gravitated to the collective type of community, or at least that those who stayed were particularly responsive to it. Looking back at their primary reasons for coming, almost three out of four present kvutza members refer to socially oriented motives, e.g., social solidarity, building a just society, changing human nature. Such motives were said to be primary by only one-third of the present moshav members. Many of the moshav members emphasized economically oriented motives, e.g., strengthening the country as a whole or their own economic position in particular.

The effect of this self-selection process may have been aided to some extent by a kvutza policy of admitting to permanent membership those candidates who receive a majority vote after a trial period ranging from six months to a year. In the early years particularly, potential members were carefully scrutinized for the characteristics which were thought to make good kvutza material. For a new person to appear to be a good worker and a harmonious comrade, it was necessary that he respond to public opinion. This ability is still tested in many subtle ways. Candidates for membership are not explicitly told all the ways of the kvutza and must learn many of them through the informal control system. In the dining hall, for example, new residents are not instructed in the complicated standards governing substitution of desired food for allotted dishes. They must learn, mainly by observing others, which kinds of foods can or cannot be taken from the waiter's cart in exchange for a dish which has already been served. Speed of learning is noted by the old-timers, and failure to learn over an extended period contributes to a negative impression of the candidate. Oftentimes individuals who fail to meet such tests are subjected to social disapproval which is sufficiently unpleasant to cause their emigration from the settlement. In general the emigration rate has been higher from the kvutza than from the moshav, and it is presumed that those who have left have been less able to conform to public opinion than those who have remained.

By contrast, no such elaborate procedures are used to determine fitness for moshav members. Most of the available farmsteads were taken years ago

---

[10]Stemming from Freud through Fromm, this distinction has been given recent expression in Riesman (1950).

by the families which still occupy them. Emigration is based primarily on inability to make a success of farming, but it is doubtful whether sensitivity to public opinion enhances or decreases the chances of success. Since a farming tradition has not yet been established, success often comes to the very individual who flouts public opinion and proceeds in accordance with his own notions. New families are accepted primarily on the basis of their promise as successful farmers and secondarily on their apparent conformity to social requirements.

Far less wasteful for the kvutza than a continuous circulation of personnel would be a system of training to increase responsiveness to public opinion. Kvutza child training practices seem to produce this effect. Children are raised from infancy in the constant company of other children of their own age with whom they sleep, eat, bathe, dress, play, and later attend school. Though control is at first the task of the nurses, it is increasingly taken over by the children themselves. Their community is organized politically in a manner similar to the adult kvutza, with children's public opinion playing a corresponding part. When one child was caught stealing bananas reserved for the babies, the Children's Assembly decided to punish the culprit by abrogating *their own* movie privileges. Though this was explained to the adults on the grounds that all were involved in the guilt of one, a reason of at least equal importance was the children's expectation that this reaction would provide such a loss to all the children that a potential wrongdoer would repeat the precipitating action at his peril. At any rate, the practice of stealing was greatly reduced following this reaction.

During their years of training, the kvutza children become very alert to their peers' opinions, on which they are dependent for virtually all their satisfactions. While they are growing up, this force is used to ensure conformity to the standards of the children's community. These standards may conflict with those of the adult community, resulting in behavior which seems wild and capricious to the adults. But adult members remark repeatedly on the suddenness with which, following their accession to formal membership at eighteen, children of the kvutza "mature," that is, learn to conform to adult standards. This is in contrast to the moshav where adolescence is a period of great stress extending over several years. Moshav children, brought up in the close-knit farm family under their parents' control, never seem to develop the great respect for public opinion characteristic of the kvutza.[11]

Supplementing migration and socialization practices are the day-to-day experiences of adult kvutza members. Quick and accurate response to public opinion enables the member to align his behavior with community standards, and thus to enhance his chances of attaining the acceptance and prestige which are needed for even small advantages. In the kvutza environment, one

---

[11] For a detailed comparison of socialization practices in these types of settlements, see Eisenstadt (1951).

is rewarded for responding to the unfavorable reaction of his comrades when he talks too long in the Assembly, does not volunteer for emergency work service, wears inappropriate clothes, or debunks a kvutza celebration. Failure to respond has been known to result in serious difficulties, such as that experienced by a teacher who so antagonized public opininon by declining to dig trenches during Israel's War of Independence that he was denied a requested change of job a full year later.

In the moshav, this kind of pressure is exerted less frequently and effectively, if for no other reason than that there are fewer gains for which the individual is dependent on the community. Near self-sufficiency in economic affairs makes it difficult for the moshav to exert informal control. Primary reliance is placed on sanctions such as fines or, in a few cases of economic failure, expulsion from the settlement.

Thus several factors appear to contribute to the relatively greater power exercised by public opinion in the kvutza. It is difficult to estimate the effects of each of these in the absence of accurate knowledge concerning the values of immigrants and emigrants, as well as changes in the values of present residents since their time of settlement. Nevertheless, processes of selection, child training and adult experience were at work which might well be expected to result in kvutza members being more sensitive to public opinion than were moshav members.

This expectation is confirmed in the verbal reports of the members themselves. A sample of adult members in both settlements were asked whether in the event of clash between their own views and the demands of public opinion they behaved in accordance with the former or the latter. Only one-third of the kvutza respondents said they would follow their own inclinations in such a case, while almost three-fifths of the moshav members said they would. Such a difference would have occurred by chance so infrequently that we are justified in considering it statistically significant.[12] These quanti-

---

[12] Four questions were asked, comprising a "Guttman scale." For a detailed description of this method see Stouffer (1950). The writer had the benefit of Dr. Guttman's advice in the construction, pretesting, and administration of this scale. A 90% sample was obtained of the adult members, but only three-fourths of these answered all the questions on this scale. Though some sample bias may have resulted from these opinions, it would have to be extreme in order to invalidate these results.

Behavior in the Event of Conflict

	Kvutza		Moshav	
	N	%	N	%
Follow own inclinations	36	33	87	57
Follow public opinion	74	67	65	43
Total:	110	100	152	100
$\chi^2 = 15.32, p < .001$				

tative data provide confirmation of differences which had already been observed by ethnographic methods.

Vicarious Learning

If the effects of sanction were confined to the behavior of sanctionees, social control would be very difficult. Because people are able to learn from the experience of others, however, the control process is greatly facilitated. Such experience has been discussed in several disciplines, ranging from psychoanalytic theories on "identification" to jurisprudential discussions of deterrence. A definitive answer has yet to be found to the very important question as to *who* vicariously learns *what* from the observed experience of *whom*.

Our theoretical orientation suggests that vicarious learning depends on the extent to which an observer perceives himself similar to an observed actor. As perceived similarity increases, so also does the likelihood that the observer will have his tendencies increased for behavior which the actor has gainfully performed. At least two factors would thus appear requisite to vicarious learning: the observer must know of the behavior of another and its consequences, and he must perceive that actor as somewhat similar to himself.

In the kvutza, both of these conditions for vicarious learning are fulfilled to a very great degree within the informal control system. Intimacy in the kvutza, as noted, permits extensive observation of other members' experiences. Moreover, there is considerable evidence that kvutza members perceive themselves as "comrades" in a homogeneous group. Their perception of similarity may well be enhanced by the mere physical resemblance among members. Men are issued the same kind of clothes, and women wear rather similar ones; even their haircuts are given without much variation by one barber who visits the kvutza. But such factors only supplement the more basic similarities of life conditions, including work schedule, consumption, and leisure activities. In all of these, members are subject to fairly uniform controls, so that they experience gain when they consider themselves similar enough to their fellow members to learn from their experiences. These factors contribute to a strong "we" feeling, one of whose effects may well be to heighten vicarious learning in the kvutza. This feeling is not challenged, as in the moshav, by the distinctive customs of individual families.

The difference between the two settlements is reflected in the responses of the members when asked to construe the phrase "amongst us."[13] Ninety-five

---

[13] Ninety percent of the adult members of both communities were sampled, and over eighty percent of the polled members responded to this question.

percent of the responding kvutza members stated that they referred to their entire community when they used this term. By contrast, more than half of all moshav respondents used the term in application to their families and fewer than a third used it to refer to the entire settlement. The kvutza thus appears to provide more of a "reference group" (see Merton and Kitt, 1950) for its members than does the moshav.[14]

This orientation sets kvutza members apart from the outside world, even from members of other collective settlements. This was reflected by the children of the settlement in holding themselves aloof from the children of other collectives, reminding each other. "We are from 'Orah.'"[15] In general, the attitude toward outsiders is one of sharper differentiation than is found in the moshav. This was manifested in the carefully correct or even suspicious manner in which kvutza members reacted to strangers, especially foreigners and Arabs, as against the tendency of moshav members to invite such persons into their homes.

NORMS

Every system of control consists of more than the simple ability to apply sanctions. In order to maximize their gain, reactors must know whether and how to react to different behaviors. By denoting given behavior as similar to a class of behaviors, reactors tend to evoke from themselves and from others the same reaction to the particular behavior as has been learned to the class.[16] Such a classification will tend to result in gain if the reaction to the class results in maximal gain, *and* if the particular behavior resembles the class in its social consequences (i.e., both cause gain or both cause loss), *and* if the learned reaction to the class affects the tendency of the given behavior as it does the class.

The effectiveness of kvutza informal controls is enhanced by a system of norms classifying all behavior with reference to desirability. This system is detailed, generally unambiguous, applicable to wide, clearly defined segments of the population, and well known to the members. As a result it provides consistent guides for the application of sanction and at the same time forewarns potential sanctionees of the consequences of their acts. Such

---

[14] Of 124 kvutza respondents, 118 used the term to refer to the entire community. Only 49 of 157 moshav respondents used it in this way ($\chi^2 = 117.49, p < .001$). These differences would have occurred by chance less than one time in a thousand.

[15] "Orah" is a fictitious name which has been substituted for the real name of the kvutza studied in order to preserve the anonymity of the members.

[16] See the discussion of legal "reasoning by example" in Levi (1949).

norms, found in every sphere of kvutza life, are particularly striking in economic matters.

Work activities in the kvutza are directed toward maximizing the production of agricultural goods and the performance of domestic services. Each able-bodied adult resident is expected to work in some unit, either an agricultural branch (e.g., orchard, poultry, or sheep) or a domestic service (e.g., kitchen, laundry, or school). Labor allocations are made by a Work Assignment Committee on the basis of economic requirements of each unit, ability of workers to meet those requirements, and lastly the preferences of each worker. Workers learn of their assignments either orally or by notice posted on the bulletin board. This assignment is understood to mean, unless otherwise specified, that the worker will report to the manager of the given unit within a reasonable time (about 15 minutes) after the morning bell has rung, and work there, except for breakfast, lunch, and siesta, until the evening bell signals the end of the working day. Some assignments (e.g., nursery, dairy, trucking, and night watch) require special hours, but these are explicitly stated and the kvutza assigns a functionary to rouse such workers and notify them of the start of their workday. Illness constitutes the major reason for exemption from this norm, and all sick persons are expected to consult the resident community physician who decides whether and for how long the patient is to abstain from work.

Each worker is expected to cooperate with the individual recognized by all as the coordinator or manager of his unit. Usually such recognition is relatively spontaneous, based upon superior knowledge, skill, leadership ability, and seniority. When no single individual is clearly superior in these regards, the Economic Council recommends reassignments which bring about this result. As a consequence, the worker typically has someone to whom he turns for guidance whenever he is uncertain as to the correct course of action. On their part, managers, though exercising considerable discretion, are expected to turn to the Economic Council for guidance in significant decisions. Ultimately, the Council itself is responsible to the General Assembly. All kvutza members are expected to perform their various activities to the best of their individual abilities. These abilities are recognized to vary widely, but kvutza members maintain that a certain level of performance exists for each worker in a given kind of job. Though a worker's prestige varies with the height of this level, he may be well esteemed if he consistently meets even a low standard of performance. Since the level of performance is set by the worker's *better* performances, he is likely to be considered a violator of this very significant norm if he is erratic and frequently falls below his standard. In an economy which has abolished wages and private profit, these work norms are of great importance in maintaining production.

Consumption activities in the kvutza are also controlled with the aid of explicit general norms. Objectives which these are supposed to serve include distribution according to need, frugality, solidarity, and of course adequate sustenance of the population. Since differential need is very difficult to ascertain, the kvutza tendency has been to distribute scarce items equally, on the assumption that need is generally equal. Exceptions are made in instances where this is obviously not the case, for example, when youth, age, illness, or pregnancy furnishes grounds for special diet, housing, or medical care. Aside from these, however, consumption of scarce goods is supposed to be as nearly equal as possible. Adults are expected to eat together in the common dining hall at specified times. There they are served meals which are planned by the dietician with an eye toward fitting the budget adopted by the General Assembly. Crops drawn directly from the land are usually sufficiently abundant to permit unrestricted consumption, but other foods such as margarine, fish, meat, hard cheese, and eggs are distributed in limited equal quantities. Though the norms governing such consumption may be a mystery to new arrivals, members are fully aware of them. Occasionally questions arise as to the kinds of dishes for which a given serving may be exchanged, but these are authoritatively settled by the dietician. Similarly, clothes are expected to be issued equally except for differences of sex and size. Women are permitted a small degree of discretion in the selection of materials, but no one may exceed the ration and standard for a given sex, of such items as work shirts, work shoes, and sweaters. In housing, correct behavior is even less complicated: one is expected to live in the room assigned by the Housing Committee, whose discretion is limited by policies established in the General Assembly. Explicit general norms also cover such matters as participation in kvutza festivals, visting of children by parents, and preservation of a minimal privacy in rooms.

Such a pervasive set of general norms may be of great aid for a system of social control. Its contribution to the system's effectiveness is dependent, however, on the uniformity of the effect of a given behavior, no matter who performs it, and on the uniformity with which a sanction tends to deter or encourage it. Kvutza goals and conditions result in a high degree of both kinds of uniformity in regard to the norms mentioned. Since the uniform effectiveness of kvutza public opinion as a sanction has already been discussed, our discussion will now concentrate on uniformity of effect of a given behavior.

Kvutza members want their society to survive and be productive. They have set up an economic system which requires diligent and cooperative work by all if it is to succeed. Any behavior which is deemed nondiligent and which does not appear to contribute to the required coordination of effort will be viewed as threatening loss to kvutza productivity. Such behavior would include failure to work at one's top ability and to comply with one's work assignment; failure in these respects would be interpreted as causing loss to the kvutza. Similarly, anyone who receives more than an equal share in food, clothes, or housing is threatening the goal of a "just society" and subjecting the other members to "relative deprivation."[17] While variations in the other direction—too much work or substandard consumption—are less of a cause for concern, they also seem to be a source of disturbance, perhaps because vicarious experience makes such behavior unpleasant to those who observe it. Whatever the reasons, strict compliance with these norms is generally considered desirable, while violation of them is typically viewed as a loss to the members as a whole.

One of the greatest weaknesses of kvutza controls arises from failure to specify the identity and special privileges of the high-prestige members.[18] Managers and old-timers are distinguished in fact from the ordinary workers and "simpletons" in the deference shown them and, within narrow limits, in the preference they may receive in housing, furniture, travel, and education for their children. Deviations from the general norms by the "important" people are less disturbing than if performed by ordinary members, since kvutza public opinion recognizes their special worth and power. But difficulties sometimes arise from uncertainty as to how important a given individual is and what privileges, if any, are due him.

Such problems tend to be minimized by a denial that important people are treated differently in any way, or that there is in fact a special managerial status. That an equalitarian society should be unwilling to recognize such privileges is not surprising. Material advantages given the important people are rationalized in terms of the norms and their accepted exceptions. For example, new housing units, built by the kvutza to accommodate an increased population, were made more elaborate than earlier ones by the inclusion of shower and toilet facilities. These units were designated from the first as "old-timers' housing," and it was explained that the increased age of this group made it difficult for them to use the central facilities. On closer questioning, however, it was revealed that these rooms were not intended for other inhabitants who were also advancing in years, namely, a few recent immigrants of middle-age and several resident parents of members. Though the physical need of such persons was at least as great as that of the old-timers, no one even considered the possibility that they should be given modern accommodations as permanent quarters. Actually the reason was a

---

[17] For development and use of this concept, see Stouffer (1951).

[18] See the discussion of this stratum in Rosenfeld (1951). The picture given there is very similar to that observed in the kvutza studied, except for Rosenfeld's observations on the attitudes of the different strata toward institutional change.

feeling of injustice that so much be given to people who had done so little for the kvutza, but this was never publicly articulated and the fiction prevailed that the distribution met the requirement of "equal or according to need." Accordingly, the behavior, which was in fact a nondisturbing deviation from the general norm, was classified as acceptable behavior and was not negatively sanctioned as were other deviations from the norm.

In most areas, however, norms have been developed which clearly distinguish acceptable from disturbing behavior in a given situation for a clearly delimited category of persons. Ambiguities which arise are usually brought before the General Assembly and are conclusively resolved by its decision. Sometimes the kvutza reaches a consensus informally. The resultant norms are applied with a high degree of certainty. Though for our purposes the reasons need not be spelled out, it would appear that kvutza norms can be unambiguous and simple because behavioral alternatives and variations are sharply limited and because a homogenous population is in general agreement in distinguishing desirable from undesirable behavior among these clear and limited alternatives.

Moshav norms, by contrast, are far less explicit, uniformly applied, or generally agreed upon. While it is important that a farmer manage his own holdings effectively and be a good neighbor, the exact pattern of actions by which this can be accomplished has never been authoritatively laid down. In most areas, the individual is likely to have his own ideas about the proper behavior in a given circumstance. On particular occasions involving the duty to aid one's sick neighbor, cooperation in the use of machinery, and a member's violation of State ration controls, widespread difference of opinion was discerned among moshav members. This difference was partly attributed to the influence on each member of such factors as the effect of the particular behavior on his own economic interest; his relations with the actor in question; and his conception of the responsibility owed to the moshav by its members.

Such crucial questions as property relations in the family and between neighbors are still being deliberated and moshav members vary widely in their views on such matters. The problem of succession is just beginning to arise with regularity, and its importance and difficulty for a village with limited, indivisible and inalienable farmsteads may hardly be overestimated. Perhaps a uniform set of norms will be evolved over a period of time to deal with such problems, or perhaps the problems, especially concerning property, defy informal concensus. At any rate, for the present, there is little agreement. It is small wonder, then, the moshav system of informal controls has been supplemented by a specialized group of deliberators able to make norms and to ensure their sanction by legal means.

THE EFFECTS OF PRIOR EXPERIENCE

Those who perceive pertinent behavior and are able to apply effective sanctions must do so frequently, vigorously, and speedily. The likelihood that they will is dependent on *past* experiences with these and alternative reactions. A given sanction is likely to be so applied at a given time if it has previously been followed by gain and if competing reactions have not. The relative gain which has previously followed a given sanction is a function, at that earlier time, of the optimality of norms[19] and the capacity of the sanction to impose the impact needed. Sanction impact, in turn, depends on information, implementation, magnitude of gain or loss, and vicarious learning at that earlier time, and on the then extant reaction tendencies. Reaction tendencies depend in turn on preceding experience and therefore on all the other factors mentioned as they existed at a still earlier period. Thus, the impact of a given sanction is dependent on its previous impact, in a way which renders the entire history of that sanction significant for the understanding of a current control system. To summarize this formally: the impact of a particular sanction, being affected by the frequency, vigor, and speed with which it is applied, is an increasing function of the reactors' previous experiences of gain following the use of this sanction in similar situations, and a decreasing function of the reactors' previous experiences of gain following the use of competing reactions in similar situations.

Tendency toward Informal Sanction

As far as could be ascertained, the conditions which promoted effective informal control existed from the first or arose early in the history of the kvutza. Since it started out as a small settlement with a homogeneous population, it was, if anything, even more of a primary group during its formative years than at present. There is sufficient evidence in reports of old-timers to indicate that pertinent behavior was readily perceived, that public opinion was an easily implemented and effective sanction, and that unambiguous norms defined the circumstances under which such sanctions should be employed. There were, to be sure, instances where these controls failed to work, as for example in regard to the use of spending money. An early norm permitted each member to take as much money from a common fund as he felt he needed for personal expenses. In practice this is said to have resulted in low expenditures by the "idealistic" members and dispro-

---

[19] An optimal norm is defined as one which produces the maximum reduction of disturbance.

portionately high ones by those with a weaker sense of social responsibility. When public opinion proved incapable of controlling this socially disturbing behavior, the General Assembly modified the norm to stipulate a yearly amount for each member's personal use. Clarification of the distinction between acceptable and disturbing behavior in this area permitted the effective application of negative sanction to the latter, with the result that few members exceeded their allotted amount thereafter. The desired result was achieved by changes which increased the effectiveness of informal sanctions rather than substituting legal controls for them.

Because effective informal control was achieved in the kvutza, the tendency for its subsequent use was increased. That this tendency was high is indicated not only by the many successful instances of its use, but perhaps even more by the persistence with which it was employed on the rare occasions when it failed. Most striking among the illustrations of this is the case of a woman who was considered by the entire kvutza to be antisocial. Soon after her arrival she began to behave very aggressively, quarreling with all her fellow workers in the kitchen and even striking them. Though the use of violence against a fellow member was shocking to the other members, only the usual mild sanctions were at first applied. For some reason, however, social disapproval failed to deter the woman. She continued the same course of behavior through seven years, during which she was subjected to more vigorous informal controls and was at the same time denied formal membership. But she was never subjected to force, expulsion, or even to material disadvantage. Only during her eighth year in the kvutza was a different type of sanction directed against her: she was given no work assignment and was deprived of the opportunity to work for the kvutza. After a year in which her isolation was thus increased, she bowed to the pressure and left the kvutza. Whether the new sanction be designated informal or legal, it is clear that it was an alternative to the traditional informal sanctions of public opinion. That it was employed only after seven years of persistent exercise of the traditional sanctions is a striking indication of the firmness with which the latter were established.

In the moshav, the tendency to exercise informal controls seems much less powerful. This is not surprising in view of previously described conditions which would minimize the effectiveness of such sanctions. Though these conditions are described as existing at the time of the study, they are traceable to the economic structure of the moshav, and thus it is reasonable to assume that they also existed at the inauguration of the community. If so, they preceded the rise of legal controls which evolved gradually during the first twenty years of the settlement's history. During this period and subsequently, informal controls have regularly been tried, but have been ineffective, presumably because of inadequate information, implementation, sanction magnitude, and norms. In the course of time, members have learned that informal controls are ineffective; the resultant lowered tendency to invoke these controls, resulting in even less frequent and less vigorous attempts to use them, has further diminished their effectiveness.[20] This attitude toward informal controls was exemplified by moshav reaction to the prank of a group of adolescents who raided a melon patch and openly ate the stolen melons. Indignation ran high because the melons had been specially cultivated for the wedding feast to be given in honor of the marriage of the farmer's daughter. Failing action by the Judiciary Committee, the feeling prevailed that there was "nothing at all to do" about it. Said one member, "If you scold those fellows, they laugh at you." So on the informal level, no serious attempt was undertaken to exert effective control.

Competing Reaction Tendencies

Infrequent and nonvigorous exertion of informal sanctions in the moshav may result in part from the competition of legal controls as an effective alternative. It is, of course, impossible to explain the original occurrence of legal controls in these terms, but once they had become established, their success as a competing reaction could have been expected to reduce the impact of informal sanctions. Within the kvutza, there was no comparable history of legal controls which might have constituted a competing alternative to the prevailing system. Free from such competition,[21] the impact of informal sanctions could have been expected to continue without abatement.

CONCLUSION

Several factors have been discussed with reference to their effect on social control. The kvutza was characterized by a number of conditions which, our theory suggests, engender a more effective informal control system. Presence

---

[20] This appears to be an instance of what has been described as the "self-fulfilling prophecy," (Merton, 1949: 179–195), although the "prophecy" is here taken not as the independent variable, but simply as a reflection of previous failure and low tendency.

[21] Another type of competition comes from other reactions which typically exert neither legal nor informal controls and may therefore be designated noncontrol reactions. Among these, two of particular interest are withdrawal from interaction and modification of values. In the kvutza, withdrawal from interaction is very difficult except through emigration. As we have seen, this occurs more frequently in the kvutza than in the moshav. If anything, by removing those individuals who were disposed toward noncontrol reactions, informal controls were strengthened and not weakened. On the other hand, kvutza members often meet disturbance by a modification of values. Some behavior which is initially thought likely to cause social loss—e.g., demand for individual radios—not infrequently comes to be accepted as socially gainful. In any event, since they are usually in competition with both informal and legal controls, the strength of such noncontrol reactions as modification of values and withdrawal from interaction generally fails to explain the form of control in a given community.

of these factors, and the effective controls which they produced, was interpreted as a partial explanation for the failure of the kvutza to develop a legal control system. By contrast, the moshav did not possess these characteristics to the same degree as did the kvutza and accordingly failed to develop an effective informal control system. The development of legal institutions in the moshav is partially explicable in these terms. Law has thus been seen to develop where disturbing behavior occurred which was not as adequately controlled informally as it could be with the aid of legal controls. If a similar process exists in the United States, its accurate description should contribute to the prediction and evaluation of our own legislative and judicial decisions.

REFERENCES

Anderson, N.
  1923   *The hobo*. Chicago: Univ. of Chicago Press.
  1940   *Men on the move*. Chicago: Univ. of Chicago Press.
Asch, S.
  1951   Effects of group pressure on the modification and distortion of judgments. In *Groups, leadership and men*, edited by Harold Guetzkow. Pittsburgh: Carnegie Press.
Baratz, G.
  1943   *Degania: The story of Palestine's first collective settlement*. Tel Aviv: Lion the Printer.
Ben Yissakhar, Y.
  1949–
  1950   The kibbutz at the crossroads. *Zionist Newsletter* **6–13** (1949–1950).
Burgess, E., and L. S. Cottrell, Jr.
  1939   *Predicting success and failure in marriage*. Englewood Cliffs: Prentice-Hall.
Clow, F. R.
  1919   Cooley's doctrine of primary groups. *American Journal of Sociology* **25** (November): 326–347.
Cooley, C. H.
  1909   *Social organization*. New York: Scribner's.
Cottrell, L. S., Jr.
  1940   *The railroader*. Stanford: Stanford Univ. Press.
Dayan, S.
  1947   *Moshave Ovdim*. Tel Aviv: Lion the Printer.
Ehrlich, E.
  1936   *Fundamental principles of the sociology of law*. Cambridge: Harvard Univ. Press. (Orig. pub. 1913.)
Eisenstadt, S. N.
  1951   *Age groups and social structure*. (Mimeo in Jerusalem).
Hayner, N.
  1928   Hotel life and personality. *American Journal of Sociology* **33** (1928): 748–795.
Hull, C. L.
  1951   *Essentials of behavior*. New Haven: Yale Univ. Press.

Kardiner, A.
1945   *The psychological frontiers of society.* New York: Columbia Univ. Press.
Levi, E.
1949   *An introduction to legal reasoning.* Chicago: Univ. of Chicago Press.
Llewellyn, K. N.
1931   Legal tradition and social science method—A realist's critique. In *Brookings Institution, Committee on Training, Essays on research in the social sciences,* pp. 89–120. Washington, D.C.: Brookings Institution.
Maletz, D.
1950   *Young hearts.* New York: Schocken Books.
Merton, R. K.
1949   *Social theory and social structure.* New York: Free Press.
Merton, R. K., and A. Kitt
1950   Contributions to the theory of reference material. In *Studies in the scope and method of The American Soldier,* edited by R. K. Merton and P. Lazarsfeld. New York: Free Press.
Messinger, S. (Ed.)
1949   *Kvutzah Moshav Kibbutz.* New York: Hechalutz Pamphlets.
Redfield, R.
1941   *The folk culture of Yucatan.* Chicago: Univ. of Chicago Press.
Riesman, D.
1950   *The lonely crowd.* New Haven: Yale Univ. Press.
Rosenfeld, E.
1951   Social stratification in a classless society. *American Sociological Review* **16** (1951): 766–774.
Schwartz, R. D.
1951   Institutional consistency in a collective society: A sociological analysis of an Israeli kvutza. Unpublished Ph.D. thesis, Department of Sociology, Yale University.
Shils, E.
1951   The study of the primary group. In *The policy sciences,* edited by M. Lerner and H. Lasswell, pp. 23–31. Stanford: Stanford Univ. Press.
Stouffer, S.
1950   *Measurement and prediction.* Princeton: Princeton Univ. Press.
1951   *The American soldier.* Princeton: Princeton Univ. Press.

Part III

LAW
AND SOCIAL
STRATIFICATION

VAGRANCY LAW IN ENGLAND
AND AMERICA

William Chambliss

WITH THE outstanding exception of Jerome Hall's analysis of theft (1939; also see Lindesmith, 1959: 48), there has been a severe shortage of sociologically relevant analyses of the relationship between particular laws and the social setting in which these laws emerge, are interpreted, and take form. The paucity of such studies is somewhat surprising in view of widespread agreement that such studies are not only desirable but alsolutely essential to the development of a mature sociology of law (see, e.g., Rose, 1962: 281–283; Geis, 1959). A fruitful method of establishing the direction and pattern of this mutual influence is to systematically analyze particular legal categories, to observe the changes which take place in the categories, and to explain how these changes are themselves related to and stimulate changes in the society. This paper is an attempt to provide such an analysis of the law of vagrancy in Anglo-American Law.[1]

---

[1] For a more complete listing of most of the statutes dealt with in this report the reader is referred to Burn (1764). Citations of English statutes should be read as follows: 3 Ed. 1.c.1. refers to the third act of Edward the First, Chapter one, etc.

Reprinted from "A Sociological Analysis of the Law of Vagrancy" by William Chambliss, *Social Problems*, Vol. 12, No. 1 (Summer 1964): pp. 67–77. Copyright © 1964 by The Society for the Study of Social Problems.

LEGAL INNOVATION: THE EMERGENCE OF THE LAW OF VAGRANCY IN ENGLAND

There is general agreement among legal scholars that the first full-fledged vagrancy statute was passed in England in 1349. As is generally the case with legislative innovations, however, this statute was preceded by earlier laws which established a climate favorable to such change. The most significant forerunner to the 1349 vagrancy statute was in 1274 when it was provided (3 Ed.1.c.1, 1274):

> Because that abbies and houses of religion have been overcharged and sore grieved, by the resort of great men and other, so that their goods have not been sufficient for themselves, whereby they have been greatly hindered and impoverished, that they cannot maintain themselves, nor such charity as they have been accustomed to do; it is provided, that none shall come to eat or lodge in any house of religion, or any other's foundation than of his own, at the costs of the house, unless he be required by the governor of the house before his coming hither.

Unlike the vagrancy statutes this statute does not intend to curtail the movement of persons from one place to another, but is solely designed to provide the religious houses with some financial relief from the burden of providing food and shelter to travelers.

The philosophy that the religious houses were to give alms to the poor and to the sick and feeble was, however, to undergo drastic change in the next fifty years. The result of this changed attitude was the establishment of the first vagrancy statute in 1349 which made it a crime to give alms to any who were unemployed while being of sound mind and body. To wit (35 Ed.1.c.1, 1349):

> Because that many valiant beggars, as long as they may live of begging, do refuse to labor, giving themselves to idleness and vice, and sometimes to theft and other abominations; it is ordained, that none, upon pain of imprisonment shall, under the colour of pity or alms, give anything to such which may labour, or presume to favour them towards their desires; so that thereby they may be compelled to labour for their necessary living.

It was further provided by this statute that (23 Ed.3, 1349):

> ... Every man and woman, of what condition he be, free or bond, able in body, and within the age of threescore years, not living in merchandize nor exercising any craft, nor having of his own whereon to live, nor proper land whereon to occupy himself, and not serving any other, if he in convenient service (his estate considered) be required to serve, shall be bounded to serve him which shall him require ... And if any refuse, he shall on conviction by two true men, ... be commited to gaol till he find surety to serve.
>
> And if any workman or servant, of what estate or condition he be, retained in any man's service, do depart from the said service without reasonable cause or license, before the term agreed on, he shall have pain of imprisonment.

There was also in this statute the stipulation that the workers should receive a standard wage. In 1351 this statute was strengthened by the stipulation: "An none shall go out of the town where he dwelled in winter, to serve the summer, if he may serve in the same town" (25 Ed.3, 1351).

By 34 Ed.3 (1360) the punishment for these acts became imprisonment for fifteen days, and if they "do not justify themselves by the end of that time, to be sent to gaol till they do."

A change in official policy so drastic as this did not, of course, occur simply as a matter of whim. The vagrancy statutes emerged as a result of changes in other parts of the social structure. The prime mover for this legislative innovation was the Black Death which struck England about 1348. Among the many disastrous consequences this had upon the social structure was the fact that it decimated the labor force. It is estimated that by the time the pestilence had run its course at least 50% of the population of England had died from the plague. This decimation of the labor force would necessitate rather drastic innovations in any society but its impact was heightened in England where, at this time, the economy was highly dependent upon a ready supply of cheap labor.

Even before the pestilence, however, the availability of an adequate supply of cheap labor was becoming a problem for the landowners. The crusades and various wars had made money necessary to the lords and, as a result, the lord frequently agreed to sell the serfs their freedom in order to obtain the needed funds. The serfs, for their part, were desirous of obtaining their freedom (by "fair means" or "foul") because the larger towns which were becoming more industrialized during this period could offer the serf greater personal freedom as well as a higher standard of living. This process is nicely summarized by Bradshaw (1918: 54):

> By the middle of the 14th century the outward uniformity of the manorial system had become in practice considerably varied ... for the peasant had begun to drift to the towns and it was unlikely that the old village life in its unpleasant aspects should not be resented. Moreover the constant wars against France and Scotland were fought mainly with mercenaries after Henry III's time and most villages contributed to the new armies. The bolder serfs either joined the armies or fled to the towns, and even in the villages the free men who held by villein tenure were as eager to commute their services as the serfs were to escape. Only the amount of 'free' labor available enabled the lord to work his demense in many places.

And he says regarding the effect of the Black Death (p. 54): ". . . in 1348 the Black Death reached England and the vast mortality that ensued destroyed that reserve of labour which alone had made the manorial system even nominally possible." The immediate result of these events was of course no surprise: Wages for the "free" man rose considerably and this increased, on the one hand, the landowners problems, and on the other hand, the plight of the unfree tenant. For although wages increased for the personally free laborers, it of course did not necessarily add to the standard of living of the serf; if anything it made his position worse because the landowner would be hard pressed to pay for the personally free labor which he needed and would thus find it more and more difficult to maintain the standard of living for the serf which he had heretofore supplied. Thus the serf had no alternative but flight if he chose to better his position. Furthermore, flight generally meant both freedom and better conditions since the possibility of work in the new weaving industry was great and the chance of being caught small (Bradshaw, 1918: 57).

It was under these conditions that we find the first vagrancy statutes emerging. There is little question but that these statutes were designed for one express purpose: to force laborers (whether personally free or unfree) to accept employment at a low wage in order to insure the landowner an adequate supply of labor at a price he could afford to pay. Caleb Foote concurs with this interpretation when he notes (1956: 615):

> The anti-migratory policy behind vagrancy legislation began as an essential complement of the wage stabilization legislation which accompanied the breakup of feudalism and the depopulation caused by the Black Death. By the Statutes of Labourers in 1349–1351, every ablebodied person without other means of support was required to work for wages fixed at the level preceding the Black Death; it was unlawful to accept more, or to refuse an offer to work, or to flee from one county to another to avoid offers of work, or to seek higher wages, or to give alms to able-bodied beggars who refused to work.

In short, as Foote says in another place, this was an "attempt to make the vagrancy statutes a substitute for serfdom." This same conclusion is equally apparent from the wording of the statute where it is stated:

> Because great part of the people, and especially of workmen and servants, late died in pestilence; many seeing the necessity of masters, and great scarcity of servants, will not serve without excessive wages, and some rather willing to beg in idleness than by labour to get their living: it is ordained, that every man and woman, of what condition he be, free or bond, able in body and within the age of threescore years, not living in merchandize, (etc.) be required to serve. . .

The innovation in the law, then, was a direct result of the aforementioned changes which had occurred in the social setting. In this case these changes were located for the most part in the economic institution of the society. The vagrancy laws were designed to alleviate a condition defined by the lawmakers as undesirable. The solution was to attempt to force a reversal, as it were, of a social process which was well underway; that is, to curtail mobility of laborers in such a way that labor would not become a commodity for which the landowners would have to compete.

Statutory Dormancy: A Legal Vestige

In time, of course, the curtailment of the geographical mobility of laborers was no longer requisite. One might well expect that when the function served by the statute was no longer an important one for the society, the statutes would be eliminated from the law. In fact, this has not occurred. The vagrancy statutes have remained in effect since 1349. Furthermore, as we shall see in some detail later, they were taken over by the colonies and have remained in effect in the United States as well.

The substance of the vagrancy statutes changed very little for some time after the first ones in 1349–1351, although there was a tendency to make punishments more harsh than originally. For example, in 1360 it was provided that violators of the statute should be imprisoned for fifteen days (34 Ed.3, 1360) and in 1388 the punishment was to put the offender in the stocks and to keep him there until "he find surety to return to his service." (12 R.2, 1388). That there was still, at this time, the intention of providing the landowner with labor is apparent from the fact that this statute provides (Foote, 1956):

> And he or she which use to labour at the plough and cart, or other labour and service of husbandry, till they be of the age of 12 years, from thenceforth shall abide at the same labour without being put to any mistery or handicraft: and any covenant of apprenticeship to the contrary shall be void.

The next alteration in the statutes occurs in 1495 and is restricted to an increase in punishment. Here it is provided that vagrants shall be "set in stocks, there to remain by the space of three days and three nights, and there to have none other sustenance but bread and water; and after the said three days and nights, to be had out and set at large, and then to be commanded to avoid the town" (11 H.8.c.2, 1495).

The tendency to increase the severity of punishment during this period seems to be the result of a general tendency to make finer distinctions in the criminal law. During this period the vagrancy statutes appear to have been fairly inconsequential in either their effect as a control mechanism or as a generally enforced statute.[2] The processes of social change in the culture generally and the trend away from serfdom and into a "free" economy obviated the utility of these statutes. The result was not unexpected. The judiciary did not apply the law and the legislators did not take it upon

---

[2] As evidence for this note the expectation that ". . . the common gaols of every shire are likely to be greatly pestered with more numbers of prisoners than heretofore . . ." when the statutes were changed by the statute of 14 Ed.c.5 (1571).

themselves to change the law. In short, we have here a period of dormancy in which the statute is neither applied nor altered significantly.

A SHIFT IN FOCAL CONCERN

Following the squelching of the Peasant's Revolt in 1381, the services of the serfs to the lord "... tended to become less and less exacted, although in certain forms they lingered on till the seventeenth century ... By the sixteenth century few knew that there were any bondmen in England ... and in 1575 Queen Elizabeth listened to the prayers of almost the last serfs in England ... and granted them manumission" (Bradshaw, 1918:61).

In view of this change we would expect corresponding changes in the vagrancy laws. Beginning with the lessening of punishment in the statute of 1503 we find these changes. However, instead of remaining dormant (or becoming more so) or being negated altogether, the vagrancy statutes experienced a shift in focal concern. With this shift the statutes served a new and equally important function for the social order of England. The first statute which indicates this change was in 1530. In this statute (22 H.8.c.12, 1530) it was stated:

> If any person, being whole and mighty in body, and able to labour, be taken in begging, or be vagrant and can give no reckoning how he lawfully gets his living; ... and all other idle persons going about, some of them using divers and subtle crafty and unlawful games and plays, and some of them feigning themselves to have knowledge of ... crafty sciences ... shall be punished as provided.

What is most significant about this statute is the shift from an earlier concern with laborers to a concern with *criminal* activities. To be sure, the stipulation of persons "being whole and mighty in body, and able to labour, be taken in begging, or be vagrant" sounds very much like the concerns of the earlier statutes. Some important differences are apparent however when the rest of the statute includes those who "... can give no reckoning how he lawfully gets his living"; "some of them using divers subtil and unlawful games and plays." This is the first statute which specifically focuses upon these kinds of criteria for adjudging someone a vagrant.

It is significant that in this statute the severity of punishment is increased so as to be greater not only than provided by the 1503 statute but the punishment is more severe than that which had been provided by *any* of the pre-1503 statutes as well. For someone who is merely idle and gives no reckoning of how he makes his living the offender shall be (22 H.8.c.12, 1530):

... had to the next market town, or other place where they [the constables] shall think most convenient, and there to be tied to the end of a cart naked, and to be beaten with whips throughout the same market town or other place, till his body be bloody by reason of such whipping.

But, for those who use "divers and subtil crafty and unlawful games and plays," etc., the punishment is ". . . whipping at two days together in manner aforesaid." For the second offense, such persons are ". . . scourged two days, and the third day to be put upon the pillory from nine of the clock till eleven before noon of the same day and to have one of his ears cut off." And if he offend the third time ". . . to have like punishment with whipping, standing on the pillory and to have his other ear cut off."

This statute (1) makes a distinction between types of offenders and applies the more severe punishment to those who are clearly engaged in "criminal" activities, (2) mentions a specific concern with categories of "unlawful" behavior, and (3) applies a type of punishment (cutting off the ear) which is generally reserved for offenders who are defined as likely to be a fairly serious criminal.

Only five years later we find for the first time that the punishment of death is applied to the crime of vagrancy. We also note a change in terminology in the statute (27 H.8.c.25, 1535):

and if any ruffians ... after having been once apprehended ... shall wander, loiter, or idle use themselves and play the vagabonds ... shall be eftsoons not only whipped again, but shall have the gristle of his right ear clean cut off. And if he shall again offend, he shall be committed to gaol till the next sessions; and being there convicted upon indictment, he shall have judgment to suffer pains and execution of death, as a felon, as an enemy of the commonwealth.

It is significant that the statute now makes persons who repeat the crime of vagrancy a felon. During this period, then, the focal concern of the vagrancy statutes becomes a concern for the control of felons and is no longer primarily concerned with the movement of laborers.

These statutory changes were a direct response to changes taking place in England's social structure during this period. We have already pointed out that feudalism was decaying rapidly. Concomitant with the breakup of feudalism was an increased emphasis upon commerce and industry. The commercial emphasis in England at the turn of the sixteenth century is of particular importance in the development of vagrancy laws. With commercialism came considerable traffic bearing valuable items. Where there were 169 important merchants in the middle of the fourteenth century there were 3000 merchants engaged in foreign trade alone at the beginning of the sixteenth century (Hall, 1939: 21). England became highly dependent upon commerce for its economic support. Italians conducted a great deal of the commerce of England during this early period and were held in low repute by the populace. As a result, they were subject to attacks by citizens and, more important, were frequently robbed of their goods while transporting them. "The general insecurity of the times made any transportation hazardous. The special risks to which the alien merchant was subjected gave rise to the royal practice of issuing formally executed covenants of safe conduct through the realm" (Hall, 1939: 23).

Such a situation not only called for the enforcement of existing laws but also called for the creation of new laws which would facilitate the control of persons preying upon merchants transporting goods. The vagrancy statutes were revived in order to fulfill just such a purpose. Persons who had committed no serious felony but who were suspected of being capable of doing so could be apprehended and incapacitated through the application of vagrancy laws once these laws were refocused so as to include ". . . any ruffians . . . [who] shall wander, loiter, or idle use themselves and play the vagabonds . . ." (27 H.8.c.25, 1535).

The new focal concern is continued in 1 Ed.6.c.3 (1547) and in fact is made more general so as to include:

> Whoever man or woman, being not lame, impotent, or so aged or diseased that he or she cannot work, not having whereon to live, shall be lurking in any house, or loitering or idle wandering by the highway side, or in streets, cities, towns, or villages, not applying themselves to some honest labour, and so continuing for three days; or running away from their work; every such person shall be taken for a vagabond. And . . . upon conviction of two witnesses . . . the same loiterer (shall) be marked with a hot iron in the breast with the letter V, and adjudged him to the person bringing him, to be his slave for two years . . .

Should the vagabond run away, upon conviction, he was to be branded by a hot iron with the letter S on the forehead and to be thenceforth declared a slave forever. And in 1571 there is modification of the punishment to be inflicted, whereby the offender is to be "branded on the chest with the letter V" (for vagabond). And, if he is convicted the second time, the brand is to be made on the forehead. It is worth noting here that this method of punishment, which first appeared in 1530 and is repeated here with somewhat more force, is also an indication of a change in the type of person to whom the law is intended to apply. For it is likely that nothing so permanent as branding would be applied to someone who was wandering but looking for work, or at worst merely idle and not particularly dangerous *per se*. On the other hand, it could well be applied to someone who was likely to be engaged in other criminal activities in connection with being "vagrant."

By 1571 in the statute of 14 Ed.c.5 the shift in focal concern is fully developed:

> All rogues, vagabonds, and sturdy beggars shall . . . be committed to the common gaol . . . he shall be grievously whipped, and burnt thro' the gristle of the right ear with a hot iron of the compass of an inch about; . . . And for the second offense, he shall be adjudged a felon, unless some person will take him for two years in to his service. And for the third offense, he shall be adjudged guilty of felony without benefit of clergy.

And there is included a long list of persons who fall within the statute: "proctors, procurators, idle persons going about using subtil, crafty and unlawful games or plays; and some of them feigning themselves to have knowledge of . . . absurd sciences . . . and all fencers, bearwards, common players in interludes, and minstrels . . . all juglers, pedlars, tinkers, petty chapmen . . . and all counterfeiters of licenses, passports and users of the same." The major significance of this statute is that it includes all the previously defined offenders and adds some more. Significantly, those added are more clearly criminal types, counterfeiters, for example. It is also significant that there is the following qualification of this statute: "Provided also, that this act shall not extend to cookers, or harvest folks, that travel for harvest work, corn or hay."

That the changes in this statute were seen as significant is indicated by the following statement which appears in the statute (14 Ed.c.5, 1571):

> And whereas by reason of this act, the common gaols of every shire are like to be greatly pestered with more number of prisoners than heretofore hath been, for that the said vagabonds and other lewd persons before recited shall upon their apprehension be committed to the said gaols; it is enacted . . .

And a provision is made for giving more money for maintaining the gaols. This seems to add credence to the notion that this statute was seen as being significantly more general than those previously.

It is also of importance to note that this is the first time the term *rogue* has been used to refer to persons included in the vagrancy statutes. It seems, *a priori*, that a "rogue" is a different social type from a "vagrant" or a "vagabond", the latter terms implying something more equivalent to the idea of a "tramp" whereas the former (rogue) seems to imply a more disorderly and potentially dangerous person.

The emphasis upon the criminalistic aspect of vagrants continues in Chapter 17 of the same statute:

> Whereas divers *licentious* persons wander up and down in all parts of the realm, to countenance their *wicked behavior*; and do continually assemble themselves armed in the highways,

and elsewhere in troops, *to the greater terror* of her majesty's true subjects, *the impeachment of her laws*, and the disturbance of the peace and tranquility of the realm; and whereas many outrages are daily committed by these dissolute persons, and more are likely to ensue if speedy remedy be not provided. [Italics added.]

With minor variations (e.g., offering a reward for the capture of a vagrant) the statutes remain essentially of this nature until 1743. In 1743 there was once more an expansion of the types of persons included such that "all persons going about as patent gatherers, or gatherers of alms, under pretense of loss by fire or other casualty; or going about as collectors for prisons, gaols, or hospitals; all persons playing or betting at any unlawful games; and all persons who run away and leave their wives or children . . . all persons wandering abroad, and lodging in alehouses, barns, outhouses, or in the open air, not giving good account of themselves," were types of offenders added to those already included.

By 1743 the vagrancy statutes had apparently been sufficiently reconstructed by the shifts of concern so as to be once more a useful instrument in the creation of social solidarity. This function has apparently continued down to the present day in England and the changes from 1743 to the present have been all in the direction of clarifying or expanding the categories covered but little has been introduced to change either the meaning or the impact of this branch of the law.

We can summarize this shift in focal concern by quoting from Halsbury. He has noted that in the vagrancy statutes (1912: 606–607):

". . . Elaborate provision is made for the relief and incidental control of destitute wayfarers. These latter, however, form but a small portion of the offenders aimed at by what are known as the Vagrancy Laws, . . . Many offenders who are in no ordinary sense of the word vagrants, have been brought under the laws relating to vagrancy, and the great number of the offenses coming within the operation of these laws have little or no relation to the subject of poor relief, but are more properly directed towards the prevention of crime, the preservation of good order, and the promotion of social economy."

Before leaving this section it is perhaps pertinent to make a qualifying remark. We have emphasized throughout this section how the vagrancy statutes underwent a shift in focal concern as the social setting changed. The shift in focal concern is not meant to imply that the later focus of the statutes represents a completely new law. It will be recalled that even in the first vagrancy statute there was reference to those who "do refuse labor, giving themselves to idleness and vice and sometimes to theft and other abominations." Thus the possibility of criminal activities resulting from persons who refuse to labor was recognized even in the earliest statute. The fact remains, however, that the major emphasis in this statute and in the statutes which followed the first one was always upon the "refusal to labor" or "begging." The "criminalistic" aspect of such persons was relatively unimportant. Later, as we have shown, the criminalistic potential becomes of paramount importance. The thread runs back to the earliest statute but the reason for the statutes' existence as well as the focal concern of the statutes is quite different in 1743 than it was in 1349.

VAGRANCY LAWS IN THE UNITED STATES

In general, the vagrancy laws of England, as they stood in the middle eighteenth century, were simply adopted by the states. There were some exceptions to this general trend. For example, Maryland restricted the application of vagrancy laws to "free" Negroes. In addition, for *all* states the vagrancy laws were even more explicitly concerned with the control of criminals and undesirables than had been the case in England. New York, for example, explicitly defines prostitutes as being a category of vagrants during this period. These exceptions do not, however, change the general picture significantly and it is quite appropriate to consider the U. S. vagrancy laws as following from England's of the middle eighteenth century with relatively minor changes. The control of criminals and undesirables was the *raison d'être* of the vagrancy laws in the U. S. This is as true today as it was in 1750. As Caleb Foote's analysis of the application of vagrancy statutes in the Philadelphia court shows, these laws are presently applied indiscriminately to persons considered a "nuisance." Foote suggests that ". . . the chief significance of this branch of the criminal law lies in its quantitative impact and administrative usefulness" (Foote, 1956: 613; also see Deutscher, 1955). Thus it appears that in America the trend begun in England in the sixteenth, seventeenth, and eighteenth centuries has been carried to its logical extreme and the laws are now used principally as a mechanism for "clearing the streets" of the derelicts who inhabit the "skid roads" and "Bowerys" of our large urban areas.

Since the 1800s there has been an abundant source of prospects to which the vagrancy laws have been applied. These have been primarily those persons deemed by the police and the courts to be either actively involved in criminal activities or at least peripherally involved. In this context, then, the statutes have changed very little. The functions served by the statutes in England of the late eighteenth century are still being served today in both England and the United States. The locale has changed somewhat and it appears that the present-day application of vagrancy statutes is focused upon the arrest and confinement of the "down and outers" who inhabit certain sections of our larger cities, but the impact has remained constant. The lack of change in the vagrancy statutes, then, can be seen as a reflection of the society's perception of a continuing need to control some of its "suspicious" or "undesirable" members.[3]

A word of caution is in order lest we leave the impression that this administrative purpose is the sole function of vagrancy laws in the U.S. today. Although it is our contention that this is generally true it is worth remembering that during certain periods of our recent history, and to some extent today, these laws have also been used to control the movement of workers. This was particularly the case during the depression years, and California is of course infamous for its use of vagrancy laws to restrict the admission of migrants from other states.[4] The vagrancy statutes, because of their history, still contain germs within them which make such effects possible. Their main purpose, however, is clearly no longer the control of laborers but rather the control of the undesirable, the criminal, and the "nuisance."

DISCUSSION

The foregoing analysis of the vagrancy laws has demonstrated that these laws were a legislative innovation which reflected the socially perceived necessity of providing an abundance of cheap labor to landowners during a period when serfdom was breaking down and when the pool of available labor was depleted. With the eventual breakup of feudalism the need for such laws eventually disappeared and the increased dependence of the economy upon industry and commerce rendered the former use of the vagrancy statutes unnecessary. As a result, for a substantial period the vagrancy statutes were dormant, undergoing only minor changes and, presumably, being applied infrequently. Finally, the vagrancy laws were subjected to considerable alteration through a shift in the focal concern of the statutes. Whereas in their inception the laws focused upon the "idle" and "those refusing to labor," after the turn of the sixteenth century, the emphasis came to be upon "rogues," "vagabonds," and others who were suspected of being engaged in criminal activities. During this period the focus was particularly upon "roadmen" who preyed upon citizens who transported goods from one place to another. The increased importance of commerce to England during this period made it necessary that some protection be given persons engaged in this enterprise and the vagrancy statutes provided one source for such protection by refocusing the acts to be included under these statutes.

Comparing the results of this analysis with the findings of Hall's study

[3]It is on this point that the vagrancy statutes have been subject to criticism. See, e.g., Lacey (1953).
[4]Edwards v. California, 314 S: 160 (1941).

of theft we see a good deal of correspondence. Of major importance is the fact that both analyses demonstrate the truth of Hall's assertion that "The functioning of courts is significantly related to concomitant cultural needs, and this applies to the law of procedure as well as to substantive law" (1939: xii).

Our analysis of the vagrancy laws also indicates that when changed social conditions create a perceived need for legal changes, these alterations will be effected through the revision and refocusing of existing statutes. This process was demonstrated in Hall's analysis of theft as well as in our analysis of vagrancy. In the case of vagrancy, the laws were dormant when the focal concern of the laws was shifted so as to provide control over potential criminals. In the case of theft the laws were reinterpreted (interestingly, by the courts and not by the legislature) so as to include persons who were transporting goods for a merchant but who absconded with the contents of the packages transported.

It also seems probable that when the social conditions change and previously useful laws are no longer useful there will be long periods when these laws will remain dormant. It is less likely that they will be officially negated. During this period of dormancy it is the judiciary which has principal responsibility for *not* applying the statutes. It is possible that one finds statutes being negated only when the judiciary stubbornly applies laws which do not have substantial public support. An example of such laws in contemporary times would be the "Blue Laws." Most states still have laws prohibiting the sale of retail goods on Sunday yet these are rarely applied. The laws are very likely to remain but to be dormant unless a recalcitrant judge or a vocal minority of the population insists that the laws be applied. When this happens we can anticipate that the statutes will be negated.[5] Should there arise a perceived need to curtail retail selling under some special circumstances, then it is likely that these laws will undergo a shift in focal concern much like the shift which characterized the vagrancy laws. Lacking such application the laws will simply remain dormant except for rare instances where they will be negated.

This analysis of the vagrancy statutes (and Hall's analysis of theft as well) has demonstrated the importance of "vested interest" groups in the emergence and/or alteration of laws. The vagrancy laws emerged in order to provide the powerful landowners with a ready supply of cheap labor. When this was no longer seen as necessary and particularly when the landowners were no longer dependent upon cheap labor nor were they a powerful interest group in the society the laws became dormant. Finally a new

---

[5] Negation, in this instance, is most likely to come about by the repeal of the statute. More generally, however, negation may occur in several ways including the declaration of a statute as unconstitutional. This later mechanism has been used even for laws which have been "on the books" for long periods of time. Repeal is probably the most common, although not the only, procedure by which a law is negated.

interest group emerged and was seen as being of great importance to the society, and the laws were then altered so as to afford some protection to this group. These findings are thus in agreement with Weber's contention that "status groups" determine the content of the law (1954). The findings are inconsistent, on the other hand, with the perception of the law as simply a reflection of "public opinion" as is sometimes found in the literature (Friedman, 1959). We should be cautious in concluding, however, that either of these positions is necessarily correct. The careful analysis of other laws, and especially of laws which do not focus so specifically upon the "criminal," are necessary before this question can be finally answered.

In conclusion, it is hoped that future analyses of changes within the legal structure will be able to benefit from this study by virtue of (1) the data provided, and (2) the utilization of a set of concepts (innovation, dormancy, concern, and negation) which have proved useful in the analysis of the vagrancy law. Such analyses should provide us with more substantial grounds for rejecting or accepting as generally valid the description of some of the processes which appear to characterize changes in the legal system.

REFERENCES

Bradshaw, F.
    1918   *A social history of England*. London: W. B. Clive.
Burn, R.
    1764   *The history of the poor laws*. London: printed by H. Woodfall and W. Strahan for A. Miller.
Deutscher, I.
    1955   The petty offender. *Federal Probation* **19** (June):12–18.
Friedman, W.
    1959   *Law in a changing society*. Berkeley: Univ. of California Press.
Foote, C.
    1956   Vagrancy type law and its administration. *University of Pennsylvania Law Review* **104** (1956): 603–650.
Geis, G.
    1959   Sociology, criminology, and criminal law. *Social Problems* **7** (Summer): 40–47.
Hall, J.
    1939   *Theft, law and society*. Indianapolis: Bobbs–Merrill.
Earl of Halsbury
    1912   *The laws of England*. London: Butterworth, Bell Yard, Temple Bar.
Lacey, F. W.
    1953   Vagrancy and other crimes of personal condition. *Harvard Law Review* **66** (1953): 1203–1226.
Lindesmith, A. R.
    1959   Federal law and drug addiction. *Social Problems* **7** (Summer): 48–57.
Rose, A.
    1962   Some suggestions for research in the sociology of law. *Social Problems* **9** (Winter): 281–283.
Weber, M.
    1954   *Law in economy and society*. Cambridge: Harvard Univ. Press. (Orig. pub. 1922.)

LEGAL PRIVILEGE IN THE ROMAN EMPIRE

Peter Garnsey

I. INTRODUCTION

... For the equality aimed at by the many (*sc., arithmetical equality*) is the greatest of all injustices, and God has removed it out of the world as being unattainable; but he protects and maintains the distribution of things according to merit, determining it geometrically, that is, in accordance with proportion and law.

T HUS A SPEAKER in Plutarch's *Dinner-Table Discussions* tried to interpret Plato's statement (authentic or apochryphal) that "God is always busy with geometry" (quoted in Farrington, 1939: 29–30). Whatever may be thought of his ingenious explanation, it does not misrepresent Plato's views on the subject of equality. Both Plato and Aristotle held that the equal distribution of things to persons of unequal merit was unequal.[1] The Roman governing classes showed by their administration of the law that they shared

[1]Plato, *The Laws*, sec. 757a, ff.; cf. sec. 744b–c: Aristotle, *Nicomachean Ethics*, 1131a, 15ff.

Reprinted with the permission of the Society and the author from "Legal Privilege in the Roman Empire" by Peter Garnsey, *Past and Present, a Journal of Historical Studies*, Vol. 31 (1968): pp. 3–24. World Copyright: The Past and Present Society, Corpus Christi, Oxford.

this conviction. So much can be deduced from the operation in Rome, Italy, and the provinces of a thoroughgoing system of legal discrimination to the advantage of certain privileged classes.

The legal system of any state may be biassed in at least three main ways. The law may favor certain parties in a relationship—for example, creditors over debtors or landlords over tenants, the poor being usually on the losing side in such relationships. Second, inequality may result from the incapacity of some through their social or economic position to enjoy the full benefits of the law even where these are not officially denied them—thus the rich can afford bail, while the poor must generally go to prison. Finally, the law as written or the law as administered may deny equal benefits and protection to different sections of the population, again in accordance with differing social and economic situations—thus a commoner might be whipped and an aristocrat fined for like offences (Carlin *et al.*, 1966). Only examples of the second and third varieties of inequality, *de facto* and *de iure* inequality, are explored in any detail in this paper. For the period that is examined, developments in procedure and in the administration of the law are of special interest.

For practical reasons, this investigation has been limited to the period from about the beginning of the Empire to about the end of the Severan dynasty, that is, from 27 B.C. to A.D. 235. These years, after the civil wars of the first century B.C., saw the emergence of a disguised monarchy which claimed to be the restored Republic. The political revolution brought in its train institutional changes in the sphere of law. New procedures grew up alongside the old ones (which, like the old political structures, were not destroyed, but allowed to wither away), and were characterized by new types of discrimination. One aim of this paper is to describe and contrast the different patterns of discrimination associated with Republican and Imperial procedures in civil and criminal law.

Three excerpts from literary sources are quoted first to indicate the kinds of people who gained preferential treatment in the law courts and to give an idea of the privileges they enjoyed. The details of the system of privilege are then assembled, and an analysis attempted of aspects of the Roman civil suit and criminal trial. Next, problems connected with the growth of the system and its basis in law are considered. Finally, the relationship between the upper-class/lower-class distinction (the so-called *honestiores/ humiliores* distinction)[2] and the citizen/alien distinction is discussed.

[2]The *honestiores/humiliores* formula is only one of several that occur in the legal sources. It is in fact confined to the "Sentences of Paulus," a late third-century compilation, which uses hardly any other terms. An earlier juristic writer employs *honestior/humilioris loci*, a close approximation. See *Digest*, xlviii.5.39.8.

II. THREE ILLUSTRATIONS

(1) L. Calpurnius Piso caused the Emperor Tiberius considerable embarrassment because of his independent attitudes and free speech. Once, according to Tacitus, Piso threatened to retire from politics in protest against the prevalence of judicial corruption and other abuses. Tiberius was able to mollify him temporarily:

> The same Piso before long gave just as vivid proof of his free and passionate spirit by summoning to court Urgulania, whose friendship with Augusta had lifted her beyond the reach of the laws. Urgulania did not obey the summons, but, scorning Piso, rode in a carriage to the Emperor's house. But Piso held his ground, despite Augusta's complaints that her majesty was being dragged in the dust. Tiberius, thinking he should so far gratify his mother as to say that he would go to the praetor's tribunal and support Urgulania, set out from the Palatium. His soldiers had orders to follow at a distance. The mob rushed up to look, as Tiberius, his face composed, and pausing every now and then for conversation, made his leisurely way, until, Piso's relations being unable to restrain Piso, Augusta issued orders for the payment of the money he was claiming. This ended an affair from which Piso emerged with glory and Caesar with an enhanced reputation.[3]

Tacitus told this story for the moral it conveyed about the way in which senators should stand up to emperors. Our present interest is less in Piso's boldness and the way the case was resolved than in the attitudes of Urgulania and Livia and, in particular, in a structural weakness of the Roman civil law procedure which the incident reveals. It was for a plaintiff, and not the authorities of the state, to see that the defendant appeared before the praetor at the start of a judicial action. However, the would-be plaintiff might find himself in difficulties if his opponent were stronger than he (or had strong supporters) and resisted or ignored the summons. Similarly, execution of sentence lay with the individual rather than the state.

Later we will ask how far the upper classes made use of the biased nature of the system of self-help as outlined here. It is doubtful whether Urgulania's behavior was typical of that of members of the privileged classes when they were faced with legal actions brought against them by their social inferiors. It might be claimed that there was no need for an upper-class defendant to flout the law—and it might be prudent of him not to do so—as there was a good chance that the natural prejudices of the judge, who invariably came from the same social milieu, might operate in his favor.

(2) A letter of Pliny the Younger gives some force to this last suggestion. The setting of the letter is provincial rather than Roman, which serves as a reminder that preferential treatment in the law courts was given not only to officials of the central administration (senators and equestrians)

---

[3] Tacitus, *Annales*, ii. 34: cf. iv.21 ff.

but also to the provincial and Italian aristocracy, the "curial" class.[4] Pliny was writing to Calestrius Tiro, who was on the point of taking up office as governor of Baetica in Spain (in succession to another governorship). As governor, Tiro would be personally responsible for the administration of justice in his province. The letter runs:

> You have done splendidly—and I hope you will not rest on your laurels—in commending your administration of justice to the provincials by your exercise of tact. This you have shown particularly in maintaining consideration for the best men,[5] but, in doing so, winning the respect of the lower classes while holding the affection of their superiors. Many men, in their anxiety to avoid seeming to show excessive favour to men of influence, succeed only in gaining a reputation for perversity and malice. I know there is no chance of your falling prey to that vice, but in praising you for the way you tread the middle-course, I cannot help sounding as if I were offering you advice: that you maintain the distinctions between ranks and degrees of dignity. Nothing could be more unequal than that equality which results when those distinctions are confused or broken down.[6]

Tiro had achieved what might seem to us the remarkable feat of paying due respect to *dignitas* (social position) while avoiding *gratia* (excessive favor).[7] Tiberius was less successful in observing this precarious distinction in his supervision of judicial affairs in Rome. This at any rate was Tacitus' judgment:

> The investigations in the Senate were not enough for Tiberius. He sat in the courts, at the side of the tribunal, so as not to drive the praetor from his chair. In his presence, many judgments were reached which disregarded the bribes and pressure of the powerful. But in his concern for truth, Tiberius undermined liberty.[8]

(3) In his treatise on criminal investigations, Callistratus, a jurist of the Severan age (A.D. 193–235), dealt with the question of the trustworthiness of witnesses:

> It is especially important to examine the status of each man, to see whether he is a decurion or a commoner; to ask whether his life is virtuous or marred by vice, whether he is rich or poor (for poverty might imply that he is out for gain), and whether he is personally hostile to the man against whom he is witnessing or friendly to the man whose cause he is advocating . . .[9]

---

[4] The legal sources do not give a complete list of those who benefited from legal privilege; but these included senators, equestrians, decurions, veterans, and soldiers (and their families).

[5] *Honestissimum quemque.* The adjective is ambiguous, implying both high moral character and social and political ascendance. See Cicero, *Brutus*, 282, and n. 17 below.

[6] Pliny, *Epistolae*, ix.5.

[7] On *gratia* see Myres (1960: 24 ff.).

[8] Tacitus, *Annales*, i. 75.

[9] *Digest*, xxii.5.3. preface (decurions were the members of the councils of cities in Italy and the provinces). The key word is *fides*, trustworthiness. Cf. Gellius, *Noctes Atticae*, XIV.2.10, where the claimant is said to be well endowed with *fides* ("fidei . . . plenum").

The questions range widely, covering not only the witness' interest in the trial, but also his character and social and economic condition. By contrast, in a modern court of law in a democratic society it would be thought relevant (in theory at any rate) to establish only a witness' impartiality—unless a previous conviction for perjury should bring his character into consideration.[10]

III. THE CIVIL SUIT

In Rome the private claims of possession, breach of contract, damage, fraud, or injury (to mention only the most important) were settled by the civil law according to the "formulary" procedure. The civil suit (or *actio*) consisted of two stages, *actio in iure* before the praetor, and *actio apud iudicem* before a private judge. The praetor was responsible for appointing the judge, with the agreement of both parties, and for passing on to him a *formula*, or a list of instructions setting out the factual and legal grounds on which the case was to be decided (see Schulz, 1951: 19 ff.).

A man who sought a civil action, therefore, approached the praetor. The praetor, however, was not obliged to grant him an action, and indeed was expected to withhold from a man of low rank (*humilis*) an action for fraud against his social superior.[11] The authority for this is Labeo, the Augustan jurist, whose commentary on the praetor's edict, in which a statement to this effect appears, was intended as a guide to magistrates and legal practitioners. The commentary probably contained little original material, for the statements of jurists were commonly based upon or were explanatory of tendencies or norms already present in the legal system. It is probable that the same rule which existed in relation to the action for fraud applied in respect of other actions which carried *infamia*, or loss of status.

The most dangerous of these actions for the higher orders in the Roman state was the action for debt. The consequences of this action, which was in effect a bankruptcy suit, included sale of property, loss of status, and political extinction. The ruling classes appear to have relied on the aristocratic prejudices of the praetor to ward off from themselves this disastrous action until the time of Julius Caesar, when a law was passed permitting impoverished aristocrats to cede part of their land to their creditors without

---

[10]Callistratus goes on to refer to Hadrianic rescripts. A rescript was a reply by the Emperor to the consultation of a governor or another official. It was meant as an order, and taken as such, probably from the early Empire.

[11]*Digest*, iv.3.11.1. The praetor's permission was needed for the issuing of any summons against parents, patrons, magistrates, priests, etc.: see *ibid.*, iii.4.2 and 4. The recurrence of the word *reverentia* in *ibid.*, 13, and *Digest* xlvii.19.28.4 is suggestive.

loss of status. Moreover, under the early Empire, a milder alternative to the *venditio bonorum* (sale of property) which was the lot of the ordinary debtor was set up or confirmed by senatorial decree. This was *distractio bonorum* (division of property). By this procedure, a part of the property was sold by a special agent, again without loss of status on the part of the former owner. *Distractio bonorum* was available to men of high status (*clarae personae*), especially members of the senatorial class.[12]

The plaintiff surmounted one barrier if the praetor granted him an action; the next obstacle was provided not so much by the magistrate who administered the civil law as by the civil law itself. The formulary procedure operated on the assumption that any plaintiff could get his opponent to court. It is true that some resistance on the part of defendants was bargained for, but the measures which were intended to cope with this eventuality (praetorian interdicts and the order for the seizure of the defendant's property preparatory to sale) did not include the use of physical force by the organs of the state. It is not difficult to imagine situations where a defendant, relying on his greater strength or influence might defy the would-be plaintiff: it will be recalled that Urgulania refused to go to court and sought sanctuary in the palace, in the knowledge that Livia would protect her.[13]

On the other side it must be acknowledged that the plaintiff of low status was not necessarily on his own in his efforts to get his opponent to justice. He might have a patron of greater influence and more substantial physical resources than himself who could perhaps bring pressure to bear on his opponent. In the case of Urgulania it was the defendant who possessed a powerful patron. Livia's friendship raised Urgulania "above the laws." If the defendant still failed to respond, the plaintiff could look for assistance from a different quarter: with the aid of the local auctioneer, who had a financial interest in the matter, he might enforce a seizure of the defendant's property.[14] A third ally of the plaintiff was the Roman social conscience. Romans in general considered it important to maintain their good name in the community and their standing with the magistrates. Probably few men were prepared to flout convention and the law by refusing to obey a summons. But there were exceptions: why else did the Julian law on violence cover the case of those who resisted a court summons with the aid of a gang of thugs?[15]

[12] For the background and context of Caesar's law *de donis cedendis*, see Frederiksen (1966: 128 ff.). For the (first century) decree, *Digest*, xxvii. 10.5.

[13] The problem discussed in this paragraph is posed forcefully by Kelly (1966: Chapter 1); also see review by Crook and Stone (1967).

[14] The latter could be rich (Cicero, *pre Caecina*, 10) and strong (*ibid.*, 27).

[15] *Digest*, xlviii.7.4 (Julian law on violence—? of Julius Caesar). Later it became a criminal offence to disobey the injunctions of magistrates: see *Digest*, xlviii. 19.5, preface.

Even if the plaintiff of low rank had been granted an action, and had secured the appearance of his opponent before the praetor, he could not have had much confidence in the outcome of the action. For a man of influence would stand a good chance of winning his case, even without corruption or the threat of force. Judges and juries (where there were juries)[16] were easily impressed by qualities such as social prominence, wealth, and good character,[17] and this was thought perfectly proper. When Aulus Gellius judged a money claim, he could not bring himself to decide against a plaintiff who was upright and trustworthy in favor of a defendant who was in his eyes a rascal, and "not possessed of good fortune" (*non bonae rei*), even though the former's case was quite unconvincing. He took the problem to the philosopher Favorinus. Favorinus quoted words of Marcus Cato to the effect that, if a cause was evenly balanced, the judge should decide which of the two parties was "better" (*melior*), a term ambiguous as between character and property, and should come down for him. Cato added that this was not a private opinion of his own, but a traditional Roman attitude. But Gellius could not declare for the claimant, and backed out of the case, pleading youth and lack of merit.[18]

Cato had held that the outcome should depend on the character of the parties only if witnesses were lacking. Gellius' plaintiff could produce "neither documents nor witnesses." The excerpt from Callistratus quoted shows that, where witnesses were called, the judge reckoned their social position and character as relevant as the quality of their evidence. Nor was this merely Callistratus' private judgment. He went on to cite a series of rescripts of Hadrian (A.D. 117–138) in support of his statement. The burden of the rescripts is that a witness with *dignitas*, *existimatio*, and *auctoritas* was especially acceptable. These are three upper-class virtues: social standing, good reputation, and prestige.

To sum up, as long as plaintiffs could have recourse only to the praetor and a private judge, both of whom shared the feelings and prejudices of the upper classes, and as long as private summons and private execution were the rule, actions by commoners against members of the upper classes were

---

[16]The juries for the public criminal courts of the Republic were drawn from the upper classes. The advisers who assisted a judge or magistrate in reaching a decision in an *extra ordinem* court characteristic of the Empire were similarly drawn from the higher orders.

[17] For the Romans, good character was in part a matter of birth and social position. It is significant that a word with a primarily moral meaning, *honestus*, should have been chosen to describe men of distinguished social position, *honestiores*. (Note that moral words such as *boni* and *optimates* were used to describe political groups under the Republic.) Quintilian, *Institutiones*, v.10.24, noted that there is sometimes a causal connection between birth (*genus*) and manner of life: " . . . et nonnumquam ad *honeste* turpiterque vivendum inde causae fluunt." Cf. *Digest*, xlvii.2.52.21, where *honestus vir* is synonymous with *vir locuples* ("rich man").

[18]Gellius, *Noctes Atticae*, xiv.2.

not likely to be frequent (Kelly, 1966: 62 ff.)[19] The end of the Republic saw an improvement in the lot of the humble plaintiff in several respects. A clause on violence from the Lex Iulia, already referred to in another connection, shows that forcible resistance to a summons was viewed as a crime in the early Empire.[20] Crimes were punishable by the state, so that neither summons nor execution was the responsibility of the individual. Further, it became possible under the Empire for a plaintiff to approach the city prefect and to seek the settlement of a claim outside the formulary procedure.[21] Again, summons and execution fell to the state—and the plaintiff might gain a fairer hearing.

Before concluding this section on the civil law, we may return once more to the role of the praetor. The praetor was in a position to discriminate against the weaker party both as the controller of the sanctions behind the judicial summons and execution, and as the granter or withholder of actions. In addition, during the first stages of some suits, notably suits for injury, he fixed the amount of compensation payable in the event of the court's deciding against the defendant. Now, according to Labeo, the *persona* of the injured party might, presumably by the praetor's decision, convert an action for injury into an action for "grave" injury, with higher penalties.[22] The word *persona* has a broad connotation, as is shown by statements of later jurists which expand Labeo's sentence. We read, for instance, in the "Sentences of Paulus," a late third-century compilation, the following:

> Injury is regarded as grave ... with respect to person, whenever the injured party is a senator or equestrian or decurion, or someone else of conspicuous prestige: for example, if a plebeian or a man of low birth has injured a senator or equestrian, or if a decurion or magistrate or aedile or judge has suffered at the hands of a plebeian.[23]

Other passages show that injury by a child against a parent or by a freedman against a patron were also automatically "grave." If all the texts dealing with this matter are put together, it can be seen that in Roman society, some persons were given special protection because and in so far as they performed certain social, political, or judicial rôles (as parents, magistrates, and judges, respectively), and others because of personal status.

---

[19] On private execution and its difficulties, see Kelly (1966: 12 ff.) In addition, many matters would have been settled out of court. Cicero often brought pressure to bear on judges on behalf of clients, who as a result were sometimes able to avoid court cases. See, e.g., *ad familiares*, xiii.54.Cf.the Piso/Urgulania affair: as far as we can tell this never reached the courts.

[20] See n. 15 above.

[21] See, e.g., *Digest*, i.12.2: the intrusion of the prefect's court into the sphere of pecuniary cases, at least from Hadrian's time.

[22] *Digest*, xlvii. 10.7.8.

[23] *Sentences of Paulus*, v.4.10; cf. Caius, *Institutiones*, iii.225; *Institutiones*, iv.4.9.

IV. THE CRIMINAL TRIAL

In the late Republic, laws were passed which defined as "public," and therefore "criminal," offences such as extortion, treason, homicide, forgery, peculation, electoral bribery, and violence, and which set up permanent jury courts to try them. The jury courts (or quaestiones) survived into the Empire, and indeed Augustus himself was behind the legislation which established a court for adultery. However, the form of criminal proceeding most characteristic of the Empire was the cognitio or extra ordinem procedure, which placed the whole trial, including the passing of sentence, in the hands of the judge. (The praetor in charge of a jury court merely chaired the proceedings and was bound by the verdict of the jury.) The jury-court system proved less durable than the formulary system in civil law, although both were Republican in origin. As late as the Severan period, those seeking redress for private injury or loss could still turn to the formulary system as a viable alternative to cognitio. By contrast, there is no evidence that "public" offences were ever investigated by a jury court after about the turn of the first century A.D. (Garnsey, 1967).

The civil action by the formulary process and the criminal trial by the cognitio procedure were very different in structure, and this difference is reflected in the patterns of discrimination which were characteristic of each. But two qualifications should be kept in mind. It is probable that criminal judges, especially provincial governors, used their discretion in granting and withholding trials, as praetors did when administering the civil law. Again, the influences to which a private judge was subjected in the course of a trial were felt equally by a criminal judge. On the other hand, discrimination in the apportionment of cases to courts was a distinctive feature of the Imperial criminal law. In addition, there was much more scope in a criminal trial by cognitio for the variation of penalty according to the social class of the defendant. The Republican system of criminal law knew neither of these methods of discrimination. Only one set of courts was provided for the trial of all defendants, and no penalties were inflicted other than those fixed by the laws which set up the courts.[24]

Under the Empire, however, several courts were capable of hearing most criminal cases, and the choice of court was sometimes of consequence for the defendant. The senatorial court was notoriously "soft" on senatorial

---

[24]Defendants before jury courts might be favored (and it is commonly assumed were favored, if of senatorial if not equestrian rank) in two principal ways. Either the court could bring in a verdict of not guilty when an acquittal was not justified (this form of favoritism was not, of course, peculiar to a jury court); or the magistrates could permit a defendant to go into voluntary exile and so avoid the necessity of having him executed (in capital cases).

defendants. Charges against equestrian officials were heard by the Emperor, to whom these officials were personally responsible, and he might be expected to have their interests at heart.[25] Again, by the late second century, governors were not allowed to execute a sentence of deportation or capital exile. In practice this meant that capital cases involving members of the provincial élite were automatically referred to the Emperor.[26] Other courts in Rome, the jury courts, for as long as they existed, and the court of the urban prefect, must have dealt principally, though not exclusively,[27] with lower-class offenders.

The *cognitio* procedure was notable for the degree of freedom it left to the judge. Not only the examination of the parties and their witnesses and advocates, but also the choice of penalty was in his hands. The laws which set up jury-courts had both defined certain crimes and prescribed fixed penalties for anyone convicted of them in those courts. The *cognitio* judge was not restricted in this way. "Today," wrote Ulpian early in the third century "he who sits in judgment in a criminal case *extra ordinem* may issue the sentence which pleases him, be it relatively severe or relatively mild, so long as he stays within the limits defined by reason."[28]

There is a further point. The judge, in choosing a penalty, could go beyond those few which had gained recognition in the law, the straight death penalty, interdiction from fire and water (a form of exile), and the monetary fine. He could apply sanctions which had been used under the Republic mainly as administrative measures against free aliens or slaves.

The "dual-penalty system," familiar to jurists of the age of the Severans, recognized the distinction between "legal" and "nonlegal" penalties. In practice, each group of penalties was aligned with a broad social category, such that members of the upper classes, or *honestiores*, suffered only penalties drawn from the first group, and members of the lower classes only

---

[25] *Senators*: see Pliny, *Epistolae*, ix.13.21. Pliny claims to have caused the indignation of "the other orders" to subside. The indignation arose from the fact that "the Senate was harsh to others and lenient only to senators, as if by mutual connivance."

Equestrians: for an early example of the trial of an equestrian by the Emperor (Claudius), see Dio, lx.33.6. In a later incident (Pliny, *Epistolae*, vi.31.7 ff.), Trajan angrily rejected the imputation that an Emperor was likely to be lenient to his own officials. In this case the defendant was a freedman-procurator (it is unclear whether the codefendant, an equestrian, was an Imperial official or not). But another "good" Emperor, Augustus, had shown favouritism to Licinus, a freedman-procurator (Dio, liv.21). (A procurator was a financial agent responsible especially for tax collection.)

[26] *Digest*, xlviii.22.6.1.

[27] See Tacitus, *Annales*, xiv.40–41, for both prefect and jury courts. The defendants, who included senators, might have been tried either by the prefect or by the jury court for *falsum* (forgery)—their crime was testamentary forgery. The prefect also had the right to deport, the *ius deportandi*: see *Digest*, i.12.1.3; xxxii.1.4; xlviii.22.6.1; etc. Deportation became an upper-class penalty.

[28] *Digest*, xlviii.19.3. The judge's freedom in choosing penalties was to a certain extent restricted by Imperial rescripts, at least from the turn of the first century. See Robertis (1939).

penalties from the second group.[29] "Deportation" and "relegation," two forms of exile, were standard penalties in the first group.[30] The former deprived the condemned of citizenship but not freedom, and the latter of neither. Execution, which was rare for *honestiores*, was by decapitation. The money fine, once the only penalty in civil law, was used as a common minor sanction. Expulsion from the senate (in the case of a senator) and from a local council (in the case of a decurion), and prohibition from officeholding, were also known. The most serious "lower-class penalty" is called by the jurists *summum supplicium* ("the highest punishment"). The term stood for aggravated forms of the death penalty, including exposure to wild beasts, crucifixion, and death by fire. Next, condemnation to hard labor in the mines was for life, and the condemned was reduced to a status akin to slavery. Condemnation to live and fight as a gladiator was just as degrading and carried a greater risk of death. A less severe penalty of the same type was labor on public works. Corporal punishment was also reserved for *humiliores*. Torture was, by tradition, applied only to slaves. But legal texts which forbid the use of torture for certain classes of free men indicate both that free men were not immune from torture in the middle and late second century, and that only well-connected free men were considered worthy of protection against it.[31] As for the treatment of accused men before trial, *honestiores* could generally avoid imprisonment. They might be entrusted to guarantors, or soldiers, or "to themselves," though not if the charge was serious.[32]

V.   LEGAL PRIVILEGE: EVOLUTION AND BASIS IN LAW

Much of our knowledge of legal privilege in Rome is derived from the writings of the Severan jurists. But legal privilege was not a phenomenon peculiar to the Severan age. The system which the jurists describe evolved in my view gradually in the course of the first century, and was well

[29]Most of the penalties listed below are mentioned and graded in an edict ("upper-class penalties," *Digest*, xlix.19.28.13) and a rescript ("lower-class penalties," *ibid*., 28.14) of Hadrian.

[30]*Relegatio* became the "legal" penalty for adultery under Augustus. See *Collatio*, ii.26.14. *Deportatio*, strictly speaking, was not a "legal" penalty, but was similar to, if it did not succeed, interdiction.

[31]See especially *Code of Justinian*, ix.41.11; *Digest*, xlviii.18.15, preface; 1.2.14; cf. xlviii.18.9.2. All texts but the second rule out torture for various privileged groups; the second implies that a freeman can be tortured if his statements as a witness are inconsistent. It is unlikely that lower-class defendants generally suffered judicial or inquisitorial torture (as distinct from "third-degree" torture, torture as a punitive measure) in the first century and early second (see, e.g., Pliny, *Epistolae*, x.96.8; slave women were tortured, but not those prisoners who were free). But the Christians at Lyons in A.D. 177 were certainly tortured: Eusebius, *The Ecclesiastical History*.

[32]*Digest*, xlviii.3.1 and 3.

established in legal practice in the second. This was true as much of the "dual-penalty system" as of other forms of discrimination.

In an important article Cardascia (1950) expressed a rather different opinion on the development of one aspect of the system of privilege, differential punishment. He granted that variation of penalty was a reality in legal practice as early as the reign of Augustus (27 B.C.–A.D. 14), but claimed that a judge was under no obligation to make concessions to rank until the time of Pius (A.D. 138–160), when, according to him, distinctions began "to pass into the law." Subsequently variation in penalty became frequent in "legislation," until under the Severans it took on "a general character."

By "the law" and "legislation" are apparently meant Imperial constitutions, the rescripts, and edicts of Emperors. It is not clear whether Cardascia holds that the rescripts of Pius and later Emperors "established" the system of privilege in a newer, more highly developed form; or whether the rescripts are supposed to have given a system which was already complete a new validity, by the fact that they refer to it and thereby indirectly sanction it. Both ideas deserve investigation.

Those rescripts issued by Pius and his successors which are at all relevant to the question of differential punishments can be divided into three groups. The first group comprises two rescripts, both of Pius, which set forth how two crimes were to be punished, the murder of an adulterer by the aggrieved husband, and thefts from Imperial mines.[33] The second group consists of four rescripts banning the use of certain penalties against children or descendants of certain privileged groups.[34] Finally, four rescripts directly concern decurions or soldiers.

It can be seen that the rescripts fail to cover the whole field of penalties, crimes, and privileged categories. Instead of a general edict launching the dual-penalty system, there are two judicial decisions in which a differential penalty scale is employed. Again, the fact that veterans, for example, are favored has to be inferred from the sentencing of their sons to exile rather than forced labor of any kind.[35] Further, it is nowhere explicitly stated by an Emperor that decurions were not to be condemned to the mines. But the Emperor Severus Alexander (A.D. 222–235) informed Demetrianus that, as his mother was the daughter of a decurion, she was not to suffer that fate.[36]

There is a second, related, difficulty. The rescripts, far from establishing a system of privilege, were apparently designed to preserve one which

---

[33] *Digest*, xlviii.5.39.8; cf. xlviii.9.1.5, xlviii.13.8.

[34] *Code of Justinian*, ix.41.11, preface (includes torture); ix.47.5;9; 12. We might add ix.41.8, preface; but the reference to soldiers is primary, so it is included in the third group.

[35] *Code of Justinian*, ix.47.5.

[36] *Code of Justinian*, ix.9.

already existed. For example, all the rescripts in the third group reaffirm known regulations, or simply make reference to them.[37] The first of the Severan Emperors, Septimius Severus (A.D. 193–211), in a reply to the petition of Ambrosius, cited the rule (*prohibitum est*) that decurions were not to be beaten.[38] His son and successor Caracalla (A.D. 197–217) wrote to Geminius that decurions patently (*manifestum est*) should not be sentenced to forced labor.[39] There was plenty of precedent for Diocletian's protection of soldiers from torture and "plebeian" penalties.[40] Finally, Marcus and Verus (A.D. 161–169), when consulted by a governor on the proper penalty for a certain Priscus, wrote that decurions ought to be relegated or deported for capital crimes.[41] Nor was this a novelty: a ruling of Hadrian which prohibited execution and prescribed exile for decurions who were murderers (except for parricides) had implied as much.[42]

The first relevant "legislation," indeed, was issued not by Pius, but by Hadrian. In addition to the ruling just mentioned, there is record of a judicial decision of A.D. 119—of the same type as the rescripts of Pius in the first group referred to above—in which Hadrian stated that exile (*relegatio*) was the proper penalty for *splendidiores personae* (which stands for *honestiores*), and two years' labor on public works (*opus publicum*) and a beating for *alii* ("the rest," equivalent to *humiliores*), for the offence of moving boundary stones.[43] We must therefore ask whether either or both of Hadrian's rescripts[44] were innovatory.

The rescript over boundary stones, if it was the first of its kind, may have actually "set up" the penalty differential. The grounds for asserting this are purely and simply that no earlier rescript is recorded in the *Digest* and other legal compilations.[45] But chance played an important part in the selection and preservation of such texts as have survived. Another band of compilers, working in A.D. 530–533 (when the *Digest* was compiled) or at another time, might have come up with a different set of rescripts, including

---

[37] In the second group, only the edict of Marcus (*Code of Justinian*, ix.41.11. preface) might have added to the ranks of the privileged class (in a very small way)—unless the edict was intended to restate an accepted rule which had been disregarded, or to make explicit an exemption which had until then been only implicit.

[38] *Code of Justinian*, ii.5.

[39] *Code of Justinian*, ix.47.3.

[40] *Code of Justinian*, ix.41.8. preface; cf. *Digest*, xlix,18.1.

[41] *Digest*, xlviii.22.6.2.

[42] *Digest*, xlviii.19.15.

[43] *Digest*, xlvii.21.2; cf. *Collatio* xiii.3.1–2. For a discussion of the text, see Cardascia (1950: 468–469).

[44] *Digest*, xlvii.21.2 and xlviii.19.15.

[45] "It is held by d'Ors (1965: 147 ff.) and Gaudemet (1954: 169 ff.) that Hadrian's rescripts were the first "true" rescripts, "des rescrits proprement dit." This doctrine rests on one text, *Vita Macrini*, 13.1, which shows that Trajan was averse to sending rescripts in reply to the petitions of private individuals (*libelli*), but not that he was unwilling to send rescripts (of the Hadrianic type) to functionaries. There are in fact numerous examples of the second type of rescript from the pre-Hadrianic era.

some from an earlier period. It is obvious that neither the classical jurists from whose works excerpts were drawn, nor the Justinianic compilers, had the intention of describing the evolution of class discrimination in the law.[46]

As for the second rescript, it was genuinely innovatory if it elevated decurions as a class. But it must be said that it does not *look* like an edict which deliberately conferred a new status and a new set of privileges, and it was very limited in application since it concerned only murder cases.[47] It cannot therefore be seen as, for instance, one of a series of edicts exempting decurions from specific penalties. Nor is there any indication that it announced or constituted a departure from previous policy. Pliny's letter to Calestrius Tiro, quoted in full above, belongs to the previous reign (it was perhaps written in 107–108), and is important evidence for the care with which the Roman administration distinguished between the local aristocracy and the rest of the provincial population. Nor was this a new attitude, originating in Trajan's reign (A.D. 97–117) and voiced first by his officials. The wealth, social status, and political usefulness of the provincial gentry had long been evident.[48] These were the qualities which made it inevitable that their most conspicuous representatives would gain the citizenship and advance into the higher orders. The actions and attitudes of courts had long respected these same qualities. It was expected of judges that they would discriminate in favor of upper-class provincials.

Thus, Hadrian may have been not so much raising decurions, or leading provincial notables, to a new status, as confirming them in one they already possessed. This would have been an appropriate measure at a time when penalties were becoming more severe, and the newer, degrading sanctions were coming into wider use—and when governors were no less inclined to arbitrary behavior than their predecessors had been. The Emperor's biographer reports that Hadrian, in his travels throughout the Empire, made it his business to correct abuses where he found them. Governors, among others, were punished.[49] Their misdemeanors may have been acts implying an unwillingness to make any distinction between decurions on the one hand, and the rest of the free population in the provinces on the other.[50]

---

[46] For the aims of the latter, see *Constitutium Tanta*, 10.

[47] This is an inference from the references in the text (*Digest*, xlviii.19.15) to the "*poema legis Corneliae (sc., de sicariis)*," and to parricide.

[48] On class division in Greek cities under the Republic and the Roman attitude to it, see Briscoe (1967).

[49] *Vita Hadriani*, xiii.10. Hadrian was a notorious "busybody": see Dio, lxix.5.1.

[50] Here is a summary of the evidence for the dual-penalty system in the time of Hadrian: the arrangement of penalties "legal" and "nonlegal" into two distinct groups is not attested before Hadrian: see *Digest*, xlviii. 19.28.13–14. Hadrian further recognized a correspondence between a category of penalties and a social class: see xlviii.21.2. *Digest*, xlviii.19.15, indeed, implies the existence of a whole system of differential punishments. The fact that Hadrian's successors made few additions to the system indirectly confirms that the system was well-established under Hadrian. *Digest*, xlvii.14.1, preface and xlviii.8.4.2 show, at the most, that the dual-penalty scale was not yet applied universally, in the punishment of every crime (cf. *ibid.*, xlvii.9.4.1, for Pius).

The "dual-penalty system," then, does not seem to have been set up by formal enactments, or, if it was (and this must be counted unlikely), those enactments are lost to us. Nor, for that matter, does a law survive which gave the senators the prerogative of trial by their peers or which maintained that privilege. Further, to my knowledge, the inequitable aspects of the formulary system, referred to above,[51] were not set up or sanctioned by any edict.

It remains for us to consider briefly the more modest suggestion that the rescripts gave the system of discrimination a new validity in law. This theory has unsatisfactory implications. Our information on the system of differential penalties comes to us through both Imperial rescripts and juristic generalizations. But, as we have seen, no Imperial pronouncements are preserved which so much as mention the bulk of upper-class privileges. It would seem to follow that only a few of these privileges were well based in law. The difficulty can be resolved if it is asked what was in the mind of a jurist when he cited an Imperial rescript, and also what was the Emperor's motive in issuing the rescript. Callistratus did not cite Hadrian's rescripts on witnesses, referred to above, because they authorized judges in a new and superior way to favor upper-class witnesses; nor was that either the purpose or the effect of rescripts. Again, Hadrian's rescript on boundaries (quoted by Callistratus) shows that he believed in the principle that criminals of different social status should be punished differently; but he did not intend, by issuing the rescript, to give that principle a legal standing which it did not have before, nor was that an indirect result of the publication of the rescript. The rescript set up new penalties for an old crime, penalties which still held good in Callistratus' day.[52] In short, differential punishment was already a feature of the judicial system, and had been tacitly if not overtly approved and sanctioned by judges, jurists, and Emperors.

VI.   THE   ROMAN   CITIZENSHIP

The Romans recognized in their society distinctions other than that between the upper class and lower class (*honestiores* and *humiliores*); for example, that between freemen and slaves, and between citizens and aliens. The relationship of these to that between *honestiores* and *humiliores* will now be considered.

For writers of juristic handbooks, the distinction between the freeman and the slave was "the basic division in the law of persons."[53] But it is evidently

---

[51] Above, III, The Civil Suit.
[52] *Digest*, xxii.5.3.1 ff. (witnesses); xlvii.21.2 (boundaries).
[53] Gaius, *Institutiones*, i.9. For a reflection of the division in penal law, *Digest*, xlviii.19.28.16.

not assimilable to that between the *honestiores* and the *humiliores*. *Humiliores*, the lower classes, included slaves, freedmen, and also any men of free birth who lacked the criteria for legal privilege, that is, the dignity and prestige associated with good birth and character and the possession of wealth and office.

The distinction between citizen and alien requires closer analysis. It has been suggested that it was replaced by that between *honestiores* and *humiliores*, which is said to have arisen in the late first or early second century (Sherwin-White, 1963: 174; Jones, 1960: 64–65). Citizens held several important advantages over aliens. They could seek the help of a tribune, or exercise their right of appeal, against the arbitrary actions of magistrates. Aliens, strictly speaking, had no standing within the civil law, and hence lacked these rights. In Jerusalem in the reign of Nero (A.D. 54–68), St. Paul staved off a beating and struck fear into a tribune with the words: "Is it lawful for you to scourge a Roman citizen, uncondemned?"[54] St. Paul had previously embarrassed the magistrates of the colony of Philippi by disclosing his citizen status *after* he and his companions had been beaten and cast into prison.[55] Considerably later, peasants on an Imperial estate in Africa protested to the Emperor Commodus (A.D. 180–193) that, even though some of them were Roman citizens, they had been beaten by a procurator and various overseers of the estate.[56] This incident indicates that appeal was not a dead letter in the Antonine period. About a generation later, Ulpian cited the section of the Julian law on public violence which dealt with appeal in his treatise on the duties of a proconsul,[57] and several sections of the *Digest* are devoted to appeal (on appeals, see Garnsey, 1966: 167 ff.).

Further, a citizen might expect to gain a less severe sentence than an alien if both were defendants on the same charge. In A.D. 17, the Senate took firm measures to stamp out astrology: among the astrologers, citizens were exiled while foreigners were put to death.[58] In A.D. 177, Christians arrested at Lyons were either beheaded or sent to the beasts, depending on whether they were citizens or aliens.[59]

The preferential treatment of citizens as opposed to aliens was therefore a long-standing form of legal discrimination, which persisted in the first two centuries of the Empire. It was based on the exclusion of aliens from the civil law (*ius civile*), but was practised also in other spheres of the law; for ex-

---

[54] *Acts*, xxii.2.4.
[55] *Acts*, xvi.37.
[56] *Fontes Juris Romani Antejustiniani*, i, n. 103, p. 496, 11.10 ff.
[57] *Digest*, xlviii.6.7.
[58] *Collatio*, xv.2.1; cf. Dio, lvii.15.8 and Tacitus, *Annales*, ii.32.5.
[59] Eusebius, *The Ecclesiastical History*, V.I.47. But Attalus, a citizen (§44), was sent to the beasts. Decapitation was the least unpleasant and least degrading form of the death penalty.

ample, in the criminal law, which under the Empire was subject to the *cognitio* of magistrates, and which covered both citizens and noncitizens.

The dividing line between the *honestiores* and *humiliores* was not identical with that between citizens and aliens, for there were citizens (and noncitizens) on both sides of it.

First, those with legal privilege included noncitizens, because decurions were a privileged group, and not all decurions were citizens. Decurions of cities of "Roman" status had citizenship. In "Latin" cities,[60] however, citizenship was won by performance of a magistracy rather than by mere membership of a city council. From the time of Hadrian or Pius it was possible for a "Latin" city to obtain a higher grade of Latinity, *Latium maius*, and so gain citizenship for all its decurions.[61] But the epigraphic evidence suggests that this had to be sued for; apparently *Latium maius* was not conferred on all "Latin" cities by an act of the central administration. Moreover, while *Latium maius* undoubtedly reduced the numbers of decurions who lacked citizenship in the West, it made no impact on the Eastern half of the Empire. Cities in the Greek East had never been anxious for either "Roman" or "Latin" status; there, citizenship was possessed by individuals and families rather than by whole city populations or ruling castes (see Sherwin-White, 1939: 194–257, esp. 236 ff.).[62]

Second, the sources imply that citizenship did not exclude the humble from cruel and humiliating penalties. The African peasants were, after all, beaten, and though this may have been strictly illegal, it could have been expected. The peasants call themselves "ordinary men of the countryside" (*homines rustici tenues*), a description which finds an echo in Callistratus:

> It is not normal for everybody to be beaten, but only free men whose standing is relatively low (*hi . . . qui liberi sunt et quidem tenuiores homines*). Members of the upper classes (*honestiores*) are exempt, and this is emphasized in Imperial rescripts.[63]

Callistratus may have had in mind a rescript of Septimius Severus which pointed out that decurions were not to be beaten.[64] This was no new development. Severus was citing an established rule (*prohibitum est*), and long before, in A.D. 119, Hadrian had ruled that the offence of moving boundary stones was to be punished in part by beating, except when the culprits were *splendidiores personae* or *honestiores*.[65]

[60]"Latinity" in the late Republic and early Empire was a half-way stage between the position of an alien and full Roman citizenship.

[61]Gaius, *Institutiones*, i.96; *Inscriptiones Latinae Selectae*, 6780 (Gigthis, N. Africa).

[62]It should be added that in no source is it stated or implied that only those decurions who were citizens were entitled to milder punishments.

[63]*Digest*, xlviii.19.28.2.

[64]*Code of Justinian*, ii.11.5(A.D. 198).

[65]*Digest*, xlvii.21.2.

Citizens were in theory protected not only against beating, but also against the execution of a death sentence in the face of an appeal. But decurions, and other members of the privileged classes, were in the more enviable position of knowing that the highest punishment to which they were liable was exile, unless they were guilty of parricide or treason.

In general, an explanation is required for the failure of the jurists to mention citizenship in those passages in which they dealt with the criteria on the basis of which the privileged class was to be identified. The omission may be due to systematic rewriting of the classical legal texts by later jurists and especially the 6th century compilers, for whom citizenship held little significance. But perhaps the classical jurists themselves considered that the distinction between humble citizens and free aliens was unimportant compared with the distinction between senators, equestrians, or decurions on the one hand, and members of the lower classes, whether citizens or aliens, on the other. If this was the case, and the evidence already adduced seems to point that way, then Justinian's men would have had no cause to make substantial alterations in the relevant texts.

The distinction between *honestiores* and *humiliores*, then, cuts across that between citizens and aliens. It is, of course, a further step to say that the former replaced the latter. That would seem to imply that the former distinction was not important in the pre-Hadrianic period; and, conversely, that the latter was once (perhaps in the first century) as fundamental as the former became (perhaps in the course of the second century).

There may be a close association between the "replacement" theory and the idea that the differential penalty system began to emerge in the reigns of Hadrian and Pius. If so, it should be stated that there is good reason for believing that the differential penalty system existed in its essentials by the reign of Hadrian[66]; and that discrimination in favor of the upper classes involved more than the assigning of milder penalties.

To reinforce the second point, it may be helpful to pick out some forms of upper-class discrimination which were practised in the course of the first century A.D.[67] The formulary procedure was in its heyday in the late Republic and early Empire. It will be recalled that it was administered by praetors and private judges with wide discretionary powers, which they used to the advantage of men of wealth and social position. Again, senators appear to have had the right to a senatorial trial in the first century, while

---

[66] See Footnote 45 above.

[67] The *honestiores/humiliores* formula will not be found in first-century sources. This is doubtless partly due to the fact that those sources are largely nonlegal: they are concerned with individual events, affecting individuals, and do not generalize (except about politics). It should also be emphasized that even the classical jurists fail to use the formula. There is a perfectly good equivalent in an excerpt from the Augustan jurist Labeo, in *Digest*, iv.3.11.1: it is unnecessary to hold that the words are Ulpian's and not Labeo's. Nor is it likely that for Labeo the phrase *qui dignitate excellet* applied only to exconsuls.

equestrians went before the tribunal of the Emperor or the Senate, and the public courts and the urban prefect dealt mainly with lower-class criminals at Rome. Third, in the matter of punishments, variation of penalty was practised as soon as *extra ordinem* courts began to operate, and it appears that while citizens were favored above aliens, citizens of low rank lost in comparison with upper-class citizens.[68] This last statement is necessarily cautious, given the nature of the evidence. The *Digest* is preoccupied with the post-Trajanic period, and, with few exceptions, the historical and biographical authors are Rome-based and caught up in the political struggle between Emperor and Senate. Hence information is lacking about the way in which penalties were normally applied to lesser men, including citizens of low station, and to provincials of all ranks.[69]

The conclusion is not that citizenship was worth nothing. There is some evidence that the Emperor was interested in the welfare of citizens in the provinces,[70] although this does not mean that he was not prepared to come to the assistance of free aliens.[71] The rights of citizens were respected by some officials at least, and the authors describe with disapproval occasions when they were ignored.[72] The relevant references are concentrated within a period of about 175 years, from the 70s B.C. to the reign of Trajan. This sug-

---

[68] *Citizens/aliens:* See Footnote 58, above; Pliny, *Epistolae*, x.96.4.

Equestrians/others: ibid., ii.11.8: an equestrian is exiled, his friends (*sc.*, of lower status) are executed: another equestrian is strangled after the application of servile sanctions—but Marius Priscus apparently demands a higher sum for this.

Senators/others: Suetonius, *Life of Augustus*, a patrician (*sc.*, a senator) asks the senate for a milder penalty because of his age and birth; Pliny, *Epistolae*, iv.11.10 ff.: an equestrian is beaten to death, an expraetor allowed to take much of his property into exile (—on the latter's complicity, see Sherwin-White (1966: iv.11.11); *ibid.*, ix.13.21 (see n. 20 above).

Foreign prince/citizen: Tacitus, *Annales*, vi.40: even Tigranes cannot escape *supplicia civium* (citizen punishments).

[69] Penalties *abnormally* applied to equestrians or to men of rank (grade unspecified): Suetonius, *Tiberius*, li (treadmill); *Gaius*, xxvii.3–4 (mutilation, exposure to beasts; condemnation to mines and road building); Josephus, *History of the Jewish Wars*, ii.308 (Gessius Florus, Nero; flogging and crucifixion); Pliny, *Epistolae*, ii.11.8. *Epistolae*, x.58 is more problematic: Flavius Archippus was sent to the mines for forgery; there is no hint of irregularity; he was a citizen, but otherwise nothing is known about his status at the time of the trial—his later prosperity may be solely due to Domitian's favor. Suetonius, *Galba*, ix is also difficult: a citizen is crucified, again for a genuine, serius crime. Was he atypical? Florus' crucifixions (above) undoubtedly were. Suetonius implies the penalty was harsh, and the man pleads his citizen status, as if expecting a milder punishment.

[70] Cyzicus lost its freedom once (perhaps twice) and Rhodes once for violence against Romans or for putting them to death: Dio, liv.7.6; lvii.24.6; Tacitus, *Annales*, iv.36.2–3; cf. Suetonius, *Tiberius*, xxxvii.3.

[71] See, e.g, Riccobono, *op. cit.*, iii, n. 185, p. 582 (Cnidus; Augustus assists free aliens). Only some of the African peasants who petitioned Commodus (see n. 55 above) were citizens. *Digest*, xlviii.6.6 may or may not be relevant: Pius instructs a proconsul to investigate a savage attack on a youth, whose name indicates he was a citizen; yet Pius describes him simply as *ingenuus* ("freeborn").

[72] *Respected: Acts*, xxii.24; cf. xxv.9 ff. (and see Garnsey, 1966: 167). Pliny, *Epistolae*, x.96.4; Eusebius, *The Ecclesiastical History*, v.i.47.

Ignored: Cicero, *ad familiares*, x.32.2 (Balbus); *2 in Verrem*, v. 162ff. (Verres); Suetonius, *Galba*, ix (Galba); Dio, lxiv.2.3 (Capito).

gests that the value of citizenship may have declined in the second century, perhaps because of the increase in the numbers of citizens.[73] Alternatively, the imbalance in the evidence may be due to mere chance. Citizenship was still sought after in the second century, (Sherwin-White, 1939: Chapters ix–x),[74] and the verdict at Lyons in A.D. 177 already referred to suggests that the reasons were not entirely sentimental. But the fact remains that the distinction between citizens and aliens was at all times only one of several which the Romans recognized, and it skated over the realities of Roman politics and social life. The Romans rejected juridical equality, the equality of all citizens before the law, as easily as they rejected political equality. Cicero viewed as unequal that kind of equality which "does not recognize grades of dignity."[75] This attitude must have been universal among those who dominated politics and the administration of justice in both Republican and Imperial Rome.

ACKNOWLEDGMENT

I wish to thank Mr. G. E. M. de Ste. Croix for his valuable advice and criticism.

REFERENCES

Briscoe, J.
   1967   Rome and the class struggle, 200–146 B.C. *Past and Present* **38** (April): 3–20.
Cardascia, G.
   1950   L'apparition dans le droit des classes d' 'honestiores' et d' humiliores. *Revue historique de droit français et étranger* **27** (1950).
Carlin, J. E., J. Howard, and S. Messinger
   1966   Civil justice and the poor: Issues for sociological research. *Law and Society Review* **1** (1966): 9–90.
Crook, J., and R. Stone
   1967   The oppressor's wrong, the proud man's contumely? (Review of J. M. Kelly, *Roman litigation*) *Classical Review* **17** (March): 83–86.
d'Ors, Pérex-Peix, A.
   1965   *Les empereurs romains d'Espagne.* Paris: Centre National de la Recherche Scientifique.
Farrington, B.
   1939   *Science and politics in the ancient world.* London: Allen and Unwin.

[73]If Tacitus was any judge, the "snob-value" of citizenship had declined anyway by the late first century. See Tacitus, *Annales*, iii.40.2: the citizenship was once "rare, and given solely as a reward for virtue." This is a conservative, upper-class Roman view.

[74]The citizen/alien distinction lost most of its meaning when Caracalla made virtually the whole free population of the Empire Roman citizens.

[75]Cicero, *de republica*, i.4.3: "... *tamen ipsa aequabilitas est inqua, cum habet nullos gradus dignitatis.*"

Frederiksen, M. W.

1966   Caesar, Cicero and the problem of debt. *Journal of Roman Studies* **56** (1966): 128–141.

Garnsey, P.

1966   The *Lex Iulia* and appeal under the empire. *Journal of Roman Studies* **56** (1966): 128–141.

1967   Adultery trials and the survival of the *quaestiones* in the Severan Age. *Journal of Roman Studies* **57** (1967): 56–60.

Gaudemet, J.

1954   L'empereur, Interpréte du Droit. In *Festschrift für Ernst Rabel*, Volume 2, edited by Wolfgang Kunkel and Hans Julius Wolff, pp. 169–203. Tübingen: J. C. B. Mohr.

Jones, A. H. M.

1960   *Studies in Roman government and law.* Oxford: Blackwell.

Kelly, J. M.

1966   *Roman litigation.* London and New York: Oxford Univ. Press (Clarendon).

Myres, J. N. L.

1960   Pelagius and the end of Roman rule in Britain. *Journal of Roman Studies* **50** (1960): 21–36.

Robertis, F. M.

1939   Arbitrium indicantis e statnizioni imperiali. Pena discrezionale e pena fissa neela cognitio extra ordinem. *Zeitschrift der Savigny-Stiftung für Rechtsgeschichte (Romanistische Abteilung)* **59** (1939): 219–260.

Schulz, F.

1951   *Classical Roman law.* London and New York: Oxford Univ. Press (Clarendon Press).

Sherwin-White, A. N.

1939   *Roman citizenship.* London and New York: Oxford Univ. Press (Clarendon Press).

1963   *Roman society and Roman law in the New Testament.* London and New York: Oxford Univ. Press (Clarendon Press).

CONTRACTS AND POWER IN AMERICA
Friedrich Kessler

WITH THE development of a free enterprise system based on an unheard of division of labor, capitalistic society needed a highly elastic legal institution to safeguard the exchange of goods and services on the market. Common law lawyers, responding to this social need, transformed "contract" from the clumsy institution that it was in the sixteenth century into a tool of almost unlimited usefulness and pliability. Contract thus became the indispensable instrument of the enterpriser, enabling him to go about his affairs in a rational way. Rational behavior within the context of our culture is only possible if agreements will be respected. It requires that reasonable expectations created by promises receive the protection of the law or else we will suffer the fate of Montesquieu's Troglodytes, who perished because they did not fulfill their promises. This idea permeates our whole law of contracts, the doctrines dealing with their formation, performance, impossibility, and damages.

Under a free enterprise system rationality of the law of contracts has still another aspect (Weber, 1925: 413 ff.). To keep pace with the constant widening of the market the legal system has to place at the disposal of the members of the community an ever increasing number of typical business transactions and regulate their consequences. But the law cannot possibly anticipate the content of an infinite number of atypical transactions into which members of the community may need to enter. Society, therefore, has to give the parties freedom of contract; to accommodate the business

Reprinted from "Contracts of Adhesion—Some Thoughts about Freedom of Contract" by Friedrich Kessler, *Columbia Law Review*, Vol. 43 (1943): pp. 629–642.

community the ceremony necessary to vouch for the deliberate nature of a transaction has to be reduced to the absolute minimum. Furthermore, the rules of the common law of contract have to remain *Jus dispositivum*—to use the phrase of the Romans; that is, their application has to depend on the intention of the parties or on their neglect to rule otherwise. (If parties to a contract have failed to regulate its consequences in their own way, they will be supposed to have intended the consequences envisaged by the common law.) Beyond that the law cannot go. It has to delegate legislation to the contracting parties. As far as they are concerned, the law of contract has to be of their own making.

Thus freedom of contract does not commend itself for moral reasons only; it is also an eminently practical principle. It is the inevitable counterpart of a free enterprise system (Pound, 1909: 454; Williston, 1921: 365; Hamilton, 1938: 450). As a result, our legal lore of contracts reflects a proud spirit of individualism and of *laissez faire*. This is particularly true for the axioms and rules dealing with the formation and interpretation of contracts, the genuineness and reality of consent. Contract—the language of the cases tells us—is a private affair and not a social institution. The judicial system, therefore, provides only for their interpretation, but the courts cannot make contracts for the parties.[1] There is no contract without assent, but once the objective manifestations of assent are present, their author is bound. A person is supposed to know the contract that he makes.[2] "A mere offer imposes no duty of action upon the offeree; there is no obligation to accept or reject or to take any notice of it" (Prosser, 1935: 45). If an offeror does not hear from the offeree about the offer, he is free to make inquiries or to withdraw his offer. but he cannot regard silence as an acceptance. Either party is supposed to look out for his own interests and his own protection. Oppressive bargains can be avoided by careful shopping around. Everyone has complete freedom of choice with regard to his partner in contract, and the privity-of-contract principle respects the exclusiveness of this choice.[3] Since

[1] Urian v. Scranton Life Insurance Company, 310 Pa. 144, 165 Atl. 21 (1933); Imperial Fire Insurance Company v. Coos County, 151 U.S. 452 (1894).

[2] In the absence of fraud or misrepresentation parties who have put their contract in writing and signed it will not be heard to say that they have not read it or did not know, understand, or assent to its contents provided the document is legible, however small the print. L'Estrange v. F. Graucob Ltd., 2K.B.394 (1934). For American cases see Williston (1936: Section 90A).

[3] Coast Fisheries Co. v. Linen Thread Co., 269 Fed. 841 (D. Mass 1921); Kaufman v. Sydeman, 251 Mass. 210, 146 N.E. 365 (1925). The evolution and gradual restriction of the privity of contract principle with the help of agency (undisclosed principal), third party beneficiary, assignment, and tort doctrines expresses our awareness of the growing impersonality of the market and of the social function of contracts. We regard the undisclosed principal doctrine no longer as a wholly anomalous doctrine which ignores the fundamental notion of the common law "that a contract creates strictly personal obligations between the contracting parties." (Huffcut, 1901: 158; Ames, 1909: 443). The privity of contract doctrine no longer perfectly insulates the producer from direct liability to the ultimate consumer, as the food and dangerous instrumentality cases illustrate.

a contract is the result of the free bargaining of parties who are brought together by the play of the market and who meet each other on a footing of social and approximate economic equality, there is no danger that freedom of contract will be a threat to the social order as a whole. Influenced by this optimistic creed, courts are extremely hesitant to declare contracts void as against public policy "because if there is one thing which more than another public policy requires it is that men of full age and competent understanding shall have the utmost liberty of contracting, and that their contracts when entered into freely and voluntarily shall be held sacred and shall be enforced by Courts of justice."[4]

The development of large-scale enterprise with its mass production and mass distribution made a new type of contract inevitable—the standardized mass contract (Issacs, 1917; Llewellyn, 1931, 1939; Raiser, 1935; Pausnitz, 1937). A standardized contract, once its contents have been formulated by a business firm, is used in every bargain dealing with the same product or service. The individuality of the parties which so frequently gave color to the old type contract has disappeared. The stereotyped contract of today reflects the impersonality of the market. It has reached its greatest perfection in the different types of contracts used on the various exchanges. Once the usefulness of these contracts was discovered and perfected in the transportation, insurance, and banking business, their use spread into all other fields of large-scale enterprise, into international as well as national trade, and into labor relations. It is to be noted that uniformity of terms of contracts typically recurring in a business enterprise is an important factor in the exact calculation of risks. Risks which are difficult to calculate can be excluded altogether. Unforseeable contingencies affecting performance, such as strikes, fire, and transportation difficulties can be taken care of.[5] The standard clauses in insurance policies are the most striking illustrations of successful attempts on the part of business enterprises to select and control risks assumed under a contract. The insurance business probably deserves credit also for having first realized the full importance of the so-called "juridical risk," the danger that a court or jury may be swayed by "irrational factors" to decide against a powerful defendant. Ingenious clauses have been the result (Patterson, 1935: 282 ff). Once their practical utility was proven, they were made use of in other lines of business. It is highly probable that the desire to avoid juridical risks has been a motivating factor in the widespread use of warranty clauses in the machine industry limiting the

[4] Sir G. Jessel, M. R., in Printing and Numerical Registering Co. v. Sampson, L. R. 19 Eq. 462, 465 (1875).

[5] For a far-reaching clause in a sales contract see Hollis Bros. & Co. Ltd. v. White Sea Timber Trust, Ltd., 3 All Eng. R. 895 (1936). Here the seller of timber from a port in the Arctic Circle open for navigation only about twenty-one days stipulated "this contract is subject to sellers making necessary chartering arrangements for the expedition and sold subject to shipments. Any goods not shipped to be cancelled."

common law remedies of the buyer to breach of an implied warranty of quality and particularly excluding his right to claim damages.[6] The same is true for arbitration clauses in international trade. Standardized contracts have thus become an important means of excluding or controlling the "irrational factor" in litigation. In this respect they are a true reflection of the spirit of our time with its hostility to irrational factors in the judicial process, and they belong in the same category as codifications and restatements.

Insofar as the reduction of costs of production and distribution thus achieved is reflected in reduced prices, society as a whole ultimately benefits from the use of standard contracts. And there can be no doubt that this has been the case to a considerable extent. The use of standard contracts has, however, another aspect which has become increasingly important. Standard contracts are typically used by enterprises with strong bargaining power. The weaker party, in need of the goods or services, is frequently not in a position to shop around for better terms, either because the author of the standard contract has a monopoly (natural or artificial) or because all competitors use the same clauses. His contractual intention is but a subjection more or less voluntary to terms dictated by the stronger party, terms whose consequences are often understood only in a vague way, if at all. Thus, standardized contracts are frequently contracts of adhesion; they are *à prendre ou à laisser*.[7] Not infrequently the weaker party to a prospective contract even agrees in advance not to retract his offer while the offeree reserves for himself the power to accept or refuse[8]; or he submits to terms or change of terms which will be communicated to him later. To be sure, the latter type of clauses regularly provides for a power to disaffirm,[9] but as a practical matter they are acquiesced in frequently, thus becoming part of the "living law." Lastly, standardized contracts have also been used to control and regulate the distribution of goods from producer all the way down to the ultimate consumer. They have become one of the many devices to build up and strengthen industrial empires.

And yet the tremendous economic importance of contracts of adhesion is hardly reflected in the great texts on contracts or in the Restatement. As a matter of fact, the term "contract of adhesion" or a similar symbol has not

---

[6] For an effort of the legislature to protect the interests of the buyer of agricultural machinery see North Dakota Laws (1919) c. 238 construed in Palaniuk v. Allis Chalmers Mfg. Co., 57 N. D. 199, 220 N. W. 638 (1928).
[7] The word "contract of adhesion" has been introduced into the legal vocabulary by Patterson (1919: 222).
[8] Cole, McIntyre, Norflect Co. v. Hollaway, 141 Tenn. 679, 214 S. W. 817 (1919), discussed by Corbin (1920: 441).
[9] See the standard form of an application for a life insurance policy, reprinted in Patterson (1932: 819); Robinson v. U.S. Benevolent Society, 132 Mich. 695 (1903).

even found general recognition in our legal vocabulary. This will not do any harm if we remain fully aware that the use of the word "contract" does not commit us to an indiscriminate extension of the ordinary contract rules to all contracts. But apparently the realization of the deep-going antinomies in the structure of our system of contracts is too painful an experience to be permitted to rise to the full level of our consciousness. Consequently, courts have made great efforts to protect the weaker contracting party and still keep "the elementary rules" of the law of contracts intact. As a result, our common law of standardized contracts is highly contradictory and confusing, and the potentialities inherent in the common law system for coping with contracts of adhesion have not been fully developed. The law of insurance contracts furnishes excellent illustrations. Handicapped by the axiom that courts can only interpret but cannot make contracts for the parties, courts had to rely heavily on their prerogative of interpretation to protect a policyholder. To be sure many courts have shown a remarkable skill in reaching "just" decisions by construing ambiguous clauses against their author even in cases where there was no ambiguity. Still, this round about method has its disadvantages as the story of the treatment of warranties in life insurance contracts strikingly demonstrates. Courts, when protecting an innocent policyholder against the harshness of the doctrine, did not state clearly that as a matter of public policy an insurance company cannot avoid liability merely because of the falsity of a statement which has been labeled "warranty." They felt that freedom of contract prevented them from saying so. Instead they disguised as "interpretation" their efforts to change warranties into representations.[10] But this makeshift solution tempted insurance companies to try the usefulness of "warranties" again and again.[11]

Society had thus to pay a high price in terms of uncertainty for the luxury of an apparent homogeneity in the law of contracts. Finally, the legislature had to step in. In many jurisdictions warrranties have been put on the same footing with representations; in fire insurance, legislation has even prescribed the contents of the standard policy. No such need has arisen with regard to contracts for reinsurance. Here parties of equal skill and bargaining power are dealing with one another.

Although the episode of warranties, because of the intervention of legislation, belongs largely to the past, another well-known controversy still lacks a satisfactory solution. Courts have been unable to agree as to who shall bear the risk of "loss without insurance" caused by an unreasonable delay on the

---

[10] Cf. Moulov. v. American Life Ins. Co., 111 U.S. 335 (1884); Ehrenzweig and Kessler (1942: 210 ff.).

[11] On the shortcomings of the "interpretation" device which results in a constant struggle between draftsman of standardized contracts and courts, see Llewellyn (1939: 703).

part of an insurance company in issuing a policy of insurance for which application has been made (Prosser, 1935). Here again the pious myth that the law of contracts is of one cloth has stood in the path of progress. The courts, because of their reliance on and preoccupation with "interpretation," were lacking experience in handling this situation.

Most courts have felt rather strongly that a recovery in contract is out of the question. According to a "thoroughly established principle of the law of contracts, within the field of which insurance largely lies," an application for insurance is a bare offer and therefore imposes no liability upon the insurance company until it is accepted. Nor does it "afford a basis for any liability by reason of delay in accepting it or the want of care in dealing with it." A decision of the Connecticut Supreme Court has summed up the arguments against an implied contract in the most persuasive form:

> It is of course true that failure to act upon it may, in such a case as this, cause loss to the applicant or to those to be named beneficiaries in the policy, against which he expected to secure protection. That situation is not, however, peculiar to the insurance law; for example, one may make an offer to buy goods which he needs at a certain price, having reason to believe the price will advance, and may incur loss through the failure of the one to whom it is made to act upon the offer within a reasonable time.[12]

To fortify the argument we are told that an implied promise for future action would be unsupported by consideration. "No legal benefit moved from the applicant to it by reason of the offer, and any detriment which the applicant suffers is not one which was contemplated by the terms of the offer or its acceptance." This is all the more true, courts assure us, since the applicant does not agree not to seek insurance elsewhere and is at liberty to withdraw his offer any time before acceptance.[13]

The argument that a recovery in contract would be "contrary to the well-settled principles of contract law" has influenced almost the whole of legal literature,[14] particularly since applications typically contain a provision to the effect that the company shall incur no liability under the application until it has been approved by the home office and a formal policy issued and delivered (Prosser, 1935: 40–41).[15] Besides, we are informed, the assumption of an implied promise to act promptly "ignores actuality." "If a court should hold that a contract to decide expeditiously on the proposal did exist, it is

---

[12] Swentusky v. Prudential Ins. Co., 116 Conn. 526, 534 (1933).

[13] *Ibid.*, p. 534.

[14] Only a few decisions have spelled out a contractual or quasi-contractual liability, for instance Columbian Nat. Life Ins. Co. v. Lemmons, 96 Okla. 228 (1923).

[15] For an analysis of the function of the clause and the efforts of courts to protect the interests of the applicant by manipulating the symbol "delivery" see Patterson (1919: 218, 221–222).

believed that, within a short time, all insurance companies doing business in that jurisdiction would incorporate in their applications stipulations expressly negativing any such promise" (Funk, 1927: 214).

And yet, although most courts subscribe to this doctrine, the majority still allows recovery by the back door, so to speak. They regard recovery *ex contractu* as impossible, but at the same time allow recovery *ex delictu*. The failure of an insurance company to take prompt action—according to these decisions—amounts to the breach of a general duty toward the public to act without undue delay on applications for acceptable risks.[16] The courts are sure that the policy of insurance cannot be treated like any other contract. The state, by granting a franchise to the insurance company, by regulating and supervising its business, recognizes the great social importance of insurance business; it is, therefore, in the public interest that applications for acceptable risks shall not be unduly delayed. Thus the courts pay merely lip service to the dogma that the common law of contracts governs insurance contracts. With the help of the law of torts they nullify those parts of the law of contracts which in the public interest are regarded as inapplicable. Disguised as tort law the courts recognized a liability for *culpa in contrahendo* thus making new law with regard to the formation of insurance contracts. This approach enables them to disregard the clause in the application by means of which the company attempted to avoid liability prior to the delivery of the policy. No wonder that this line of reasoning has been sharply criticized not only for its inconsistency[17] but also for undermining legal certainty and the stability of the insurance business. To impose upon an insurance company, because it acts under franchise from the state, a duty to act promptly on an application

> would be to open a field of legal liability the limits of which we cannot encompass, and which would go far to introduce chaos in the entire business of insurance, indeed, would almost necessarily reach out into the field of other specially chartered corporations occupying not dissimilar relations to the public, as banks, utility companies, and the like. Public interest more requires that stability of the insurance business which is necessary to guard the great body of persons who enter into relations with it for their own protection and that of those dependent upon them, than it does that certain individuals should be saved the loss which may result by adherence to established legal principles.[18]

[16] Duffie v. Bankers' Life Ass'n, 160 Iowa 19, 139 N.W. 1087 (1913); for further cases, see Prosser (1935: 41 ff.).

[17] Savage v. Prudential Life Ins. Co., 154 Miss. 89, 121 So. 487 (1929). "To hold that there is no contract, nor breach of a contract, in failing to insure this applicant, or to notify him that he was not insured, and then to hold that a tort arises, is to hold that there was created a legal duty, and to this we cannot subscribe" *Ibid.*, p. 489. The situation is unlike that in the early history of contract law where contractual liability was developed with the help of the action on the case. In the insurance cases contract and tort analyses represent conflicting ideologies.

[18] Swentusky v. Prudential Ins. Co., 116 Conn. 526, 532 (1933).

This lineup of arguments brings out clearly the basic issue with which the courts in the insurance cases are confronted—can the unity of the law of contracts be maintained in the face of the increasing use of contracts of adhesion? The few courts which allow recovery in contract and the many which allow recovery in tort feel more or less clearly that insurance contracts are contracts of adhesion, and try to protect the weaker contracting party against the harshness of the common law and against what they think are abuses of freedom of contract. The courts denying recovery, on the other hand, cling to the belief that an application for insurance is not different from any other offer, and they are convinced that efforts to build up by trial and error a dual system of contract law must inevitably undermine the security function of all law, particularly since courts are ill equipped to decide whether and to what extent an insurance contract has compulsory features.

To be sure, the task of building up a multiple system of contract law is eminently difficult, particularly since courts are not commissions which are able to examine carefully the ramifications of the problem involved and can see only the narrow aspect of the total problem which comes up for litigation. Equally difficult is the job of determining whether and to what extent a contract, for instance that of insurance, is a contract of adhesion. Still, the predicament to which an applicant for insurance is exposed by an unreasonable delay in handling his application is deserving of more serious consideration than the assertion that in case of unreasonable delay the applicant can withdraw his offer and apply elsewhere. The denial of liability may very well put a premium on inefficiency. It is submitted that in this respect the attitude of the courts which allow the applicant to recover as if he were insured is more realistic, provided the risk was acceptable and the insurance company, in dealing with the application, deviated from its standard pattern of behavior, on which the applicant could reasonably rely.[19] There has been no evidence that the insurance business has been unable to adjust itself to the new law created by the decisions allowing recovery. This is not surprising since deviations from the standard practice in handling applications which result in "loss without insurance" are the exception.[20]

The idea implicit in the cases which allow recovery seems very fruitful

[19] Until now decisions allowing recovery in tort have been rather lax in requiring evidence that the delay in handling the application has caused "loss without insurance." For a decision insisting that the plaintiff can recover only if he had reason to believe that a policy would be issued to him and if he were precluded to his damage from procuring other insurance, see Wallace v. Metropolitan Life Ins. Co., 212 Wis. 346, 248 N.W. 435 (1933).

[20] The practice of antedating insurance by using premium receipts is a step in the right direction but hardly goes far enough. The applicant, if he is protected at all against the risk of delay, is only protected if he has paid the first premium in full. He is not protected for instance if he has only made a down payment on the first premium, as illustrated by Swentusky v. Prudential Ins. Co., 116 Conn. 526, cited *supra* note 17. Whether and to what extent the applicant is protected depends further on the type of the premium receipt used. For a description of the various types of premium receipts used and their shortcomings, see Comment (1935: 1223).

indeed. In dealing with standardized contracts courts have to determine what the weaker contracting party could legitimately expect by way of services according to the enterpriser's "calling," and to what extent the stronger party disappointed reasonable expectations based on the typical life situation (Llewellyn, 1939: 704).[21] It can hardly be objected that the resulting task of rewriting, if necessary, the contents of a contract of adhesion is foreign to the function of common law courts; the judge-made law in the field of constructive conditions is amply proving the opposite and refutes the contention that a contract implied in fact does not differ from an express contract except that the intention of the party is circumstantially proved (Prosser, 1935: 49).

The task of adjusting in each individual case the common law of contracts to contracts of adhesion has to be faced squarely and not indirectly. This is possible only if courts become fully aware of their emotional attitude with regard to freedom of contract. Here lies the main obstacle to progress, particularly since courts have an understandable tendency to avoid this crucial issue by way of rationalizations. They prefer to convince themselves and the community that legal certainty and "sound principles" of contract law should not be sacrificed to dictates of justice or social desirability. Such discussions are hardly profitable.

To be sure "case law and the feeling of justice are certainly not synonymous" (Cohen, 1927: 470); it is just to obey laws of which one does not approve. But it is equally true that the rules of the common law are flexible enough to enable courts to listen to their sense of justice and to the sense of justice of the community. Just as freedom of contract gives individual contracting parties all the needed leeway for shaping the law of contract according to their needs, the elasticity of the common law, with rule and counter-rule constantly competing, makes it possible for courts to follow the dictates of "social desirability." Whatever one may think about the possibility of separating the "law that is" from the "law that ought to be," this much is certain: In the development of the common law the ideal tends constantly to become the practice. And in this process the ideal of certainty has constantly to be weighed against the social desirability of change, and very often legal certainty has to be sacrificed to progress. The inconsistencies and contradictions within the legal system resulting from the uneven growth of the law and from conflicting ideologies are inevitable.[22]

---

[21] Llewellyn calls our attention to the case law on oral contracts to ensure which indeed shows the ingenuity of common law courts in making contracts for the parties on the basis of the typical life situation. See, for instance, Aetna Ins. Co. of Hartford, Conn. v. Licking Valley Millings Co. (C. C. A. 6th, 1927) 19 Fed. (2d) 177, Patterson, 1935: 59 ff., 64 ff.).

[22] Still, in a time of transition like ours where the dichotomy between political freedom and economic insecurity belongs to the experience of everyday life and where the widespread feeling of economic insecurity threatens even political freedom the psychological urge to rely on the law for certainty is particularly powerful. For a penetrating psychological analysis of the emotional dilemma of modern man, see Fromm (1941).

It is not even profitable to spend "the energy of counsel, the money of clients and the time and analysis of judges" (Douglas, 1929: 594) in discussing the problems presented by contracts of adhesion in terms of established legal principles and to proclaim that recovery is "contrary to the well settled principles of contract law." This approach tries to create the impression that the rules concerning the formation of contracts are a closed and harmonious system. But this is hardly the case. The doctrine of consideration,* for instance, more than any other doctrine, is in a constant process of evolution, full of contradictions and inconsistencies (Corbin, 1937: 453 ff.). It has responded to the belief in freedom of contract, as the peppercorn theory of consideration illustrates. It can also be used to protect a creditor against the risk of economic duress of his debtor *(Foakes v. Beer).*[23] Diametrically opposed social policies have thus been defended in the name of consideration. Furthermore, the harshness of the rule of *Thorne v. Deas,*[24] which seems to support the theory of the courts which deny liability in contract, is mitigated by a counterrule which is constantly gaining in strength and has found expression in Section 90 of the Restatement. Even the mere risk of reliance has been regarded sufficient consideration,[25] a doctrine which comes in handy here to offset the argument that the applicant could have withdrawn his application and applied for insurance elsewhere. It is true that acceptance of the application can hardly be inferred from silence for an unreasonable length of time since the standard clause in the application expressly warns the applicant that the company shall incur no liability under the application until it has been approved and a formal policy has been issued and delivered. But is this clause sufficiently unequivocal to negative not only an acceptance by silence but also an implied collateral promise (as it is technically called) to take prompt action on an application for an acceptable risk?[26] More serious is the argument that the assumption of an implied promise to act promptly is unrealistic because insurance companies,

---

*(Editors' note: The Anglo-American doctrine of consideration holds that a contract is enforceable only if both parties receive a specifiable benefit. This exchange need not be equal. An early legal principle has it that even a peppercorn may serve as consideration.)

[23] L. R. 9 App. Cas. 605 (1884); Sharp (1940: 253). Thus interpreted the rule in *Foakas v. Beer* is not so conceptualistic as its critics contend.

[24] 4 Johns. 84. (N.Y. 1809). It is difficult to believe that the efforts on the part of some courts [e.g., Comfort v. McCorkle, 149 Misc. 826,268 N.Y. Supp. 192 (1933)] to reconcile §§ 45 and 90 of the Restatement by limiting the application of promissory estoppel to charitable subscriptions and promises to make gifts (noncommercial cases) will be successful in the long run.

[25] For a collection and discussion of authorities see Note (1939: 133 ff.).

[26] The risk of reliance furnishes the needed consideration. The situation is in a way the reverse to that presented by Los Angeles Traction Co. v. Wilshire, 135 Cal. 654, 67 Pac. 1086 (1902) and similar cases envisaged by § 45 of the Restatement of Contracts.

once subjected to such an implied promise, would immediately negative it by express stipulation in the policy. But is this argument not begging the question? The crucial problem is not whether insurance companies would insert such a clause but whether they could do so with impunity.

Thus, technical doctrines of the law of contracts cannot possibly provide the courts with the right answers. They convince only those courts which are already convinced. For instance, which consideration doctrine the court is going to choose as the correct one depends upon its attitude with regard to freedom of contract. All the technical doctrines resorted to by the courts in the insurance cases denying liability are in the last analysis but rationalizations of the court's emotional desire to preserve freedom of contract. Even the cases which hold the insurance company liable in tort pay tribute to the dogma; otherwise it would have been unnecessary constantly to emphasize that the plaintiff is not seeking recovery in contract. The freedom of contract dogma is the real hero or villain in the drama of the insurance cases, but it prefers to remain in the safety of the background if possible, leaving the actual fighting to consideration and to the host of other satellites—all of which is very often confusion to the audience which vaguely senses the unreality of the atmosphere.

Still, the tort cases are a constant though indirect challenge to the claims of the freedom of contract dogma. They keep alive the question whether or not the "received ideas" (Pound, 1930: 554) on freedom of contract which form the background of the insurance cases represent a cultural lag.

The individualism of our rules of contract law, of which freedom of contract is the most powerful symbol, is closely tied up with the ethics of free enterprise capitalism and the ideals of justice of a mobile society of small enterprisers, individual merchants, and independent craftsmen. This society believed that individual and cooperative action left unrestrained in family, church, and market would not lessen the freedom and dignity of man but would secure the highest possible social justice. It was firmly convinced of a natural law according to which the individual serving his own interest was also serving the interest of the community. Profits can be earned only by supplying consumable commodities. Freedom of competition will prevent profits from rising unduly. The play of the market if left to itself must therefore maximize net satisfactions. Justice within this framework has a very definite meaning. It means freedom of property and of contract, of profit making and of trade (Hamilton, 1937: 142). Freedom of contract thus receives its moral justification. The "prestabilized harmony" of a social system based on freedom of enterprise and perfect competition sees to it that the "private autonomy" of contracting parties will be kept within bounds and will work out to the benefit of the whole.

With the decline of the free enterprise system due to the innate trend of competitive capitalism toward monopoly, the meaning of contract has changed radically. Society, when granting freedom of contract, does not guarantee that all members of the community will be able to make use of it to the same extent. On the contrary, the law, by protecting the unequal distribution of property, does nothing to prevent freedom of contract from becoming a one-sided privilege. Society, by proclaiming freedom of contract, guarantees that it will not interefere with the exercise of power by contract. Freedom of contract enables enterprisers to legislate by contract and, what is even more important, to legislate in a substantially authoritarian manner without using the appearance of authoritarian forms. Standard contracts in particular could thus become effective instruments in the hands of powerful industrial and commercial overlords enabling them to impose a new feudal order of their own making upon a vast host of vassals (Note, 1931: 830 ff.). This spectacle is all the more fascinating since not more than 100 years ago contract ideology had been successfully used to break down the last vestiges of a patriarchal and benevolent feudal order in the field of master and servant (*Priestley v. Fowler*). Thus the return back from contract to status which we experience today was greatly facilitated by the fact that the belief in freedom of contract has remained one of the firmest axioms in the whole fabric of the social philosophy of our culture.

The role played by contract in the destruction of the institutional framework of capitalistic society is constantly obscured to the lawyer by the still prevailing philosophy of law which neglects to treat contract as the most important source of law. According to conventional theory contract is only a convenient label for a number of "operative facts" which have the consequences intended by the parties if the law so ordains (Williston, 1936: Sec. 1; Restatement, Contracts, 1928: Sec. 1; Pound, 1937: 323). In this respect the great philosophers of natural law thought quite differently; society, in proclaiming freedom of contract—according to their teaching—has delegated to individual citizens a piece of sovereignty which enables them to participate constantly in the law-making process. Freedom of contract means that the state has no monopoly in the creation of law. The consent of contracting parties creates law also. The law-making process is decentralized. As a result, law is not an order imposed by the state from above upon its citizens; it is rather an order created from below. This was a realistic insight (Cohen, 1933: 585). Unwarranted, however, was the optimistic belief that capitalism meant a permanent advance over the preceding social system, feudalism, because of the fact that contract and not status had become the chief means of social integration. Nor can we subscribe to the thesis of natural law philosophers that the progress in any society toward freedom is to be measured by the extent to which all political relations can be reduced to contract, "the perfect form of obligation."

In the happy days of free enterprise capitalism the belief that contracting is law-making had largely emotional importance. Law-making by contract was no threat to the harmony of the democratic system. On the contrary it reaffirmed it. The courts, therefore, representing the community as a whole, could remain neutral in the name of freedom of contract. The deterioration of the social order into the pluralistic society of our days with its powerful pressure groups was needed to make the wisdom of the contract theory of the natural law philosophers meaningful to us. The prevailing dogma, on the other hand, insisting that contract is *only* a set of operative facts, helps to preserve the illusion that the "law" will protect the public against any abuse of freedom of contract. This will not be the case so long as we fail to realize that freedom of contract must mean different things for different types of contracts. Its meaning must change with the social importance of the type of contract and with the degree of monopoly enjoyed by the author of the standardized contract.

REFERENCES

Ames, J. B.
 1909   Undisclosed principal—His rights and liabilities. *Yale Law Journal* **18** (May): 443–453.
Cohen, M. R.
 1927   Positivism and the limits of idealism in the law. *Proceedings of the Sixth International Congress of Philosophy* **6** (1927): 469–481.
 1933   The basis of contract. *Harvard Law Review* **46** (1933): 553–592.
Comment
 1935   *Yale Law Journal* **44** (1935): 1223–1232.
Corbin, A. L.
 1920   When silence gives consent. *Yale Law Journal* **29** (February): 441–444.
 1937   Recent developments in the law of contracts. *Harvard Law Review* **50** (1937): 449–475.
Douglas, W. O.
 1929   Vicarious liability and administration of risk. *Yale Law Journal* **38** (1929): 548–604.
Ehrenzweig, A., Sr., and F. Kessler
 1942   Misrepresentation and false warranty in the Illinois insurance code. *University of Chicago Law Review* **9** (February): 209–223.
Fromm, E.
 1941   *Escape from freedom.* New York: Farrar & Rinehart.
Funk, C. W.
 1927   The duty of an insurer to act promptly on applications. *University of Pennsylvania Law Review* **25** (1927): 207–226.
Hamilton, W. H.
 1937   Competition. In *Encyclopaedia of the social sciences*, Volume 2, edited by E. R. A. Seligman, pp. 141–147. New York: Macmillan.

1938   Freedom of contract. In *Encyclopaedia of the social sciences*, Volume 3, edited by E. R. A. Seligman, pp. 450–455. New York: Macmillan.

Huffcut, E. W.
1901   *The law of agency.* (2nd ed.) Boston: Little, Brown.

Issacs, N.
1917   The standardizing of contracts. *Yale Law Journal* **27** (1917): 34–48.

Llewellyn, K. N.
1931   What price contract—an essay in perspective. *Yale Law Journal* **40** (1931): 704–751.
1939   Review of *The standardization of commercial contracts in English and continental law*, by O. Pausnitz, *Harvard Law Review* (1939): 700–705.

Note
1931   "Mutuality" in exclusive sales agency agreements. *Columbia Law Review* **31** (1931): 830–871.

Note
1939   Promissory obligations based on past benefits or other moral obligations. *University of Chicago Law Review* **7** (December): 124–136.

Patterson, E. W.
1919   The delivery of a life insurance policy. *Harvard Law Review* **33** (1919): 198–222.
1932   *Cases and other materials on the law of insurance.* New York: Commerce Clearing House, Inc.
1935   *Essentials of insurance law.* New York: McGraw-Hill.

Pausnitz, O.
1937   *The standardization of commercial contracts in English and continental law.* London: Sweet & Maxwell.

Pound, R.
1909   Liberty of contract. *Yale Law Journal* **18** (April): 454–487.
1930   The new feudalism. *American Bar Association Journal* **16** (1930): 553–558.
1937   Contract. In *Encyclopaedia of the social sciences*, Volume 2, edited by E. R. A. Seligman, pp. 323–329. New York: Macmillan.

Prosser, W. L.
1935   Delay in acting on an application for insurance. *University of Chicago Law Review* **3** (1935): 39–60.

Raiser, L.
1935   *Das Recht der Allgemeinen Geschäftsbedingungen.* Hamburg: Hanseatische Verlagsanstalt.

Restatement of the Law of Contracts
1928   Philadelphia: The American law institution.

Sharp, M. P.
1940   Promissory liability, II. *University of Chicago Law Review* **7** (1940): 250–280.

Weber, M.
1925   Rechtssoziologie. In *Wirtschaft und Gesellschaft. Grundriss der Sozialökonomik, III (Abteilung).* (2nd ed.) Tübingen: J. C. B. Mohr. (Orig. pub. 1922.)

Williston, S.
1921   Freedom of contract. *Cornell Law Quarterly* **6** (1921): 365–380.
1936   *A treatise on the law of contracts.* (Rev. ed.) New York: Baker, Voorhist, and Co.

CHAPTER

11

SOCIAL CLASS AND LEGAL SERVICES IN AMERICA*

Leon Mayhew
Albert J. Reiss, Jr.

E VERYONE FROM time to time defines his affairs as legal matters or experiences violations of his legal rights. Yet little is known of how citizen affairs come to the attention of attorneys or official legal agencies. Particularly lacking is an understanding of how both the organization of citizen affairs and of the legal system leads citizens to define affairs as legal matters and to seek advice from a lawyer. This paper presents some findings on problems citizens define as legal matters and their contact with attorneys.

To prevent confusion and to forestall inappropriate criticism, we should also stress what the study is not. It is not, as are a number of recent studies, an attempt to assess the "objective" legal requirements of a population from a value or organized system perspective. Nor is it an attempt to evaluate the quality of legal services. Rather it is based entirely on citizen reports of perceived problems and of their actual experience in problem solving, including contact with lawyers.

*Being a revised edition of a paper presented at the annual meetings of the Midwest Sociological Association, Omaha, Nebraska, April 19, 1968.

Reprinted from "The Social Organization of Legal Contacts" by Leon Mayhew and Albert J. Reiss, Jr., *American Sociological Review*, Vol. 34 (1969): pp. 309–318.

The findings result from 780 completed interviews from an original sample of 957 households in the Detroit SMSA, a completion rate of 82%. The refusal rate was 12%, with the remaining noncompletion rate of 6% assigned to failure to locate a respondent after at least three call backs.

The sampling design set the probability of selecting a Detroit City household at twice that (1:785) of a household outside the central city (1:1570) so as to insure inclusion of more Negro citizens in partial analyses. There are 173 Negro and 349 white interviews in the central city and 3 Negro and 255 white interviews outside the central city. All estimates of proportions are based on the weighted sample of 1038 residents: 859 white and 179 Negro.

THE PREVALENCE OF SEEKING LEGAL ADVICE OR HELP

Each resident was asked whether he had ever gone to a lawyer or talked with a lawyer in order to get help or advice on problems that can be legal matters. Approximately seven of every ten residents in the weighted sample reported seeing a lawyer at least once about a legal matter. One in four reported seeing a lawyer in the last five years. The actual hiring of lawyers is overestimated somewhat by these proportions, since after seeing a lawyer some citizens decided they did not want or could not afford legal services.

Contact with lawyers is nevertheless a prevalent experience among Detroit area residents. Indeed, inspection of Table 1 shows that for all major race, sex, age, and socioeconomic status groups, contact with attorneys is higher than is commonly supposed. In the socioeconomic status group with least contact with attorneys—Negro females with a family income of less than $7000 a year–40% reported seeing a lawyer about a legal problem.

Despite the high incidence of contact with lawyers for all structural status groups shown in Table 1, contact with a lawyer does vary with status. It might be objected that ever having seen a lawyer is a very weak index of legal contact since one visit to an attorney places a person among the "haves." But, within our sample, stronger indicators of legal contact such as seeking a lawyer about three or more separate types of incidents do not increase the difference in the legal experience of socioeconomic status groups.

The best predictors of contact with attorneys are family income and property ownership as indicated by the consistent and substantial differences among classes of income and home ownership, even when race and sex are controlled. Among respondents with annual family income of over $15,000, 83% reported seeing a lawyer, as compared to 56% among persons with an income of less than $7000. Education, occupational status, age, and sex have a moderate to strong effect but none is as discriminating as family income or home ownership.

It might be supposed that the full relation between income and legal contact is being suppressed by the fact that we are comparing lifetime legal experience to family income during the year immediately preceding the study. Many older respondents may have visited lawyers only in earlier years when they had more income. Though plausible, this objection is not well founded. Twenty-six percent of the 711 respondents who had ever visited a lawyer were in the lowest income group; 24% of the 263 who visited a lawyer within the previous year were in the same low income group.

On first glance race appears to have a substantial effect on seeking legal services. Fifty-nine percent of Negroes and 71% of whites said they saw a lawyer about a legal matter. Closer scrutiny indicates that this difference is largely accounted for by the asymmetric position of Negro females who saw lawyers less frequently than either Negro males or white females. Negro males, despite the facts of low income and education, report nearly as much contact with attorneys as their white counterparts. On the other hand, Negro males are also more likely to report that they have been "cooled out" during a visit to an attorney. Seventeen percent of Negro males said that they had been discouraged from taking legal action by an attorney. The comparable figure for white males is only 7%. These socioeconomic differences in the use of legal services are consistent with differences found in studies of other cities (Carlin and Howard, 1965: 382–383).[1]

SOCIAL ORGANIZATION AND CONTACT WITH ATTORNEYS

Previous studies of this type have regularly shown a strong relation between income and the use of professional legal services. Differences by income are then attributed to the fact that the poor cannot afford legal representation, that they are unaware of legal problems and services, and that they distrust attorneys (Carlin and Howard, 1965: 381–382, 423–429).

[1] Carlin and Howard examined studies from California, Texas, Iowa, Missouri, and Ohio and concluded that roughly two-thirds of upper income groups and one-third of lower income groups had ever employed the services of a lawyer.

184

TABLE 1
PERCENT OF ALL RESIDENTS WHO SOUGHT ADVICE FROM A LAWYER BY SOCIAL BACKGROUND FACTORS: WEIGHTED SAMPLE OF DETROIT SMSA, 1967

Social background factors	Percent seeking advice from lawyer	Social background by race and sex	Percent seeking advice from lawyer	Social background by race and sex	Percent seeking advice from lawyer
		Race–sex–education		Race–sex–education	
Race		White male		White male	
White	71	$6999 or less	59	High school or less	71
Negro	59	$7000–$14,999	78	Some college	82
		$15,000 and over	84		
Sex		White female		White female	
Male	73	$6999 or less	61	High school or less	67
Female	66	$7000–$14,999	71	Some college	75
		$15,000 and over	83		
Race–sex		Negro male		Negro male	
White male	74	$6999 or less	58	High school or less	69
White female	69	$7000–$14,999	72	Some college	*
Negro male	69	$15,000 and over	*		
Negro female	53	Negro female		Negro female	
Home ownership		$6999 or less	40	High school or less	52
Owner	76	$7000–$14,999	82	Some college	60
Renter	52	$15,000 and over	*		

Catholic		68
Protestant		70
Jewish		88

Age		
Under 35		65
35–54		73
55 and over		69
Income		
$6999 or less		56
$7000–$14,999		74
$15,000 and over		83
Education		
High school or less		67
Some college		77
Social status		
White collar		75
Blue collar		66
All residents		69

Race–sex–social status

White male		
	White collar	79
	Blue collar	70
White female		
	White collar	72
	Blue collar	67
Negro male		
	White collar	77
	Blue collar	67
Negro female		
	White collar	57
	Blue collar	52

Race–sex–home ownership

White male		
	Owns	77
	Rents	64
White female		
	Owns	76
	Rents	46
Negro male		
	Owns	72
	Rents	66
Negro female		
	Owns	71
	Rents	36

*Fewer than 15 sample cases.

This view can be described as a "resources" theory of legal representatio
Those who have resources such as income, and to a lesser extent oth
resources such as education, confidence, and social connections, are mo
likely to perceive the need for, afford, and gain access to legal servic
Resources, therefore, account for the distribution of the use of lawyers
the population.

That resources make a difference is most clearly supported by the assoc
tion between income and using attorneys within populations who ha
experienced a given legal problem. Conard *et al.* (1964: 225–227), 1
example, report a positive association between income and legal represen
tion among a sample of persons who have been injured in automob
accidents.

Nevertheless, the resources theory fails to account for the extent of u
of legal services even among those with the least résources. More serious
the resources theory fails to predict the differences in patterns of use
legal services across socioeconomic categories. Access to resources, thou
it may account for the *adequacy* of legal services, is not a sufficient explar
tion of the patterns of contact between attorneys and the public, 1
attorney–client relations occur in the context of a complicated netwo
of social organization.

The resources theory appears to contemplate an approach to the use
legal machinery which echoes the doctrine of "economic man." There
a "litigious man" who weighs the costs of his problems against the co
of taking legal action and comes to a rational decision. In other contex
this has been shown to be an inadequate basis for predictions about t
use of legal agencies (Mayhew, 1968a: 424–425). It is more important
know something about the character of routine, organized activity with
the legal agency, the social organization of the institutional arena subj
to legal regulation. Out of the social links between these spheres flow
routine pattern of contact between the legal agency and the public (Mayhe
1968b: 152–198).

A parallel approach can be applied to the problem at hand. We kn
from a series of studies of the legal profession that legal practice is bo
specialized and stratified. The stratification of access to resources in t
population parallels this differentiation and stratification of legal practi
The demand for legal services produces a response from competitive lawy
who move in to fill vacant niches so that distinctive patterns of pract
emerge in various problem areas, e.g., estate, tax, criminal, and contra
(Carlin, 1962, 1966).[2] Competition among lawyers likewise leads to le

---

[2] Of course, one may not assume that the quality of representation is equal for all who use l
services. Indeed, the fact of stratification in the legal profession suggests the opposite.

·vices at fees adapted to the means of clients. These responses of lawyers
ιy be inadequate from the point of view of public policy but they are
netheless responses. Specialization and stratification of legal practice
cordingly mitigate the relation between resources and access to attorneys.
·e also observe a set of distinctive patterns of use of legal services which
lect variations in the patterns of problems experienced in various struc-
·al locations (such as by communities, or by race and ethnic groups), and
·rresponding differences in the social organization of legally relevant
·ivity.

INCOME AND PROPERTY

One important weakness of the resources theory is its failure to
·tinguish between resources as facilities and resources as constraints. The
ual interpretation placed on the association between income and the use of
·al services is that income *enables* the citizen to make use of legal services.
·ght the influence be more indirect? Income brings one into participation
the institution of property, and property as an institution is socially organ-
·d so as to bring its participants into contact with attorneys. Anyone who
·s been caught up in the inescapable constraints of, say, a probate court is
·ely to agree. In other words, not only are resources essential to purchase
·al services, but given the institution of property, the purchase of legal
·vices often is necessary to acquire, maintain, and increase property.
Our data support the proposition that a substantial portion of the income
·ferential in contact with attorneys is accounted for by the greater partic-
·tion of high income persons in the institution of property. Table 2
·icates that income differences in legal contact are considerably reduced
·en contact about matters other than property is considered alone.

TABLE 2

PERCENT OF ALL RESIDENTS WHO SAW LAWYER ABOUT PROPERTY AND
NONPROPERTY MATTERS, LIFETIME AND LAST VISIT TO LAWYER BY FAMILY
INCOME: WEIGHTED SAMPLE OF DETROIT SMSA, 1967

| | Percent who saw lawyer | | | | | |
| | Lifetime | | | Last visit (respondents with visits) | | |
·ome	About property only	About other matters	Total	Property	Non-property	Total
ɔ $6999	22	34	56	50	50	100
000 to $14,999	32	42	74	61	39	100
·er $15,000	40	43	83	67	33	100
·respondents	30	39	69	59	41	100

Although 69% of our sample had sought advice from attorneys, only 3⁹ had ever sought advice on matters other than property. The remaining 3(had seen an attorney only about wills, estates, transactions in real esta advice about entrepreneurial activity or business and property taxes a assessments. For nonproperty matters, that is, domestic problems, neighb‹ hood problems, automobile accidents, personal injuries, problems w public authority, and disputes about purchases and repairs of automobi and other expensive consumer goods, we find that persons with family comes under $7000 still have the least contact with attorneys. Thirty-f‹ percent of this low income group sought professional advice, as compar with 42% of the group with family incomes over $7000 but under $15,0(However, this difference is considerably smaller than the difference betwe these groups in total contact with attorneys. Further, beyond $7000, fam income has no effect on contact with attorneys about nonproperty matte Those with incomes over $15,000 are more likely to seek legal help but o‹ *on matters relating to property.*

In sum, the association between income and legal contacts is in part organizational effect. The legal profession is organized to service busine and property interests. The social organization of business and proper is highly legalized. Out of this convergence emerges a pattern of citiz contact with attorneys that is heavily oriented to property.

The dominance of property in the pattern of contact is evident in t fact that of our respondents' most recent consultation with attorne three-fifths concerned property. Even for the lowest income group, th‹ with family incomes under $7000, one-half had seen a lawyer most recen‹ about a property matter.

OTHER BACKGROUND VARIABLES

More refined analyses of the various types of legal contact social background variables show other examples of organizational effe on the pattern of legal contacts. These effects are shown in Tables 3 and Although there is a rough similarity in the distribution of legal proble across all socioeconomic categories, a number of remarkable differen‹ are also apparent.

One of the most striking differences is the racial variation in seeing lawy‹ about property matters, a fact reflecting the prevalence of home ownersh in the Detroit area. Seventy-seven percent of white respondents and 5⁹ of Negro respondents are homeowners. Home ownership clearly has broug Negroes into contact with the legal profession; 36% of Negroes have se‹

TABLE 3

PERCENT OF ALL RESIDENTS WHO SAW LAWYER BY FOURTEEN TYPES OF LEGAL PROBLEMS AND RANK ORDER OF THESE PERCENTS, BY RACE AND SEX OF RESPONDENT: WEIGHTED SAMPLE OF DETROIT SMSA, 1967

| | Percent of all R's | | | | Rank order of percents | | | | Total | |
| | White | | Negro | | White | | Negro | | Per- | Rank |
saw a lawyer about	M	F	M	F	M	F	M	F	cent	order
ying/selling/										
building a house	45	31	47	30	1	1	1	1	37	1
king a will	25	23	7	—	2	2	6.5	19	20	2
tting an estate	17	22	4	6	5	3	8	6	17	3.5
dvice on business										
matters	19	16	21	11	3	4.5	3	3	17	3.5
urance claims	18	16	11	8	4	4.5	4	4	16	5
vorce/alimony/										
child support	8	12	22	16	8	6	2	2	12	6
ntract disagreements	12	10	7	7	6	7	6.5	5	10	7
x problems/										
disputes with officials	11	7	3	4	7	8	10	7.5	8	8
ffic tickets	7	3	8	4	9	11	5	7.5	5	9
ighborhood	4	4	1	2	10.5	9	12	9.5	3	10.5
cused of crime/										
disturbance	4	3	3	1	10.5	11	10	11	3	10.5
mestic-family	2	3	—	—	12.5	11	13.5	13	2	12
nployer/employee										
disputes	*	1	3	2	14	14	10	9.5	1	13.5
ndlord–tenant	2	2	—	—	12.5	13	13.5	13	1	13.5

—, no frequency; *0.5% or less.

lawyer about buying a home, a figure virtually identical to the 37% of whites who have seen a lawyer for this purpose. But the introduction of Negroes the property complex through home ownership has not yet become sufficiently institutionalized to incorporate Negroes fully into the organized stem for the transmission of property. Only 3% of Negroes had seen a wyer about making a will; among whites, making a will is the second most mmon occasion (23%) for visiting a lawyer.

Seeing a lawyer about a will is not viewed as a pressing legal problem nong Negroes. In response to the query "Have you ever wanted to go to a wyer but didn't for some reason?" Negroes and whites answered "Yes" approximately equal proportions, 19% among whites and 17% among egroes. Yet only one Negro informant mentioned a will in this regard. contrast, 35% of the problems of whites who wanted to talk to a lawyer, ut did not, involved wills. That the passing on of property is less embedded a legal context among Negroes is also indicated from the fact that 20% whites and only 5% of Negroes had seen a lawyer about settling an estate.

		Family income		
R Saw a Lawyer about	All residents	$6,999 or less	$7,000–$14,999	$15,000 or more
Buying/selling/building a house	37	21	46	46
Making a will	20	19	16	42
Settling an estate	18	14	17	29
Advice on business matters	17	11	16	31
Insurance claims	16	8	19	18
Divorce/alimony/child support	12	11	13	12
Contract disagreements	10	7	13	11
Tax problems/disputes with officials	7	6	6	15
Traffic tickets	5	4	5	8
Neighborhood	4	2	4	6
Accused of crime/disturbance	3	2	4	2
Domestic–family	2	1	2	4
Employer/employee disputes	1	—	2	—
Landlord–tenant	1	1	2	—

—, no frequency; *0.5% or less.

These differences by race status in the use of legal advice to handle pe
sonal property parallel rather closely the Negro's integration into America
society. Consider an institutionalized cycle of personal property whe
legal advice pertains first to its acquisition, then to its sale, transformatio
or taxation, then to advice on disposition in the event of the death of i
owner, and finally to the settling of an estate. It seems clear that the Negr
in major metropolitan areas, such as Detroit, is institutionally integrate
in seeking legal advice for the acquisition of personal property and ha
organized access to legal resources for that end. Given the recency of th
acquisition, there is less integration with respect to other phases of th
personal property cycle.

Nonetheless, given the high rate of acquisition of personal propert
among Negroes, particularly in the form of housing, one would foreca:
that Negroes will increasingly seek legal advice for other property matter
as well, although perhaps at a lesser rate. Some indication of this can b
gained from the fact that the only Negroes in the sample to have seen
lawyer about making a will were males aged 55 and older. Twenty-si

PES OF LEGAL PROBLEMS BY SOCIAL BACKGROUND VARIABLES:
:TROIT SMSA, 1967

			Social background variables								
Social status		Education		Home ownership		Age			Religion		
Blue collars	White collars	High school or less	Some college	Rents	Owns	Less than 35 years	35–54 years	55 years and older	Protestant	Catholic	Jewish
35	40	35	43	15	45	30	43	36	36	39	56
15	28	16	33	10	24	9	16	35	19	22	32
12	26	14	30	11	20	7	18	25	15	22	24
11	26	15	24	13	18	13	19	17	18	15	12
13	20	14	23	13	17	18	18	10	13	19	32
12	11	12	11	15	11	14	13	9	14	8	20
9	12	10	12	8	11	14	11	7	11	10	8
7	9	7	11	7	8	7	9	8	9	6	8
4	6	4	6	5	5	4	6	4	4	7	—
2	5	3	5	3	4	5	3	3	3	3	—
3	3	3	3	5	2	5	3	1	4	2	—
1	3	2	2	2	2	4	2	*	2	3	—
2	—	1	2	1	1	3	1	—	1	2	—
1	2	1	2	1	1	2	1	2	1	1	4

:rcent of these Negro males had seen a lawyer about making a will, as
)mpared with 35% of white females and 41% of white males of this age
'oup.

The incomplete involvement of Negroes in the property complex may
·so be related to the much noted fluidity of Negro family structure. This
suggested not only by the fact just cited—that only older Negro males
.ake wills—but by the prevalance among Negroes of seeing lawyers about
.vorces, alimony, and child support. Among Negroes this type of problem
the second most common occasion for seeing a lawyer, with 18% seeking
.e service of a lawyer in this connection. Among whites the problem ranks
1ly seventh at 10%.

It is worth noting in passing that this problem area of divorce, alimony,
1d child support is the only major area where the incidence of seeing a
·wyer shows no relation to income, occupational status, or education.
For all major categories of legal problems other than divorce and related
.atters, Negroes have had somewhat less contact with attorneys than whites.
·owever, as mentioned before, Negro females account for much of the

race difference. Comparing only Negro males to white males, we find th
Negro males are *more* likely to have seen a lawyer about buying, selling,
building a house, about advice in business matters, about traffic ticke
about disputes with employers, and about divorce, alimony, and child su
port. Except in the case of divorce, however, the differences are quite sma
In view of the fact that our Negro males have much less income on t
average than the white males, we can conclude that the Negro male parti
ipates in a number of organized systems that bring him into conta
with lawyers more than might be expected on the basis of income. Looki
at middle income ($7000–$14,999) males, for example, we find that 23
of Negroes and only 8% of whites have seen a lawyer about a divorce o
related matter. On the other hand, even when income is introduced as
control, the greater proportion of whites who have seen a lawyer abo
making a will or settling an estate remains unchanged. Looking only at lc
income males ($6999 and less), we find that 27% of whites and 8% of Negro
had seen a lawyer about a will, and 10% of whites and 8% of Negroes h.
seen a lawyer about settling an estate. Among middle income males ($700
$14,999), the corresponding figures are 19% of whites and 5% of Negro
in regard to a will, and 17% of whites and 2% of Negroes in regard to settli
an estate. In short, income differences play a part in determining acce
to attorneys, but differences in patterns of participation in social organiz
tion, particularly the social organization of property and familial relatior
also affect the patterns of contact between citizens and attorneys.

SEEING A LAWYER: RATES AND INCIDENCE

The preceding data refer primarily to the incidence of seei
lawyers about various types of legal problems. To compute a rate, we wou
need to know what proportion of the sample had experienced a given type
legal problem and then what proportion of that group had seen a lawy
about it. In some contexts this is a less serious problem than in othe
Thus, in a sense, everyone has a problem in connection with making a w
since, though some estates are small, everyone owns something and, thou
some are young, everyone will ultimately die. Further, in some cases, we ha
rough denominators for rates. Because we know who are now home owne
we are led to believe that the rate of consulting attorneys is higher f
Negroes than whites. Holding sex and income constant, Negroes are as like
to have seen a lawyer about buying a home even though *fewer* Negroes a
homeowners. Other matters, such as accidents, can be assumed to be re
atively evenly distributed across socioeconomic categories. Nevertheles
in some categories, e.g., disputes with government agencies and tax pr

ms, it is more difficult to estimate an appropriate denominator for com-
ting a rate. The problem is exacerbated by the fact that the more one
ves for compatibility of problems through applying restrictive definitions
various types of problems, the smaller becomes the number of persons
o have had that particular type of problem, and, in some cases, the
mber who have seen a lawyer about that precise problem becomes too
all to study.

At one point in our interview we attempted to generate case histories
out the respondents' most serious problems. First we took an inventory
the informants' problems in five areas: relations in the neighborhood;
dlord–tenant relations; relations with the sellers of expensive objects;
ations with public organizations; and discrimination because of race,
t, age, religion, nationality, or beliefs. Then we asked for detailed
tories of the two problems which were considered by the respondent
have been the most serious or to have caused the most problems.
r both most serious and second most serious problems considered
parately, about 9% reported seeing a lawyer about the problem. Table 5
mbines the most serious and second most serious problems and examines
em by respondent's race and sex, and by type of problem, indicating the
rcentage who saw a lawyer.

Few gross differences by race status are apparent in Table 5. One dif-
ence merits brief attention since it illustrates differences that may emerge
en rates rather than incidence is made the focus of study. Negroes are
parently more likely to visit lawyers when they face serious trouble with
blic organizations. The percentage who saw a lawyer among those who
ose problems with public organizations as one of their two most serious
oblems is 19% for Negroes and 10% for whites. Yet the corresponding in-
ence figures for seeing a lawyer about a problem with public organizations
cluding police) appear to be higher for whites than for Negroes. In other
rds, whites are more likely to see lawyers about problems in relation to
vernment, but Negroes appear to be more likely to see lawyers about their
st serious problems with government authority. Beyond merely illustrat-
g differences that emerge from variable ways of expressing degrees of con-
t with the legal profession, this difference reinforces an organizational
erpretation of patterns of contact.

Mere differences in access to resources cannot account for patterns of
cess to attorneys in regard to problems of public authority. Not only does
e *possession* of resources create demand for certain kinds of legal services,
t their *lack* also creates demands for certain kinds of services. Citizens
different income levels in different structural locations experience dif-
ent types of problems and are connected to government in different ways.
cordingly they have different probabilities of becoming involved with

TABLE 5

NUMBER OF CITIZENS REPORTING LEGAL PROBLEM AS SERIOUS AND PERCENT DISTRIBUTION OF CITIZENS CONSIDERING LEGAL PROBLEMS AS SERIOUS, PERCENT OF PROBLEMS FOR WHICH LEGAL ADVICE WAS SOUGHT, FOR RACE–SEX GROUPS: WEIGHTED SAMPLE OF DETROIT SMSA, 1967

Type of legal problem	Number of citizens with serious legal problems						Percent of citizens reporting problem as serious						Percent of serious problems where legal advice was sought					
	White			Negro			White			Negro			White			Negro		
	M	F	Total	M	F	Total	M	F	Total	M	F	Total	M	F	Total	M	F	Total
Neighborhood	169	195	364	18	40	58	53	55	45	35	50	44	8	6	7	6	5	5
Landlord–tenant	19	43	62	9	19	28	6	12	9	18	24	21	5	5	5	11	—	4
Purchase of expensive object	172	178	350	22	26	48	54	50	52	43	32	37	17	10	13	9	12	10
Public organization	112	98	210	12	19	31	35	28	31	24	24	24	12	8	10	17	21	19
Discrimination	29	39	68	23	19	42	9	11	10	45	24	32	10	—	4	4	10	7
Total number	501	553	1054	84	123	207	—	—	—	—	—	—						
Total percent	—	—	—	—	—	—	82	76	79	72	74	73	12	7	9	8	9	9

—, no frequency.

194

torneys in relation to government authority. Thus, Negro citizens report
wer difficult problems in relation to government, but their serious pro-
ems with government are more likely to be with police and with welfare
encies and to require legal aid. White citizens report more problems with
blic organizations and more contact with attorneys about public organi-
tions, but their worst problems concern taxes and government services
ther than police and welfare agencies. Their most serious problems with
blic authority do not seem to have the same capacity to draw them into
ntact with attorneys.

In sum, income and location in the social structure may affect contact
h attorneys not only through providing relevant resources but by deter-
ning what types of problems people have. Each problem has its own
terns of constraints and requirements for the use of legal services. Citizens
not brought into contract with the legal profession merely by their
ources but by their problems, institutionalized definitions, and the
cial organization of problem solution.

CONCLUSION

The emphasis on the social organization of legal institutions
the source of patterns of contact between citizens and attorneys must be
en as a corrective to the common view that income in the form of funds
pay for legal representation is the crucial determinant of use of legal
rvices. At the same time this argument must not be misconstrued as a
affirmation of the view that the poor have no legal problems. This allega-
n is occasionally heard within the legal profession, but the claim can hard-
stand against the extensive documentation of the actual and potential
gal problems of the poor. The poor have fewer legal problems only in the
rrow sense that they have fewer problems that the legal profession
bitually serves.

The implication of our findings is that untreated problems exist for all
gments of the community. Organized to serve property and a few other
oblems, notably divorces and accidents, the legal profession provides
latively little professional representation and advice in relation to a broad
noply of problems surrounding such daily matters as the citizens' relation
merchants or public authority. It cannot be said that such problems do not
ist; our survey of citizen problems shows otherwise. But the institution of
gal advocacy is not organized to handle these problems on a routine basis.
is an interesting commentary on the legal frame of reference to note that
e legal scholar has argued that such interests as rights to welfare benefits,

job and retirement rights, and civil rights will only be adequately protect
when lawyers come to see them as property rights (Reich, 1964).

One of our interviews provides a particularly telling example of t
reach of the problem across social strata. One informant, himself a succe
ful attorney, was rather contemptuous of the survey. He could not belie
that our standardized questions could apply to him since he had such rea
access to legal services. Yet, in another section of the interview, this
formant said that he had been cheated by a "gypsy" roofing contractor a
that he had neither initiated legal action on the matter nor consulted ar
one about such a possibility. This respondent was able to combine a comfo
able sense of legal efficacy and a rather restricted concept of the limits
legal action.

Our findings suggest that those who advocate the extension of leg
services through such devices as the neighborhood law office, group leg
service, lay advocacy, and the ombudsman could well found their claim
failures beyond the denial of legal services to the poor.

REFERENCES

Carlin, J. E.
  1962   *Lawyers on their own.* New Brunswick: Rutgers Univ. Press.
  1966   *Lawyers' ethics.* New York: Russell Sage Foundation.
Carlin, J. E., and J. Howard
  1965   Legal representation and class justice. *UCLA Law Review* 12 (January): 381–437.
Conard, A. F., J. N. Morgan, R. W. Pratt, Jr., *et al.*
  1964   *Automobile accident costs and payments.* Ann Arbor: Univ. of Michigan Press.
Mayhew, L.
  1968a   *Law and equal opportunity.* Cambridge: Harvard Univ. Press.
  1968b   Action theory and action research. *Social Problems* 15 (Spring): 420–432.
Reich, C.
  1964   The new property. *Yale Law Journal* 73 (April): 733–787.

Part IV

LAW
AND SOCIAL
MORPHOLOGY

DISPUTE SETTLEMENT AND COMMUNITY
ORGANIZATION:
SHIA MOSLEM AND MEXICAN ZAPOTEC*

Laura Nader

INTRODUCTION

IN AN ARTICLE on "The Use of Typology in Anthropolo
ical Theory" Clyde Kluckhohn (1960) called for more exploratory studi
into typologies of relations. In the field of kinship much of this kind
investigation has been carried on, but what we have done in comparati
law is indeed minimal. Although we do not have abundant data on leg
procedure we probably have sufficient information about cultures fro
different parts of the world so that one could at least construct a descripti
typology illustrating the range of variation in legal procedure. The work
Hoebel (1954), in his book *The Law of Primitive Man*, was in part an attem
to describe this range of variation and to relate complexity in the law
different levels of subsistence.

---

*This paper was presented at the 1962 meetings of the American Anthropological Association in Chica
Illinois. I wish to thank Michael Moerman for his useful suggestions in the preparation of this manuscri

Reprinted by permission of the American Anthropological Association from "Choices in Legal P
cedure: Shia Moslem and Mexican Zapotec" by Laura Nader, *American Anthropologist*, Vol. 67, No
(1965): pp. 394–399.

In this paper I compare the formal conflict-settling procedures in two
llages which share the same subsistence level. They are both peasant
llages and thereby share certain features. There are also many differences
:tween them, but only three differences are specifically relevant in this
scussion: (1) patterns of social grouping; (2) formal political organization;
) the mechanics of settling conflicts by public means. My general aim is to
iderstand what factors affect the choice of settling disputes by court or by
her means. More specifically, I am interested in the relation between legal
·ocedure and types of social grouping

DESCRIPTION[1]

The first village, Libaya, is a Shia Moslem community of the
.etwalli sect with a population size of approximately 1400 people. This
wn, located in the southern Beqá Valley in Lebanon, is not easily found on
map because villages do not get on maps if they are not connected by road,
id this village only had its road a few years ago. It is a town of mud and
one houses interrupted only by the tall whiteness of the village mosque.
·ie people who live here are peasant farmers, some of whom also specialize
carpentry, stone masonry, and other activities. The major crops, wheat
id barley, are subsistence crops and a few people grow the cash crop
·bacco.
The land is divided for use into individual family plots but much of the
nd is owned by one landlord who is absentee. At different times in the life
·cle the household may be extended with two or more nuclear families, or
may be only nuclear. The villagers recognize ten lineage groups in this
mmunity. These lineages are not localized; rather their members are
·attered throughout the village.
Excluding the political and economic control which may be exerted by the
ndlord, there is little of what may be called village government in Libaya.
ccording to Lebanese statute any community of 50 persons or more should
ect a mukhtar and a council. During my stay no mention was made of any
juncil (the members of which are theoretically supposed to function as
ablic decision makers); nor did mention of such a group crop up in the
:hnographic material. Libaya does, however, have a mukhtar, a mayor, who
supposedly elected every four years by the village men. The duties of this

[1] The data upon which this paper is based were gathered during two field trips. Between 1957 and 1959 I
ent nine months working among the Zapotec of Oaxaca, Mexico. This work was sponsored by the Milton
ind at Harvard University, Radcliffe College, and the Mexican government. Fieldwork in the Shia Moslem
mmunity was carried out during the summer of 1961 and supported by a grant from the Institute of Inter-
.tional Studies, University of California.

mukthar are primarily organizational and administrative. He signs deeds
sale, identity cards, bills of assessment, etc. He is theoretically responsib
to the central government for maintenance of peace and for collection
taxes. His position is unpaid and primarily prestigious. There is no villa
court; there is no village police force. If there is a serious dispute, the loc
government gendarmerie will be called in by one or both parties.

In Libaya the position of *mukhtar* has alternated for several generatio
between the two leading and opposed families of the town—the Akls and tl
Abrahams. And when one of these two families succeeds in getting in
power, it usually holds on to the position for ten to fifteen years. Libaya
a village which for as long as anyone can remember has been split into tv
opposing factions based on family alliances—one headed by the Akls, ar
the other by the Abrahams. Each faction (except for the rare marriage l
capture) is endogamous. The balance of power between factions shifts fro
time to time, according to one informant, because one or two of the small
families, described as being peripheral, may ally themselves one way or tl
other. All the recreative as well as political activities and family or life cyc
activities are patterned along lines of this dual division. No one from tl
Abraham group attends funerals, weddings, or participates in the men
winter discussion groups with the members of the Akl group or vice vers
There is almost a touch of humor about this avoidance, especially whe
informants are reporting on face-to-face "noninteraction."

In order to get at the procedures or processes for settling conflicts
collected a series of conflict stories. For our purposes here, I will differentia
between two classes of conflict—the first involves persons within one or tl
other half, and the second involves conflict between individuals belongi
to the two opposing groups or between an individual and an outsid
(i.e., a member of another town). The procedure involving the settlement
conflict within one-half of the town is described as friendly and peacefu
often these quarrels are mediated by older members of the families, or t
awadeem—respected individuals who may be from the same half or fro
nearby Shia towns. Conflicts that arise between the two sides or between
member of the village and an outsider are by far the more serious and are n
settled in this way, although a kind of intermediary is used. This second cla
of conflict usually ends up in the district's civil court at Jeb Jannine, or, if n
settled there, in the Zahle civil court. Remember, there is no court in Libay
Remember also that the *mukhtar*, theoretically at least, is a man who
supposed to maintain peace. But he does not in fact function very effective
as a village peacemaker because of the dual division in the village. He may t
consulted to settle problems for his own side, but he is never called upon t
settle conflicts between the two sides because he is "biased." How then d
Libayans settle such conflicts? This can best be illustrated by citing one sho
case:

There was a man named Hassan from Libaya. He bought a goat in order to feed his three youngsters from her milk. One day Hassan decided to send the goat out to the prairie with the shepherd for one day. At the end of the day the shepherd returned without the goat. Hassan started to look around the village and to ask this one and that if he had seen the goat, but the goat was nowhere to be found. He went to the *mukhtar* and told him the story asking him to accompany him in search of neighbors' homes—that is, those houses which the goat would have had to pass on the way home. They went out and began to search in various homes but did not find anything. The owner of the goat then turned to the *mukhtar* and said "I would like to look in your house to see if my goat is there."

The *mukhtar* and the owner of the goat entered the animal shelter and found the goat lying down on the floor with a young man sitting on her in order to prevent her from raising her voice. The *mukhtar* went over and struck the young man, a cousin of his named Moh. The owner of the goat, one of the worst enemies of the *mukhtar* and a leading member of the 'other side,' left the *mukhtar's* house with his goat shouting and screaming "I found my goat in the house of the *mukhtar*. . . ."

The police came and took the story from both sides. . . . Weeks later the case had been scheduled at the district court. The judge ordered the *mukhtar* of Libaya to come as a witness, since he had indeed been one of the two men who had caught the thief. The *mukhtar* complied once but then refused to return to the court trial because his father and the father of the young thief were first cousins; they had pleaded with him not to go as a witness in the case. When the judge insisted that the *mukhtar* be present, the *mukhtar* began to see various doctors in order that he be given sick permission to be absent. This was done with the help of K.N., the Bekka congressman. The judge would not, however, give his final decision until the *mukhtar* was present.

Now K.N. paid a great deal of attention to this case because the *mukhtar* and his cousin paid him to untie the knot of the case. They did this because K.N. knows the judge personally, and if there was anyone who could make a *wasta* he could. K.N. went to see the judge in Jeb Jannine and talked with him, principally asking him to set the thief free, which the judge actually did. When the goat owner heard that the thief had been freed, he went to Zahle and began to ask, "Who knows the judge, who has influence with the judge? He found such a person. His name was S.H., a man who had been a close friend of the judge since they were studying law together. S.H. prepared for a lone meeting with the governor and pleaded rights for Hassan. . . . The judge then set a hearing date. The *mukhtar*, Hassan, and the two 'lawyers' were there to hear the *mukhtar* tell the story of the goat thief. The *mukhtar* could not lie because what he had said previously was still in the hands of the judge. The judge, finding himself in a dilemma between two friends, decided the case according to the law, and did not pay any attention to any of the *wastas*. He judged that the thief should pay 100 liras to the owner of the goat, that he should spend one month in prison and pay 25 liras to the court. When S.H. heard the decision he refused to accept it, convinced that K.N. had pressured the judge. After this decision in the Jeb Jannine court, S.H. took the case to Zahle, and until this time the case is still with the courts. K.N. is still working by means of the *wasta* method for his client; as for the goat owner, S.H. and J.S., Zahle's congressman, are making *wastas* for him.[2]

There are several interesting things to note about all of the cases. First there is almost no mention made of Moslem written law at the village level. Second, *wastas*—or remedy arrangements—are made by specialists, and for

---

[2] Unfortunately I was unable to witness any court cases during my field trip to Lebanon. Because of a national strike of practicing lawyers, court business was suspended during the summer of 1961.

the most part these *wasta* specialists are Lebanese politicians. Another way to state this is that Lebanese politicians, or aspiring politicians, must by definition be professional *wasta* makers. It is considered the duty of a Lebanese politican to settle the grievances of his constituents and these grievances may deal with murder or stolen goats. Their interest in the settlement of a case is a political one, and not so much an interest in "justice." A single case won in Libaya can mean the votes of half the village. On the other hand, the villager in trouble, if he is to find the right *wasta*-maker, must have a most detailed knowledge of interpersonal relations among the politico-elite of Lebanon, and it is a rather admirable game they play—both plaintiff and defendant—to see who can get to the best connections fastest. In looking for a *wasta*, the Shia Moslem villager comes into contact with a whole series of people, and they may be of almost any religious affiliation (except perhaps Sunni Moslem). The arrangements made about a case are usually made outside of any courtroom and always outside of the village itself—often in the homes of politicians. I was visiting in such a Beirut household and awoke at 6:30 one morning to note that along with the first cup of coffee, the head of the household and his wife received, while still in bed, villagers in singles, in groups, even in busloads. The professional *wasta*-maker, unlike the tribal *sheikh*, is not to judge a situation but rather to use his personal influence to swing the decision of the judge in favor of his constituent. There is a kind of adversariness involved except that the decision of the judge is usually based on the relative efficacy of personal power rather than on the facts of the case.

The Zapotecan town of Ralu'a is both similar and different. It has a population of 2000 people. These, too, are mountain, peasant farmers, with mud houses surrounding not a mosque but a large Catholic church. The inhabitants grow corn, beans, and sugar cane as subsistence crops, and coffee as their cash crop. This town has also been relatively isolated and was connected by road to the state capital the same year that Libaya acquired its road.

There is no landlordism here as in Lebanon; 90% of all Ralu'ans have their own land. Although some households are extended, the predominant family pattern is nuclear. There are no recognized lineages or large family groups as in Libaya. There is general village endogamy.

In very strong contrast to Libaya, there are many ties which link citizens in Ralu'a: ties of kinship, locale, common work groups; there are musicians' groups, savings and loan groups, religious associations—all kinds of ties which link a number of men together in a group or as individuals, but other ties which divide them by linking some of them with different groups. Whereas in Libaya all of the ties that bind merge within one group to cause a dual, deep rift in town, in Ralu'a the groupings by not coinciding, but by countering each other, cause a complexity in relations serving to unify the village as a whole.

The presence of village government, which is outlined in the Oaxacan state code, is immediately symbolized by a large town hall. And within this town hall there are many officials: the *presidente*, the *sindico*, the *alcalde*, the *policia*, the *regidores*, the *secretario*, the *tesorero*, etc. Apart from this village officialdom, there are frequent town meetings.

Three of these men, elected by the town citizens for one year's service, constitute the town court of justice: the *presidente*, the *sindico*, and the *alcalde* (Nader, 1964). The *presidente* and the *sindico* have administrative and judicial duties while the duties of the *alcalde* are only judicial. The following case illustrates how conflicts are publicly settled in Ralu'a:

> Having been detained over night in jail, Francisco Chavez appeared in court today to render his declaration. The plaintiff Manuel Gonsalez, also present, told the following story. The previous night at about 11:00 there were various people in his *cantina* drinking *mezcal*. When Manuel Gonsalez refused to serve Francisco Chavez any more alcohol on credit, the defendant struck Manuel a blow that made him fall over. At this point, the defendant grabbed the machete behind the table and attempted to stab (kill) the plaintiff. It was only because of the other men present that the machete was torn away from him. The plaintiff took advantage of this scuffle to run and call the police. At this point, the *presidente* asked the defendant to speak. The defendant declared that it was true that he had committed all these acts, but that it was only because he was so drunk. "As everybody knows," he said "he has never had reason to fight with Manuel Gonsalez." The defendant asked that the court fine him. The *presidente* decided to fine both parties. The owner of the *cantina* was fined 25 pesos because he had violated the closing hour rule set by the *municipio*. The defendant had to pay 100 pesos on a charge of battery and threat to kill. (If this case had not been settled by the *presidente*, it would have been referred to the *alcalde*.)

DISCUSSION

In summary, then, both towns are peasant farming villages, homogeneous in religion—one being Moslem, the other Catholic. They differ, however, in the following important respects: Libaya is divided into two endogamous groups; it lacks a development of secondary groups not based on kinship or strong alliance to one of the two factions; it lacks a viable organization for village government. Loyalties are unidirectional and directed to the half in which an individual belongs. Conflicts within the half are resolved by the use of go-between intermediaries; conflicts between halves or between a member of one half and an outsider are settled ultimately at appeal courts in larger towns by means of *wasta*-makers who act as biased intermediaries between villager and judge. At the village level, conflict divides by accentuating the hostility which members of each half have toward each other. At the national level, it may be argued, the mechanics of conflict resolution function as an integrative factor. Villagers involved in serious disputes must rely on the formal and informal processes of a civil court which they can often influence only by manipulation of interpersonal relations. Usually this forces Shia villagers, for example, out of the Shia community, into interaction with members of other religious groups. Winning a case in a civil court means learning how to deal successfully with Lebanese officials.

Ralu'a is a village composed of many groups which serve to cross-link town citizens. Loyalties are multidirectional, certainly none being directly antithetical to the village as a united whole. There is a proliferation of secondary groups not based on kinship factors. Conflicts between individuals and groups are publicly solved by means of a court system which succeeds in terminating most cases without referring them to courts outside of the village.

The data suggest that villages with dual organization are incompatible with village court or council systems of settling conflict.[3] It also suggests the reverse: that wherever village court systems do develop (in contrast to where they are imposed), secondary groupings which cross-link citizens will be found. If, as in Libaya, loyalties within the village are only attached to a large kin group or to the intermarrying half of the village, this situation will compete with any system of adjudication that may pretend to be impartial. Villages which have a proliferation of secondary groupings which cross-link citizens, like Ralu'a or Zuni, for example, provide a good setting for councils or courts of adjudication. Also, societies like Tzintzuntzan in Mexico, where in place of various groupings we have a series of social relations based on the dyadic contract, there is absent a unit which can serve as a basis for feuding (Foster, 1961). In Libaya there are two units which may well serve as a basis for feuding and it is more than likely that before Libaya was linked to the Lebanese national scene they probably did settle disputes by means of institutionalized feuding.

Perhaps the reader will object that the contrast presented here ignores the problem of comparable units. This is a question to be considered seriously in any kind of comparison. It is possible, for example, that I should have compared the village court of Ralu'a with conflict settling procedures in one-half of the Shia village, in which case I would have been comparing a court system with the proceedings as carried out by go-betweens. Or I could have contrasted the Ralu'an court with the civil court in Jeb Jannine, in which

---

[3] H. T. Nuñez reports the presence of a dual division and the absence of a village court system for Cajititlán, Galiaco, Mexico.

case I would be contrasting a court of elected peers, as among the Zapotec, with a court of politically appointed, professionally trained judges. In this paper, however, I chose to compare the village unit, that is, the largest number of people who share a common settlement, and recognize that it is common regardless of other differences they might have, because my central question evolved about this unit.

REFERENCES

Foster, G. M.
  1961   The dyadic contract: A model for the social structure of a Mexican peasant village. *American Anthropologist* **63** (1961): 1173–1192.
Hoebel, E. A.
  1954   *The law of primitive man: A study in comparative legal dynamics.* Cambridge: Harvard Univ. Press.
Kluckhohn, C.
  1960   The use of typology in anthropological theory. In *Selected Papers of the Fifth International Congress of Anthropological and Ethnological Sciences*, edited by A. F. C. Wallace, pp. 134–140. Philadelphia: Univ. of Pennsylvania Press.
Nader, L.
  1964   An analysis of Zapotec law cases. *Ethnology* **3** (1964): 404–419.

LEGAL CHANGE AMONG THE CHAGGA OF EAST AFRICA*

Irving Kaplan

COURTS MAY be a source of rule change and one of the institutions contributing to the development of a body of law in a changing society. But if the precepts and notions that emerge in the course of their dispute-settling activity are to have any consequences, they must be communicated to relevant segments of the society. Communication is, however, problematic; it may be facilitated or inhibited by the characteristics of the courts, of their personnel, and of the society in which they function. In this paper I consider some of the dimensions, suggested by the Chagga materials, in terms of which these characteristics may be analyzed. The Chagga, Bantu speakers, live on the slopes of Mount Kilimanjaro in northeastern Tanganyika.

I am concerned with the factors affecting the communication of decisions and the bases of decisions among the courts and between courts and the society at large. The factors here considered are (1) the scale and the degree of differentiation of the societies in which the courts function, (2) the presence or absence of techniques for intercourt communication and the question of the dependence of such techniques on the specialization and pro-

*A preliminary draft of this paper was read at the 60th Annual Meeting of the American Anthropological Association, November 18, 1961.

Reprinted from "Courts as Catalysts of Change: A Chagga Case" by Irving Kaplan, *Southwestern Journal of Anthropology*, Vol. 21 (1965): pp. 79–96.

fessionalization of personnel, and (3) the status of courts and court personnel in the society at large. I discuss only one case the subject of which I believe to be of intrinsic interest, but other materials support my argument.[1]

THE CHAGGA MATERIALS

Understanding of the case and my interpretation of its meaning require a brief description of the Chagga judiciary. In 1952, shortly before I arrived in the field, a new judicial order had been instituted in Uchagga as part of a more general constitutional change. As a result of a curious convergence of British administrative policy and the tactics of a tribal political movement hostile to chiefs, the judiciary had been separated from the executive.[2] Separation was mandatory at the level of the Chagga Appeal Court, the highest court staffed by Chagga, and at the level of the intermediate (divisional) courts, of which there were three. At the level of the local chiefdom (that unit corresponding most closely to the traditional maximal political unit), the members of each chiefdom had the option of choosing a magistrate or retaining the chief as judge. More than half the seventeen chiefdoms chose magistrates; the chiefdom in which the case cited below took place did not. At first appeals lay from the local magistrate's or chief's court to the intermediate courts and thence to the Chagga Appeal Court. Beyond that, cases went to the District Commissioner. A little later the system was altered so that cases went directly from the local courts to the Chagga Appeal Court, and the intermediate court was reserved as a court of first instance for certain types of cases. The intermediate magistrates constituted the membership of the Chagga Appeal Court.[3]

All magistrates were recruited on the basis of educational and other nontraditional achievement criteria. The requirements for the intermediate magistrates—who were also the appeal court—were higher than those for local magistrates. The latter were quite variable in education and experience. The three (later four) appeal court magistrates spoke good to excellent English, although only one had some formal education at the college level. All had worked in or out of the tribal area as teachers or as responsible

---

[1] Much of this material is in Kaplan (n.d.) Some of the issues treated in this paper are considered from a different perspective in Kaplan (1957).

[2] A preliminary account of Chagga political development is given in Kaplan (1956).

[3] In addition to the magistrates, there were assessors. At first they were three elected members of the Chagga Council; but when the Appeal Court became a circuit court, assessors were chosen in each chiefdom on an *ad hoc* basis for each case.

personnel in government posts or in one of the specialized enterprises that have emerged in modern Chagga. All were in their thirties. Only one was of chiefly lineage, but the others were of fairly prominent families.

Now to the case: During the rainy season a local chief was traveling in his own car, which slid into a rut and was bogged down. At a nearby cluster of shops he asked the help of those present. Among them was a local leader of the Chagga Citizens Union, the tribal political movement referred to above. He and a henchman sought to persuade the others not to help the chief. Some were persuaded; others helped.

The local leader of the political group and his supporter were charged by the chief with disobeying an order of the Native Authority (then the official term for a chief). The local court, staffed by the deputy chief and three assessors, found them guilty. The defendants lodged an appeal with the Chagga Appeal Court, which reversed the decision. Its judgment began by lecturing the appellants on their un-Chagga behavior: it had been wrong for them not to respond to an appeal for help and to encourage others to reject such an appeal. But, said the court, a chief traveling in his own car is a private person. His appeal for help was that of a private person to other such persons. He was not, in these circumstances, acting in his official capacity, and the charge of disobeying the order of a Native Authority must be dismissed.

The distinction between action in an official and in a private capacity had not been part of traditional Chagga political ideology. As we shall see, the development of chieftainship during the colonial period had made the emergence of such a distinction possible, but it was not explicitly held by the chief, his antagonists, or Chagga generally. It may be that in a situation more obviously official, for example, the clearing of a public road, these Chagga Citizens Union leaders might have obeyed a chief's order, but this does not mean that they would have been operating in terms of an explicitly held principle.

In this respect, then, the Chagga Appeal Court had made explicit, if it had not introduced, a distinction which could serve as a basis for decision in other cases, affect the behavior of chiefs, and diminish the frequency of some kinds of disputes. Did the event have the consequences mentioned or any others? It is often difficult to determine whether certain effects may be traced to an event of the kind described. It is even more difficult to assert with confidence that such an event had no significant consequences. It is necessary, therefore, to indicate the status of my observations. First, I was in the field at the time the case was decided, although I did not live in the chiefdom in which the case took place. I learned of it only through conversations on tribal political matters with one of the appeal court magistrates. In short, the information was not conveyed to me by public comment or record but by a participant.

Second, I remained in the field for a year after the decision and heard no citation of it, no spontaneous discussion of it, saw no public record of it (despite the existence of a tribal newspaper in which, conceivably, it might have been mentioned). Third, I heard of no case in this period which was decided in similar terms. All of this is not proof that the decision and its grounds had no influence beyond the particular case. It is possible that no case to which the principle applied arose in that period. More to the point, it is possible that the scale and degree of differentiation of Chagga society, to which I shall refer below, prevented my learning of the effects of the decision among some segments of the population. Finally, a year may not be enough to judge the effects of a particular event. Nevertheless, I think it safe to assert that the event had no significant consequences for the development of Chagga law. Moreover, I submit that it was unlikely to have them.

I do not attribute such lack of effect to impenetrable values and existential premises held by the Chagga. Although the distinction drawn by the Chagga Appeal Court was not part of Chagga vocabulary in 1953, Chagga political culture seems to have been open to the Appeal Court's innovation. Obviously the idea was familiar to the members of the court because (a) they had had—for Chagga—considerable exposure to formal, British-controlled education and (b) much of their work experience, especially their current positions, involved such a distinction. They were, after all, "civil service" magistrates. The experience and education of some other Chagga put them in a similar position. Still, such a background was limited to relatively few.

Important too for the Chagga view of chieftainship was British policy, its implementation, and the changing society within which that implementation took place. Little by little the chiefs had been turned into paid administrative officers who had to meet and maintain nontraditional standards in order to get and hold their posts. However, in an attempt to couple traditional legitimation with modern requirements, the local chiefs were chosen from chiefly lineages. At the same time, traditional chiefly functions and prerogatives had been altered, sometimes as a result of official policy. Moreover, the ties between chief and people had withered away. In the years after World War II many Chagga were at odds with their chiefs. This is not the place to spell out the sources and nature of the antagonism. We need only note that it found expression in the intratribal political movement mentioned and helped to provide a milieu in which a redefinition of the chief's role was possible. Granted the assumption that Chagga experience permitted the acceptance of the Chagga Appeal Court's formulation of the role of the chief, what were the obstacles to the formulation serving as a basis for further development of the law?

THE COMMUNICATION OF LEGAL DECISIONS

I turn first to the related dimensions of social scale and degree of differentiation, and their relevance for the communication of legal decisions and their bases among dispute settlers and between them and other members of the society. The contrast between pre-Colonial and modern Chagga with respect to these dimensions helps to elucidate this aspect of the communications problem.

Pre-Colonial Chagga chiefdoms were autonomous and ranged in size from under 5000 to no more than 15,000 persons. In the 50–60 years of European (German, then British) control, thirty-odd chiefdoms were administratively consolidated to fifteen. The population grew from fewer than 100,000 to about 250,000 by 1952. Consolidation and population growth resulted in chiefdoms ranging from 10,000 to 30,000 persons each.[4] Over the years a governmental hierarchy developed, unifying these once autonomous entities. A relatively powerless council of chiefs established in the 1920s gradually gave way to three-tiered administrative, legislative, and judicial structure under a paramount chief by 1952.

An increase in scale is apparent. Here we are concerned primarily with the increase in the numbers of people within the jurisdiction of each local court and, above all, of the appeal court. Given that increase, how are people to be made aware of what the courts do and why they do it?

Social and cultural differentiation have several implications for communication. One of these is so important that it must be mentioned here, although it pertains to the substance rather than the process of communication. Social differentiation implies distinctive channels of experience and ordering of experience, which, in turn, imply that meanings may not be wholly shared and that communication may be difficult in one degree or another. The normative and existential assumptions explicit or implicit in a statement or series of statements by any "transmitter" may differ so much from those of the "receivers" that the latter will not recognize the communication. On the other hand, the statements may be translated or interpreted so that some, if not all, of the meaning is conveyed and takes effect. Thus, in the case at hand, the Chagga Appeal Court magistrates' education and experience were such that they could distinguish clearly between office and incumbent. That education and experience were not shared by many other Chagga, but the political situation was such that a statement of the distinction might have conveyed something to the latter had they received it. The effect of differentiation just discussed is important to the analysis of the problem of the

---

[4]The Chagga political structure included two smaller, non-Chagga chiefdoms in the plain below Kilimanjaro, but these are not considered here.

effect or lack of effect of law-making. As I suggested at the beginning of this paper, however, that problem is not at issue until the communication, at least in part, has been received.

But differentiation has other effects of more immediate concern. Again a contrast between old and new Chagga helps to clarify the issue. Role differentiation in pre-Colonial Chagga was relatively slight. In addition to a chief, there were headmen and a few other political officers. A patron–client relationship based on cattle or land also existed. Finally, there were a few magico–religious specialists and metal workers. There is no indication that the styles of life of any of these differed substantially or that their notions of the way the world works varied significantly. Most important for our problem, Chagga males, by virtue of their participation in the age–set system, had the right and the duty to participate in dispute settling. True, there were some who, because of their closeness to the chief or their recognized capacity in legal matters, were more actively engaged in dispute settling, but genuine adulthood required some involvement of all.

Although the vast majority of Chagga are now peasants, engaged in a varying combination of subsistence and cash crop farming, Chagga society is differentiated in that there is considerable variation in education, religion, occupational experience, and experience of the wider world generally. Most males under sixty have worked or are working for wages, or they are engaged in some enterprise other than or, more usually, in addition to cultivation. The duty to participate in dispute settling no longer obtains (the age–set system disappeared long ago), and the right to do so is limited to being part of an audience. But that right is not often actualized. Coffee cultivation and other gainful activity require an allocation of time such that few Chagga spend much time at court. Many Chagga have some experience of dispute settling, either in the courts of record as parties or partisans or in the informal hearings that take place at a level below that of the local court, but authoritative decisions are not made at that level. Change has brought differentiation and an end to direct, routine, universal participation in legal life, creating another obstacle to communication. There are mechanisms which permit communication, and I shall refer to them later, but they were either ineffective or inoperative among the Chagga of 1953.

COMMUNICATION, SPECIALIZATION, AND PROFESSIONALIZATION

If a court system is to contribute to the development of law in a changing society, the courts must communicate among themselves. Fallers' (1956) treatment of Soga law and some of its developmental problems provides a point of departure from which to approach this aspect of the Chagga situation.[5] The Soga legal system of the 1950s confronted some of the problems faced by that of the Chagga and had not yet solved them. Fallers, focusing primarily on land law, notes that there was little communication among the courts and that decisions in Soga land cases were characterized by inconsistency. He suggests that one way of achieving both consistency and flexibility is to institute a system of case reports which would serve as a source of precedents. Such reports might contribute to the end sought, but several other conditions must also be met if the reports are to be something more than insect fodder. Fallers assumes that court personnel would be concerned or encouraged to use the reports systematically. I suggest that such personnel also would have to be sufficiently specialized (i.e., full time) and sufficiently professional (i.e., committed to and educated in a task and its techniques) to do so. The Chagga met some of these conditions to a degree and others hardly at all.

If we examine the Chagga system in terms of the conditions noted, we find that the courts' records were full and judgments set out at length, both in the upper and lower courts. However, upper court judgments were transmitted only to the local court from which the appeal had been taken and not to lower courts generally. In 1953–1954, the appeal court traveled from chiefdom to chiefdom so that its judgments were heard only by locals.[6] During my stay in the field, occasional meetings of some or all of the court personnel were held, but the matters discussed were administrative and procedural. Substantive law was not dealt with. The physical processes of duplicating and transmitting reports would, of course, have been relatively easy to manage. But here we must come to terms with the notion of precedent and ask whether the Chagga courts did and do—as of 1954—make use of the idea and practice of precedent.

It must first be noted that Fallers's reference to precedent in the context of a discussion of consistency and flexibility in the law assumes an ongoing interchange between a society and its dispute-settling system in which the latter has some autonomy, that is, does not merely reflect what goes on in social life, but channels and chooses. Discussion of law and change often emphasizes the promulgation by an agency of single major changes in a society's rules. Such immediate changes or efforts at change are fairly easily communicated, either because of their rarity or, often, their revolutionary

---

[5] Busoga has roughly twice the population of Uchagga and is, in some ways, quite different (Fallers, 1965), but the similarities referred to in the text and some others warrant comparison.

[6] When the system was first established in 1952, and earlier when selected members of the Chagga Council heard cases on appeal, parties and others concerned would attend a central court, where decisions on cases from one chiefdom might be heard by a few people from other chiefdoms. But there is no indication that effective diffusion was established in that way.

character. When, however, the aim is consistency and flexibility, which require a continuous process of choosing and channeling, the communications problem is more complex. In order to achieve this aim, it may be necessary to have a set of specialists, working in terms of a set of techniques for receiving communications and, after reception, for accepting or rejecting them. That is, reasonably intensive knowledge of some set of principles governing choice, as well as knowledge of substantive law, is demanded of court personnel. Fallers seems to suggest such a set of techniques when he refers to the notion of precedent. He does not, however, elaborate on his understanding of that term.

For the purposes of this paper there are two relevant meanings to the idea of precedent. The first of these is the more or less common sense, nontechnical meaning. Precedent here refers to a tendency to see previous cases as guides to the application of the law, insofar as those cases are thought to be similar to the one at hand. In this sense of the term, precedent plays some role in Western legal systems other than the Anglo-American ones. Even in this sense, however, it did not and does not—as of 1954—play a role in Chagga law. The second notion of precedent, operative in Anglo-American law, is a refinement of the broader one indicated above, but cases are thought of as defining, rather than simply exemplifying, the application of the law. Subsequent decisions take account of previous ones; but which previous case is relevant is not always easy to determine, since no cases are thought of as defining, rather than simply exemplifying, the applica-or its applicability. In this lies the significance of precedent for change *and* continuity.[7] Precedent in the broader sense has similar implications, although previous decisions are not conceived of as controlling subsequent ones in the same way as in the Anglo-American system. Either system is alien to Chagga legal thinking, and the introduction of one of them would require not only a change in that thinking, but the training of technical personnel.

Chagga courts do not refer in any explicit fashion to other cases as illustrations of the way in which a given substantive rule has been applied or its scope and relevance defined.[8] Chagga court personnel do, of course, incorporate experience of previous cases in the background which they bring to cases at hand, but the incorporation is not systematic, and the

---

[7]For an analysis of the role of precedent in American law, the logic involved in the comparison and alignment of cases, and the significance of precedent for change, see Levi (1949). Judicial and legal personnel are not always aware of the nature of the process in which they participate, but they are thoroughly steeped in its specific techniques.

[8]Cf. Gluckman (1955: 255–256 *et passim*) for a similar situation with respect to precedent in the Barotse courts. Gluckman, however, is concerned with whether precedent is or is not an element in Barotse judical process; he does not focus especially on precedent in relation to change.

experience remains unexamined. Chagga Appeal Court magistrates and, very likely, some of the local magistrates are aware of the notion of precedent as it has filtered into their English vocabulary. The best educated of them, the person to whom I owe my being informed of the case cited, used the term in referring to that case ("It might even set a precedent"). But he was using a word derived from one body of experience in a different context, more as part of intellectual play with the anthropologist (who, by the way, did not raise the issue) than as an expression of conviction or as prediction.

While the nontechnical notion of precedent may require a less specialized education than does the more technical one, a higher level of education than that characteristic of most lower court personnel would still be necessary if precedent were to be communicated. Some experience or training in the comparison of cases would have to be part of that education if consistency and flexibility are to result. The foregoing is given more significance if we think of legal development as something more than the addition and subtraction of specific rules. It is probably easier to transmit a rule of the form "chiefs may not order people to pull their cars out of the mud," than to transmit a principle of the sort offered by the Chagga Appeal Court, a principle which has implications beyond what is to be done about a chief's car when it is bogged down. If both consistency and flexibility in change are the ends in view, then principles as well as specific rules must be developed and transmitted.

It may be argued that, even in the absence of a tradition of precedent and personnel educated in the examination of cases, communication might have occurred had two other conditions prevailed, viz., specialization insofar as it refers to full-time activity, and commitment to roles.

All upper and lower magistrates worked full-time at their tasks. Although all were or expected to be holders of homesteads, which ordinarily implies participation in the cultivation of subsistence and cash crops, magistrates were not normally expected to engage in that activity. It was not only a matter of dignity. While their case loads varied with the seasons, magistrates were usually fairly busy. Chagga litigiousness alone did not keep them so. All concerned—British and Chagga—felt that cases ought to be heard quickly and that there should be no backlog. The additional time called for by Fallers' suggestion would probably require an increase in personnel. The Chagga magistrates of 1953–1954 had little time to devote to the total output of appeal court judgments, let alone that of other lower courts. Those chiefs who still acted in a judicial capacity also had administrative tasks. True, administrative and judicial activities were shared with deputies,[9] but neither

---

[9] Before the institution of magistrates (1952), each local chief had a deputy who heard many if not most cases, although the right to act as judge was believed to inhere in chieftainship. Where the chief continued as judge, this practice also continued.

a chief nor his deputy could give the kind of time demanded by a systematic use of court reports.

In the case of commitment, I am concerned chiefly to indicate how court personnel conceived of their tasks and the degree of devotion they brought to them. The appeal court magistrates were interested in what they were doing, and they felt their tasks to be important. In a general and vague way they thought of themselves as contributing to the development of Chagga law, in addition to their acknowledged duty to render judgments efficiently and justly. However, they had no definite notions on how such development was to take place, nor was any attempt made to guide them along these lines. The foregoing remarks on the appeal court magistrates apply to one or two local magistrates who could have met the standards for appeal court magistrates had additional posts been open. The other local magistrates and those chiefs who remained judges were concerned to mete out justice as they understood it, but they had no wider perspective on the law than this essentially tradition-al one. In at least one or two cases, the local magistracy was seen as an available, desirable post, but no commitment to the law seems to have been involved.

The foregoing remarks must be placed in perspective. In any set of roles—in this instance a court system—some incumbents are just "doing a job." To the extent that there are certain prescriptions for role behavior, to the extent that continued role incumbency depends upon such behavior, and to the extent that incumbents may wish to continue in roles for reasons (e.g., wealth, prestige, power) other than commitment to their tasks,[10] the job will get done. When, as in the Chagga instance, there are possibilities but no prescriptions for certain kinds of behavior in a given role, the per-spective of the incumbents and their commitment to that perspective may make a difference as to what gets done. Concretely, in the Chagga situation, if the lower courts were to receive communications from the upper court or from each other, those concerned would have to make a special effort above and beyond the call of duty.

The foregoing may be summarized thus: Some of the obstacles to com-munication among Chagga courts were (a) the absence of a tradition of precedent or the development thereof in recent times; (b) a relative lack of time for existing personnel to devote themselves to tasks other than the hearing and deciding of cases; (c) a lack of commitment to role possibilities other than traditional ones on the part of most personnel. I suggested that,

[10] When roles are open to aspirants—rather than ascribed—those who aspire to and achieve such roles may do so for various reasons. I do not suggest that those committed to (or involved with) certain roles are motivated solely by that commitment. Indeed, one may become involved with a role after he has acted in it for a time. Nevertheless, the notion of commitment is useful for considering performance in roles.

even in the absence of the first, the presence of the last two might have been conducive to greater intercourt communication. I argued further—stimulated by Fallers' suggested solution to Soga problems—that the notion of precedent, were it to be introduced, would require a major reorientation of Chagga legal thought and a specialized education for Chagga judicial personnel.

THE STATUS OF DISPUTE SETTLERS AND OF THE COURTS

The preceding discussion has suggested that, were certain requirements for communication met, the courts might have an important role in the channeling of change, but such a role demands that the courts be recognized arbiters of conflicting alternatives as these are manifest in disputes. Fallers (1956: 144), in his discussion of the Soga situation, remarks:

> The adjustment of differences created by rapid and uneven changes is often made more difficult by the lack of generally accepted "referee institutions"—institutions for the resolution of conflict. Courts and councils, whether traditional or European introduced, are often inadequate for this purpose because their own authority is questioned by one or another section of the community.

In this connection it may be argued that some societies are traditionalist in that rules are not seen as subject to change. Quite recently, Pospisil (1958) felt constrained to argue, on the basis of his New Guinea material, that legal change does occur in relatively simple societies.[11] The basic distinction, nonetheless, is that between those societies in which law is not *routinely* subject to change (although this does not preclude occasional legal innovation or choice of alternatives) and those in which legal development, change, and systematization are institutionalized.[12]

Although pre-European Chagga do not seem to have had an explicit traditionalist ideology,[13] they tended to see their law as given. We must note, however, that their traditional history, particularly as it relates to political

[11] A variety of other materials shows this to be the case, among them that on the Cheyenne; cf. Llewellyn and Hoebel (1941: 127–129).

[12] My statement would require elaboration and qualification if it were to be satisfactorily explained, but such explanation would be beyond the purpose of this paper. Cf. Redfield (1953: 134–135).

[13] Gutmann (n.d.), the chief source on traditional Chagga law, does not deal with this issue. My statement rests on my own work and on the impression I received from Gutmann's discussion.

structure, is one of change,[14] and that there are instances reported from the nineteenth century of innovation or contemplated innovation in specific social relationships (Gutmann n.d.: *passim*).

The modern Chagga view of legal change is complex. They do make new rules. Over the years, councils at various levels and of varying compositions have been given the power to legislate. At times, indeed, the Chagga have seemed much like Americans in demanding that laws be passed prohibiting or controlling behavior that they consider undesirable but in which many of them indulge. With rare exceptions, the rules tend to be either attempts to cope with behavior seen as contrary to traditional Chagga or Christian-influenced morality, or they are rules to deal with quite new situations and relations. Rarely do the councils intrude where customary law is believed to hold sway.

The Chagga are aware of changes in that law, but they accept them as the result of a kind of drift,[15] manifested in cases rather than made by the courts in the process of deciding cases. If there is talk of organizing the law, it is in terms of a code, the basis for which is to be a systematic inquiry of knowledgeable elders, chiefs, and so on. Not included is an examination of court decisions. True, the elders are or have been assessors, and the chiefs have, of course, heard many cases; their notion of the contents of customary law is bound to be influenced by what they have experienced in the course of years of dispute settling. But they are oriented towards the "real," that is, received, law.

Approaches to law similar to that of the Chagga are probably fairly widespread. In the Chagga situation, however, the courts could be more influential in developing the law provided that they were firmly legitimated and the status of their personnel high. The firmness of that legitimation and the status of Chagga court personnel is open to question. I noted earlier that the modern form of the Chagga Appeal Court resulted from a convergence of administrative policy and political conflict. For many Chagga in 1953–1954 the appeal court magistrates were to be perferred to the divisional chiefs or

---

[14] Dundas (1924, Chapter II) recounts some of the oral history of the Chagga, in which a major theme is the development of chieftainship in an acephalous society. Whatever charter functions such a history may have, it is also possible that it represents historical truth to a degree.

[15] Llewellyn and Hoebel (1941: 278) consider *drift* a relatively unnoticed lumping and shifting of behavior, a mode of change contrasted to *drive*, which involves conflict and tends to force issues into consciousness. In other words, a drift is established by the observer-analyst. I use the term in a related but different way, viz., to refer to the way in which a people see change in their law. In this perspective, the behavior governed by rules has drifted, and the behavior of the courts, reflecting these changes, has also drifted. Insofar as we are dealing with behavior which has led to dispute and resulted in a decision, some of the issues will have been brought to consciousness. Nevertheless, when behavior has firmly shifted, the Chagga usually see it as "just having happened," an attitude quite consistent with a legal culture which is not case oriented.

their deputies, and the local magistrates to the local chiefs. Some of the more fiery antichief people expected the magistrates to be an arm of their movement. While the appeal court magistrates, at least, were responsive to political trends insofar as these signified modernization to them, they were not responsive to immediate political demands. The courts did not, therefore, acquire immediate popularity. In short, the new system was more or less acceptable to many Chagga for negative rather than positive reasons.

Where the local courts were still in the hands of chiefs, the appeal court magistrates were sometimes seen as upstarts; the magistrates felt this. In these circumstances what the appeal court did was even less likely to be construed as directive for the lower courts. Where magistrates sat in the lower courts, they were sometimes closely tied to the chief, despite the fact that they had been chosen as alternatives to him. In any case they did not look to the appeal court as a source of law or to its members as their leaders in law. Within the chiefdom, the magistrates had no extraordinary prestige. Their office too had come into being out of an antipathy for incumbent chiefs, and they had yet to establish their legitimacy in positive fashion.

It may be argued that any functioning court system has *some* legitimation, that its personnel have *some* status. The foregoing discussion is predicated precisely on that assumption. If the Chagga courts were completely divorced from Chagga social life, if the Chagga rarely resorted to them for dispute-settling purposes, there would be no point in asking why the courts did not communicate to the members of the society or to the Chagga powers-that-be (chiefs, Chagga Council, and so forth) on matters pertaining to legal development and change.[16]

Finally I should like to examine an unrealized possibility in Chagga legal development in the context of my remarks on legitimation and the notion of precedent.

At the time of my stay in the field, two elements in the governmental system seemed to enjoy high regard—the Paramount Chief and the Chagga Council, the latter to the extent that it was identified with its elected members,[17] most of whom were also members of the Chagga Citizens Union. The paramount chieftaincy had been established in large part because of the pressure of the Chagga Citizens Union, and its incumbent had been

---

[16]Victor LeVine has reminded me that there are communities in Africa where traditional dispute-settling arrangements are preferred to parallel arrangements instituted by colonial or post-Colonial governments. In such instances, where the imposed system is barely legitimated in the eyes of most of the community, it would be futile to raise some of the issues here discussed. In the Chagga instance, however, the courts recognized by the higher authorities are also the courts recognized by the people, and it is useful to pose problems as to the kind and degree of legitimation they enjoy.

[17]The nonelected members were mostly chiefs, but they had relatively little power in the Council if the Paramount Chief and the elected members acted together. Moreover, the chiefs were then behaving as official members, i.e., taking direction from the Paramount Chief.

the choice of the Union, although he was not himself a member. Communication from these two elements (Paramount Chief and Chagga Council) to governmental units at lower levels (chiefs and councils) and to the Chagga generally were good in the sense that they were heard, if not always accepted. Both Paramount Chief and Chagga Council benefited from a kind of charismatic legitimation, but they also had available to them a variety of communications mechanisms, official and unofficial, formal and informal, written (including a tribal newspaper) and oral. Transmissions from various authorities to the courts were heard by the latter.[18]

The relatively firm legitimation enjoyed by the Paramount Chief and the Chagga Council might have permitted them to act as a communications link between the courts, which did not enjoy such legitimation, and the people. Just as important, the chiefs in council, had they heard and responded to communications in the form of decisions from the courts, might have given the courts an opportunity to play a role in legal development. Courts may play such a role even if they do not function in quite the same way as they do in systems of the Anglo-American tradition. Whatever the ideal or actual functions of the courts, the issue is whether their decisions are considered not merely as settlements of particular disputes but also as attempts to deal with the underlying problems of the relation of rules to behavior and of rules to other rules. This issue must be clearly understood if the contemporary Chagga situation is to be compared with developed systems generally rather than with Anglo-American systems alone. Moreover, insofar as change starts from a given base, any analysis of the Chagga instance, which has no tradition of precedent, must deal with existing potential. The point is best illustrated if we note that, in the particular Chagga case treated in this paper, the decision of the Chagga Appeal Court need not have been treated as precedent in any technical sense in order to have been meaningful in the development of the law. The Chagga Council need only have taken the case and the judgments of both courts as indications of an issue needing legislative resolution.

SUMMARY AND DISCUSSION

In the foregoing analysis of some Chagga materials, I suggested that the process in the development of substantive law and the relation of such legal development to behavior depend, at least in part, on communication among the dispute settlers and between them and the society in which

---

[18] Although magistrates were chosen by the councils from among those who applied, and the courts were linked to different levels of local administration for some administrative purposes, general supervision was exercised by a district officer.

they operate. I then considered some factors affecting communication in the Chagga situation. I argued that increases in the scale and degree of differentiation in Chagga society constitute obstacles to communication between courts and people, and that the lack of time and the absence of sufficient commitment on the part of court personnel are obstacles to communication among the courts. Finally, I suggested that the status of the courts and their personnel in Chagga society are not conducive to communication between them and the members of the society, and that status relations among judical personnel tend to limit intercourt communication.

Historically, the onset or increase of differentiation has tended to accompany an increase in scale. The relationship is not a simple one and, in any case, the dimensions of scale and differentiation may be analytically separated.

It is suggested, as the first hypothesis, that communication between courts and people decreases as the scale of the society increases. An increase in scale (in this case, the size of the population over which the dispute-settling institution has jurisdiction) tends to remove members of the society from direct participation in dispute settling. Ecological considerations may, however, have an effect. Specifically, an increase in scale may mean an increase in population density or it may involve population dispersal over a larger area. Conceivably, an increase in density may enhance certain kinds of communication (e.g., back-fence gossip).

I noted earlier that the Chagga had developed no mechanism to mitigate the decrease in communication entailed by the increase in scale that had taken place among them. In the Chagga instance, the increase in scale was accompanied by an increase in differentiation. If, however, we consider the dimension of scale alone, obstacles to communication might be dealt with by the institution of representation in a society where the representatives are not significantly different in experience and outlook from those represented, although they might devote much of their time to the activity and may know and use better what some know and use to a lesser degree. Such representatives would mediate a flow of communication—in both directions—between courts and people. An increase in scale may also be met by an increase in the number of dispute-settling units, but such a solution may lead to another kind of communications difficulty—that among courts.

The second hypothesis is as follows: Communication between courts and people decreases as differentiation increases. In my discussion of the Chagga I was concerned chiefly with the consequence of differentiation for the allocation of time, such that those who once typically participated in dispute settling no longer do so. Again, the Chagga developed no mechanism to deal with this obstacle to communication. Representation is one such mechanism, but the legitimation of representation may be difficult where differentiation rather than scale alone is at issue. One institution, the Chagga Council, might have acted in this representative capacity, but it did not.

Here a caveat may be entered. Historically, societies of high differentiation and great scale (complex societies) have a high rate of communication between courts and people. Writing, printing, and, most recently, telecommunications, as well as a specialized corps of persons (lawyers) who represent the society and the courts—all contribute to a two-way flow of communication. The hypotheses worked out in dealing with the Chagga material apply, therefore, to like societies, that is, those which have begun to increase in scale and degree of differentiation but have not developed those specialized mechanisms or institutions which effectively take over the communications task.

The Chagga materials do not suggest directly testable hypotheses with respect to the dimensions of specialization (time allocation) and professionalization. My earlier comments on these matters do provide some queries or perspectives in terms of which other situations may be considered.

Important conditions controlling communication from courts to people and among courts are those having to do with the status of court personnel and the legitimation enjoyed by the courts.[19] I point up the issues by contrasting briefly Chagga society of the 1950s with old Chagga society on the one hand and modern society on the other.[20]

Old Chagga society seems to have been one in which the distribution of status and power was not altogether settled. Nevertheless, status arrangements (prestige and deference), control over economic resources (cattle, land), and the allocation of authority (rights, powers, privileges) were more or less congruent in the sense that one who ranked at a given point with respect to any one of these values tended to rank at relatively the same level with respect to the other two. This schematic analysis is, of course, a simplification of the facts; there were aspects of old Chagga stratification arrangements which do not fit neatly into it, but they are not relevant to our present concerns. It is possible that some or all of the members of the society might have rejected the substance of a communication from a chief, but it is highly unlikely that they would have failed to receive it.

In modern societies, incongruities in and among stratification systems exist: persons are differently or ambiguously placed in, for example, the

---

[19] The notions of social stratification and legitimation here used derive, with modifications, from Weber (1947, 1954, 1958).

[20] The comparison of two concrete systems with an abstraction—modern society—is a device and does not imply more than the terms of comparison indicate.

power and status hierarchies; the bases or criteria for stratification may be uncertain or even conflicting. Even so, if governmental systems are firmly legitimated, the institutionalized communications system will work; that is, relevant members of the governmental system and those members of the society to whom decisions apply will hear about and be influenced by them. The substance of the communication may be rejected, but as in the old Chagga society it will not go unheard.

Unlike old Chagga society, Chagga society of the 1950s was characterized by stratificational incongruity. Unlike modern stable societies, it was not characterized by a firmly legitimated governmental system, although segments of that system varied in the extent to which they were legitimated. Traditional Chagga criteria for status and authority had given way to a mixed and uncertain set of criteria which included wealth, education, and ascriptive considerations. The formulation of authority roles and the allocation of personnel to them was not a settled matter in the view of many Chagga. Among other things, persons who were not members of the society, such as colonial administrators, had an important voice in that formulation and allocation. Moreover, the system of authority was a matter for political debate, and Chagga life was sufficiently politicized so that status was, in some respects, a political question; for example, the granting of deference might depend on one's political stand.

To summarize: in societies marked by stratificational incongruity and an insufficiently legitimated court system, communication from courts to people decreases as the status of court personnel decreases; and communication from higher to lower courts decreases as the degree of consistency between the hierarchical position of personnel in the court system, on the one hand, and in the general status system, on the other, decreases.

Most or all of the independent variables in the hypotheses offered above are likely to be relevant in any concrete situation. It may be difficult, therefore, to determine their relative power in specific situations. They are, however, analytically distinguishable; they provide perspectives from which situations may be approached; and they are so formulated that data may be brought to bear to support, negate, or modify them.

ACKNOWLEDGMENTS

Victor LeVine of Washington University provided helpful comments on the first version, and Lloyd A. Fallers on the penultimate one. I obtained the Chagga materials as a predoctoral area research fellow of the Social Science Research Council, 1952–1954.

REFERENCES

Dundas, D.
1924   *Kilimanjaro and its people*. London: J. F. and G. Witherby.
Fallers, L. A.
1956   Changing customary law in Busoga District of Uganda. *Journal of African Administration* 9 (1956): 139–144.
1965   *Bantu bureaucracy: A study of integration and conflict in the political institutions of an East African people*. Chicago: Univ. of Chicago Press.
Gluckman, M.
1955   *The judicial process among the Barotse of Northern Rhodesia*. New York: Free Press.
Gutmann, B.
n.d.   *Chagga law*. New Haven: Human Relations Area Files. (Orig. pub. 1926.)
Kaplan, I.
forth- Land, law and change among the Chagga. Ph.D. dissertation, Department of
coming Anthropology, Harvard University.
1956   Chiefs and intra-tribal politics: A Chagga case study. *Anthropology Tomorrow* (Graduate Anthropology Club, University of Chicago) 4 (1956): 107–130.
1957   Truth, land litigation and social change: Chagga. Paper presented at the 59th Annual Meeting of the American Anthropological Association.
Levi, E.
1949   *An introduction to legal reasoning*. Chicago: Univ. of Chicago Press.
Llewellyn, K., and E. A. Hoebel
1941   *The Cheyenne way: Conflict and case law in primitive jurisprudence*. Norman: Univ. of Oklahoma Press.
Pospisil, L.
1958   Social change and primitive law: Consequences of a Paupan legal case. *American Anthropologist* 60 (1958): 832–837.
Redfield, R.
1953   *The primitive world and its transformation*. Ithaca: Cornell Univ. Press.
Weber, M.
1947   *The theory of social and economic organization*. New York: Oxford Univ. Press. (Orig. pub. 1922.)
1954   *Law in economy and society*. Cambridge: Harvard Univ. Press. (Orig. pub. 1922.)
1958   *From Max Weber: Essays in sociology*. New York: Oxford Univ. Press.

Part V

LAW AND COLLECTIVE ACTION

REVOLUTIONARY LAW IN SOVIET CENTRAL ASIA*

Gregory Massell

INTRODUCTION[1]

THIS STUDY is concerned with a problem central to comparative politics in a world of new nations pursuing stupendous goals: how, and to what extent, political power—and specifically, legal engineering—may be deliberately used in the revolutionary transformation of societies, especially those we generally call "traditional societies." It pursues that concern through a study of the interaction between central power and local traditions in one of thee peripheral areas of the Soviet land mass, Soviet Central Asia. And it is most especially concerned with the meaning and impact of large, abstract, impersonal political blueprints of great

*This article is a slightly revised version of a paper read at the Annual Meeting of the American Political Science Association, Chicago, Illinois, Sept. 8, 1967. It is a by-product of a general inquiry into the problems of strategy in planned social change in which I am engaged with the support of the Center of International Studies at Princeton University. I am grateful for the facilities the Center has placed at my disposal.

[1]I have not taken for granted in this paper any previous acquaintance with the literature on Soviet Central Asia—the sociocultural context from which the data for this study are drawn.

Reprinted from "Law as an Instrument of Revolutionary Change in a Traditional Milieu: The Case of Soviet Central Asia" by Gregory Massell, *Law and Society Review*, Vol. 2, No. 2 (1968): pp. 179–211. This is a shortened version of the original paper.

movements and figures when pursued by ordinary men in the small, concrete, and intimate worlds of human relations, on the manipulation of which the achievement of all revolutionary goals ultimately depends.

Specifically, this study examines the role of legal rules and institutions (pertaining to personal status and family relationships, and hence, in this context, to sexual equality) in inducing, in conjunction with a series of other political drives, a full-scale revolution in traditional Islamic societies under Soviet rule in the late 1920s—that is, in the early, experimental stages of communist revolutionary attempts in Central Asia.[2]

LAW AS AN INSTRUMENT OF REVOLUTIONARY CHANGE: THE QUEST FOR REVOLUTIONARY ACCESS AND INFLUENCE IN A TRADITIONAL MILIEU

At the inception of Soviet experiments in social engineering (mid-1920s), Central Asia combined enormous size (almost half the size of the United States) with a relatively small population (circa 15 million). The population included three principal ethnic groups: Turkic (Uzbeks, Turkmens, Kirghiz, and Kazakhs); Iranian (mainly Tadzhiks); and—about 10% of the total—Slavic (Russians, Ukrainians, and Belorussians). Formally, most of the indigenous population had been Moslem ever since the Arab invasions in the eighth century. The structure of traditional occupations in the area comprised sedentary pursuits of the oases and lowlands (agriculture, commerce, and artisan trades), and nomadic pastoralism of the steppes, deserts, and high plateaus (stockbreeding and caravan trade). The educational pattern was overwhelmingly traditionalist in nature; the few schools were staffed and controlled by Moslem clergymen. The illiteracy rate at the time of the October Revolution was almost 100%. The social structure of indigenous communities tended to reflect basic subsistence patterns: local traditional societies were organized around kinship units in relatively self-sufficient communities, by and large along patriarchal, patrilineal, and patrilocal lines, with residues of tribal organization most pronounced among the pastoral nomads and, to a lesser extent, among the mountaineers.

A highly complex pattern of social and cultural pluralism was amply reflected in the region's legal institutions. What is very important, Tsarist

[2]The substantive material in the text that follows, including direct quotations as well as specific references to Soviet views and to events in Central Asia, is based almost entirely on Soviet sources—all of them in Russian, and none of them available in English translation.

colonial administrators had made no significant deliberate and concerted attempt to transform the prevailing sociocultural and legal patterns, after Russia completed the conquest of the area toward the end of the nineteenth century. This meant that, at the inception of the Soviet experiment, the revolutionary regime confronted in the legal realm no less than in others a heterogeneous and multilayered universe. Aside from Russian statutory law (governing primarily the relationships of the region's European newcomers), two major categories of law were in operation here, affecting especially in the civil realm the bulk of the indigenous population: codified Moslem law (*shariat*) and local customary law (*adat*). As a rule, *shariat* was administered by formal canonical courts staffed by qualified Moslem religious personages. In this form, the system was operative primarily in urban and sedentary agricultural locales. The *adat* depended neither on a written code nor on formal administration; the resolution of disputes tended to be entrusted to tribal leaders, to clan and village notables, and/or to local Moslem clergymen. This system tended to be operative primarily in tribal, nomadic–pastoral milieus. In terms of Georges Gurvitch's legal typology, the legal systems of Central Asia's traditional Islamic principalities (such as Bukhara and Khiva) had a "theocratic-charismatic" base; the legal systems of primitive "polysegmentary" social organizations (especially among nomads and mountaineers) had a "magical–religious" base (see Gurvitch, 1942: Ch. 4; cf. Almond and Powell, 1916: Chs. 6 and 9). Yet even these two broad categories of judicial legitimation and arrangements are ideal-typical in nature. Reality was considerably more complex. Central Asia subsumed an extremely variegated patchwork of religious and tribal tribunals, usages, and laws. In such a context, conflict resolution could be formal or highly informal, public or private, and the prevailing legal forms, norms, and practices depended to a large extent on the particular region, communal organization, and ethnocultural milieu, as well as on the personal charisma of the particular judicial mediator.

The social pattern could hardly offer serious direct resistance to the establishment of Soviet power in the period between 1917 and 1921. Yet as bolshevik strategists were shortly to realize with growing unease, the very pattern of local traditional solidarities and orientations that had made the cluster of Central Asia's traditional societies so fragmented, communo-centric, and insular, and thus so accessible and vulnerable to the determined thrust of modern Soviet power, tended also to make them particularly elusive to attempts not merely to "establish" a mechanism of power but to use it for rapid revolutionary transformation and efficient integration.

The modernization process, even when relatively sedate, always contains elements of suspenseful confrontation. In few cases, however, has it been quite so dramatic as in the attempted modernization of Central Asia under

Soviet auspices. One reason for this is that the drive toward modernization did not, by and large, come out of Central Asia itself, nor primarily from a local elite, nor even a local counterelite commanding the support of an "expectant people." The outside powers, moreover, had an exceptionally extravagant vision and explicit ideology, as well as remarkable revolutionary elan and impatience. *Per contra*, the societies to be transformed were at an especially low level of social and economic development, as different from that postulated by the Marxist theory of revolution as they could possibly have been; they were also, relatively speaking, highly intact and integrated, that is, lacking in relatively large, significant, and politically experienced groups that were both alienated and marginal. The drama of modernization in Soviet Central Asia thus arose from a huge gap between the social structures existing and those envisioned; from the lack of significantly disintegrated structures readymade for refashioning; and from great verve and urgency on one side and a deep imperviousness to manipulation on the other.

This drama involved only partially, however, the confrontation of traditional society and revolutionary men. Equally dramatic were the conflicts engendered by that confrontation among the revolutionaries themselves, men (and women) whose ideology—originated, developed, and intended for application in Western industrialized societies—had in no way prepared them for dealing with what existed in Central Asia. To be sure, in Leninism the Bolsheviks had an ideological weapon that combined a strong voluntaristic and teleological bias with equally strong organizational, interventionist, and manipulative dispositions. But Leninism was also markedly ambivalent regarding specific transformationist strategies to be employed in the conquered societies, especially in the Central Asian context. Thus, the Bolsheviks' experiences in Central Asia, even more so than elsewhere in the Soviet Union, compelled them to rethink many problems and to reconstitute many organizations and instrumentalities, but since they were men of firm—and rapidly rigidifying—philosophy, and since there were vested interests in the organizations, this process did not come about without grave internal strains.

At first, then, we have in Soviet Central Asia a rather simple encounter between revolution and tradition, reflecting the simplicities of early Soviet politics in the large. There was a belief that disadvantaged men (and most men in traditional society were "disadvantaged") would readily take to a social transformation carried out by dedicated reformers operating new formal and legal institutions superior to the old. This belief was encouraged by the apparent ease with which the revolutionary takeover was accomplished in Central Asia; by the Marxist–Leninists' apocalyptic view of revolution itself, a view considering violent revolution as a final and definitive act, a consummation rather than a mere beginning; and the belief, shared by communists with other children of the Enlightenment, in the great strength of rationally devised social machinery as against the implicit norms and networks of informal expectations of prerational society. There was to be revolutionary machinery, and revolutionary products would issue from it as a matter of course.

The failure of that wonderfully hopeful approach, perhaps more crushing in Central Asia than anywhere else, was the first great trauma of Soviet rule. It was not so much that the revolutionary machinery was attacked and incapacitated by reactionary strata. Rather it was that the new institutions could not even begin to permeate the vast regions of society outside of the urban administrative centers, and that, in so far as they did gain entrance, they tended not to transform accustomed ways but to be themselves "traditionalized," to provide merely a new setting in which affairs proceeded much as before. As Marx and Engels would have visualized this, Central Asia's traditional elites (religious, tribal, and communal) turned out to stand "in the midst of society," in that they continued to command respect and authority at the grassroots. The agents of the Soviet state stood "outside and above" that society (Engels, 1942: 156).

There were several possible responses. One was to use the coercive power of the regime to excise the more manifest obstructive elements (especially the traditional elites) and to force the general population into compliance with revolutionary ways, thus accomplishing quickly revolutionary ends. Another was to find a weak link in society, a surrogate proletariat where no proletariat in the real Marxist sense existed, to recruit from it reliable native cadres and to use them, by slow and systematic processes, first to loosen and disintegrate traditional social relationships, then to rebuild society when its very dissolution compelled reconstitution. Access to the traditional structures to be transformed could then be viewed either as a negative process of forcibly removing obstructions or as a positive one of finding willing and useful collaborators, or as a combination of the two. But both approaches have a crucial point in common, one that has wide significance for the deliberate transformation of any and all societies: transforming social institutions that still are going concerns presupposes a prior weakening, if not utter destruction, of the institutions to be transformed, and hence the discovery of crucial actors whose deliberately engineered alienation and separation from the institutions will cause these to be drained of vitality.

The initial Soviet political reflex in this case was essentially an orthodox one, reverting to a hard, fundamentalist Bolshevik bias—to attack the obstructive elements head-on, and to excise them from the local body politic. Without waiting for either political, or economic, or cultural development to take its course, the party decided to attack directly the network of traditional authority relationships, and to strike it at a point that could logically be considered its nerve center and its head. It called upon its cadres to subordinate everything to the requirements of "class struggle" in the traditionalist countryside, and to concentrate, first of all, on "undercutting . . . isolating . . . [and then physically] removing" the traditional elites of Soviet Central Asia. Such a decision involved more or less explicit expectations: that the liquidation of traditional elites would presumably amount to a political decapitation of the traditional command system; that it would thus serve to remove the linchpin from the formal organizational structures of local communities and tribes. As a result, local social structures would presumably collapse, the hold of primary and local groups upon their members would break down, and minds as well as bodies would be released from the previous equilibrium and set adrift, as it were, and be delivered into the Soviet fold.

Yet, what seemed to disturb the regime above all while the attack was in progress was that the separation of traditional leaders from their followers, even when successfully carried out—which was not everywhere the case— did not make a community automatically available for Soviet-sponsored mobilization. Far from being supplanted by considerations of property and bureaucratic status, the old unities based on kinship, custom, and belief showed signs of persisting even in the absence of traditional figureheads and presented just as great an obstacle to the diffusion of Soviet influence as before. As perceived by Soviet analysts, these obstacles continued to group themselves around two basic, and intimately correlated, traditionalist propensities in the dealings of local groups with outsiders: secrecy and solidarity. If anything, intensified Soviet pressures upon tribal and communal leadership seemed, at least in the short run, to strengthen the resolve of communities and groups—or even to activate fresh or previously dormant dispositions—to guard the walls of secrecy and internal solidarity.

What came to be perceived in this context, at the apex of the party, as a crucial desideratum in Central Asian conditions was nothing less than a "cultural revolution." As communist organizers saw it, the blow dealt to tribal–patriarchal elites was but one blow, and possibly not the most crushing and important one. One needed to deliver "a second blow," one that would destroy the residues of "tribal–patriarchal . . . ideology"—an ideology that, through persistent loyalties and habits, made it possible for old kin and custom-based unities to survive even when the old elites were gone. One needed approaches that would reliably disengage human beings from the matrix of traditional ties, values, and beliefs. Where was one to begin? The answer, as one party analyst saw it, could be as dramatically unorthodox as it was apparently simple: "the real battle against harmful . . . tribal–

patriarchal residues ... [against] the survivals of the old order ... [blocking the path of Soviet development], must begin from the destruction of the old ... family—of that primary cell of the conservative [Central Asian] village, [a cell] that refuses to surrender its positions to [the forces of] the new ... [world]." Moreover, if the key to a genuine cultural revolution was in the destruction of traditional family structures, the undermining of the kinship system itself could most speedily be accomplished through the mobilization of those of its members who were the most consistently "humiliated ... [and] exploited," who were, as a rule, segregated, secluded, and constrained, who were in effect, "the lowest of the low," "the most enslaved of the enslaved": its women.

Accordingly, while the overall Soviet assault on Central Asia's Moslem traditional societies proceeded on a number of levels, and with widely varying degrees of success, one essential facet of that assault came to be the deliberate attempt to stimulate and manipulate sexual and generational tensions that would help to induce an upheaval in a traditional system of values, customs, relationships, and roles, beginning with the primary cell of that system: the extended, patriarchal Moslem family.

The Quest for Strategic Leverage Points in a Traditional Milieu: Moslem Women as a Surrogate Proletariat

REVOLUTIONARY ACTION AS STRATEGIC LEVERAGE

At least three basic propositions were implicit in the decision to use women to break up Moslem traditional societies. First, that "class struggle," in some socieites, did not need to express itself exclusively through social strata conventionally designated on the basis of property and relation to the means of production. Second, that "patriarchism" characterized authority relationships not only in large and complex social organizations in Central Asia but also, and perhaps most strikingly, in the primary cell of the native traditional world, that is, in the extended family. Third, that in such a milieu, social status, and hence potentially social tensions, could be based as much on sexual as on economic or other roles.

There was at least one congenial ideological precedent for such a view. Engels had written (1942: 51, 58):

> The *first division of labor* is that between man and woman for the propagation of children. . . . The *first class opposition* that appears in history coincides with the development of the antagonism between man and woman in monogamous marriage. . . . The *first class oppression* coincides with that of the female sex by the male. . . . The modern family contains in germ not only slavery (*servitus*) but also serfdom, since from the beginning it is related to agricultural services. It contains *in miniature* all the contradictions which later extend throughout society and its state (partially quoting Marx—eds.).

One factor made such an analysis particularly relevant where Central Asia was concerned. Marxist references to female inferiority in a capitalist industrial system were relatively marginal illustrations of the hypocrisy and inequality accompanying the struggle between the classes. In the case of the emergence of the patriarchal family, however, the thrust and imagery of the analysis placed male–female relationships at the center of the class struggle.

It helped to strengthen conclusively the arguments of those who had been insisting all along that there were highly unusual opportunities for revolutionary action in Moslem traditional societies, and that women were the key to those opportunities. To deliberately proceed on the assumption of a woman's dumb, isolated, subordinated, exploited, depersonalized, will-less, and loveless existence could presumably help the party find more than merely additional social leverage in Central Asia. Deliberate and planned utilization of this issue could prove to be social dynamite par excellence. It could attack what might be potentially the weakest link in the solidarities of native kinship systems, and could thus speed up immensely the processes both of social disorganization and of reintegration under Soviet auspices.

In this sense, it seems fruitful to visualize Soviet experience in Central Asia as a complicated search for strategic factors in a revolutionary transformation—for techniques, instrumentalities, and targets that would provide the regime with relatively high leverage in undermining and transforming a Moslem traditional milieu. In other words, it was a quest for a structural weakpoint through which particularly intense conflict could be engendered in society and leverage provided for its disintegration, the recruitment of sympathetic elements from its ranks, and, finally, its reconstitution.

Of course, to the extent that Soviet goals involved the deliberate disruption of an entire milieu, one of the primary problems in such a purposive enterprise was that of control. Soviet experience suggests—to borrow Anatol Rapoport's terms (1966) from another context—an attempt to induce a strategic conflict at the nerve centers of a social order and to avoid a cataclysmic one; commensurately, control of the revolutionary process turned out to be one of the most sharply perceived imperatives in Soviet experiments with social engineering, perhaps more so in Central Asia than in other parts of the Soviet Union.

REVOLUTIONARY ACTION AS ACTIVATION OF
A SURROGATE PROLETARIAT

To turn from conventional categories of class struggle to the role of the family and its members meant to turn from macrocosmic perceptions of social revolution to microcosmic ones; from abstract to intimate and detailed preoccupations in social engineering; from settled notions of social process and action to research, experiment, and improvisation; from class struggle to the novel, and unfamiliar, realms of sexual and generational tension; from a real proletariat to a surrogate for it.

Where a Moslem woman was concerned, party activists could reason—certainly not without some psychological justification—that under the seeming bedrock of her traditional entrapment there seethed deep currents of humiliation, frustration, and hatred; and that these currents could be shaped into elements not just combustible in the short term but inherently and fundamentally subversive to the entire spectrum of traditional behavior, relationships, and norms. It was not of decisive significance whether a woman's fate was, in her own perception, as bleak as the party saw it, or wished it to be seen. More relevant: there was a possibility that the very terms of contact with unprecedented concepts of human existence would hold up an extraordinary mirror to a woman's eyes, letting her see herself as she had never seen herself before; that they would activate currents of unaccustomed restlessness, agitating minds and feelings into a search for ways to establish the newly perceived identity, to realize a novel sense of human worth and potentialities; that they would, in effect, raise to a conscious level the sense of outrage on account of existence that could not fail but be perceived as being, relative to men, dramatically inferior. A woman might endure perpetual inferiority, degradation, and segregation, but only as long as she lacked the capacity to visualize, and the opportunity to grasp, alternative possibilities. As soon as the psychological and organizational barriers were breached—as soon as the past and future were perceived in a radically new light—a dramatic turnabout could not fail to take place.

The party's tasks were thus twofold. To maximize female revolutionary potential, it was necessary to maximize female discontent, and to minimize the obstacles in the way of a woman's perceiving, articulating, and acting upon that discontent. Along with this, it was the party's task to find the right keys to the latent revolutionary currents, and the right molds for harnessing the unleashed forces and channeling them in desirable directions —that is, to find optimal social controls for unleashed social energies. This would require careful engineering: as good an estimate as possible of the linkages, in every conceivable sphere, between female mobilization and broader social transformation; of the specific advantages and forms of utilizing female revolutionary energy; and of the ways in which the latter could contribute to, or endanger, the stabilization, legitimation, and development of the revolutionary regime itself.

Given such requisites, what were Soviet expectations regarding the actual operational opportunities and potentials? How could women be used to help in the revolutionary transformation of a traditional society, and what impact could such use be expected to have? The Soviet plan of action (a plan that crystallized only gradually, and that was by no means consistent and continuous) may, perhaps, best be visualized in a series of propositions—propositions that constitute a brief and selective projection of the imperatives and premises underlying the Soviet action-scheme, that relate immediate means to ultimate ends, that are interdependent, and that fluctuate in emphasis within a spectrum from moral to instrumental considerations, from revolutionary idealism to cold political pragmatism.

1. *To emancipate women as individuals—and, with women, the young generation:* from "slavery in the feudal-patriarchal order" of kinship, custom, and religion, and thereby fulfill the egalitarian strictures of Marxism with respect to the family, as well as engage the humanitarian and reformist impulses of important segments of the emerging male and female elites in Russia and Central Asia.

2. *To undermine the prevailing patterns of traditional authority:* based on lineage, kinship, conquest, custom, religion, and age, as well as on the absolute superiority of men—by endowing women with unprecedented sociopolitical roles, and backing these roles with an organizational framework, with educational and material opportunities, and with the legal and police power of the new state. By the same token, to undermine the backbone of a traditional community's political cohesion, and ease and hasten, thereby, the grafting and assimilation of new Soviet authority patterns at the grassroots.

As a corollary, *to politicize the latent or actual grievances of the most disadvantaged females*—especially of orphans exploited and tormented by a hierarchy of guardians, and ready to run away; of girls separated from lovers by elders' authority and force; of girls feeling themselves deprived and stifled under parental authority; of child brides married to old men; of young women married to unloved and cruel men; as well as of widows and divorcees—making them especially disposed to burn their bridges to the old world altogether, to enter the Soviet fold, and to actively seek vengeance. This would help the regime to gain, in effect, a political fifth column in the Moslem traditional milieu. By being disposed to act in such a role, women could be uniquely suitable elements in depriving native kinship units and village communities of their salient traditional advantages in dealing with outsiders—their secrecy and solidarity.

3. *To undermine the kinship system and the village community:* revolving around clan loyalties, and ties of family and custom—by endowing women with unprecedented social, cultural, and economic roles, by encouraging and sponsoring divorces initiated by women, and by involving them in massive and dramatic violations of traditional taboos, such as mass-unveiling in public, playing of dramatic female roles on stage, open competition with

males in sports events, and assumption of martial roles in paramilitary formations, including the operation of airplanes, the use of parachutes, and the handling of guns.

As a corollary, *to compound the power of attraction upon male as well as female youth,* by stressing a new accessibility of the sexes to each other, an accessibility based on free choice and no longer dependent on customary and religious rules, or on tribal, communal, or paternal authority, an accessibility involving unprecedented dimensions of contact, courtship, and romantic love. By the same token: either to subvert the traditional realms and hierarchies of loyalty and socialization, and thus release women and/ or youth into Soviet socializing media, or gain inside those realms exceedingly important allies in bringing up the young generation—present or future mothers.

4. *To significantly weaken some crucial moorings of Islam in native societies:* especially the codified religious laws of *shariat,* and the main repository of local customary laws, the *adat*—by endowing women with unprecedented civil rights, by backing those rights with a new and especially tailored judicial system, and by staffing that system, in part, with women. To revolutionize traditional attitudes toward the clergy, by suggesting, among other things, that the latter's presumed spiritual guidance of a man's wives and daughters could easily go hand in hand with sexual exploitation; and by wooing especially women—traditionally the most numerous and submissive clients—away from the influence of Moslem "teachers," village "wise men" and "holy men," and tribal shamans.

As a corollary, *to break the monopoly of knowledge, and of political, adjudicative, intellectual, educational, spiritual, and consecrative functions,* held by males in general, and by traditional elites—religious, tribal, and communal —in particular, thus helping to undermine the status, authority, as well as livelihood of these elites. To help subvert, thereby, not only the claims of religion and custom upon human beliefs, values, commitments, and ties, but, also, the hold of religious and customary institutions upon the hierarchies of society and family, the administration of justice, the system of education, property relations, and the overall pattern of daily life.

5. *To disorient and weaken the prevailing concepts of property:* by bringing into question the woman's role as, in bolshevik interpretation, her father's means of exchange, and her husband's beast of burden, chattel, and property in marriage; by forcefully stressing and challenging the entire range of her legal and customary inferiority, particularly with respect to her control and inheritance of property, including land; and by endowing her with unprecedented roles and capabilities in the sphere of economic activity.

As a corollary, *to compound the power of attraction upon poor and socially disadvantaged males*, by stressing a new availability of brides that would no longer be dependent on the social status of a man and his family or clan, or on the requirements of property in the form of the locally traditional bride price (*kalym*) and thus endowing the males' sense of sexual deprivation with overtones of social, economic, and political deprivation, making the conflict over women into a potential fulcrum for a sharpening class conflict.

6. *To gain, in the heretofore secluded female masses, a large and reliable labor pool, and a potentially important reservoir of technical cadres:* so as, in the short run, to maximize the scope and tempo of economic development (particularly in the growing of cotton, the production of silk, and the expansion of textile, clothing, and food industries) and, over the longer term, to release the productive and creative potentials of a traditional society. By the same token, by recruiting women *en masse* into novel forms of economic activity, and by encouraging them to play unprecedented roles in that sphere, to remove the traditional "middlemen"—fathers, brothers, and husbands—standing between women and the economic market place, and thus to create optimum conditions for their economic independence from husbands, families, or clans, and for their attraction to, and socialization in, the Soviet system. Simultaneously, by gaining in women a maneuverable labor force, to free corresponding contingents of men for tasks wherein women were relatively less suitable, such as exceptionally heavy labor or service in the army.

As a corollary, *to compound the emotional pressures upon the whole male population—by exposing it, in every role, in every enterprise and sphere of life, to unprecedented competition from women*, thus, at a minimum, depriving men of the traditional haven of unquestioned acceptance and superiority in the family and in public life; making it, therefore, necessary for men to seek new—that is, Soviet—criteria of self-assertion, self-esteem, competence, and accomplishment; and, hence, stimulating their economic performance and political cooperation—if not outright loyalty and full-fledged participation.

7. *To recruit, through and among women, political, administrative, medical and educational cadres:* cadres that would reliably staff and expand the network of Soviet influence and control, including the new system of communications, health, education, and welfare; cadres that would thus not only dramatize the new relations of the sexes, but would serve directly as sharp political tools, and assist deliberately and actively in the fragmentation of tradition. In this fashion, to gain in women, and especially in young women, unique agents as well as catalysts in the overall revolution of modernization, and in the shaping of new foci of sociopolitical integration under the auspices of the Soviet regime.

As a corollary, because the endowment of Moslem women with unprecedented social, cultural, economic, and political roles would take place entirely under Soviet auspices, and because women's training, organization, and socialization could thus be substantially *de novo*, it could be expected not only to elicit the women's exceptional gratitude and cooperation, but also to allow the Soviet regime exceptionally broad leeway in the allocation of values, skills, resources, and manpower, in the collectivization of handicraft and agricultural production, and in the overall coordination of initiatives called for by both modernization and control.

8. *To compound the power of attraction upon other traditional societies— sharing ethnic identity or cultural and historical experience with Central Asia's peoples—outside Soviet borders*, and hence spur revolutionary ferment in the colonial and semicolonial world, through the buildup of egalitarian and high-achievement imagery in the realms of youth and sex; to open up, thereby, unprecedented potentials for the formation of a revolutionary and modernizing elite and elan.

REVOLUTIONARY LEGALISM AND SOCIAL ENGINEERING: THE USES AND LIMITS OF SUPERIMPOSED RULES

The multifaceted justifications for work with Moslem women were, of course, designed to secure the party's acquiescence in ideologically unorthodox initiatives, as well as its maximum support with cadres and funds. But, if the party's high command came to see the promise of such action, and accordingly proceeded to set in motion a number of initiatives on this account, it also came to perceive sharply the dangers implicit in such an undertaking. To attempt a sudden and full-fledged mobilization and emancipation of Moslem women, to stage an all-out, undifferentiated assault on the realities and symbols of sexual apartheid and female inferiority in a traditional Islamic world, was to initiate what was perhaps the most overtly illegitimate action in that world.

Revolutionary Action as Insurgency by an Incumbent

The perception of, and responses to, this dilemma undoubtedly played a crucial role in the evolution of Soviet approaches to female mobilization in Central Asia. Concerned ever more concretely with the extension of Soviet influence from urban hubs to a vast countryside, with the creation of reliable access routes to the grass roots of Central Asia's societies, with the subversion of established native solidarities, and, simultaneously, with laying a groundwork for an efficient mobilization system, the Soviet regime found itself in need to strike a balance between a host of conflicting impera- tives. While these were subject to repeated questioning and revision, and were affected not only by the Central Asian milieu but also by the ferocious struggle of wills and views inside the party, *the action-scheme that evolved in the process was analogous to insurgency—albeit insurgency generated and controlled by the incumbent and, therefore, governed both by the requirements of social revolution and by the imperatives of incumbency itself.*

As such, insurgency by an incumbent could not but entail some inherent paradoxes. In Soviet Central Asia it was designed to set in motion a course of tensions, conflicts, and selective violence, and hence an upheaval in the traditional system of values, customs, relationships, and roles within the existing structures of society. In effect fundamentally reversing the essential order of Marxist expectations, it marked an incumbent's deliberate effort to induce insurgent attitudes, a deliberate effort to induce a pervasive sense of alienation from traditional commitments, orientations, and modes of life, and a commensurate attraction to radically new ones—those furthered by victorious revolutionaries. Basically, then, this process had twin purposes: that of inducing a psychological and organizational revolution at the nerve centers of a relatively intact social order, and that of consolidating and legitimizing the incumbent's power. It turned out to be of fundamental importance that the imperatives of insurgency could not be reconciled with the imperatives of incumbency, since both sets of imperatives were gener- ated, and needed to be weighed, by one and the same party—the incumbent revolutionary Soviet regime.

Not all of the relevant implications of this dilemma were anticipated by the party's organizers, and some were anticipated with greater sensitivity than others. Moreover, some of the consequences, while anticipated quite perceptively by a number of the party's field workers in Central Asia, were either underestimated or deliberately ignored by leading echelons on ideo- logical grounds, and were acted upon only after precipitous political initia- tives revealed just how disastrous the consequences could be. Nonetheless, Soviet initiatives tended to order themselves into a definite pattern. Soviet experience suggests three paths to making a revolution beyond the mere winning of political incumbency. These are "revolutionary legalism," "administrative assault," and "systematic social engineering." While this typology involves a rather high level of abstraction, it does reflect quite closely the predilections, commitments, and actions entertained in Soviet ranks in the early experimental stages of revolutionary transformation. The three strategies of planned social change may be conceived as three main steps in a learning process on the part of Soviet revolutionary elites, a process with what were at first rudimentary, though by no means negligible, feed-back mechanisms. This process led, over a relatively short period of time, to repeated assessments of costs and payoffs of a particular strategy, and to a periodic quest for courses of action that would combine optimal fulfillment of Soviet goals with minimal risk, given the resources available to the regime. For the purposes of this paper, we have concentrated primarily on revolutionary legalism, and on the specific perceptions and pressures that led Soviet leadership to repeated redefinitions of that strategy in the broader context of revolutionary social action (see Massell, forthcoming).

Revolutionary Law as a Tension-Management System[3]

The use of law as one of the Communist Party's strategic approaches to revolutionary change may be said to have involved the intro-duction of a *specialized tension-management system into a traditional milieu*, a system combining tension-inducing and tension-controlling purposes. Specifically, the strategic objectives came to be: to induce (positive) tensions that would fundamentally undermine the traditional order (the target sys-tem), and, at the same time, to control those (negative) consequences of induced tensions that threatened to affect the stability of the Soviet regime (the sponsor system) and the safety of its developmental objectives. In other words, a new legal system had both to encourage and to maintain a delicate balance between disequilibrium and stabilization, fragmentation and inte-gration, social revolution and orderly development. Moreover, it had to take into account not one homogeneous universe of clients, but, as we shall see, many—and overlapping—social interests and groups.

Implications of Tension-Inducing Action:
Law as a Heretical Model

Soviet views of law were, from the very beginning, frankly instrumental. As perceived by the regime, Soviet law was designed for three basic purposes: to destroy the antecedent social order; to ensure the dis-cipline of a population mobilized to create a new industrial system, as well as to ensure the security of the Party-State that generated and administered this system; and to serve as a means in building a communist society. This paper is primarily concerned with the first of these purposes.

---

[3] Moore and Feldman (1962) have proposed to view society itself as a tension-management system. It should be fruitful to explore the linkages between their and our analytical approaches to society and to law, respectively.

Revolutionary legalism as a strategy of social change emphasized reliance on a newly superimposed judicial system for the routinization of revolutionary norms in traditional society. It reflected expectations that by supplanting traditional adjudicative institutions, and by vigorously championing and applying the principle of equality of the sexes before the law, the new judicial system would set in motion a full-fledged revolutionary process. As the highest Party and State echelons affirmed in the mid-1920s, "the Eastern woman's ... actual emancipation [will be attained through] the full and exact implementation ... of Soviet laws" pertaining to women's rights in all realms of social life, beginning with family, marriage, and property. In other words, the desired shift in female status would occur primarily as a result of the regime's emphasis upon, and of popular acceptance in Central Asia of, the new legal norms and institutions simply because they were legal. Female emancipation was viewed, at this point, as primarily a juridical problem, to be solved by a stress on strict legalistic consistency. It is in this sense that revolutionary legalism may be characterized—to paraphrase Judith Shklar (1964)—as an ethical and political attitude that holds moral and politically requisite conduct to be a matter of rule-following, and moral as well as instrumental relationships to consist of duties and rights determined by rules that are imposed and enforced by revolutionary elites.

Potential Functions of a Heretical Model

In its norms, forms, procedures, and personnel, and in its massive and detailed concentration on sexual equality, the new legal system in Soviet Central Asia constituted a fundamental challenge to the structure and life-style of local communities. Indeed, it constituted a powerful *heretical model*.

It was heretical in that

a. in and of itself, it constituted deliberate and absolutely autonomous legislative action by secular authority in any and all, including the most sacred, realms of life—something that Islamic orthodoxy has long regarded as by definition not only heretical and illegal but a contradiction in terms, given the avowedly revealed, comprehensive, and perfect nature of Moslem law;

b. rather than merely questioning the interpretation of one or another belief, it called into question the basic assumptions underlying the prevailing belief and value systems, and thus invited radical skepticism about the moral basis of society;

c. rather than merely calling for some adjustment in one or another dimension of social esteem, it threatened a *total* abrogation of the primordial status system, beginning with the structure and hierarchy of sexual and generational roles;

d. by assigning drastically new meanings to authority and domination, and to religious, communal, and affinal obligations, it negated ancient paradigms of solidarity and trust, sanctioned the abrogation of traditional social controls, and cast grave doubt on the justice, utility, and hence legitimacy of the entire social order;

e. in addition to engendering a revolutionary interpretation of the present and the past, it formulated radically new goals for the future, thus engendering unprecedented aspirations with respect not only to rights but also to roles, possibilities, and opportunities, and hence encouraging individual concerns deeply at variance with and apart frnm those of the local group;

f. in making tabooed issues a matter of open concern, it threatened, in effect, to make many latent conflicts manifest.

While, in this sense, the new legal system was profoundly heretical, it could also serve as a tangible model in that

a. rather than involving merely the sporadic propagation of whispered or printed doubts on the part of deviant men or groups of men, it was a negation of the social order embodied in a system of laws and courts forcefully grafted and backed by the overwhelming power of a state;

b. in marking not only a departure from particular precedents but a complete abolition of all antecedent judicial channels and procedures, it claimed a monopoly of the legal universe;

c. in turn, no matter what its intrinsic merits in the eyes of the population, it was always visible and available, perennially calling for utilization, and thus serving as a constant catalyst and exerting constant leverage;

d. insofar as Moslem women, for example, pioneered in using its services, enacting its precepts and, most important, joining the ranks of its personnel, it constituted a palpable standard, a consistent alternative, for comparison and choice.

Implicit in such operations of a heretical model were aspects that were both defensive and offensive, therapeutic and punitive, integrative and disruptive, purposes that involved both learning and unlearning. Hence, in a deliberately induced revolutionary situation, the new legal system might be expected to function, at one and the same time, (a) as a repository of new ideal norms, (b) as a parental surrogate, (c) as a focus of grievances, (d) as an instrument of mobilization, (e) as an arena of participation and recruitment, (f) as a trip wire, (g) as an instrument of class struggle, (h) as an instrument to extirpate the antecedent legal system, (i) as a protective shield for revolutionary agents and converts.

There might have been expected to be at least four basic categories of clients affected in diverse ways by the function of Soviet law as a heretical model. If short-term Soviet operational objectives—based at least in part on female mobilization and emancipation—involved the productive intensification of class struggle in the traditional milieu and the resultant unraveling of the traditional social fabric, the attitudes and responses of these four client-categories had to be taken into account.

(1) *A principal beneficiary client group*, including of course primarily women.

(2) *A secondary beneficiary client group*, including primarily unmarried young and poor men, owning neither land nor flocks, that is, men socialized in traditional values and solidarities, but lacking authoritative standing both in private and in public realms, lacking significant access to material and spiritual goods, and lacking significant access to women as well, such access having been traditionally delimited by ritual, hereditary, authoritarian, and financial considerations.

(3) *A secondary adversary client group*, including primarily married (monogamous) men, either poor or moderately well off, that is, men with a large but limited stake in the traditional order in the sense of having access to women and commanding patriarchal authority in the kin group, but having relatively little authoritative influence at the supra-familial level of community or society, and relatively narrow access to material and spiritual goods.

(4) *A principal adversary client group*, including primarily polygamous, well-to-do, or socially esteemed patriarchs, and the surviving authoritative traditional elites (religious, tribal, and communal), that is, men with a very high stake in the traditional order in the sense of having relatively broad access to, or actually controlling the allocation of, a community's social and political statuses as well as material, spiritual, and sexual objects.

On purely rational grounds, the Soviet regime could expect to find in the first group not only natural followers and friends but also enthusiastically devoted agents. In turn, the successful mobilization of the first group might have been expected to intensify the adherence and participation of the second group, and its delivery of what could be viewed as the regime's natural allies. While the third group had relatively greater cause than the first two to be repelled by Soviet initiatives and goals, it might have been expected to have commensurately little incentive to stake its life on the defense of the status quo; it could be expected to remain at least cautiously neutral and tacitly accommodationist to Soviet revolutionary approaches through law. For obvious reasons, the fourth group could certainly be expected to muster the regime's staunchest and natural enemies. Yet, given its originally small size, the thinning of its ranks through Soviet-sponsored deportations and executions, a measure of internal division (e.g., into red/progressive and black/reactionary *mullahs*), the shattering impact of large-scale defections from tradition on the part of kinswomen, kinsmen, parishioners, and countrymen, as well as the ever growing threat of draconic Soviet sanctions, it might have been confidently expected that the fourth group would find itself increasingly isolated and shorn of influence, and that it could in any case do very little damage.

The cumulative effect could thus be assumed to be obvious: a marked acceleration of a shift in the psychocultural and political orientations of virtually *all* clients. Explicitly or implicitly, nuances of precisely such expectations were advanced by communist field organizers in justifying Soviet revolutionary initiatives. The concurrence of the highest echelons of the party was indeed reflected, in part, in official proposals that the revolution in Central Asia be spearheaded by a political alliance of "landless farmhands . . . poor peasants [and nomads] . . . and women."

Yet, even this relatively subtle turn of political judgment ran afoul of social reality. It turned out to be exceedingly difficult, if not impossible, to distinguish friend from foe in any meaningful or reliable way. First, the perceptions and responses of the women themselves turned out to be far from homogeneous in intensity, orientation, and value. Second, the attitudes and behavior of male clients turned out to be determined at least as much by old unities based on kinship, custom, and belief as by new, legally ensured considerations of property, bureaucratic status, and sex. Third, and perhaps most important in the short run, the performance of the new Soviet apparatus—the "sponsor system"—composed in the lower echelons of largely native cadres was itself subject to the same complex parallelogram of loyalties. In other words, it was found to be difficult to replicate in reality the simple "rational" dichotomy between "we" and "they," between "sponsors" and "targets" of action, between the worlds of "revolutionary agents" and "traditional clients." There were numerous additional complications, such as

a. the extent to which a native Soviet official was a self-selected or deliberately planted representative of his kin, communal, or ethnic group;
b. the extent to which he wished or felt obliged to maintain contacts with the traditional milieu;
c. the extent to which his professional activity in the Soviet apparatus placed him in the traditional hinterland or in the largely Russian and Soviet urban milieu;

d. the extent to which his arrival in, and benefits from, the Soviet apparatus were due to his own or to the regime's exertions, and due to ideological or to instrumental considerations;
e. the extent to which his joining the new agencies involved traversing great cultural distance, as well as recruitment from relatively low social, economic, and political status;
f. the relative position he occupied in the new Soviet hierarchy of authority and status;
g. the nature and intensity of his political convictions.

Needless to say, this meant that the sponsor groups could contain at least as many self-perceiving beneficiaries and adversaries, in this case, as the client groups, and that the challenge-and-response flows between them could not be as simply drawn as in a one-to-one relationship. Ironically, then, the revolutionary potential of a surrogate proletariat turned out to be as problematic and elusive as history has shown the political moods of the real proletariat itself to be.

Initial Moves

Soviet approaches to revolutionary change through law proceeded on two planes: (1) the decreed abolition of traditional court structures, including religious and customary tribunals, and their replacement by a secular, uniform, centralized, bureaucratic, and hierarchical system of Soviet courts; and (2) the decreed abolition of religious and customary law, applying (for the purposes of this study) to personal status and family matters, and their replacement by a secular, egalitarian, uniform, and written code of statutory laws.

In the period between 1918 and 1927 traditional courts were subjected to gradually increasing pressure. This included (a) growing competition from a parallel Soviet court structure, (b) separation from sources of material support, (c) infiltration of judicial personnel, and (d) delimitation and successive amputation of jurisdictional realms. In September 1927, traditional courts were formally proscribed and abolished.

In the course of the same decade, successive legislative enactments gradually extended the list of proscribed customary relationships and conduct. In April 1928, a new and fairly exhaustive code of laws—*On Crimes Constituting the Relics of the Tribal Order*—was enacted by the Russian republic (for the non-European minorities on its territory) and incorporated within a few months, with only minor variations, in the legal systems of the Central Asian republics. In addition to proscribing a number of customary forms of intertribal and interclan relations (such as blood vengeance and blood money for claimed loss, damage, or dishonor) the new code addressed itself virtually to the entire range of manifestations denoting status inferiority on the part of women. The catalog of proscribed acts included bride-price (*kalym*, carrying sanctions against both giver and receiver of payment), child marriage, forced marriage (involving either physical or psychological coercion), marriage by abduction, rape (with or without intent to marry), polygamy, levirate, as well as mistreatment and killing of wives. The sanctions ranged from a year of hard labor for polygamy, to up to three years of jail for forcing a girl into marriage, to death for the murder of a wife.

A separate series of decrees and constitutional guarantees were promulgated with the express purpose of ensuring the absolute equality of the sexes. Thus, on the one hand, marriages concluded under traditional religious auspices were declared to be invalid; only registration in appropriate Soviet state agencies, accompanied by proper evidence regarding age, health, and mutual consent of the marital partners, could make the unions legal. On the other hand, a number of women's rights were spelled out, contravening the very core of religious and customary prescriptions regarding sexual apartheid and female inferiority: the right to initiate divorce (as against a Moslem male's prevailing right to unilateral divorce action through simple repudiation); the right to equal succession (as against religious or customary provisions for female inequality in the inheritance of property); the right to equal witness in court (as against specific Islamic stipulations that the testimony of two female witnesses be required in contesting the testimony of one man); as well as the right to full-fledged participation in public life—including general education, professional training, and participation in all sociocultural, economic, and political pursuits, services, and organizations on equal terms with men. The latter denoted not only voting but also service in all, including the highest, elective and appointive public offices in the land—with early and special emphasis given to service in judicial roles in the new Soviet court system. In recognition of the obvious possibility that overt acceptance of legal rights might go hand in hand with covert denial of real opportunities to exercise these rights, Central Asian republican constitutions incorporated explicit provisions for sanctions in cases of "resistance [by anyone and in any form] to the actual emancipation of women."

At the same time, an attempt was made to set three interrelated processes in motion outside of the legal realm, all designed as enabling vehicles to spur female mobility and self-assertion, and thus to undermine the mainstays of female dependence, segregation, and seclusion not only in public life but also in the private realms of family and home.

(1) Cadres of the Party's *zhenotdel* (Department for Work with Women) were instructed to commence, in cooperation with appropriate industrial, agricultural, labor, trade, health, education, and welfare agencies of the

state, the organization of "Councils of Women's Delegates," clubs, stores, vocational centers, literacy and hygiene circles, and health centers catering especially to women, and to use such new associational foci as forums for political agitation and recruitment.

(2) *Zhenotdel* cadres were assigned to the task of personally encouraging Moslem women to sue for divorce from cruel, unloved, polygamous, or otherwise unacceptable husbands, and personally supervising and assisting them toward this end in court.

(3) The entire party and state apparatus in Central Asia, including *zhenotdel* cadres, was instructed (a) to elicit public demands, especially on the part of Moslem women, to ban female veiling; to float such demands as trial balloons in all mass media, and to determine the feasibility of a legal prohibition of the veil; (b) to organize (beginning with March 8—Soviet Woman's Day—1927) mass meetings and demonstrations of women in a number of Central Asia's larger population centers; at these meetings to encourage–through the personal example of native communists' wives and daughters, through the example of especially assembled Turkic (particularly Tatar, and hence unveiled) women from outside the region, and through special provisions for police protection—the massive and dramatic unveiling of Moslem women in public, and the burning of their veils in great bonfires on village and city squares, including squares bordering on Central Asia's holiest Islamic shrines.

Initial Results: The Pattern of Popular Response—Females[4]

The response of indigenous Moslem women to the norms and thrust of Soviet legal engineering was varied in the extreme. It tended, at least at first, to be dependent on the attitudes and actions of males in general and the tug-of-war between traditionalist and Soviet forces in particular. Broadly speaking, female response may be said to have ranged from what might be called avoidance and selective participation to militant self-assertion and uncontrolled involvement.

1. AVOIDANCE

During the initial period of Soviet emancipatory initiatives in Central Asia in legal and extralegal fields (1925–1926), what appears to have been the majority of Moslem women showed few if any signs of being interested in, or affected by, the unprecedented developments. They did not unveil; they

---

[4]It should be kept in mind that not even a rough quantitative distribution of modes of response on the part of the relevant actors can be attempted at this point. Accessible Soviet sources have so far given no meaningful cues on this account. When Soviet Central Asian archives are opened to scholarly perusal, some rough estimates might become feasible.

failed to vote or otherwise assert their newly proffered rights; they avoided contact with Soviet agents and institutions; and, most importantly, they failed to bring their grievances to Soviet courts.

In attempting to explain this peculiar lack of response, communist field organizers came to the following conclusions:

Moslem women in the traditional hinterland were not really aware of the new Soviet legislation and of the rights and opportunities it promised. In most cases the only people who could inform them about their civil rights, and urge them to utilize these rights, were native (i.e., male) Soviet officials, and they in particular were not going out of their way to do so. Thus, the disadvantaged either did not know about, or did not know how to take advantage of, the new world embodied in the new law.

The psychic world in which a Moslem woman lived constituted a "primordial wall" which one needed to break through. This wall was made up of "primordial habits and religious fanaticism," of "wild customs and superstitions," and it stood guard over a "slough of darkness and culturelessness." That world had made the woman "passive," engendering the feeling that "her slave-like position in the family and her isolation from society were predetermined from above [were decreed in heaven], were eternal and inviolable." Laws alone—"no matter what kind . . . and how good . . . they were"—could hardly be expected to make a dent in such a world.

Precisely because—without "long-term preparatory enlightenment work" by the party—these women were "not fully aware of their own slave-like existence," they considered all contacts with strangers as a "[mortal] sin," compounded by their living in perpetual fear of their fathers, husbands, brothers, or guardians, and of condemnation by the community as a whole.

In certain situations a woman had especially pressing, concrete reasons not to bring her grievances to a Soviet, or any other court. This was especially true in cases of human interaction in intimate situations. Thus, if a woman was abducted with intent to marry, and raped on the way, she either had to marry her abductor or risk becoming an outcast in her own community, since she had no other place to go. Under these circumstances, she was not likely to report the violation in a Soviet court lest she burn all her bridges behind her.

2. SELECTIVE PARTICIPATION

Under certain circumstances, and in certain locales (especially in urban and within close proximity to urban locales), women did show signs of willingness to assert, albeit selectively, their new rights. If contacted by a woman (especially by a kinswoman or a woman of the same ethnic and cultural background) and in circumstances considered natural and harmless by the dominant male in the family, they were disposed to bring up relatively frankly their grievances, needs, and hopes. If provided with segregated electoral districts, they appeared, even if hesitantly at first, at the polls. If provided with tangibly practical incentives (such as scarce consumer's goods, vocational and household counsel, medical assistance for themselves and their children, a chance to earn extra income or merely a chance to enjoy and participate in collective entertainment), and if assured of a secluded (i.e., segregated) situation, they showed an interest in joining a Soviet-sponsored club, a handicraft or consumer's cooperative, or a literacy circle in close vicinity of their homes. But in all cases they tended to retain their veils—at least on the way to and from the new milieu—to remain completely within the confines of their traditional community, and to shun communication, commitments, and actions that would in any way violate traditional taboos and provoke opprobrium or wrath from the community or kin group.

3. MILITANT SELF-ASSERTION

In relatively urbanized locales, in especially engineered emotional situations, and under close personal guidance by congenial leaders, some women (especially maltreated wives, wives of polygamous men, recent child-brides, menial employees in well-to-do households, orphans, and divorcees) showed themselves willing to exercise their rights and challenge the traditional status quo through massive, public, and dramatic violation of traditional taboos. Encouraged and trained in the relative isolation of the first women's clubs, some indigenous women were persuaded to enact (unveiled) female roles in the theater, and to give concerts and to dance in public. Especially recruited by female agents of the communist party's *zhenotdel* (Department for Work with Women), some Moslem women volunteered to run on the party's ticket and to be elected to public posts in "Councils of Women's Delegates," in soviets and in the administrative and judicial apparati. Some, albeit relatively few, joined the party.

Befriended, supported, and coached by *zhenotdel* representatives, a rapidly growing number of women in Soviet courts initiated divorce proceedings, accompanied by demands for equitable division of property and assignment of children. By mid-1926 communist organizers reported a veritable "divorce wave" in some Central Asian districts, or simply "massive ... epidemic [abandonment]" of husbands by their wives. In March 1927, the party succeeded in organizing in Central Asia the first great marches of female crowds in public. Exhorted by fiery recitations, revolutionary songs and music, and agitators' calls for immediate female liberation and sexual desegregation, great crowds of women not only entered into public quarters traditionally reserved for men, but also marched into locales sanctified for special religious purposes. There, thousands were moved into collective, simultaneous, and public burning of their veils, and then surged through the streets unveiled, chanting challenges to the old order. Throughout 1927 and early 1928, groups of women appeared at labor exchanges in Central Asia's major cities demanding jobs and equal employment opportunities. Other groups, led by communist *zhenotdel* officials, and accompanied by Soviet militiamen, roamed city streets, tearing veils off other women, hunting for caches of food and cotton hidden by peasants and traders, and hunting as well for members of traditional elites subject to arrest and deportation. Some reported to the Red Army and the secret police the hideouts of remaining local guerrillas. Even in some isolated outposts in the hinterland, party officials reported cases of especially aggressive Moslem women arriving in local party headquarters, offering their services as village organizers, and only asking for "guns, secretaries [and body-guards]" to settle old accounts in the countryside.

4. Uncontrolled Involvement

By 1928 communist officials in Central Asia reported with increasing frequency and unease that in locales where divorce proceedings, public unveiling, and overall female mobilization had gone farthest, conditions were "verging on [mass] prostitution." They offered two basic reasons for such an unprecedented turn of events: economic and psychocultural. Women abandoning—or being obliged to leave—their communities and kin groups, with or without a divorce, had neither the means and skills nor the requisite attitudes and opportunities to support themselves. Women emerging suddenly from a Moslem traditional milieu, and coming into unrestricted contact with men in a variety of social situations, were emotionally unprepared for the occasion. As one Tadzhik party organizer put it, speaking about herself as well as her peer group:

> It is generally the adventurous, daring, and naturally enough, rather good-looking woman who flings aside her *paranja* (veil) . . . As a reaction to her previous enforced meekness, she now tends to become more self-assertive and unrestrained than is good for her . . . [for] . . . in her relations with the opposite sex she is helpless. Not having been trained since childhood to meet men, she has not built up the particular defenses which a woman needs if she is to meet men freely, on an equal basis. In her work she mingles among men without being emotionally prepared to ward off their equivocal remarks and persistent advances. Whenever she is in a mixed group, the atmosphere becomes charged—passion, jealousy, fear—much more so than you probably find among European men and women. The woman here needs a good deal of discipline and balance, particularly when her habitual defenses have been surrendered and no new ones have as yet been erected. . . . In my own case this resulted in tragedy. Meeting men was to me a novel and thrilling experience. A compliment or an embrace was a grand experience. I lost my head.

If, then, suddenly emancipated Moslem women appeared to be acting like harlots it was because "this new freedom was too much [for them]"; they were "doomed to burn their wings in their heedless dash for freedom" (referred to in Kunitz, 1935: 298–300).

Initial Results: The Pattern of Popular Response—Males

The pattern of male response within the traditional milieu may be said to have ranged from evasion and selective accommodation to limited retribution and massive backlash.

1. EVASION

Moslem males, in both traditionally authoritative and nonauthoritative roles, were found as a rule to evade the newly imposed rules and to avoid entanglement with the new judicial institutions. The reasons were manifold. As in Islamic contexts elsewhere, their cultural reflex was to pay, overtly, elaborate and even reverent obeisance to formal requisites imposed by a predominant outside power, but, at the same time, covertly, to expend inordinate energies on evading the law, including even the laws of the *shariat*—whenever the latter conflicted with locally valued mores and customs or with the perceived self-interest of individuals, local communities, and groups. The rules, procedures, and structures of the new legal system could be viewed, especially in this case, as directly antithetical to legitimate institutions. In addition to being, on general grounds, profoundly heretical and fundamentally subversive in traditional Moslem and customary tribal context, the new system embodied three specific features making it especially repellent. Its institutions were rigidly formal, bureaucratic, and impersonal, hence lacking the familiar, flexible, sacred, and charismatic attributes of mediation and control long considered requisite and legitimate in local communities. It was sponsored and staffed by aliens and infidels—Russians, communists, and native reformers. And its emphasis on sexual equality was tantamount to subversion and regulation of the most deeply embedded, sensitive, intimate, and sacred aspects of private life. Thus, as Soviet court officials reported uneasily from Central Asia, native males not only regarded the new laws as "sinful," and hence evaded them, but when apprehended and indicted for "crimes based on custom"—"crimes constituting survivals of a tribal way of life"—they "[experienced] no sense of guilt . . . [and] . . . could not understand why they were being punished." In some instances, to follow the new rules meant to incriminate oneself immediately and automatically. For example, two fathers (representing two extended families or clans) planning the marital union of their children and arriving in a Soviet agency to register the union, could at once be liable to imprisonment and fine—if, as was customary, a bride price was involved, if the explicit consent of both marital partners was not secured, or if the boy's, or more usually the girl's, age was under the legal limit. Further, a male planning to acquire a second or third wife, who agreed to register his new marriage in a Soviet agency, would likewise be subject to prosecution. Under such circumstances, Moslem men tended not to utilize the legal auspices of formal Soviet institutions, not even to report the birth of a child, lest its age be thus incontrovertibly established. They continued, instead, to use the services of a *mullah* in traditionally sanctioned, private ceremonies. And if it was impossible to hide the fact of a traditional marriage, for example, and if pressed to register it under the law, male heads of families and clans simply invented new modes of negotiations for a bride price that evaded official detection. They also supplied as many false witnesses as needed, including false grooms and brides, in order to legalize a traditional union in a Soviet institution.

2. SELECTIVE ACCOMMODATION

Under some circumstances, and in some realms, males in general and traditional elites in particular, showed signs of interest in responding to the challenge of female emancipation through selective accommodation. The response in such cases was essentially competitive in nature. In some districts where women turned out in significant numbers to vote, men, made uneasy—as Soviet voting officials reported—by the implications of leaving the field to female majorities, showed up in unprecedented numbers at the polls.

Aroused by the visible and potential consequences of Soviet-sponsored mobilization among women, some Moslem clergymen and village and clan notables launched what was in effect the first conscious organizational effort in local cultural history directed along tribal and religious lines to "win back" women and youth. It included tribal and village sponsorship of "women's meetings" and elaborate celebrations—*toy* and *ash*—prominently involving women; material help in furthering cooperative arrangements in the community, for example, simple machinery for the manufacture of dairy products; the formation under clerical auspices of Moslem youth groups, for boys as well as girls, to rival the Komsomol; the establishment of special girls' schools for "religious enlightenment"; the attraction of women into the mosque; the denial, at least in some cases, that the *shariat* necessarily ordained the veiling of women and their inequality in marriage, divorce, inheritance, and court proceedings; and even the establishment, in what were projected as centers of Moslem administration, of special "Women's Departments" under a female *kadi*, to rival the party's *zhenotdel*. This was a series of awkward, isolated, small-scale attempts, in self-defense, to formulate a response to the challenge of a secularist revolution under communist auspices. It was an effort to introduce some flexibility into the customary and Islamic view of social relations and roles, and to provide some alternatives to the rights proffered and the opportunities promised by the Soviet regime.

3. Limited Retribution

When faced with growing female participation, or pressure to participate, in the public realm, males responded—albeit largely as individuals, and largely in private—by applying proscriptive counterpressures. Their motives were explicitly reported by Soviet organizers. They were, primarily, the fear of female economic and political competition; the fear of the effect that social participation would have on the attitudes, morality, and fidelity of daughters and wives (and hence the fear of other men's sexual competition); and the fear, ultimately, of the loss of authoritative male dominance over females.

In widely scattered locales, especially in the countryside, girls and women were persuaded, sometimes forcefully, to keep away from schools, clubs, and voting booths. Heads of families tended to permit a modest degree of such participation only when assured of complete sexual segregation in these realms, or when confronted, as on voting days, by police and the Red Army. While some husbands and fathers were tempted by the promise of extra income, they were reported to have deep misgivings about their females' going to work in a factory. Here the degree of the community's supervision over its members was bound to be much lower, and the chances of unrestricted contact with other men much higher than usual. In parallel fashion, while unmarried and relatively poor males showed signs of welcoming greater access to females, they were reported to feel deeply threatened by women's arrival in the economic market place in general and in factories in particular.

When faced with divorce proceedings initiated by women, and with the first acts of female unveiling, Moslem husbands and kinsmen responded with privately administered beatings, and to a growing extent, with the expulsion of these women from home. What seemed particularly ominous in the eyes of Soviet officials was the fact that, with or without a divorce, women were being thrown out unceremoniously into the streets, and were left without property that legally belonged to them, "without a roof over their heads, and without a piece of bread . . . [to keep body and soul together]." Likewise, when apprehended and pressed to dissolve a polygamous marriage, native males tended simply "to throw the [extra] wife [or wives]—in most cases the old ones and the cold ones—out the door, denying them even the least bit of property." It appeared, then, that by pressing the issue the regime was likely to wind up with a vast throng of old, lonely, and destitute women on its hands.

4. Massive Backlash

When faced with a mounting wave of divorces and organized public unveiling, and with the concomitants of women's spatial and social mobility, including widespread desegregation, political denunciations, and prostitution, Moslem men reponded with an explosion of hostility and violence unequaled in scope and intensity until then on any other grounds.

Two sets of mutually reinforcing perceptions seem to have been set in motion here. First, under the umbrella of Soviet rule a native male's opportunities for martial, acquisitive, and hegemonic self-assertion had been severely circumscribed. This meant that the act of asserting himself vis-à-vis a woman was one of the very few realms—if not the last one—left to him for the assertion of authority and virility. Under these circumstances, *khudzhum*—the "cultural revolution" launched through legal and extralegal channels—by suddenly and powerfully intensifying men's apprehensions and anxiety stemming from the threat of impotence, apparently precipitated a crisis in the male's self-esteem. Moreover, the sudden threat to the nexus of authority relationships in the most intimate circle of a man's life—the sense of being *dispossessed* in sexual and generational realms—served to provide the vehicle that fused men's unease and resentment stemming from the entire spectrum of Soviet-inspired actions in the traditional milieu. By the same token, despondency, hatred, and violence heretofore devoid of clearly identifiable objects for blame could suddenly focus upon the sponsors of *khudzhum*: female defectors from tradition, male communists, infidels, and aliens.

Second, both the Islamic and customary components of Central Asian folkways had always carried expectations that unrestricted female mobility and unveiling would inevitably lead to widespread social disorganization, demoralization, promiscuity, and harlotry. Some aspects of female mobilization seemed to confirm these traditional expectations, thus providing the makings of a self-fulfilling prophecy.

The resulting backlash, beginning on a large scale in the spring of 1927 (i.e., immediately after the first organized public unveilings), marked the massive consummation of two interrelated trends: the radicalization of male attitudes to women and the radicalization of native male attitudes toward the Soviet regime.

The backlash patterns included the following manifestations which in turn constituted stages following each other in rapid succession and reaching their most violent forms within weeks of the pattern's inception: an insidious rumor campaign by *mullahs* associating Soviet-sponsored emancipatory and related activities with whatever actual or potential calamities might befall individuals or entire communities of believers; framing or casting out (amounting to excommunication) of men who acquiesced in their womenfolk's participation in public unveiling; public prophesying that Bolsheviks would turn all Moslem women into harlots; shaming, raping, and killing of unveiled women in the streets (including the disemboweling of pregnant women) as traitors to tradition and prostitutes; vilification, persecution, and murder (including lynching) of female activists and organizers, and of their families, wholesale murder of anyone even distantly connected with the "cultural revolution"; indiscriminate generalized violence—that is "a wave of terror" directed against any and all representatives of the Soviet regime, male or female, native or Russian.

As Soviet organizers reported from the field, both the causes and the process of the backlash tended to lead to the closing of traditionalist ranks and to the hardening of traditionalist attitudes. The specter of massive and dramatic emancipatory activities in public seemed to drive traditionalist males—"poor" as well as "rich"—and the sacred Moslem intelligentsia and clan notables closer together, for all of them felt challenged as Moslems, as heads of kin groups, and as males. This meant that, instead of sharpening the class struggle, as the communists had hoped, precipitate Soviet initiatives tended to mitigate that struggle. Instead of leading to the alienation of substantial segments of society from the traditional way of life, sudden and massive female mobilization tended to lead to widespread and intense alienation from the Soviet system and its works, accompanied by cleavages running along primarily sexual and ethnic lines. Instead of helping to induce conflicts that would be socially, culturally, politically, and economically productive from the Soviet point of view, precipitate female mobilization was activating conflicts that were highly destructive. . . .

CONCLUSION

To sum up:

(1) The realization through Soviet law of new ideal norms in Central Asia tended to be inversely related to the degree of forcible attempts to apply it in reality.

(2) Statute law, while evidently a suitable parental surrogate (Berman, 1963: Sec. III) in the Russian milieu, lacked the cultural underpinnings for such a role in Central Asia, and therefore could not be easily transplanted there in its specific Soviet-Russian forms.

(3) While law successfully elicited, reinforced, and focused grievances, it tended to be dysfunctional to the extent that it encouraged hopes it could not satisfy.

(4) The functioning of law as an instrument of mobilization (as both a repository of ideal norms and a focus of grievances), while powerful in its

revolutionizing impact, tended to be directly related to the degree that extra-legal integrative and supportive arrangements were provided for, and coordinated with the mobilizational thrust.

(5) Given its vivid imagery of justice and of equality of the sexes before the law, the operation of the Soviet legal system as an instrument of recruitment unquestionably made a highly important contribution to Soviet revolutionary objectives, since recruitment through the legal milieu tended to net female cadres that were the toughest, the most disaffected from tradition, the most vengeful, and hence, politically, the most reliable from the Soviet point of view. But the impact of the system, in this case, tended to be diluted to the extent that the manipulations of its native male personnel made female judicial roles purely honorary or menial, and it was relatively narrow in that it tended to appeal primarily to female personalities with aggressive and authoritarian, but not necessarily imaginative and creative, characteristics.

(6) To the extent that Soviet law was intended to be a warning system (a "trip wire") designed to prevent transgressions and resulting conflicts it tended to be relatively useless (since it was regarded as irrelevant, or disregarded altogether, by traditionalist males) and decidedly dysfunctional (in that, far from preventing conflicts, it helped to trigger and aggravate them).[5]

(7) Deliberately fashioned and used as an instrument of class struggle—an instrument dispensing distinctly political justice (Kirchheimer, 1961)—Soviet law tended to be eufunctional (from the Soviet point of view) only if class enemies could be readily detected and safely indicted, but tended to be dysfunctional to the extent that the local traditional milieu was alienated in the course of the regime's crude and indiscriminate attempts to identify and apprehend "class enemies."

(8) Having to function not only as a conveyor of new norms but also as an instrument to extirpate the entire antecedent legal system, Soviet law enjoyed the advantages of (a) a formal monopoly of the legal universe; (b) a formal monopoly and overwhelming superiority of force; (c) a centralized and potentially efficient bureaucratic apparatus; and (d) the backing of an authoritarian party-state committed to an overarching ideology and uninhibited by moral and democratic constraints. It was at a disadvantage, however, and hence was congenitally unattractive, or at least not immediately useful, in that (a) it lacked the sacred qualities and personalities of the antecedent system; (b) it tended to be abstract, rigid, and impersonal; (c) it could not easily gain access to traditional communities either because the latter were physically distant, or nomadic–pastoral (hence elusive), or

---

[5]This confirms Stanley Hoffman's conclusion in another context (1963); cf. Röling (1966).

because they were governed by a combination of religious and customary law, and could thus be independent of, and elusive to, formal legal structures.

(9) To the extent that it had to function as a protective shield for revolutionary agents and converts, Soviet law tended to be not only useless (in that it could do little or nothing to protect defecting Moslem women from violent retribution), but decidedly dysfunctional (to the extent that it obliged the Soviet regime to risk the lives of valuable and scarce political activists in the impossible task of protecting the rights and lives of masses of individuals scattered in an extremely hostile milieu).[6]

(10) Viewed as an heretical model, the impact of Soviet law on the traditional milieu was exceptionally great. Perhaps no other instrument could hold out to the traditional community, and especially its women, revolutionary standards of human relationships and potentialities as palpably, consistently, and authoritatively as Soviet laws did. Perhaps no other instrument could, in the short run, be as powerful a catalyst of systematic alienation in, and fundamental transformation of, the traditional milieu. But law as a heretical model tended also to be dysfunctional to the extent that (a) it was felt to be forced upon traditional communities by men who were ethnically or ideologically outsiders; (b) it not only posed a threat to the traditional unities and values, but impinged directly upon the most intimate and sacred realms of local life styles; (c) it stimulated the self-assertion of both Soviet-oriented heresy and traditionalist orthodoxy; (d) it put a discipline-oriented, implicitly authoritarian system in the position of encouraging iconoclastic and libertarian propensities that showed themselves capable of turning just as easily against the Soviet regime as against the traditional order.

(11) As a regulative mechanism in a revolutionary situation, Soviet law was at one particularly pronounced disadvantage, apart from all those already mentioned. It had neither the legitimate authority, nor the judicial resources, nor yet the extralegal supportive structures to be able to control tensions as widespread, pervasive, and corrosive as those induced by the heretical model. A revolutionary instrument that was itself not easily controllable, and was itself seeking legitimation in a traditional world, could not very well control tensions and ensure order in that world while it was enforcing with all the power at its command the very quintessence of illegitimacy: heresy.

(12) Therefore, in its role as a specialized tension-management system designed to induce and control revolutionary change, Soviet law turned out to be an exceedingly volatile, imperfect, inexpedient, and in certain circumstances, dangerous instrument. It tended to be volatile in the sense that it

---

[6] This calls for some significant qualifications in Arnold's Rose's proposition (1956) regarding the role of law as a shield protecting innovators and daring minorities.

could just as easily go too far as not far enough inducing and managing change. It was imperfect in the sense that, if devoid of supportive institutions and arrangements that would permit the translation of legal rights into real roles and opportunities, it tended to define new goals while failing to supply the means to reach them. It was inexpedient in the sense that it could undermine the traditional status quo, but could not really transform it. It tended also to be dangerous in that as a heretical model, it maximized undesirable as well as desirable tensions, while, as a regulative mechanism, it could not minimize the impact of those tensions on the political structures and developmental objectives of the incumbent Soviet regime.

Revolutionary legalism as a strategic approach to social engineering could be self-delusory to its sponsor as well as dangerous. Its perfectionist emphasis on adherence to uncompromising, if seemingly rational, rules, and its heavy stress on the strength and promise of rationally devised legal machinery, served to deemphasize to the point of neglect or exclusion precisely those initiatives that were needed most for the attainment of revolutionary and developmental objectives, and for the legitimation of the legal system itself—initiatives involving comprehensive, systematic, and coordinated social action whereby human needs, potentialities, and expectations would find a reasonable chance to be fulfilled. Given such omission, revolutionary legalism, intended to induce a strategic conflict in a traditional milieu for the purpose of changing it, tended, instead, to precipitate cataclysmic conflict, verging on civil war.

Faced with the full panoply of implications of massive enforcement and repression, the Soviet regime had the following options: to continue inducing revolutionary tensions as before, to contain them by selective rather than indiscriminate enforcement, to deflect them by retaliating primarily against selected targets, to suppress them at all cost and with all the means at its disposal, or to reduce them at the source. While predispositions to all these choices continued to assert themselves in Soviet ranks, the regime's chief reaction was to attempt mitigating the tensions at their source— through a deliberate reduction of legalistic pressures and a calculated attempt to construct a complex infrastructure of social service, educational, associational, expressive, and economic facilities.

By early 1929, only two and one-half years after the inception of the "cultural revolution" in Central Asia, the communist party felt obliged to bring the "storming" activities on behalf of female emancipation and the massive and overt forms of the cultural revolution itself to an abrupt halt. The retrenchment pattern included the following components:

(1) Emphasis on specialized cadre formation, stressing selective recruitment of indigenous personnel and its training in protected cultural islands, rather than general social mobilization.

(2) Planning of a new social infrastructure, stressing actually felt needs rather than political agitation, and intended to allow a gradual but comprehensive and coordinated approach to social reconstruction.

(3) Temporary exemption of some especially sensitive Central Asian districts from the sanctions of the new legal code.

(4) Tailoring of some provisions in the code to bring them into closer accord with local mores.

(5) Scaling down sanctions for some "customary crimes."

(6) Withdrawal of official encouragement from female-initiated divorces, designed to halt the divorce wave altogether.

(7) Preservation, where necessary, of segregated facilities for Moslem women.

(8) Prohibition of massive and dramatic violations of traditional taboos, and especially of administered female unveiling in public.

(9) Shelving, indefinitely, all official proposals for outlawing female veiling and seclusion in Moslem societies under Soviet rule.

Thus, within two and a half years of the beginning of their experiment the Soviet authorities reversed their emphasis: from precipitate legal change for the sake of social transformation to long-term social rebuilding for the sake, in part, of meaningful legal change.

Can this be regarded as a valid general maxim about the relation of law to revolutionary social change?[7] If we consider that the Soviet campaign took place under almost "ideal" conditions—a determined commitment to revolutionary purposes by a radical modernizing elite; the incumbent's undisputed and centralized political power, overwhelming superiority of force, and authoritarian dispositions coupled with the absence of democratic constraints; isolated and small target populations denuded, in large part, of their traditional elites; the incapacity or unwillingness of neighboring states to intervene in the affairs of their ethnic brethren; and, therefore, the sponsor-regime's relative freedom both to *initiate* and to *retreat* from a revolutionary experiment—then there are grave questions about the utility of law as an autonomous strategic instrument of rapid, administered social change under less favorable circumstances.

It is true that Soviet objectives were unusually large, and Soviet Central Asian societies especially distant from these objectives. Yet one wonders whether this very fact does not permit one to see, enlarged and accentuated, what is less apparent, but nonetheless true, in all confrontations between legally expressed ideals and social actualities.

---

[7] For a recent, excellent review of the literature on law and (evolutionary) social change, accompanied by some highly incisive propositions on the relationship between law and social process, see Friedman and Ladinsky (1967).

To be sure, neither Soviet experience in Central Asia nor the lessons derived therefrom may be literally applicable in other milieus. They do not tell us, for example, to what extent other methods of legal codification and judicial organization, applied under other political auspices, might have been more effective than the ones used; or whether legal means might have been more effective when focusing on less explosive issues than sexual and generational relationships; or whether social engineering through law might be more effective in societies where supracommunal agencies (e.g., those of a modern state) are collectively expected to play (by way of political manipulations in general and legal engineering in particular) a more powerful regulative and transforming role than is evidently the case in relatively intact traditional Islamic milieus. Nonetheless, both the experience and the lessons appear to be most pertinent for the identification and evaluation of factors that determine the role, and the success or failure of law as an instrument of revolutionary change. They might be useful in establishing a firm empirical base, and in developing and testing a propositional inventory, for the comparative study of strategies of modernization. Likewise, the systematic evaluation and comparison of the requisites of social engineering through law should lead to more fruitful correlations between jurisprudence and empirically based social science, between the sociology of law and political sociology.

REFERENCES

Almond, G. A., and G. B. Powell, Jr.
  1966 *Comparative politics: A developmental approach.* Boston: Little, Brown.
Berman, H. J.
  1963 *Justice in the U.S.S.R. An interpretation of Soviet law.* (Rev. ed.) New York: Vintage Books.
Engels, F.
  1942 *The origin of the family, private property, and the state.* New York: International Publishers. (Orig. pub. 1884.)
Friedman, L. M., and J. Ladinsky
  1967 Law as an instrument of incremental social change. Paper presented at the Annual Meeting of the American Political Science Association, Chicago.
Gurvitch, G.
  1942 *Sociology of law.* New York: Philosophical Library and Alliance Book Corp.
Hoffman, S.
  1963 The study of international law and the theory of international relations. *Proceedings of the American Society of International Law* 57 (April): 26–35.
Kirchheimer, O.
  1961 *Political justice: The use of legal procedure for political ends.* Princeton: Princeton University Press.
Kunitz, J.
  1935 *Dawn over Samarkind: The rebirth of Central Asia.* New York: Covici, Priede.

Massell, G. J.
forthcoming   *The strategy of social change and the role of women in Soviet Central Asia.*
Moore, W., and A. Feldman
    1962   Society as a tension-management system. In *Behavioral science and civil defense* (Disaster research group study no. 16.), edited by G. W. Baker and L. S. Cottrell, Jr., pp. 93–105. Washington, D.C.: National Research Council.
Rapoport, A.
    1966   Models of conflict: Cataclysmic and strategic. In *Conflict in society*, edited by A. de Reuck and J. Knight, pp. 259–287. Boston: Little, Brown.
Röling, B. V. A.
    1966   The role of law in conflict resolution. In *Conflict in society*, edited by A. de Reuck and J. Knight, pp. 328–350. Boston: Little, Brown.
Rose, A.
    1956   The use of law to induce social change. *Transactions of the Third World Congress of Sociology* 6 (1956): 52–63.
Shklar, J.
    1964   *Legalism.* Cambridge: Harvard Univ. Press.

CHAPTER
15

KINSHIP AND POLITICAL POWER IN FIRST CENTURY ROME

Robert Nisbet

I

MY SUBJECT in this essay is a problem that has long been of interest to historians and sociologists of legal institutions: kinship authority (*patria potestas*) and its decline in ancient Rome. Quite apart from the intrinsic interest of the subject, we can learn much from it, I believe, of what is more generally involved in the shift of authority from one institution to another, in the rise of legal individualism, and in the dislocation of important social groups from functional significance in a social order.

Exactly a century ago, Sir Henry Maine gave brief but striking attention to the problem, and his own statement is worth repeating. Whereas, Maine pointed out, we find the housefather possessing in early Rome the *jus vitae necisque*, the power of life and death, over his children and others under his power, along with comparable authority in other spheres—economic, religious, and educational—the Imperial Age reveals the decline of the *patria potestas* to a level scarcely greater than that to be found in the modern family.

Reprinted with permission of the Macmillan Company from "Kinship and Political Power in First Century Rome" by Robert Nisbet, in *Sociology and History*, Werner J. Cahnman and Alvin Boskoff, editors, pp. 257–271. Copyright © 1964 by the Free Press of Glencoe, a Division of The Macmillan Company.

The unqualified right of domestic chastisement has become a right of bringing domestic offenses under the cognizance of the civil magistrates; the privilege of marriage has declined into a conditional veto; the liberty of selling has been virtually abolished, and adoption itself, destined to lose almost all its ancient importance ... can no longer be effected without the assent of the children ... in short we are brought very close to the ideas which have at length prevailed in the modern world (Maine, 1917: 81–82).

It would be difficult to state the problem more concisely, and, as we shall see, Maine has some penetrating observations to make on the factors involved in the decline. The principal objections to Maine's presentation —apart from a lack of data that more recent scholarship has supplied—are, first, the view he takes of the general nature of change and, second, the strict and uncompromising legalism of his treatment.

Like most of his contemporaries, Maine wrote under the spell of the evolutionary perspective. He regarded change in an institution as endogenous, proceeding as does growth in an organism, in a slow, gradual, and continuous manner. Past phases of any social institution are deemed to be immature or imperfect, mere steps in a development whose true and proper nature lies ahead. Thus, Maine tells us, the *patria potestas* could not have been a durable institution; it was inherently unstable and imperfect. The essential problem of change is not that of accounting for actual transformation in the *patria potestas* but rather "to guess at the causes which permitted the *patria potestas* to last as long as it did by rendering it more tolerable than it appears" (Maine, 1917: 88).

This leads to the second difficulty of Maine's approach—that of dealing with his subject in an exclusively legal manner. Writing as a lawyer—albeit a broadly educated one—Maine chose to regard the *patria potestas* as a power much like sovereignty in the modern state—abstract, impersonal, and remote—rather than as an institution embedded in religion, morality, and economics. It was because Maine fixed his attention almost strictly on the power aspects that the problem of the *patria potestas* could appear as one of accounting for the length of time it was able to maintain itself, rather than that of uncovering the historical forces which were in fact necessary for the dislocation of one of the most durable institutions in all Roman history.

Most subsequent students of the Roman family have dealt with the subject in substantially the same terms. Sociologists, in particular, have done so in the same way that they have handled social change in general—as the consequence of internal forces and tensions, only moderately and perhaps catalytically affected by external factors.[1]

---

[1] This is, of course, one of the consequences of the continuous influence exerted upon European thought by the Greek concept of organism; from Aristotle down to contemporary functionalists in the social sciences, there is scarcely an exception to the view that change is inherent in the institution or culture.

Major social change is not, however, the consequence of internal tensions, nor of immanent variations and mutations proceeding in ways best known to biologists. It is, on the contrary, the result of intrusion, external impact, or conflict.

It will be the primary purpose of this paper to show that the *patria potestas*, far from being unstable and driven to its decline by innate difficulties, was in fact a powerful and tenacious institution, one that did not change in any important respect until it was subjected to the force of another—and eventually greater—authority, the military *imperium*. It was the unequal conflict between these two forces, as we shall see, that transformed the kinship system in Rome and, with it, the basis of the larger society.

II

We have no difficulty in describing the nature and significance of the *patria potestas* in the Republic—that is, the period down to approximately the end of the first century B.C. An imposing body of scholarship gives us a clear and detailed view of our subject. What has too often been overlooked or underemphasized, however, is the key role of the *patria potestas* in the larger structure of power in the total society of the Republic. As we shall see, the fateful change in kinship authority came only where there began to take place a massive rearrangement of this larger structure of power.

To properly see the picture of early Roman society, Strachan-Davidson writes (1912: 28–29, 38):

> We must imagine a number of households, each united under its own *paterfamilias*. Inside the household the father is the sole judge, beholden to no one for his actions and performances.... No Roman writer ever attributed the *patria potestas* either to the magistrate, whether king or consul, or to the sovereign people itself, and there is no trace of the power exercised by the state authorities developing out of those exercised by the head of the family.

Strachan-Davidson's last point is an important one to our problem. So many anthropologists and historical jurists in the modern world have treated political sovereignty as if it were the simple outgrowth of family authority that the essential separateness of the two has been minimized or overlooked. In the final section of this paper, I will expand upon the significance of this separateness to the problem of change. Here it suffices to emphasize that the *patria potestas* was an original and autonomous power within Roman society, drawing its vast authority over individual behavior from immemorial tradition, not from any higher agency within the Roman state.

Strictly speaking, the *patria potestas* was much more than power. It stood for the unity of the family, its continuity in time, and as the irreducible atom of society as a whole. The word for father, *pater*, did not connote generation, but authority and protection. The basis of the Roman family, Fowler has emphasized, was the right of ownership, inseparable "from the idea of land settlement and therefore essentially *das Hauswesen*, the house itself, with persons living in it, free or servile, with their land and all their property, all governed and administered by the *paterfamilias*, the master of the household" (Fowler, 1911: 70).

The centrality of the family in law was reinforced by its agnatic character. The framework of the Roman family was not common birth; blood brothers were not *ipso facto* members of the same family. Two people were related agnatically if they were in the *patria potestas* of the same man, or if there was some common ancestor in whose power they would both have been were he still alive. Thus, given Roman male succession, a father and his brother were agnates; so were a father and his son. But a Roman male and his married daughter or sister were not agnatically related. For there was only cognatic relationship, and to this the Romans, in the Republic, attached little importance of any kind, and no legal importance whatsoever.

The reason for strict insistence upon the agnatic tie in all matters of law, property, and religion is not far to seek. The organization of Roman society would have been disrupted if men had claimed relationship to their mother's blood relatives. For then a person would have fallen under more than one *patria potestas*, with all the related confusion that would prevail in a society that did not possess a centralized political power over persons. "As long as the family was an *imperium in imperio*, a community within a commonwealth, governed by its own institutions of which the parent was the source, the limitation of relationship to the agnates was a necessary security against a conflict of laws in the domestic forum" (Maine, 1917: 88). It was only after the public power penetrated and became eventually sovereign in private matters that the principle of agnation could be safely abandoned. And, as history records, by the second century of the Empire, the agnatic relationship meant little more than it does in modern society. It had ceased to be the center of gravity of Roman society (Roby, 1902: Book 2, Chapter 7).

Individualism did not exist in the Republic—legally, economically, morally, or socially. Tradition united with overt authority in making each Roman feel, first, a member of a group, with duties, and, only second, an individual with rights. Until very late in the Republic the family bore responsibility for most individual offenses, and it was the prime agency of retribution for injuries suffered by one of its members. Not until 149 B.C. did true criminal law make its appearance, in the statute known as the *Lex Calpurnia de Repetundis*, resulting in the establishment of the first *Quaestio Perpetua*—that is, a permanent commission for consideration of public crimes. Prior to this date such offenses were dealt with by the Senate as a whole, much as they did with any other public responsibility (Schisas, 1926: 125–129; Maine, 1917: 227). In the execution of criminals, even when the offense was against the whole state (e.g., treason), it was the family itself that served as the vehicle.

> Over and over we find the actual execution of punishment, capital or otherwise, committed to the relatives of the culprits instead of being carried out by servants of the state. The noticeable point is that this occurred not only with those who were under the *potestas* of father or husband ... but with women who were *sui juris*, but who were nevertheless put to death or banished by *propinqui* or *cognati* (Strachan-Davidson, 1912: Vol. 1, 32).[2]

Repeatedly we are struck by the autonomy of the family in the law and custom of the Republic. Magistrates and censors could exhort, but little more.

> The officers of the commonwealth, the consuls and other magistrates, did not dare cross the threshold of a father's house; they assumed no power to interfere within his doors. The head of the family was its sole representative; he alone had *locus standi* in the tribunals of the state. If a wrong was done by or to any member of his family, he and not they must answer for it or demand compensation (Hunter, 1934: 14).

The legal majesty of the *patria potestas* could not have endured as long as it did, and been as difficult to dislodge in the end, had it not been for roots in the religious, economic, and social life of Rome. This is the point that has been too often overlooked by historians and jurists. And when the *patria potestas* did come to an end as a major part of Roman society, it did so, as we shall see, within a larger context of change that included religious and economic, as well as political dislocations.

Thus, religion, throughout most of the Republic was hardly more than a spiritualization of family life, reaching back to earliest ancestors and forward to the unborn. Public pontiffs had few and limited rights of supervision. The *Lares* and *Penates*, being gods of the household were private; ceremonies were secret. Nothing violated the priestly authority of the father over his hearth, and religion was deemed as inextinguishably a function of kinship as was life itself. Birth, marriage, and death were the ceremonial high points, and in each ritual the authority and unity of the family were, in effect, reaffirmed. No child was born into the family; he had to be accepted. What else were death rites but the means whereby one left the earthly members of the family to join the departed—who were deemed not the less living for their eternal stay elsewhere? To allow others—strangers—into

---

[2]Poste writes (1925: 402): "Injuries which in modern law are punished exclusively as crimes could throughout the history of Roman law be vindicated by the private party as private wrongs."

the religion of the hearth was to risk alienation of the departed; and for a family to fail to make food offerings at each meal to the gods of the household, or, most direly, to permit the sacred flame to go out, was to risk extinction of the departed souls. Similarly, marriage, far from creating a new family, was the ceremony (purely private) whereby the young woman, the intended wife of a son under power, was, in effect, cleansed of the worship under which she had previously lived, and made the subject of a new religion, that of her husband.[3]

Finally, and equally crucially, property and wealth were regarded as possessions of the family, never of individuals. At no time in the Republic could a son under power, however important he might be in military or public affairs, or whatever his age, legally own property. Nor could he even retain income personally earned, unless with the consent of the father. Beyond this, there was the strict limitation of rights of inheritance. Property could not easily be alienated from the agnatic family. Law and custom joined in stress upon the corporate, kinship character of property (Declareuil, 1924, 1927: 156 ff.).

Let us summarize briefly the character of the society within which the *patria potestas* flourished.

(1) It was the very opposite of an individualistic society, for the family was the irreducible unit in law, economics, religion, as well as other functional areas.
(2) It was a society strong in descriptive law—tradition, convention, custom—rather than prescriptive law.
(3) Pluralism, rather than monism, was the essence of the social system, although we should not underestimate the ease and effectiveness with which the early Romans could mobilize into military unity.
(4) It was a society based upon legal decentralization rather than centralization, a condition emanating naturally from its pluralism.

For the *patria potestas* could hardly have flourished in a society where the power of the state directly impinged upon each individual.

III

So much for the background of the problem. We must turn now to the events and changes which specifically and decisively changed the character of the *patria potestas* in Rome and, with it, the foundations of order in Rome. Our subject is intimately involved in the social transforma-

---

[3] By all odds the finest and most beautiful account of the religious basis of the Roman family may be found in Fustel de Coulanges (1956: Book 2, Chapter 2).

tion which characterized the end of the Republic and the rise of the Empire at the very end of the first century B.C.

We can do no better than quote some words of the Roman historian, Dio Cassius, as the means of introducing this section. "So it was," he wrote of the fateful accession of Augustus in 27 B.C., "that all the power of the people and the Senate passed over to Augustus, and from that day pure monarchy was established."[4] Monarchy is perhaps not the word we would apply to a personal absolutism founded, not upon tradition or right of succession, but rather upon military power united with popular appeal to the masses that is best known as Caesarism. Julius Caesar had offered the vision, and, for a moment, the actuality of absolutism founded upon mass appeal; Augustus Caesar now supplied both the blueprint and the implementation of a form of totalitarian power that was to survive in one form or another for half a millennium.

The façade of the Republic was maintained in the form of the Senate, but after 27 B.C., as Rostovtzeff, among others, has emphasized, the crucial elements were "the now permanent army and its commander-in-chief, the Emperor Augustus, *Imperator Caesar divi filius Augustus*. . . . The army was the master of the State, and, in the restored Roman republic, the Emperor ruled wholly through the army and for so long as the army was willing to keep him and obey" (1926: 39–40, 41). There was, to be sure, much to recommend the new form of government. A century of bitter, destructive civil wars among the rival military commanders—based, as Rostovtzeff has pointed out, upon no social programs or objectives; merely the struggle for absolute supremacy in the state—had so thoroughly weakened the traditional foundations of the commonweal that effective rule by the Senate was impossible. It is, of course, tribute to the majesty of the idea of the Senate that Augustus strove to make his government at all times seem to rest upon the Senate. But every Roman historian who touched upon the matter makes clear that, in fact, Augustus was the unrivaled and absolute ruler of Rome. All else was convenient fiction.

Time does not permit an examination of all the changes which were the consequence of the penetration of Augustan political power into the recesses of the social structure in Rome. Our specific concern here is the *patria potestas* and the role of the family in the new order. It is enlightening, however, to note by way of preface that changes in the *patria potestas* were themselves parts of a larger program that involved also the reconstitution of social classes in Rome, new foundations of property and wealth, the character of religion, and even the social origin of members of the Senate.

---

[4]Dio Cassius, Liii, 17. Dio together with Tacitus and Suetonius form the basic source of all that we know of this fateful period.

As Pelham has written, legislation on the family "formed an integral part of the general policy of social and administrative reconstruction in Rome and Italy which Augustus kept steadily before him from the beginning to the end of his long reign, and it is only in connection with that policy that it can be properly studied and understood" (Pelham, 1911: 94).[5]

I will merely summarize the consequences of this broad program. There was, first, the centralization of political power. No longer would Rome be, in political terms, a decentralized and cellular society as it had been for centuries in the Republic. In the same way that the Senate had been supplanted by the Emperor as the effective source of public power, so would all other social bodies that lay intermediate to the individual and the government: social classes, gilds, and the family itself. Gradually there took form the doctrine that was, within a century, to become the basis of the texts of Roman jurists (the texts which, after their codification in the age of Justinian, were to comprise the powerful and historically significant code of Roman law). The essence of this doctrine was the axiom that law—in contrast to mere custom or tradition—flows from the sovereign alone, who must be, by definition, above the law.

Second, and functionally related to the doctrine of centralized sovereignty, was the rise of legal individualism. A century of social atomization caused by civil war and political turmoil greatly facilitated this, but the theoretical essence of legal individualism lay in the idea, closely related to the idea of sovereignty, that individuals alone are the true units of the state, not social units; and such individuals, and all the relations among them, exist under the contemplation of the legal sovereign. Everything between the state and the individual inevitably had, now, an insecure existence, for it was the state alone that could give sanction to a corporate unity. From this fateful perspective of legal individualism arose, within a century, the important doctrines of legal fiction and legal concession. By legal fiction was meant the proposition that no social group, however old and embedded in tradition, has true or real character. It is a concept in the contemplation of the sovereign—nothing more, so far as law is concerned. Reality lies in individuals, not groups. More important was the related but distinguishable idea of concession. Those groups and only those groups may legally exist whose foundations have been created, so to speak, by specific concession of the sovereign.

This is, stated simply and baldly, the Roman doctrine of corporations, and it means, in the words of the great Maitland, that "all that stands between the individual and the state has but a derivative and precarious exis-

---

[5] The entire essay on the domestic policy of Augustus (pp. 89–151) is a brilliant sociological analysis of one of the greatest ages of change in Roman history.

tence." I do not suggest that this momentous doctrine, which was to aid the transformation of Europe a thousand years later with the revival of Roman Law, took its full shape in the Age of Augustus. We must wait a century for this. But there can be no doubt that the specific measures of centralization and individualization that took place in the Roman polity under Augustus, at the end of the first century B.C., were the true source of later legal formulations (Declareuil, 1927: 152–154, 354–355; Willems, 1888: 611).[6]

What happened to the *patria potestas* in 18 B.C. is of a piece with the other measures which were being taken to bring power firmly into the central government over associations and classes throughout society. If public order was to be restored and Rome's greatness secured in the world, there must be no *imperium in imperio*, no social allegiance, not even the agnatic family, which could detract from necessary political centralization.

The professed object of the famous *Leges Juliae* in 18 B.C.—and in particular the two laws *de adulteriis* and *demaritandis ordinibus*—was moral: to clean up the moral delinquencies and to restore marriage to its once proud estate. We need not question motive. The austerity of Augustus' personal life—unchallenged by contemporaries—is perhaps sufficient proof of this. But neither can we overlook the fact that in the establishment of these laws on morality and marriage, we are dealing with the first *official* limitations in Roman history of the historic authority of the *patria potestas* over these matters. It must further be kept in mind that the new laws, far from being isolated manifestations of moral reform, constitute an integral part of that larger reconstruction of Rome which, whether dealing with water supply, fire control, education, religion, or corn dole, was to lead to complete centralization. As Pelham has written (1911: 95–96):

> When we turn to the measures of reform adopted by Augustus it becomes clear that his efforts were by no means limited to the removal of the obstacles which impeded the growth of material prosperity or the repression of the vices which disgraced society. Great statesman as he was, he realized from the first the necessity, if either the political system which he had established was to stand or his other reforms were to have any lasting effect, of creating in a people demoralized by faction and civil war a healthy and vigorous public feeling.

For centuries, however imperfectly at times, the sole authority over adultery and other moral matters had been the power of the corporate family. Exile for personal delinquencies was not uncommon, but it was a power wielded under the authority of the *patria potestas*, not by a public magistrate nor even by the Senate unless damage to the commonweal had

---

[6] F. W. Maitland dealt with the centralizing and the individualizing characteristics of Roman imperial law as profound forces of change in the rise of modern Europe (see Maitland, 1911: Vol. 3, 309).

been done. Similarly, responsibility for marriage, for its motivation as well as for its operation, was, as we have also seen, a sacred function of the family. No public officer intruded into the decisions and ceremonies involved.

Now, at a stroke, these matters are brought within public jurisdiction. In the case of adultery, the nature of the offense was defined, the procedure fixed which was to be followed when a case arose, and the penalty laid down.

> For the primitive and probably decaying jurisdiction of the *paterfamilias* and the equally primitive right of private vengeance where the guilty parties were caught in the act, the *Lex Julia* aimed at substituting the more regular procedure of the law (Pelham, 1911: 115).

So it did, but it also, as Pelham himself points out, suggests, as do Augustus' other social and moral reforms, his anxiety not merely to restore social order by assigning to each class an appropriate career, a definite status, and definite privileges, but to connect each class with himself and his rule by special ties.

So far as we know, the first object of the new law was Augustus' own daughter, a young woman who, apparently, deserved exile for the reasons given. But the genius of the punishment lay in the fact that, having just established a public law which for the first time in history arrogated such punishment to the public agency, any possible sting in its first application was taken away by the familiar spectacle of a father exiling his own daughter. Further genius was shown when, for a time, he showed considerable mercy in dealing with others guilty of adultery, turning them over to their own families. But the all important precedent had been set, and under the head of *de pudicitia* in the law, various other regulations governing public decency— behavior at public games and shows, women's attendance at athletic contests, extravagances in dress, and undue expenditures on banquets—were passed under the authority of the *Legas Juliae* (Haight, 1922: 335–376).

The same kind of transfer of authority is to be seen in the sections on marriages. Here too the ostensible aim is the encouragement of marriage and the production of children, an aim on which Augustus could indeed claim the sanction of ancient custom and opinion. The aim had more than once, in earlier times, been made the subject of exhortation by various censors. But there is more in the Augustan decree. For the first time in history marriage becomes a matter of state concern and supervision. Marriage is made obligatory upon all men between the ages of 20 and 60 and upon all women between 20 and 50. Childlessness in men over 25 and in women over 20 was made punishable. Widows and divorced women were also ordered to remarry within a specified time. "To enforce these regulations a system of penalties and rewards was devised. The unmarried were declared incapable of inheriting property or accepting legacies; the childless were mulcted of half the amount of such bequests (Pelham, 1911: 120).

Perhaps even more significant was the limitation placed upon the right of marriage among certain classes, specifically with persons who were not freeborn. Marriage between the freeborn and those who were not—the freedmen were a large and growing class—was forbidden to patricians. Marriages to freedmen were forbidden not only to senators but to their children, grandchildren, and great-grandchildren. Here too it might be said that the aim was moral—the reduction of the license that had grown up, often leading to the exploitation of the lower class member as well as to dilution of ancient families. But, from our point of view the result is the same: for the first time the state intervened in a matter that had been traditionally private, reserved to the *patria potestas*.

The penalty forbidding the unmarried from inheriting property was, of course, an invasion of what we have seen to be the autonomy of the family in matters connected with its own property and income, and it is closely related to a separate act of Augustus during this period. This was the *peculium castrense*, which permitted the sons under power to retain all booty, income, and property they had acquired during military service. It will be remembered that at the basis of the *patria potestas* was its economic solidarity, the corporate possession of property by the family alone, not its individual members. In this decree, plainly, lie the beginnings of economic individualism and, with it, of contractualism, a concept that was also to become primary in later Roman law codes. Later emperors, beginning with Hadrian, were to extend this right of individual ownership to all public employees and civil servants, eventually to all citizens. Not unrelated to Augustan decrees on property and family were those touching on membership in the Senate. Senatorial status was no longer inherited through family lines; it was to be conferred by the Emperor.[7]

There was, finally, the religious aspect of the *patria potestas*. As we have seen, family authority was deeply rooted in the religion of the *Lares* and *Penates*. Privacy of the corporate religion of the family was one of the very pillars of the *patria potestas*. This, too, was radically modified. In 12 B.C. Augustus became Pontifex Maximus, thus uniting the political and religious life of the commonweal. But far more important from our point of view is the political penetration of the family hearth. Images of Augustus began to make their appearance within family domiciles, thus giving root to the novel and exotic efflorescence of emperor worship, a form of religion in the East that had aroused the revulsion of Romans a century or two before.

[7]On this momentous economic invasion of the *patria potestas* see Hadley (1931: 213; Declareuil, 1927: 159–160).

Along with the image of the *Lares* and *Penates* was placed that of Augustus. So this "genius" shared with the *Lares* the libations poured in their honor and the offerings placed for their acceptance. The worship which thus established Augustus as a household god in the homes of the people and gave him a place in one of their oldest worships was admirably fitted to serve his interests and those of the empire on a larger scale (Pelham, 1911: 109).

Thus, in three decisive ways, the *patria potestas* was challenged by the military *imperium*—in control of marriage and descent of family property; in the fragmentation of economic ownership; and, finally, in the invasion of the religious sphere. All of these momentous changes took place in the decade, 18–8 B.C., and they are at the heart of that simultaneous rise of individualism and political centralization in the Empire.

Relations between the state and the individual became ever more direct. The various situations in which the juridical person found himself affected him alone, and there was no more need to break or form any bond with a jealous and exclusive family group. Being no longer the foundation of the Republic, the *paterfamilias* ceased to interpose between the individual and the state . . . (Declareuil, 1927: 314).

IV

Let us turn, finally, to the question of what social forces, over a considerable period of time, had combined to form the effective bases of the Augustan decrees. Obviously these decrees did not take effect in a society totally unprepared for them. Change in an institution or concept may be the consequence of impact and intrusion from external forces, but conditions for the assimilation of this intrusion must be present—as studies of diffusion have made clear.

Here it is tempting to take refuge in such abstractions as secularism, commercialism, and religious skepticism in Rome during the century or two leading up to Augustus. These, it is said rightly enough, formed the context that alone permitted acceptance of the radical Augustan inroads on the family and other forms of association. No one familiar with the history of Rome in this period would doubt that such generalized forces were indeed involved.

Without pretending to exclude these forces, I would like, however, to put the matter in somewhat different terms—terms that are at once more precise and more sociological. I shall illustrate this in a context that had been potentially present in Roman society from earliest days. This is the conflict between the *patria potestas*—the ancient authority of the family, and the *imperium militiae*—the authority over soldiers that came into being at the outbreak of any war.

The *imperium militiae* was not, strictly speaking, military power alone. "The Romans," writes Strachan-Davidson, "knew no such thing as a severance between supreme military and supreme civil authority. They merely distinguished between the space inside the walls (*domi*) and the rest of the world which was comprehended in the locative case by the word *militiae* 'on service.' This full imperium, then, governs all the world, less the city of Rome" (Strachan-Davidson, 1912: 100). So much is true, but the fact remains, and it is crucial, that it was in a military context that "the rest of the world" became of significance to the Romans, and, more important, it was in its intrinsic military role that the *imperium militae* first conflicted with the *patria potestas*.

I stressed earlier the fact that the public power did not and could not deal with the multitude of private and social matters that came under the *patria potestas*. The opposite, however, is also true, and here I present a brilliant clarifying insight from Maine (1917: 81):

> In every relation of life in which the corrective community might have occasion to avail itself of his wisdom and strength, for all purposes of counsel and war, the *filius familias*, the son under power was as free as his father. It was a maxim of Roman jurisprudence that the *patria potestas* did not extend to the *jus publicum*. Father and son voted together in the city, and fought side by side in the field; indeed, the son, as general, might command the father, or as magistrate, decide on his contracts and punish his delinquencies.[8]

Here, I suggest, is a potential conflict of roles, a tension, that lies at the heart of our subject. So long as the public role of the *filius familias*, the son under power, was minimal, just so long was the claim of the *patria potestas* upon his allegiance an unqualified and undistracted one. There could be little conflict of authority and role. On the other hand, all that tended to maximize the son's public role—either in quality or extent—tended equally to weaken the prestige and moral authority of the *patria potestas* if only because of the greater relative sphere of matters in the son's life over which the *patria potestas* had no influence.

We are justified in assuming from the evidence that it was in times of war that the maximization of a son's public role—and, correspondingly, his sporadic releases from the *patria potestas*—was heightened. Historically, as we know, war puts a premium upon the services of the young, not the old. Ordinary civil affairs in Rome, like ordinary business affairs, could be, and were, handled by those who were *sui juris*, those who held the *patria potestas* and were not under it. The most honored title indeed of the members of the Senate was the *Patres Conscripti*. But in war, different requirements

---

[8] It is this kind of insight that makes Maine one of the great sociological minds of his age.

prevail, and when warfare is extended and intensified, as it became in the later Republic, these requirements can become decisive.

The conflict between kinship society and the military is, as Jenks (1908: 308 ff.) has brilliantly emphasized, one of the key conflicts of history.[9] Kinship society is inherently cellular—composed of compact and largely autonomous groups, families, clans, and *gentes*—whereas the military, as we find it in its earliest forms is, by comparison, individualistic. Between the power of the commander and the individual soldier there is no intermediate authority, for such authority would weaken both the unity and the necessary directness of command. The very directness of the military *imperium* therefore induces a kind of potential individualism in social relations if only because of its corroding effects upon intermediate groups. In the second place, military society operates primarily in terms of command—not custom, tradition, and the *mores*. In the interstices of command, accordingly, there is a degree of moral freedom unknown in kinship society, which is governed not by prescriptive law, but by the less specific and infinitely more inclusive ties of custom which, by its nature, fills in every possible crevice. In short, there is a kind of secularizing and individualizing quality in military life.

In the third place, military society, unlike kinship, is, or by its nature aspires to be, rational in its distribution of function and authority; that is, whether explicitly or implicitly, both authority and function tend to fall into hands that are most competent, irrespective of considerations of age or social prestige. It does this, that is, if it is to be successful. Kinship society, on the other hand, tends, as we have seen, to accept seniority and age as the crucial qualities of leadership, with such matters as descent and inherited prestige close in importance. We may summarize the difference between the two societies by saying that in the first—kinship—it is ascribed status that counts, whereas in the second—the military—it is achieved status that is alone significant, if victory is the prime consideration.

We know that the Romans were well aware of the differences between the two types of society and the potential consequences of military service to kinship and ordinary civil authority. An ingenious variety of checks existed to prevent possible thrusts to ascendancy of victory-intoxicated returning soldiers. For centuries there was the custom by which no militia could form within the walls and no returning militia could enter the city gates until it had disbanded outside. When the individuals reentered the city, they were thus symbolically, as well as actually, freed from the *imperium* and once again under normal civil authority, and especially the *patria potestas* (see, e.g., Mommsen, 1895: Vol. 1, 335). Such checks, however, whether custom-

[9] My comparison of the two types of society here is greatly indebted to Jenks' work.

ary or constitutional, could not forever withstand the growing number of wars, the increasing size of the forces themselves, and, perhaps most important, the constantly growing pressure for a regular standing army with continuous command.

One by one, from the end of the second century on, the old checks upon the military ceased to function. There began that fateful affinity between military service and popular following, between military triumph and political success, that, in Rome, as in many another society, was to have a transforming effect upon government and society. The key personage, undoubtedly, was the powerful and ruthless Marius at the beginning of the first century B.C. "Marius was not content to supplement his army by drawing upon the 'bravest men of Latium' and recalling to the colors *evocati* or discharged veterans known to him by reputation. He employed another method of enlistment. The proletariat ... now legally qualified for enrollment, were signed on for a definite period of service, in all probability for twenty years" (Parker, 1928: 24). The soldier might be a citizen when he joined up, he might be uncomplainingly under civil and paternal power, but the mere length of service that he among tens of thousands of young Roman males was now to look forward to—making him in effect a mercenary, knowing little and caring less about traditional matters—would make him restive, to say the least, when he returned on furlough or following separation:

> The army strongly detached from civil institutions, had chiefs who were absolute chiefs. Soldiers entered the service because they liked it; they hoped for loot and allotments of land. Who could give them this privilege? The General. So there grew up between the general and his men a closer association based not on the old discipline, nor even on the religion of the standard, but on mutual interest and greed (Homo, 1930: 164).

It is therefore, I suggest, in the rising incidence of war in Roman history, especially from the second century B.C. on, that we find the setting for the tensions that were eventually to reduce the *patria potestas* to innocuousness. For it was in the circumstances of increasing warfare that more and more sons under paternal power found themselves for lengthening periods of time under the *imperium militiae*, a form of authority that differed vastly from the *patria potestas* and provided, for all its own stringency, the essential conditions of that special type of individualism that was to sap the foundations of kinship society.

As Maine has reminded us (1917: 82):

> The military tribune and the private soldier who were in the field three-quarters of a year during the earlier contests and, at a later period the proconsul in charge of a province and the legionaries who occupied it, cannot have had practical reason to regard

themselves as the slaves of a despotic master; and all these avenues of escape tended constantly to multiply themselves ... We may infer, I think, that a strong sentiment in favor of the relaxation of the *patria potestas* had become fixed by the time that the pacification of the world commenced on the establishment of the Empire.

REFERENCES

Declareuil, J.
  1924   *Rome et l'organization du droit*. Paris: La Renaissance du livre.
  1927   *Rome the law-giver*. London: K. Paul, Trench, Trubner.
Fowler, W. W.
  1911   *The religious experience of the Roman people*. London: Macmillan.
Fustel de Coulanges
  1956   *The ancient city*. Garden City, New York: Doubleday. (Orig. pub. 1885.)
Hadley, J.
  1931   *Introduction to Roman law*. New Haven: Yale Univ. Press.
Haight, E. H.
  1922   Reconstruction in the Augustan Age. *Classical Journal* **17** (April): 335–376.
Homo, L.
  1930   *Roman political institutions*. New York: Knopf.
Hunter, W. A.
  1934   *Introduction to Roman law*. (9th ed.) London: Sweet and Maxwell.
Jenks, E.
  1908   *Law and politics in the Middle Ages*. New York: Holt.
Maine, H. S.
  1917   *Ancient law*. New York: Dutton, Everyman's Library. (Orig. pub. 1861.)
Maitland, F. W.
  1911   *Collected papers*. London and New York: Cambridge Univ. Press.
Mommsen, T.
  1895   *History of Rome*. (Rev. ed.) New York: Scribner's.
Parker, H. M. D.
  1928   *The Roman legions*. London and New York: Oxford Univ. Press.
Pelham, H. F.
  1911   *Essays on Roman history*. London and New York: Oxford Univ. Press (Clarendon).
Poste, E.
  1925   *Gai institutiones*, or, *Institutes of Roman law*. (4th ed.) London and New York: Oxford Univ. Press.
Roby, H. J.
  1902   *Roman private law in the times of Cicero and the Antonines*. London and New York: Cambridge Univ. Press.
Rostovtzeff, M. I.
  1926   *The social and economic history of the Roman Empire*. London and New York: Oxford Univ. Press (Clarendon).
Schisas, P. M.
  1926   *Offences against the state in Roman law*. London: University Press.
Strachan-Davidson, J. L.
  1912   *Problems of the Roman criminal law*. London and New York: Oxford Univ. Press.
Willems, P.
  1888   *Le droit public romain*. Paris: Louvain, C. Peeters.

POLITICAL ORGANIZATION AMONG AMERICAN INDIANS

Robert H. Lowie

I N A GROSS description of continental areas the American aborigines figure as separatistic and democratic, contrasting in the former respect with the African Negro, in the latter with both African and Polynesian. The illuminating studies on African politics edited by Drs. Fortes and Evans-Pritchard have demonstrated decisively what readers of P. A. Talbot or Henri Labouret had long known, to wit, that the traditional picture of Negro government is oversimplified. To be sure, there have been many powerful monarchies in African history, but east of the Niger, in the Upper Volta region, and in the Anglo-Egyptian Sudan not a few tribes resist integration as much as any people in the world. In 1931 the 69,484 Lobi on French soil in the Upper Volta country were spread over 1252 mutually independent sham villages (*prétendus villages*); a single one had over 600 residents, while 44 of these hamlets numbered fewer than 100, so that M. Labouret properly speaks of a *particularisme accusé*. Within no unit were there any chiefs, and assemblies convened to adjudicate particular issues had no means to execute their decisions. In short, the gamut of possible variations is realized in Negro Africa: we find there vast kingdoms on the pattern of Uganda and Benin, but also minute, headless, "anarchic" groups (Fortes and Evans-Pritchard, 1940; Labouret, 1931: 51, 56, 215, 386).

Reprinted from "Some Aspects of Political Organization among the American Aborigines" by Robert H. Lowie, *Journal of the Royal Anthropological Institute*, Vol. 78 (1948): pp. 11–24.

In the present essay I shall examine the corresponding phenomena in aboriginal America. In a discussion of this sort it is convenient, if not inevitable, to use such terms as "the State," "law," "government," "political," "sovereignty." Conforming to the views of Max Weber, Professor Radcliffe-Brown, and Professor Thurnwald as I understand them, I take these words to imply the control of physical force so far as a given society recognizes it as legitimate. Thus, the King of Uganda could rightfully order the execution of a subject, no matter how arbitrary the decree might seem from our point of view; and in West Africa the Mumbo Jumbo organization properly flogged malefactors. On the other hand, similar acts by the Ku Klux Klan are in usurpation of functions monopolized by the State in Western civilization.

However, a genetic view of political structure must reckon with the fact that primeval anarchy could not suddenly blossom forth into a modern State claiming absolute dominance within its territorial limits. It is, indeed, a documented fact that the states of the most advanced modern peoples did not develop contemporary pretensions until relatively recent times, yet their immediate antecedents did have a political organization, in other words, laws and government. A simple society may be differentiated so as to foreshadow government, yet the coercive element may be lacking. The Yurok of northwestern California and the Ifugao of Luzon have no chiefs or judges whatsoever, yet a dispute in their midst is settled by unofficial go-betweens approved by public opinion, who offer their services, though without an iota of authority. A logical dichotomy of societies on the rigid definition of Statehood indicated would rule out such phenomena as quite irrelevant to a study of government, but the common sense of comparative jurists regards them as highly significant. In the following inquiry, then, I shall indeed retain the exercise of force as the criterion of a full-fledged political organization, but I shall also consider what seem evolutionary stages toward that consummation.

The question I ask concerning American Indians may be phrased as follows: Within what territorial limits does authority create some measure of solidarity? And what is the nature of the authority encountered? Specifically, where, in America, was a state of modern type realized? What trends can be discerned toward its evolution?

SEPARATISM AND INTEGRATION

Notwithstanding my initial qualifications, African systems on the whole do differ noticeably from those of the New World. According to Roscoe, the Baganda once numbered three million; by 1911 civil wars and sleeping sickness had sadly reduced them, but not below the million mark. In

1668 Dapper credited Benin with a regular army of 20,000, which at a pinch could be increased to five times as many; the capital was five or six Dutch miles in circumference and had thirty main streets. In about 1870 Schweinfurth set the Shilluk at over a million; partly because of wars recent estimates are far more modest, yet they fluctuate between 50,000 and 100,000. Shortly before this explorer's visit a million Mangbettu had been under the sway of a single ruler. More recently the king of Ashanti had a quarter of a million subjects (Roscoe, 1911: 6; Talbot, 1926: 162ff; Schweinfurth, 1873: Vol. 1, 15; Vol. II, 35).

Except in the few higher civilizations of Mexico, Yucatan, Colombia, and Peru, there is nothing to match even the least of these figures, apparent parallel proving deceptive. To be sure, aboriginal Chile is said to have been inhabited by from half a million to a million and half Araucanians, but "there was no peacetime overall chief, no centralization of authority." There were, indeed, greater and lesser territorial units, but the subordination of the smaller "must have been close to purely nominal." Only during the nineteenth century "the earlier atomistic peacetime political structure assumed somewhat greater unity, cohesion and hierarchization." To take a humbler figure, the 55,000 Navaho now rank as the largest native tribe in the United States. But, in the first place, theirs has been a mushroom growth: in 1868 they did not exceed 15,000—possibly not 9000. Second, it is not clear that even this number was ever under a single government (Cooper, 1946: 694, 724; Kluckhohn and Leighton, 1946: 73).

As a matter of fact, a tendency to separatism was general. So advanced a people as the Hopi—some 3000 in all—live in eleven villages, mislabeled "towns" by grandiloquent ethnographers. Yet even this paltry population neither has nor has had a common head: "between pueblo and pueblo there is an attitude of jealousy, suspicion and subdued hostility" (Titiev, 1944: 59–68).

Much ado has been made about the Creek Confederacy in the southeastern United States and the Iroquois League of northern New York State. Unquestionably both prove wider political cooperation than was common in the New World, but their achievements must not be overrated. Authenticated occurrences reduce the cohesion involved in these alliances to a proper scale. It so happened that one of the Creek tribes, the Kasihta, became friendly with the alien Chickasaw. When the latter were at war with the Confederacy in 1793 "the Kasihta refused to take up arms with the other Creeks and their right to act in this independent manner was never questioned." Strictly parallel conduct among the federated Iroquois during the American Revolution was noted by Morgan. Each tribe was permitted to decide upon its course of action: the Oneida and half of the Tuscarora sided with the colonists, the other "leagued" tribes with the English. It was as though in 1914 Bavaria and half of Baden had joined the Allies to fight their fellow Germans. Apart from this disintegration in a crisis, earlier claims on behalf of the League's influence have been exploded by Fenton's historical researches. The Iroquois did raid far and wide, but it hardly holds true that "their dominion was acknowledged from Ottawa River to the Tennessee and from the Kennebec to Illinois River and Lake Michigan." In any case, at its peak in the seventeenth century the League never embraced over 16,000 or at most 20,000 persons (Swanton, 1930: 368–76; Hewitt, 1907; Fenton, 1940; Morgan, 1877: 2, Chapter 5).

Since the one-eyed is king among the blind, the two faltering attempts at consolidation by the Creek and the Iroquois remain noteworthy "climactic" results, as my colleague Professor Kroeber might phrase it. In world perspective, however, they are unimpressive.

If skillful farming populations showed no greater sense of nationalism, little can be expected of the hunters. The Caribou Eskimo lacked permanent political units altogether, each community being in Professor Birket-Smith's judgment "an incoherent conglomerate of families or households, voluntarily connected by a number of generally recognized laws." The largest settlements have a population of about 50, and all of them jointly do not exceed ten times that figure. Earlier reports, to be sure, suggest a recent decline, due largely to famine, but even half a century ago the largest separate tribe of the area was not credited with over 178 souls. To turn toward the southern tip of the New World, the Ona population at its peak is set at between 3500 and 4000. Since this embraced 39 wholly independent territorial hordes, the average size of the political unit was about 100 (Birket-Smith, 1929: 65–75, 260; Gusinde, 1946: 97).

Extreme as the Eskimo and the Fuegian instances may seem, they are paralleled on varying levels of cultural complexity. The exceptionally favorable food supply of Northwest Californians failed to produce solidarity beyond the bounds of kinship and of immediate proximity. Of the seventeen independent Yurok hamlets listed in 1852, the largest had only 165 inhabitants; three other had over 100; five, well under 50.

Up and down the Pacific coast of North America similar conditions prevailed. In northeastern Washington something less than 1500 Sanpoil were spread over twenty villages, each of which, except for those conspicuously small, was autonomous. The Quinault, in the southwestern part of the same state, probably numbered 800, divided among roughly 20 villages. The Lemhi of Idaho and associated Shoshoneans are set at 1200 about the beginning of the nineteenth century, and this included more than a single group; Lewis and Clark estimated one group at 100 warriors and 300 women and children; another at 60 warriors. In eastern Brazil the Botocudo stock was split into several distinct tribes, some of them subdivided into bands from 50 to 200. Notwithstanding the existence of tribal chiefs, an authority reports "the constancy of their blood feuds, not only between distinct ribes, but even between bands of the same tribe." The Foot Indians of the Gran Chaco gathered in bands approximating the Botocudo pattern (Kroeber, 1925: 16; Ray, 1932: 21–24, 109; Olson, 1936: 22; Steward, 1938: 188 ff.; Nimuendajú, 1946a: 97 ff.; Métraux, 1946a: 536, 1946b: 302).

No doubt an intermediate order of magnitude occurred. The Cheyenne of the Northern Plains at one time probably numbered not far from 4000. Of the Ge stock, some members were inconsiderable enough: the recent Canella fluctuated about the 300 mark, but earlier travellers describe the villages of their congeners as rather larger. In 1824, for example, one Apinayé settlement had a population of 1400; and the more remotely related Sherente display a sense of solidarity beyond the immediate local group. Though a paramout head is wanting, the several village chiefs sometimes jointly depose a grossly deficient colleague and appoint his successor. Characteristically, however, the Sherente had long been at bitter enmity with the Shavante, their closest linguistic and cultural kin (Llewellyn and Hoebel, 1941: 78; Nimúendajú, 1939: 7; 1942: 9 ff.).

Similar qualifications apply to the instances from the eastern United States. The League of the Iroquois has already been discussed. The Cherokee and the Choctaw were the two largest southeastern tribes, being estimated at 22,000 and 15,000 souls, respectively, in 1650. However, once more the *political* unit is incomparably smaller than the linguistic. For the Choctaw, Swanton reasonably suggests some 40–50 synchronous communities "constituting small States, each with its chief." An anonymous French writer of ca. 1755 does speak of a *grand chef* of the nation, but adds that his authority was negligible. The Cherokee were scattered over at least 80 towns. "These people came under the domain of one tribal chief only in time of great emergency and then most imperfectly." On the whole, it seems likely that the figures set for the Natchez in 1650 and for the Powhatan in 1607—4500 and 9000—approach the limits attained within the area by any governmental entity (Gilbert, 1943: 363; Swanton, 1931: 90, 95, 243; 1946: 114, 123, 161, 175).

At this point it is well to recall the phenomenon luminously illustrated by Durkheim for Australians, by Mauss and Beuchat for the Eskimo, and since demonstrated elsewhere. The seasonal rhythm of life, rooted in economic exigencies, transforms the constitution of a group and, as a corollary, its social life. The consequences we shall consider later. For the present, we merely note that some of the figures quoted would hold only for a relatively brief portion of the year; at other times, the tribe breaks up into minute fragments in order more effectively to exploit the environment (Durkheim, 1912; Mauss and Beuchat, 1904–1905).

To review the argument, American figures of a population approximating or exceeding 10,000 rarely, if ever, refer to permanently integrated political units.

How far does this conclusion apply to the four higher civilizations? As for the Aztec, the moot question of whether they totaled three or many more millions need not concern us; we are interested solely in what number belonged to the same state. That the hoary idea of an Aztec empire is untenable, seems certain in the light of modern research. All we find is a belated league of three tribes which remained mutually distrustful: "the Aztecs had no sense of unity," no national spirit. Within the present limits of Mexico City, Tenochtitlan, and Tlatelolco long persisted in complete independence of each other. At the time of the Spanish invasion the Texcocans joined the intruders against their former ally, Tenochtitlan. A quarter of a million people, or thereabouts may possibly have had a single government on a strict definition (Vaillant, 1941: 91, 134, 213 ff.).

Maya ruins are spread from northern Yucatán to Honduras, but they belong to different periods, and it is not easy to estimate the residents of any one state. Possibly in about A.D. 1000, according to legendary history, there was a league of three cities, of which Mayapan gained the ascendancy, establishing a centralized government two or three centuries later. This was followed by disintegration, leaving only petty chieftains for the Spaniards to contend with. In their era the rulers of Mani were "the most powerful in Yucatán." The tribute list for that province demonstrates 13,480 adult males. If we multiply this by six, or even ten, we still get no total population that looks spectacular by an African scale (Tozzer, 1941: 64; Morley, 1915: 2–12; Roys, 1933: 188–195).

The Chibcha numbered possibly a million, but they too, were divided up among several distinct states, of which Zipa, the largest, is credited with 300,000 souls. The untrustworthiness of early estimates is indicated by a fantastic reference to armies of 50,000 whereas no more than 600 Zipa braves attacked the Spanish troops (Kroeber, 1946: 887–909).

In short, the solitary convincing instance of grandiose expansion in the Western Hemisphere is that of the Incas of Cuzco, Peru. Their realm did extend from Ecuador to northern Chile, embracing possibly 6,000,000 subjects. However, we must recollect that aggrandizement was a very late pre-Columbian achievement. "In early times neither the *Inca* nor any of their neighbours thought of organizing their conquests as a permanent domain." Until the reign of Pachakuti (ca. A.D. 1438) "towns very near to

Cuzco preserved complete freedom of action and raided one another's territory whenever there seemed to be a good opportunity for plunder" (Rowe, 1946: 184 ff., 201–209, 257 ff.).

With a unique exception, then, the American Indians must be regarded as eminently separatistic.

However, there was certainly no sudden mutation from an Ona-like to an Inca-like condition. The Creek and the Iroquois schemes indicate a stage of solidarity, however imperfect, on a larger than normal scale. Still more illuminating are phenomena within the historic period. Whereas the two well-known leagues united mainly communities of like or closely related speech, Pontiac (1763) and Tecumseh (died 1813) brought together wholly unconnected tribes. The Ottawa chief rallied not merely his own people and their Algonkian congeners, but also the Seneca and the Wyandot of Iroquoian stock and the Siouan Winnebago. The Shawnee leader arrayed Algonkians, Wyandot, and even Creek Indians against the United States. Though both uprisings proved abortive, though they culminated in negation of British and American overlordship rather than in the creation of a close-knit aboriginal state, they do prove that under strong emotional stimulus exceptional natives could and did visualize cooperation of major scope. Individuals of comparable organizing skill, however diverse their motivation, must be credited with the nascent forms of Andean imperialism (Mooney, 1896: 668 ff., 681–691).

COERCIVE AUTHORITY

I now turn to my second theme—the manifestation or adumbration of coercive authority in aboriginal America. As in Africa, so here too, the range of observable phenomena is very great. At one extreme we find the "anarchic" Eskimo, Northwest Californians, and Fuegians; at the other, the Incas of Peru. But in the New World, the latter must be regarded as atypical, and an intermediate condition represents the norm. By this I mean a condition with differentiation of one or more individuals or headmen, even though their actual power is circumscribed or even negligible. For convenience of exposition I shall call these officials "titular chiefs" in contrast to the "strong chiefs" possessing unquestioned authority. After discussing the functions of these two types of civil heads, I shall examine the factors that many have strengthened the titular chief's hands in the American milieu; and I shall likewise consider what agencies aside from chiefs of either category have assumed State functions.

Titular Chiefs

Titular chiefs vary considerably in actual status. The Chipewyan individuals who bear the title exercise so little influence apart from the accident of personality that one might perhaps just as well put this north Canadian tribe into the chiefless category with the Eskimo and the Fuegians. Elsewhere the office is not only honorific, but also fraught with definite public functions. In order to overcome semantic difficulties it will be best to emphasize what the titular chief is *not*, before trying to indicate his positive attributes. That he cannot, in many American societies, correspond to an African chief is apparent whenever a single band or tribe has more than one title-bearer. Three hundred Canella are headed by three "chiefs"; another Ge people, the Pau d'Arco Kayapo, generally had two; the related Gorotire band, five (in 1940). Until 1880 the Omaha had two principal chiefs, with a varying number of lesser ones; this oligarchy was then superseded by a septet of uniform rank. Among the Arapaho there were four chiefs, and the Cheyenne with a population never greatly exceeding 4000 had 44! (Birket-Smith, 1930: 66; Dorsey, 1884: 357; Nimuendajú, 1943; Llewellyn and Hoebel, 1941: 67 ff.). A series of examples from diverse culture areas will elucidate what American chiefs typically lacked.

The Ojibwa (around Lake Superior) had a council "with vague and limited powers." It selected a chief "whose power was even vaguer than that of the council," and who was "less able to work his will against an existing custom." Tanner, who lived in this region from 1789 until 1822, mentions "the unstable power and influence of the chiefs." In an assembly of 1400 Assiniboine, Cree, and Ojibwa, he remarks "not one would acknowledge any authority superior to his own will." A chief was, indeed, entitled to some deference, "but this obedience . . . continues no longer than the will of the chief corresponds entirely with the inclination of those he leads." About the same time the trader Tabeau notes that among the Teton Dakota "all authority is as naught before the opposition of a single individual," and for the related Assiniboine, Denig—himself the husband of a woman of that tribe—offers an eyewitness's priceless corroboratory evidence. At a council attended by him the "leading chief" advocated peace with the Crow; a tribesman of lesser dignity vigorously and successfully opposed the idea, carrying the assembly with him. The historian Parkman, on the basis of personal experience in 1846, declares that very few Oglala Dakota "chiefs could venture without instant jeopardy of their lives to strike or lay hands upon the meanest of their people" and correctly notes the paradox that the "soldiers," that is, police, "have full license to make use of these and similar acts of coercion." This institution will be discussed later. Among the Shoshoneans of Nevada "any family was at liberty to pursue an independent course at any time"; in Arizona the head of the Maricopa had functions "more admonitory than coercive"; and among the Yuma the tribal leader, though appealed to in a dispute, was "more significant as an embodiment of spiritual power than as a lawgiver or executive." Equivalent testimony comes from Oregon and Washington (Jones, 1906: 137; Tanner, 1940: 151; Tabeau, 1939: 105 ff.; Denig, 1930: 430–56; Parkman, 1856: 291; Spier, 1930: 35; 1933: 158; Ray, 1932: 111; Steward, 1947: 246–60; Goodwin, 1942: 178 ff.; Forde, 1931: 134 ff.).

Superficially the stratified societies of coastal British Columbia are different, but only superficially in the questions at issue. What they emphasize is social eminence, not political power. A Haisla chief "gives orders only in matters directly concerned with feasts and potlatches"—not in cases of quarrels, theft, or murder; the Tsimshian equivalent was responsible for his followers' safety in battle and indemnified the mourners if their kindred had been killed. How different from an African potentate who owns his subjects' bodies and collects all damages for injuries sustained by them (Sapir, 1915; Olson, 1940: 182; Boas, 1916: 429 ff., 499).

South America yields corresponding testimony. In British Guiana a Barama headman has limited authority. Each of the three Canella dignitaries works like everyone else; none of them wears a badge of higher status, or interferes in private affairs, or issues commands, or imposes penalties. Among the related Apinayé, the headman does initiate measures against a sorcerer, but he cannot order an execution without popular assent. To take two more Brazilian examples, Karaya villagers simply desert a chief whose actions they resent; and though a Nambikuara leader enjoys a good deal of influence, he "has no coercive power at his disposal." In short, the typical American chief may enjoy social standing, but he lacks sovereignty (Gillin, 1936: 98, 140; Nimuendajú, 1939: 19 ff., 131 ff., 1946b: 93, 159–62, 239 ff.; Krause, 1911: 321; Lévi-Strauss, 1944: 23).

What, then, are the titular chief's positive attributes and functions? The outstanding one forthwith explains the deficiency I have harped on: he refrains from attempting physical force, because many societies conceive him as primarily a peacemaker. It would be a contradiction in terms for him to mete out punishment when his business is to smooth ruffled tempers, to persuade the recalcitrant, coax and even bribe the justly aggrieved into foregoing vengeance. He is, indeed, a go-between of the Yurok or Ifugao order, but with the essential difference of being the official, recognized, permanent moderator instead of a self-appointed one *ad hoc*. In order to compass his end—maintenance of communal harmony—he might stoop to eating humble pie and to personal sacrifices. A Sanpoil chief presents each litigant with a blanket; his Cree colleague is expected to give up thoughts of revenge on his own behalf, such as other men freely indulge. A Winnebago went still further: "If necessary, the chief would mortify himself, and with skewers inserted in his back have himself led through the village to the home of the nearest kinspeople of the murdered person." By thus arousing compassion he hoped to avert a feud (Mandelbaum, 1940: 222; Radin, 1923: 209).

No wonder that an appeaser *ex officio* was not associated with warfare, was often—in his official capacity—deliberately divorced from violence and discipline. An Iroquois sachem's duties, Morgan reports, "were confined to the affairs of peace. He could not go out to war as a sachem." His position was sharply separated from the military leader's, being hereditary in the clan, whereas a successful captain gained a "chiefly" title of another category by personal bravery. This polarity was widespread. In a Fox Indian (Wisconsin) council, the Quiet and the War Chief were complementary figures, as are the Pueblo Town and War Chiefs—the former being prescriptively a man of peace who must not even go hunting, the latter a policeman who threatens punishment. The Omaha neither let a chief head a raid nor even allowed him to serve as a subordinate officer of one. Again, "a man who has often been on the warpath," say the Pawnee, "becomes imbued with the desire to take scalps and capture ponies and is no longer fit to be chief." A Winnebago chief always belongs to one clan, a policeman to another (Morgan, 1877: Part II, Chapters II, IV, V; Jones, 1939: 82; Titiev, 1944: 59–68; Parsons, 1939: 154 ff.; Dorsey, 1884: 217; Dorsey and Murie, 1940: 112 ff.).

This dichotomy prevails even where a fusion of civil and military pre-eminence seems at first blush easily realized. In several South American tribes the "chief" did lead war parties, but whereas he became a virtual autocrat on a raid he relapsed into his usual impotence on his return. On this point early sources on the Kariri and the Tapuya (eastern Brazil) agree with recent ones on the Taulipang (south of the Roroima) and the Jivaro (Ecuador). One North American phenomenon is instructive in this context. The Iroquois League found it desirable to create two generals "to direct the movements of the united bands," but these officials never aspired to a dictatorship. To quote Morgan, "the essential character of the government was not changed. ... Among the Iroquois this office never became influential" (Koch-Grünberg, 1923: 94; Nantes, 1706: 103; Pompeu Sobrinho, 1934: 18; Karsten, 1923: 7 ff.; Morgan, 1877: Part II, Chapter V).

In short, the conceptions of civil and of military leadership were distinct in America. There was sporadic tyranny even in the democratic Northern Plains societies, but it sprang from individual bullying, usually supported by a powerful body of kin or from putative supernatural sanction, not from the *coup d'état* of a captain returning drunk with success and filled with the ambition of a despot.

Besides being a skillful peacemaker, the ideal chief was a paragon of munificence. This may hold more often in North than in South America, but instances are not wanting in the south. Thus, a Nambikuara headman constantly shares with his tribesmen whatever surplus of goods he may have acquired: "Generosity is the quality . . . which is expected of a new chief." In the north, this demand is constant. In Alaska, where the Eskimo were affected by the ideology of their Indian neighbors, the title of "chief" automatically devolved on that Nunivak who entertained most lavishly at village feasts. A chief of the Tanaina Athabaskans (about Cook Inlet) feeds and cloths the destitute, provides for the households of men away on hunting trips, adopts orphans, and even pays for shamanistic services that are beyond a poorer tribesman's means. The coastal tribes of British Columbia, not withstanding their emphasis on hereditary status, insisted that a headman should validate his claims by frequent distribution of property. In the Plains area chieftainship and niggardliness were mutually exclusive. To quote Wissler "no Blackfoot can aspire to be looked upon as a headman unless he is able to entertain well, often invite others to his board, and make a practice of relieving the wants of his less fortunate band members." The Cheyenne or the Crow had identical standards of behavior (Lévi-Strauss, 1944: 24; Lantis, 1946: 248; Osgood, 1937: 132; Sapir, 1915; Wissler, 1911: 23; Llewellyn and Hoebel, 1941: 79).

A third attribute of civil leadership is the gift of oratory, normally to be exercised on behalf of tribal harmony and the good old traditional ways. Speaking of the Sherente, Nimuendajú reports: "On many evenings . . . I saw the chief assemble the village. Stepping in front of the semi-circle . . ., he would impressively and vividly harangue the crowd for possibly an hour. Usually he began circumstantially explaining the half-forgotten ceremonial of some festival. . . . There followed a lengthy admonition . . . to preserve ancient usage. In conclusion, he would urge all to live in peace and harmony. . . ." The extinct Tupinambá of coastal Brazil regarded a species of falcon as the king of his zoological class: *"ils se fondaient sur le fait que cet oiseau se levait de bon matin et haranguait les autres oiseaux, tout comme le chef de la hutte le faisait chaque jour, à l'aube, dans les villages tupinamba."* In the Chaco the contemporary Pilaga merely postpone oratory until nightfall: *"Ce prurit d'éloquence est commun à tous les caciques et constitue . . . un des principaux attributs de leur dignité. . . . Le thème habituel de ces harangues est la paix, l'harmonie et l'honnêteté, vertus recommandées à tous les gens de la tribu."* In characteristic fashion a Chiriguano explained to Nordenskiöld the existence of a female head of the tribe: her father had taught her to speak in public. Thousands of miles to the north, in the Shoshone vernacular a headman figures as "the talker," which "designates his most important function." Maricopa and Apache chiefs, too, were matutinal lecturers; and among the Havasupai (Arizona) Spier says: "it might be said not that a chief is one who talks, but that one who talks is a chief" (Métraux, 1928: 179; 1937: 390; Nordenskiöld, 1913: 229; Steward, 1938: 247; Spier, 1928: 237 ff.; 1933: 158; Goodwin, 1942: 165 ff., 178).

In my opinion, then, the most typical American chief is not a lawgiver, executive, or judge, but a pacifier, a benefactor of the poor, and a prolix Polonius.

Strong Chiefs

But not all chiefs were only titular. A relatively small, but significant number of societies had genuine rulers. It is best to begin with an unexceptionable example, the Inca state, the outstanding American sample of Drs. Fortes and Evans-Pritchard's category A—political systems with a well-developed governmental apparatus (1940: 5).

The Inca emperor, ruling by divine right, undoubtedly did control means of coercion. Through an elaborate "bureaucracy" he exacted tribute from his subjects and directed their labors, even their private lives. He did not scruple to transfer masses of the population from one province to another in the interests of the dynasty. What elsewhere in the New World were private wrongs here became offences against the Crown and called for summary official penalties.

Emblematic of autocracy were the trappings of royalty otherwise conspicuously rare in America. The ruler wore and carried impressive regalia, traveled in a litter borne by special attendants, kept a large harem, and surrounded his court with an elaborate etiquette. His corpse was prepared for preservation in the palace, and his favorite wives together with a suitable retinue were strangled to accompany their master to the hereafter (Rowe, 1946).

Concerning the Aztec chief the authorities yield contradictory and confusing evidence, but it seems clear that he did not conform to the Inca pattern. He was apparently not closely identified with the supreme deity; and, notwithstanding fixed succession within a lineage, he could be deposed. The hereditary *halachuinic* of the Maya probably wielded greater power, claiming tribute as well as military service and periodically examining subordinate chiefs in order to weed out pretenders. Significantly, both he and the sacred war leader traveled in a litter, a symbol of exalted rank also attached to a Chibcha monarch, who resembled his Peruvian parallel in other respects. He, too, received tribute, kept a seraglio, hedged himself about with ceremonials, and was buried with several wives and slaves. When he expectorated, an attendant caught the spittle in an extended cloth—a form of flunkyism hardly conceivable among the Crow or Cheyenne

(Roys, 1933: 192 ff.; Tozzer, 1941: 165, 222; Kroeber, 1946; Vaillant, 1941: 113 ff.).

It may be natural to find a full-blown political system among the materially advanced populations whose very numerical strength requires some central control if there is to be any solidarity. But, interestingly enough, the outlines of such a system appear also in the tiny states of the southeastern culture area of North America. This anomaly has been recently stressed by Steward. Indeed, the Natchez sovereign came very close to the Inca conception of royalty. He claimed relationship with the solar deity, his kinsmen ranking as "Little Suns"; held power over life and death; traveled in a litter and in death was followed by wives and servants, his bones being laid to rest in a temple near those of his predecessors. His subjects were obliged to keep at least four paces away from his person and would hail him "with genuflections and reverences." Elements of this complex, such as the litter, characterize the Timucua of Florida and the Chickasaw of Northern Mississippi; and though the monarchical principle is generally weaker in the southeast as a whole than among the Natchez, it reappears in full force in Virginia. "As halfe a God they esteeme him," Captain John Smith reports in writing of the Powhatan chief. This ruler arbitrarily ordered his subjects to be beaten, tortured, and killed, and kept a sizable bodyguard to execute his will. "What he commandeth they dare not disobey in the least thing." He demanded tribute of skins, beads, corn, and game; and numerous concubines waited upon him. Here and there undemocratic usages turn up as far north as New England, where they have been plausibly ascribed to southeastern influences. However that be, the specific resemblances among Peruvians, Natchez, and Powhatan suggest a common origin for so atypical an American polity (Swanton, 1911: 100–10, 139 ff.; 1946: 161, 175, 598 ff., 641–654, 728, 730; Flannery, 1939: 116 ff., 122 ff., Steward, 1947: 97). Of course, this does not imply that the social scheme diffused from the Inca Empire itself, a chronologically impossible assumption, but rather that certain elements of a monarchical system crystallized somewhere between Yucatán and Peru and spread in a period considerably antedating the expansion of Inca sovereignty. If I understand Professor Steward correctly, this agrees with his recent interpretation of the facts.

Given the marked libertarian bias of most American aborigines, how can we conceive the growth of absolutism? What could convert the titular chief who cajoled his tribesmen into preserving the social equilibrium into a veritable king?

Evolutionary Germs

In reexamining the chiefless or virtually chiefless tribes we discover here and there that the Indians willingly subordinate themselves to some individual for a particular enterprise. In a rabbit drive the Washo and neighboring Shoshoneans of the western Basin temporarily followed a leader noted for his skill as a hunter, though "apart from that special occasion his authority was nil" (Lowie, 1924: 196 ff., 284 ff., 305).

An exceptionally large gathering may favor the similarly spontaneous acceptance of a director. The Yahgan, who normally move about in very small groups, unite up to the number of eighty when a beached whale provides food for the participants at an initiation ceremony. Without an election some mature man well posted in traditional usage emerges as the master of ceremonies and henceforth plans the daily routine. What is more, he appoints a constable, who in turn chooses a number of deputies. These policemen exercise genuine legal authority: they forcibly drag refractory tyros to the initiation lodge, overpower a troublemaker, bind him, and let him lie for half a day without food or drink. The Yahgan, furthermore, have a men's club: the members as a whole bully their wives into fetching fuel and food for the assemblage, and one man has the duty of keeping women from prying (Gusinde, 1937: 199–208, 653, 779 ff., 805–961, 1319–1376).

Informally established offices are not necessarily ephemeral. The Nambikuara illustrate the rise of a relatively stable chieftaincy, as suggestively described by Lévi-Strauss (1944). A man with inborn gifts of leadership forms the nucleus for a group that voluntarily acclaims him, thereby shifting responsibility to his shoulders. He directs the food quest during the difficult dry season, shares his surplus freely, prepares arrow poison for his adherents, and plans their entertainments. In requital, they concede him certain prerogatives, such as plural marriage, but without their approbation he is powerless. Here, then, there emerges a titular chief with genuine influence, though still not a ruler.

By way of contrast there is a short-lived but absolute authority of the war leader as already noted for several South American groups. For North American parallels we have fuller data. A Crow supposedly organized his raid only when prompted by a supernatural patron, whence the leader's ascendancy over all who joined his expedition: theirs were the menial tasks, his the loot to dispose of as he chose, but also the responsibility for failure and losses. The equalitarian attitudes of everyday life recede, supplanted by a transitory overlordship. Omaha captains even appointed policemen who had the right to beat refractory or lagging warriors. Fleeting dictatorship of this limited range is not irrelevant to our problem. About 1820 the Cheyenne conceived themselves as one huge war party, whose leader thus automatically became supreme, supplanting the tribal council of "chiefs." Yet in consonance with native ideology he retained not a vestige of his special authority when his task was done (Dorsey, 1884: 321; Llewellyn and Hoebel, 1941; 163).

Undisputed supremacy for a restricted period was also granted during religious festivals. When a Hopi ceremony is in process, Stephen (1936: 728) learned, "the chief of it is chief of the village and all the people." Similarly, the priest who directed a Crow Sun Dance was not merely the master of ceremonies, but the temporary ruler of the tribe, superseding the camp chief.

Nonchiefly Authority

Perhaps the most remarkable instances of authority, full fledged and not altogether ephemeral, turn up in connection with important, economic undertakings which are to be safeguarded in the common interest.

A pertinent phenomenon from northern Brazil seems to have eluded general notice. The Apinayé chief, if properly qualified, succeeds his maternal uncle in the office, by virtue of which he guards the villagers' interests and orders the execution of evil sorcerers. But at the planting season a pair of men representing the moieties begin to act as independent executives. One of them collects the seeds, invokes the Sun to prosper them, and is the first to plant a plot. Both of these officials watch the crops, chant daily songs to promote growth, and *forcibly prevent or punish premature harvesting*. "Woe to any Indian woman who should dare to remove clandestinely even the most trifling product from her own plots before maturity is officially announced!" If the rule is broken, they "attack the houses of the village or the camp, raging and throwing everything about pellmell, breaking the vessels and flogging with thorny whips any women who have not fled in good season, or gash them with a special weapon. . . ." Even the chief's wife was once severely chastised for transgressing the law. Apart from the religious feature, the phenomenon reminds an Americanist of the Winnebago or Menomini constables who punished overhasty gatherers of wild rice (Nimuendajú, 1939: 13, 19, 89, 131 ff., Radin, 1923: 226 ff., Skinner, 1913: 26).

The last-mentioned officers from the Woodlands of North America are obvious variants of the familiar Plains Indian "soldiers" mentioned by Parkman. Their activities developed most spectacularly during a communal hunt, upon whose outcome the very life of the natives would depend. In order to ensure a maximum kill, a police force—either coinciding with a military club, or appointed *ad hoc*, or serving by virtue of clan affiliation—issued orders and restrained the disobedient. In most of the tribes they not only confiscated game clandestinely procured, but whipped the offender, destroyed his property, and, in case of resistance, killed him. The very same organization which in a murder case would merely use moral suasion turned into an inexorable State agency during a buffalo drive. However, Hoebel and Provinse have shown that coercive measures extended considerably beyond the hunt: the soldiers also forcibly restrained braves intent on starting war parties that were deemed inopportune by the chief; directed mass migrations; supervised the crowds at a major festival; and might otherwise maintain law and order (Wissler, 1911: 22–26, 1912:17, 24, 1922: 161, 178; Richardson, 1940: 9 ff.; Jenness, 1922: 11, 41; Mandelbaum, 1940; 203, 225; Kroeber, 1908: 147 ff.; Hoebel, 1936: 443–448, 1904: 82; Provinse, 1937: 347).

Here, then, we find unequivocal authoritarianism. Theoretically, the police acted, at least in a number of tribes, under the direction of the tribal chief or council. The foundation was thus laid for either an autocracy or an oligarchy. Why did this logical end fail to be consummated?

In the first place, let us revert to the seasonal rhythm of the Plains Indians. During a large part of the year the tribe simply did not exist as such; and the families or minor unions of families that jointly sought a living required no special disciplinary organization. The soldiers were thus a concomitant of numerically strong aggregations, hence functioned intermittently rather than continually.

Second, the "constitutional" relationship of chief and police was by no means so simple as might appear. It was definitely not that of the head of a modern state toward his army. Denig, whose observations on the impotence of Assiniboine chiefs have been quoted, ascribes to the police "the whole active power of governing the camp or rather of carrying out the decrees and decisions of the councils." He himself witnessed "two killed and many severely thrashed for their misdemeanours." Were the soldiers, then, strictly subordinate to the *council*, as Denig's phraseology implies? Well, according to the same authority, if councillors threatened to grow violent at a meeting "two soldiers advanced to the middle of the lodge and laid two swords crosswise on the ground, which signal immediately restored order and quiet." There was thus a dispersal of sovereignty: the titular chief had none, the council was in principle a governing board controlling a police squad that carried out their decisions, but *de facto* the theoretically subordinate police acted with considerable independence (Denig, 1930: 436, 439, 442, 444 ff., 448, 455, 530 ff.).

The much fuller data on the Cheyenne collected by Messrs. Llewellyn and Hoebel (1941: 67–131) corroborate this interpretation. Here a self-perpetuating council of 44 "chiefs" with safe tenure during a ten-year term of office was headed by five priest-chiefs, one of whom took precedence as the representative of the mythical culture here, Sweet Medicine. This did not make him the equivalent of a Shilluk king, for he "wielded no consequent special political authority" nor was he above the traditional law. Unlike other Plains peoples, the Cheyenne for ritual reasons conceived homicide as a crime. When Little Wolf, the head chief and man of superb record, killed a tribesman, though under mitigating circumstances, he did not escape the penalty, but went into voluntary exile. A lesser chief is known to have been severely flogged by the soldiers for a similar offence and was likewise banished, though not demoted in rank.

To turn to the council as a whole, it is true that they appointed one of the five existing military clubs to oversee a migration or a communal hunt. But, apart from such matters as directing travel, the "chiefs" were little concerned with secular affairs, sometimes waiving the right to a definitive decision and thus leaving a great deal to the discretion of their appointees. Accordingly, the police became the final authority in a large number of issues either beyond the competence of their electors or deliberately turned over to them by the council for settlement. The soldiers thus could, and repeatedly did, inaugurate legal precedents, nor does it appear that these were even challenged by the "chiefs."

Llewellyn and Hoebel draw attention to an extraordinary illustration of police autonomy. During a march directed by the Fox society, a councilor named Sleeping Rabbit answered a taunt by shooting the interlocutor, a member of the Dog organization. The arrow could not be extricated. The Foxes severely mauled and kicked the criminal; and when the victim's arm grew worse, they decreed that Sleeping Rabbit must amputate it, a novel verdict. Public sentiment, crystallized in the four other societies, favored exiling the culprit, but he avowed his guilt and, in self-infliction of a fine, presented the Foxes with five good horses. This settled the matter.

As our authorities show, this was emphatically not an example of composition. Damages accrued neither to the victim nor to his kin nor to his society, but to the Foxes. *They* were the State in this case, receiving the indemnity as a Bantu ruler might in corresponding circumstances. Of course, so far as we know, the case is unique and might have remained so throughout Cheyenne history; but the mere possibility of its occurrence is significant.

The relations of the Cheyenne council and soldiers were, of course, determined by the general American conception of chieftaincy. If more than temporary sovereignty were to be attained at all, it would thus more naturally center in the police. Here we encounter a third factor that militated against autocracy or oligarchy. In this culture area the constabulary force was rarely fixed, being as a rule recruited differently for different seasons or even for specific occasions. In a Pawnee village, for example, the chief's adjutant and three of his deputies acted as police, but for a buffalo hunt a priest chose one of four societies as a nonce police (Dorsey and Murie, 1940: 113). The Cheyenne, we have noted, had five such organizations; it was not likely that four of them would calmly submit to the oligarchical pretensions of one rival body.

It so happens that in this tribe the Dogs did enjoy an unusual advantage over the other clubs: by an accident of history, a century or more ago, the males of one band collectively joined this society, so that in this solitary instance society and band coincided in adult male membership. The chief of the Dogs was thus *ipso facto* head of his band, and the Dog men remained united during the winter when rival clubs were scattered over various local divisions. Here, then, the germ for hegemony occurred, but it never reached fruition.

A further point must be mentioned. Within any one of the military clubs its chief was supreme, issuing orders like a war captain and sometimes ruling his members with an iron hand. Yet the libertarian impulses of these Indians would not brook servility in an absolute sense; in 1863, characteristically, the Dogs *forbade* their chief to attend a treaty council with American commissioners!

In short, though the Plains Indians indubitably developed coercive agencies, the dispersal of authority and the seasonal disintegration of the tribes precluded a permanent State of modern type. Generalizing for the whole of America, there were sundry gropings toward centralization of power, but counteracting trends made them fall short of permanent results. Yet such results were achieved in Peru and in so relatively simple a setting as that of the Powhatan. What were the circumstances involved in these cases? And is it possible to detect similar factors in the normally libertarian societies?

The Religious Factor

When Alexander the Great aspired to imperial grandeur, he was not content with the glory of a successful general, but claimed divinity and, as a mark of its acceptance, prostration. This sacred character, we have seen, supposedly belonged to the Inca ruler and to the Natchez Great Sun; the obeisances and genuflections in their presence are the equivalent of Alexander's demand for *proskúnésis*. With frankly evolutionary aim I shall assemble some data from the simpler American tribes in order to show that religious beliefs were used to attain political influence there; and I suggest that the awe which surrounded the protégé of supernatural powers formed the psychological basis for more complex political developments. It is possible for a titular chief to add to his standing by combining spiritual blessings with civil eminence, or he may enter an alliance with the religious functionary, thus foreshadowing the familiar spectacle of State and Church joined in the support of the established order.

The latter contingency is classically exemplified in Gayton's (1939) study on the Yokuts, a central Californian stock of some 18,000 souls divided into over fifty autonomous tribelets, probably never exceeding 800 in population.

In each of these units an acceptable member of the Eagle lineage served as chief, representing the mythical Eagle who had ruled the world in dim antiquity. Notwithstanding this lofty role, the chief was not an autocrat, but he did hold more than nominal precedence. Provided with food by his tribesmen, enjoying a monopoly of trade in highly prized products, entitled to a share in doctors' fees, he was the wealthiest man in the community. By way of reciprocity, it was his duty to entertain visitors, to help the poor, and to contribute generously to the cost of festivities. He determined movements from and to the village and alone could authorize the death penalty for a public enemy. In general, he adhered to the part of a peace-preserving headman, rarely making a vital decision without previously consulting other venerable men.

Nevertheless, a chief could *de facto* magnify his power with the aid of a favourite shaman. In lieu of taxation the Yokuts expected the persons attending a festival to defray the expenses. If a wealthy villager evaded this obligation, the chief's medicine man would smite him with illness and impoverish his victim by exorbitant fees for sham treatment. Since the chief's consent was essential for violent measures against the doctor, he could always dismiss complaints on the subterfuge of insufficient evidence. It is important to note that public opinion as a rule sympathized with the chief and the shaman, for the miser who failed to contribute at festivals thereby imposed extra burdens on his fellows.

Given the native faith, an unscrupulous chief could evidently work his will in collusion with a shamanistic accomplice. Yet in the long run, Dr. Gayton explains, such knavish tricks led to a revulsion of feeling. A chief could not safely give rein to his malevolent inclinations. In the face of continuous suspicion his prestige would wane, in extreme instances he might even be supplanted in office by a less objectionable scion of his line. As for his accessory, the attitude toward doctors being ambivalent here, as in much of North America, a persistently malevolent leech was likely to be killed by the enraged family of his victim. In short, the Yokut system involved a considerable strengthening of chiefly influence without, however, approaching anything like despotic rule. Its instructiveness lies largely in demonstrating religion as a prop of the civil head on the relatively low plane of a simple hunting people.

In a not inconsiderable number of South American societies there is a personal union of temporal and spiritual functions. In Colombia, the Kágaba and the Ijca (the latter linguistic relatives of the Chibcha) do not dissociate the concepts of priest and chief. Among the Yaruro (Venezuela) each moiety recognizes a shaman as its head. In the Matto Grosso the Tupi-Kawahib chief is "first of all, a shaman, usually a psychotic addicted to dreams, visions, trances and impersonations." Another Brazilian group, the Botocudo, had as the leader of a band the "strongest" man, the epithet designating not muscular strength, but spiritual ascendancy. And, suggestively enough, these chiefs played a greater role than their colleagues in neighboring populations and were in higher measure responsible for their bands, which sometimes took their names from the leaders (Bolinder, 1925: 111 ff., 126 ff.; Preuss, 1919–1920: 364–368; Petrullo, 1939: 215; Nimuendajú, 1946a: 97 ff.; Lévi-Strauss, 1944: 25).

But even the Botocudo chief's influence pales before that of the prophets who periodically arose in both Americas (Mooney, 1896: 662, 672 ff., 676, 686, 700; Spier, 1935; Métraux, 1931; Nimuendajú, 1914). In my opinion, Nimuendajú, Spier, and Métraux have demonstrated that these messiahs did not so much react against white aggression, which represented merely a special case of the generic problem of evil, as against the supposed doom that threatened to engulf the moribund universe. Typically, the prophets promised salvation to their adherents, whereas unbelievers were to be transformed or destroyed. Given the mental atmosphere of the aborigines, the more dynamic of the messiahs undoubtedly gained an extraordinary sway over their fellows. One of the early Guarani deliverers affected the pomp of royalty: refusing to walk, he had himself carried on the shoulders of his attendants; the common herd were not allowed to approach his person. Such pretensions rested on a claim to supernatural inspiration or to divinity itself. Many of the self-styled saviors tyrannically imposed their will against common sense and, what is far more, against previously entrenched beliefs. In order to dance and chant as required, Obera's Guarani followers ceased to plant and harvest their crops in 1579. In the nineteenth century, under the spell of successive prophets, the Apapocuva band of this people repeatedly chased the will-o'-the-wisp of an earthly paradise, undertaking lengthy migrations to escape the menacing catastrophe. A little over a century ago an Algonkian messiah successfully ordered his people to kill their dogs and to abandon their hitherto prized sacred bags. For a while, about 1805, Tenskwatawa, the Shawnee prophet, even held the power over the lives of his tribesmen, having his opponents burned as witches.

It is a far cry from the unstable sovereignty of these prophets to the close-knit Inca state, but the gap is far greater between the nominal chiefs described by Tanner among the Central Algonkians and the messiah he met in the very same tribe. The former were obeyed when the people so chose; at the latter's behest they humbly killed their dogs, gave up their strike-a-lights at the expense of "much inconvenience and suffering," and threw away their hitherto holiest possessions. Assume the urge to leadership, as found by Lévi-Strauss in the Matto Grosso, to be combined with an awe-inspiring supernatural sanction, and the way is clear to a formative stage on the way toward a government by divine right. What military prowess failed to create in aboriginal America is demonstrably possible even in a democratic environment under the hypnosis of religious exaltation and the moral duress that follows in its wake.

CONCLUSION

It is not part of my plan to squeeze out of the evidence conclusions it will not bear. I cannot trace in detail the sequence of events that led from Ona "anarchy" to the close-knit structure known as the Inca state. I rest content with sketching a probable line of development. The totalitarian concentration of power in Inca Peru is an historic fact; so is the absence of any comparable official authority over most of the New World. If, for the sake of throwing the problem into relief, we assume an otherwise unwarranted teleological point of view, we discover sundry gropings toward the establishment of political authority, which, however, lose themselves in blind alleys. On analogy, what seems simpler than a military despotism under the two Iroquois generals? Yet nothing of the sort arose in the face of an antagonistic cultural tradition. Similarly, the workings of the Cheyenne military societies seem to predestine the tribe to an oligarchical system; but that, too, was precluded by the regnant pattern of social life.

Nevertheless, equalitarianism recedes when confronted with putative supernatural favor. The very same men who flout the pretensions of a fellow brave grovel before a darling of the gods, render him "implicit obedience and respect." It is probably no mere coincidence that Pontiac was a higher priest in the most sacred organization of this people, that Tecumseh was seconded by his brother, the prophet, and on occasion himself laid claim to supernatural powers. The foundation of a major state, I suggest, was due to men of this type—men who both imagined a unity beyond that of immediate kinship and contiguity and who simultaneously succeeded in investing their mission with the halo of supernaturalism. When not pitted against the terrible odds actually encountered by Pontiac and Tecumseh, natives of their mentality would be able to overcome both the dominant separatism and the dominant liberatariansim of their fellows and create the semblance of a modern state.

REFERENCES

Birket-Smith, K.
  1929   *The Caribou eskimos. Report of the Fifth Thule Expedition, 1921–24*. Vol. 5. Copenhagen: Gyldendal.
  1930   *Contributions of Chipewyan ethnology. Report of the Fifth Thule Expedition, 1921–24*. Vol. 6. Copenhagen: Gyldendal.

Boas, F. B.
  1961   *Tsimshian mythology*. Annual Report 31. Washington, D.C.: Bureau of American Ethnology.
Bolinder, G.
  1925   *Die indianer der tropischen Schneegebiete*. Stuttgart: Strecker und Schroder.
Cooper, J.
  1946   The Araucanians. In *Handbook of South American Indians*, pp. 687–760. Bulletin 143, Vol. 2. Washington, D.C.: Bureau of American Ethnology.
Denig, E. T.
  1930   *Indian tribes of the upper Missouri*. Annual Report 46. Washington, D.C.: Bureau of American Ethnology.
Dorsey, G. A., and J. R. Murie
  1940   *Notes on Skidi Pawnee society*. Vol. 27. Chicago: Field Museum of Natural History.
Dorsey, J. O.
  1884   *Omaha sociology*. Annual Report 13. Washington, D.C.: Bureau of American Ethnology.
Durkheim, E.
  1912   *Les formes élémentaires de la vie religieuse*. Paris: Alcan
Fenton, W. N.
  1940   *Problems arising from the historic North-Eastern position of the Iroquois*. Miscellaneous Collection 100. Washington, D.C.: Smithsonian Institute.
Flannery, R.
  1939   *An analysis of coastal Algonquin culture*. Series 7. Washington, D.C.: Catholic Univ. of America Press.
Forde, D.
  1931   *Ethnography of the Yuma Indians*. Vol. 28. Berkeley: Univ. Publications in American Archaeology and Ethnology.
Fortes, M., and E. E. Evans-Pritchard (Eds.)
  1940   *African political systems*. London: Oxford Univ. Press.
Gayton, A. H.
  1939   *Yokuts-Mono chiefs and shamans*. Vol. 24. Berkeley: Univ. of California Publications in American Archaeology and Ethnology.
Gilbert, W. H.
  1943   *The eastern Cherokees*. Bulletin 133. Washington, D.C.: Bureau of American Ethnology.
Gillin, J.
  1936   *The Barama River Caribs of British Guiana*. Vol. 14, No. 2. Cambridge: The Peabody Museum of American Archaeology and Ethnology.
Goodwin, G.
  1942   *The social organization of the Western Apache*. Chicago: Univ. of Chicago Press.
Gusinde, M.
  1937   *Die Feuerland indianer. Die yamana; vom leben und denken der wassernomaden am Kap Hoorn*. Vol. 2. Mödling bie Wien: Verlag Anthropos.
  1946   *Urmenschen in Feuerland*. Berlin: Zsolnay.
Hewitt, J. N. B.
  1907   Iroquois. In *Handbook of American Indians north of Mexico*. Bulletin 30, No. 1. Washington, D.C.: Bureau of American Ethnology.
Hoebel, E. A.
  1936   Associations and the state in the plains. *American Anthropologist* 38 (1936): 433–438.

1940   *The political organization and law-ways of the Comanche Indians.* No. 54. Menasha, Wisconsin: American Anthropological Association.

Jenness, D.
1922   *Life of the Copper Eskimos. Report of the Canadian Arctic Expedition, 1913–1918.* Vol. 12. Ottawa: Acland.

Jones, W.
1906   Central Algonkin. In *Annual archaeological report*, pp. 136–146. Toronto: Provincial Museum and Art Gallery of Ontario.
1939   *Ethnography of the Fox Indians.* Bulletin 125. Washington, D.C.: Bureau of American Ethnology.

Karsten, R.
1923   *Blood revenge, war, and victory feasts among the Jibaro Indians of eastern Equador.* Bulletin 79. Washington, D.C.: Bureau of American Ethnology.

Kluckhohn, C., and D. Leighton
1946   *The Navaho.* Cambridge: Harvard Univ. Press.

Koch-Grünberg, T.
1923   *Vom roroima zum Orinoco.* Vol. 3. Berlin: D. Reimer.

Krause, F.
1911   *In den wildnissen Brasiliens.* Leipzig: R. Voiglander.

Kroeber, A. L.
1908   *Ethnology of the Gros Ventre.* Vol. 1. New York: The Trustees of the American Museum of Natural History.
1925   *Handbook of the Indians of California.* Bulletin 78. Washington, D.C.: Bureau of American Ethnology.
1946   The Chibcha. *Handbook of South American Indians.* Bulletin 143. Vol. 2. Washington, D.C.: Bureau of American Ethnology.

Labouret, H.
1931   *Les tribus du Rameau Lobi.* Paris: Institute d'Ethnologie.

Lantis, M.
1946   The social culture of the Nunivak Eskimo. *Transactions of the American Philosophical Society, New Series* **35**, Part 3 (1946): 153–323.

Lévi-Strauss, C.
1944   The social and psychological aspects of chieftainship in a primitive tribe: the Nambikuara of north-western Mato Grosso. *Transactions of the New York Academy of Sciences, Series 2*, **7** (November): 16–32.

Llewellyn, K. N., and E. A. Hoebel.
1941   *The Cheyenne way: Conflict and case law in primitive jurisprudence.* Norman: Univ. of Oklahoma Press.

Lowie, R. H.
1924   *Notes on Shoshonean ethnology.* Vol. 20. New York: American Museum of Natural History.

Mandelbaum, D. G.
1940   *The Plains Cree.* Vol. 37. New York: American Museum of Natural History.

Mauss, M., and H. Beuchat
1904–   Essai sur les variations saisonnières des sociétés Eskimos: étude de morphologie
1905   sociale. *L'Année sociologique*, **9**.

Métraux, A.
1928   *La religion des Tupinamba.* Paris: E. Leroux.
1931   Les hommes-dieux chez les Chiriguano et dans l'Amerique du Sud. *Revista del Instituto Ethnográfico del Universidad Nacional de Tucuman* **2** (1931): 61–91.

1937   Etudes d'ethnographie Toba-Pilaga. *Anthropos* **32** (1937): 171–194, 378–401.
1946a   The Botocudo. *Handbook of South American Indians.* Bulletin 143, Vol. 1. Washington, D.C.: Bureau of American Ethnology.
1946b   Ethnology of the Chaco. *Handbook of South American Indians.* Bulletin 143, Vol. 2. Washington, D.C.: Bureau of American Ethnology.

Mooney, J.
1896   *The ghost dance religion and the Sioux outbreak of 1890.* Bulletin 14. Washington, D.C.: Bureau of American Ethnology.

Morgan, L. H.
1877   *Ancient society.* New York: H. Holt.

Morley, S. G.
1915   *An introduction to the study of Maya hieroglyphs.* Bulletin 57. Washington, D.C.: Bureau of American Ethnology.

Nantes, M. de
1706   *Relation succinte et sincere de la mission du pere Martin de Nantes.* Paris. (publisher unknown—eds.)

Nimuendajú, C.
1914   Die Sagen von der erschaffung und vernichtung der welt als grundlagen der religion der Apapocuve-Guarani. *Zeitschrift für Ethnologie* **21** (February): 284–403.
1939   *The Apinaye.* Vol. 8. Washington, D.C.: Catholic Univ. of America Press.
1942   *The Sherente.* Vol. 4. Los Angeles: Publication of the Frederick Webb Hodge Anniversary Publication Fund.
1943   A note on the social life of the Northern Kayapo. *American Anthropologist* **45** (1943): 633–635.
1946a   Social organization and beliefs of the Botocudo of Eastern Brasil. *Southwestern Journal of Anthropology* **2** (1946): 93–115.
1946b   *The Eastern Timbira.* Vol. 41. Berkeley: Univ. of California Publications in American Archaeology and Ethnology.

Nordenskiöld, E.
1913   *Indianerleben.* Leipzig: G. Merseburger.

Olson, R. L.
1936   *The Quinault Indians.* Vol. 6. Seattle: Univ. of Washington Publication in Anthropology.
1940   *The social organization of Haida of British Columbia.* Berkeley: Univ. of California Press.

Osgood, C.
1937   *The ethnography of the Tanaina.* Vol. 7. New Haven: Yale Univ. Press.

Parkman, F., Jr.
1856   *Prairie and Rocky Mountain life; or the California and Oregon Trail.* Columbus, Ohio: Miller.

Parsons, E. C.
1939   *Pueblo Indian religion.* Chicago: Univ. of Chicago Press.

Petrullo, V.
1939   *The Yaruros of the Capanaparo River.* Bulletin 123. Washington, D.C.: Bureau of American Ethnology.

Pompeu Sobrinho, T.
1934   Os Tapuias do nordeste e a monografia de Elias Herckman. *Revista del Instituto Ceara* **48** (1934).

Preuss, K. T.
1919   Gorschungsreise zu den Lagaba-Indianern der Sierra Navada de Santa Marta in
-1920   Kolunbien. *Anthropos* **14–15** (1919–1920): 314–404, 1040–1079.

Provinse, J. H.
  1937   The underlying sanctions of Plains Indian culture. In *Social anthropology of North American tribes*, edited by F. Eggan, pp. 341–376. Chicago: Univ. of Chicago Press.
Radin, P.
  1923   *The Winnebago tribe.* Annual Report 37. Washington, D.C.: Bureau of American Ethnology.
Ray, V. F.
  1932   *The Sampoil and Nespelem; Salishan peoples of north-eastern Washington.* Vol. 5. Seattle: Univ. of Washington Press.
Richardson, J.
  1940   *Law and status among the Kiowa Indians.* New York: Augustin.
Roscoe, J.
  1911   *The Baganda.* London: Macmillan.
Roys, R. L.
  1933   *The book of Chilam Balam of Chumayel.* No. 438. Washington, D.C.: Carnegie Institute.
Rowe, J. H.
  1946   Inca culture at the time of the Spanish conquest. In *Handbook of South American Indians*, pp. 183–230. Bulletin 143, Vol. 2. Washington, D.C.: Bureau of American Ethnology.
Sapir, E.
  1915   *The social organization of the West Coast Tribes.* Ottawa: The Royal Society of Canada.
Schweinfurth, G.
  1873   *The heart of Africa.* London: Low, Marton, Low and Searle.
Skinner, A.
  1913   *Social life and ceremonial bundles of the Menominee Indians.* Vol. 13. New York: The Trustees of the American Museum of Natural History.
Spier, L.
  1928   *Havasupai ethnography.* Vol. 29. New York: The Trustees of the American Museum of Natural History.
  1930   *Klamath ethnography.* Berkeley: Univ. of California Press.
  1933   *Yuman tribes of the Gila River*, Chicago: Univ. of Chicago Press.
  1935   *The prophet dance of the Northwest and its derivatives; The source of the ghost dance.* Menasha, Wisconsin: Banta Publ.
Stephen, A. M.
  1936   *Hopi journal.* New York: Columbia Univ. Press.
Steward, J. H.
  1938   *Basin-plateau aboriginal sociopolitical groups.* Bulletin 120. Washington, D.C.: Bureau of American Ethnology.
  1947   American culture history in the light of South America. *Southwestern Journal of Anthropology* 3 (1947): 85–107.
Swanton, J. R.
  1911   *Indian tribes of the lower Mississippi Valley and adjacent coast of the Gulf of Mexico.* Bulletin 43. Washington, D.C.: Bureau of American Ethnology.
  1930   An Indian social experiment and some of its lessons. *Scientific Monthly* 31 (1930): 368–376.
  1931   *Source material for the social and ceremonial life of the Choctaw Indians.* Washington, D.C.: Bureau of American Ethnology.

1946 *The Indians of the southwestern United States.* Bulletin 137. Washington, D.C.: Bureau of American Ethnology.

Tabeau, P. A.
1939 *Narrative of Loisel's expedition to the Upper Missouri.* Norman: Univ. of Oklahoma Press.

Talbot, P. A.
1926 *The peoples of Southern Nigeria.* London and New York: Oxford Univ. Press.

Tanner, J.
1940 *An Indian captivity (1789–1812): John Tanner's narrative of his captivity among the Ottawa and Ojibwa Indians.* Occasional Papers, Reprint Series, No. 20. San Francisco: Sutro Branch, California State Library.

Titiev, M.
1944 *Old Oraibi.* Vol. 22. Cambridge: Peabody Museum.

Tozzer, A. M.
1941 *Landa's relacion de las cosas de Yucaten.* Vol. 18. Cambridge: Peabody Museum.

Vaillant, G. G.
1941 *Aztecs of Mexico.* Garden City, New York: Doubleday.

Wissler, C.
1911 *The social life of the Blackfoot Indians.* Vol. 7. New York: The Trustees of the American Museum of Natural History.

1912 *Societies and ceremonial associations in the Oglala division of the Teton-Dakota.* Vol. 11. New York: The Trustees of the American Museum of Natural History.

1922 *The American Indian.* New York: McMurtrie.

Part VI

LAW AND CULTURE

THE DIFFERING REALMS OF THE LAW
Paul Bohannan

ANTHROPOLOGY, including legal anthropology, is faced
with a problem that may be unique in social science: In order to present
the results of our field research without seriously warping the ideas, we
must undertake a second job of research, on the homologous institutions of
our own society, and in the scientific disciplines that have investigated those
institutions. This paper is an exercise in the anthropological investigation of
jurisprudence. It investigates three things: (1) definitions that jurisprudence
has used, and the anthropological usefulness of such definitions, (2) the
"double institutionalization" of norms and customs that comprises all
legal systems, and (3) some of the problems of the association between legal
institutions and certain types of political organization.

LEGAL LANGUAGE

It is likely that more scholarship has gone into defining and explaining the concept of "law" than any other concept still in central use in
the social sciences. Efforts to delimit the subject matter of law—like efforts
to define it—usually fall into one of several traps that are more easily seen

Reprinted by permission of the American Anthropological Association from "The Differing Realms
of the Law" by Paul Bohannan, *The Ethnography of Law*, supplement to *American Anthropologist*, Vol. 67,
Pt. 2 (December 1965): pp. 33–42.

than avoided. The most naïve, on the one hand, beg the question and use "law" in what they believe to be its common sense, dictionary definition— apparently without looking into a dictionary to discover that the word "law" has six entries in Webster's second edition (1953), of which the first alone has thirteen separate meanings, followed by five columns of the word used in combinations. The most sophisticated scholars, on the other hand, have been driven to realize that, in relation to a noetic unity like law, which is not represented by anything except man's ideas about it, definition can mean no more than a set of mnemonics to remind the reader what has been talked about.

Three modern studies, two in jurisprudence and one in anthropology, all show a common trend.

Hart (1954) concludes that there are three "basic issues": (1) How is law related to order backed by threats? (2) What is the relation between legal obligation and moral obligation? (3) What are rules, and to what extent is law an affair of rules? Stone (1965) sets out seven sets of "attributes usually found associated with the phenomena commonly designated as law": Law is (1) a complex whole, (2) which always includes norms regulating human behavior, (3) that are social norms; (4) the complex whole is "orderly," and (5) the order is characteristically a coercive order (6) that is institutionalized (7) with a degree of effectiveness sufficient to maintain itself. Pospisil (1958) examines several attributes of the law—the attribute of authority, that of intention of universal application, that of *obligatio* (the right-obligation cluster), and that of sanction. In his view, the "legal" comprises a field in which custom, political decision, and the various attributes overlap, though each may be found extended outside that overlapping field, and there is no firm line, but rather a "zone of transition," between that which is unquestionably legal and that which is not.

It was Hermann Kantorowicz (1958) who pointed out that there are many subjects, including some of a nonlegal nature, that employ a concept of law. He proceeded to a more questionable point: that it was up to "general jurisprudence" to provide a background to make these differing concepts sensible. Kantorowicz' method for supplying such a jurisprudential background is very like Pospisil's in anthropology— examination of some characteristics of law that are vital to one or more of the more specific concepts. Law, he tells us, is characterized by having a body of rules that prescribe external conduct (it makes little immediate difference to the law how one feels about it—the law deals in deeds). These rules must be stated in such a way that the courts, or other adjudging bodies, can deal with them. Each of the rules contains a moralizing or "ought" element—and Kantorowicz fully recognizes that this "ought" element is culturally determined and may change from society to society and from era to era. Normative rules of this sort must, obviously, also be distinguished from factual uniformities by which men, sometimes with and sometimes without the help of courts and lawyers, govern their daily round of activity. Law is one of the devices by means of which men can reconcile their actual activities and behavior with the ideal principles that they have come to accept in a way that is not too painful or revolting to their sensibilities, and a way that allows ordered (which is to say predictable) social life to continue.

DOUBLE INSTITUTIONALIZATION

Law must be distinguished from traditions and fashions and more specifically, it must be differentiated from norm and from custom. A norm is a rule, more or less overt, which expresses "ought" aspects of relationships between human beings. Custom is a body of such norms— including regular deviations and compromises with norms—that is actually followed in practice much of the time.

All social institutions are marked by "customs" and these "customs" exhibit most of the stigmata cited by any definition of law. But there is one salient difference. Whereas custom continues to inhere in, and only in, these institutions which it governs (and which in turn govern it), law is specifically recreated, by agents of society, in a narrower and recognizable context— that is, in the context of the institutions that are legal in character and, to some degree at least, discrete from all others.

Just as custom includes norms, but is both greater and more precise than norms, so law includes custom, but is both greater and more precise. Law has the additional characteristic that it must be what Kantorowicz calls "justiciable," by which he means that the rules must be capable of reinterpretation, and actually must be reinterpreted, by one of the legal institutions of society so that the conflicts within nonlegal institutions can be adjusted by an "authority" outside themselves.

It is widely recognized that many peoples of the world can state more or less precise "rules" which are, in fact, the norms in accordance with which they think they ought to judge their conduct. In all societies there are allowable lapses from such rules, and in most there are more or less precise rules (sometimes legal ones) for breaking rules.

In order to make the distinction between law and other rules, it has been necessary to introduce furtively the word "institution." I use the word in Malinowski's sense (Malinowski, 1945; Bohannan, 1963).

A legal institution is one by means of which the people of a society settle disputes that arise between one another and counteract any gross and flagrant abuses of the rules (as we have considered them above) of at least some of the other institutions of society. Every ongoing society has legal institutions in this sense, as well as a wide variety of nonlegal institutions.

In carrying out the task of settling difficulties in the nonlegal institutions, legal institutions face three kinds of tasks:

(1) There must be specific ways in which difficulties can be disengaged from the institutions in which they arose and which they now threaten and then be engaged within the processes of the legal institution.
(2) There must be ways in which the trouble can now be handled within the framework of the legal institution.
(3) There must be ways in which the new solutions which thus emerge can be reengaged within the processes of the nonlegal institutions from which they emerged.

It is seldom that any framework save a political one can supply these requirements.

There are, thus, at least two aspects of legal institutions that are not shared with other institutions of society. Legal institutions—and often they alone— must have some regularized way to interfere in the malfunctioning (and, perhaps, the functioning as well) of the nonlegal institutions in order to disengage the trouble-case. There must, second, be two kinds of rules in the legal institutions—those that govern the activities of the legal institution itself (called "adjectival law" by Austin, and "procedure" by most modern lawyers), and those that are substitutes or modifications or restatements of the rules of the nonlegal institution that has been invaded (called "substantive law").

Listed above are only the minimal aspects that are all shared by all known legal institutions. There may be other aspects, as for example the commonly recognized fact that legal institutions on both the procedural and the substantive sides can be in the fullest sense innovatory.

Seen in this light, a fairly simple distinction can be made between law and custom. Customs are norms or rules (more or less strict, and with greater or less support of moral, ethical, or even physical coercion) about the ways in which people must behave if social institutions are to perform their tasks and society is to endure. All institutions (including legal institutions) develop customs. Some customs, in some societies, are reinstitutionalized at another level: they are restated for the more precise purposes of legal institutions. When this happens, therefore, law may be regarded as a custom that has been restated in order to make it amenable to the activities of the legal institutions. In this sense, it is one of the most characteristic attributes of legal institutions that some of these "laws" are about the legal institutions themselves, although most are about the other institutions of society—the familial, economic, political, ritual, or whatever.

One of the reddest herrings ever dragged into the working of orderly jurisprudence was Malinowski's little book called *Crime and Custom in Savage Society*. It is unfortunately almost the only anthropological book that appears on the standard reading list used in many law schools, "The Dean's List," and it has had an undue and all but disastrous influence on the rapprochement between anthropology and jurisprudence. Malinowski's idea was a good one; he claimed that law is "a body of binding obligations regarded as right by one party and acknowledged as the duty by the other, kept in force by the specific mechanism of reciprocity and publicity inherent in the structure of . . . society." His error was in equating what he had defined with the law. It is not law that is "kept in force by . . . reciprocity and publicity." It is custom, as we have defined it here. Law is, rather, "a body of binding obligations regarded as right by one party and acknowledged as the duty by the other" *which has been reinstitutionalized within the legal institution so that society can continue to function in an orderly manner on the basis of rules so maintained*. In short, reciprocity is the basis of custom; but the law rests on the basis of this double institutionalization. Central in it is that some of the customs of some of the institutions of society are restated in such a way that they can be "applied" by an institution designed (or, at very least, utilized) specifically for that purpose.

One of the best ways to perceive the doubly institutionalized norms, or "laws," is to break up the law into smaller components, capable of attaching to persons (either human individuals or corporate groups) and so to work in terms of "rights" and their reciprocal duties or "obligations." In terms of rights and duties, the relationships between law and custom, law and morals, law and anything else, can be seen in a new light. Whether in the realm of kinship or contract, citizenship or property rights, the relationships between people can be reduced to a series of prescriptions with the obligations and the correlative rights that emanate from these presumptions. In fact, if it is not carried too far and unduly formalized, thinking in terms of rights and obligations of persons (or role players) is a convenient and fruitful way of investigating much of the custom of many institutions (Hohfeld, 1923; Hoebel, 1954). Legal rights are only those rights that attach to norms that have been doubly institutionalized; they provide a means for seeing the legal institutions from the standpoint of the persons engaged in them.

The phenomenon of double institutionalization of norms and therefor of legal rights has been recognized for a long time, but analysis of it has been only partially successful. Kantorowicz (1958), for example, has had to create the concept of "justiciability" of the law. It would be better to say that legal rights have their material origins (either overtly or covertly) in the customs of nonlegal institutions but must be *overtly restated* for the specific purpose of enabling the legal institutions to perform their task.

A legal right (and, with it, a law) is the restatement, for the purpose of maintaining peaceful and just operation of the institutions of society, of some but never all, of the recognized claims of the persons within those institutions; the restatement must be made in such a way that these claims can be more or less assured by the total community or its representatives. Only so can the moral, religious, political, and economic implications of law be fully explored.

Law is never a mere reflection of custom, however. Rather, law is always out of phase with society, specifically because of the duality of the statement and restatement of rights. Indeed, the more highly developed the legal institutions, the greater the lack of phase, which not only results from the constant reorientation of the primary institutions, but also is magnified by the very dynamic of the legal institutions themselves (Stone, 1964: Chapter 1, Section 1).

Thus, it is the very nature of law, and its capacity to "do something about" the primary social institutions, that creates the lack of phase. Moreover, even if one could assume perfect legal institutionalization, change within the primary institutions would soon jar the system out of phase again. What is less obvious is that if there were ever to be perfect phase between law and society, then society could never repair itself, grow, and change, flourish, or wane. It is the fertile dilemma of law that it must always be out of step with society, but that people must always (because they work better with fewer contradictions, if for no other reason) attempt to reduce the lack of phase. Custom must either grow to fit the law or it must actively reject it; law must either grow to fit the custom, or it must ignore or suppress it. It is in these very interstices that social growth and social decay take place.

Social catastrophe and social indignation are sources of much law and resultant changes in custom. With technical and moral change, new situations appear that must be "legalized." This truth has particular and somewhat different applications to developed and to less highly developed legal systems. On the one hand, in developed municipal systems of law in which means for institutionalizing behavior on a legal level are already traditionally concentrated in political decision-making groups such as legislatures, nonlegal social institutions sometimes take a very long time to catch up with the law. On the other hand, in less developed legal systems, it may be that little or no popular demand is made on the legal institutions, and therefore little real contact exists or can be made to exist between them and the primary institutions (Stone, 1965: Chapter 2, Section 17). Law can, as we have seen in another context, become one of the major innovators of society, the more effective the greater a people's dependence on it.

BEYOND THE AUSTINIAN SOVEREIGN

To summarize the position so far, it is the essence of "law" to present a double institutionalization of norms. A secondary criterion was added: a unicentric political unit (no matter how pluralistic) is the device most commonly utilized to carry out the secondary, or legal, institutionalization (a "sovereign"). Such a theory—although it may be charged with being simplistic—is, it would seem, consonant with the state type of organization. However, the theory of double institutionalization seems inadequate thus far to explain three related situations: the situations of (1) law in a stateless society, (2) law in a colonial society, and (3) international law.

So far we have two assumptions. First, we have assumed a power or a state, whether it be seen as an Austinian sovereign, or as the greater entity that assumes the court whose actions are to be predicted with greater or lesser accuracy. Second, we have assumed that there is also only one legal culture in such a situation—no matter, for the moment, how many contradictions are to be found in it. A legal culture, for the present purposes, is that which is subscribed to (whether they know anything about it or not, and whether they act within it or "agree" with it or not) by the people of a society. The secondary institutionalization forms a more or less consistent cultural unit.

With these ideas in mind, it is possible to question both assumptions and hence to build a four-square diagram in order to extend our views for examining the realm of the legal (see figure). Municipal systems, of the sort studied by most jurists, deal with a single legal culture within a unicentric power system. Subcultures in such a society may create vast problems of law's being out of phase with the customs and mores of parts of the society, but it is a problem of phase.

Colonial Law

Colonial law is marked by a unicentric power system, with greater or lesser problems of conjoining the colonial government with the

	Unicentric power	Bicentric (or multicentric) power
One culture	Municipal systems of "law"	Law in stateless societies
Two (or more) cultures	Colonial law	International law

THE LEGAL REALM

local government, and more and less overt theories (such as the British "indirect rule") of accomplishing the conjunction. All are marked, however, by two (or more) legal cultures. Sometimes this situation is recognized, as it was in preindependence Kenya with its two hierarchies of courts, one for "European" law and the other for African law joined only at the top in the Supreme Court. The mark of a colonial situation might be said to be a systematic misunderstanding between the two cultures within the single power system, with constant revolutionary proclivities resulting from what is, at best, a "working misunderstanding."

In colonial law, the problem of disengaging a problem case from the milieu in which it arises is often complicated by the existence of directly opposed ideas about the motives and goals to be achieved in resorting to court action. Once disengaged, the culture of the court officials may be completely different from that of the principals and witnesses in the cases, so that the outcome at best may seem arbitrary. Once "settled" in this more or less arbitrary way, the reengagement in the institutions of society may be very imperfect, because of lack of consensus about what was decided or lack of agreement about the binding qualities and the justice of it.

We are only now far enough removed from colonies—now that they are obsolete—to begin a thorough examination of the effect that colonial powers had, via such a system, on the legal systems of the countries in which they were found.

Law in Stateless Societies

The mark of the stateless society is the absence of a unicentric power system. All situations of dispute that occur between people not within the same domestic unit *ipso facto* occur between two more or less equal power units. The prime example of a bicentric system is, of course, the lineage system based on the principle of segmental opposition, but there is no reason that this type of solution need be limited to such situations. There is, however, only a single culture: the principals and witnesses in a case may be at vast odds about who did what and to whom, and hence where justice lies. But they understand one another's activities and plots—perhaps they understand them only too well.

In such a situation, all trouble cases are settled by some form of compromise, more or less in accordance with a set of overt "rules." Instead of "decisions" there are "compromises." In a unicentric system, it is possible to have judicial decision and a recognized mechanism of enforcement which presents problems merely of efficiency, not of substance. In a bicentric situation, nobody can be in a position to make decisions—it is organized so that there cannot be. The "judges" must make compromises, and their compromises must be enforced from two power centers, which often—to a citizen of a "state"—looks like no enforcement at all. Instead of implementing decisions, the parties are made to accept the principles and provisions of a compromise.

It is my feeling—but I cannot claim it is any more than that—that the compromise, bicentric solution of problems leads to very much less precise restatements of norms as law than does the decision-based unicentric solution. Bodies of rules in stateless societies seem to be less precise, scarcely made into anything resembling a *corpus juris* although, of course, the anthropologist or the intellectually inclined informant can create a system—even a system of precedents—from the regularities that result from compromise between units in terms of their common cultural recognition of their common institutions.

In some societies the compromiser may be quite firmly institutionalized. Among the Nuer (Evans-Pritchard, 1940), for example, the leopard-skin chief is a firmly institutionalized compromiser who may or may not be resorted to in any specific instance. If he is, his task is to create a compromise to which both parties will concur, saving the face of all by his religious position and "sanctions."

Most specifically, perhaps, the court—a body of men representative of the political power—cannot have any part in a bicentric system, unless there is some mode of organizing multiple judges. The more common methods of procedures are moots, contests, oracles, and self-help. In short, the bicentric, unicultural system may not have a very great potential for organized, neat systems of "law."

International Law

This section is set forth with great circumspection, because I know very little about international law. Yet it is obvious, even to a rank amateur, that there has been a long dispute in jurisprudence about whether international law is *really* "law" (Williams, 1945).

The difficulty arises among scholars who derive their model too narrowly from that law which is associated with a unicentric power system. It is undoubtedly true that the most "developed" legal systems occur within organizations such as states that have a single power system—indeed, the growth of states has been coincident with the growth of such legal systems. For all that such a power system may be pluralistic, it nevertheless is not legally divisible into warring and treating factions. "Law" is seen as one of the supreme activities of such an institution. The elements of coercion and prediction that have been emphasized in the definitions of law have lent credence to the point. These qualities have carried over and indeed obscured discussions of international law.

The situation in international law is, however, made more complex in that two or more unicentric power systems are bound together by means other than a more inclusive unicentric power system. In each of them, custom is "legalized." In international law, then, the process of "reinstitutionalization" must take place yet again—but with the qualitative difference that this time it must be done within the limitations of a multicentric power system. The difficulties in this secondary reinstitutionalization of international law are compounded because there are likely to be cultural differences in the two or more primary legal systems.

The "law" must, in short, be reinstitutionalized not out of a single related set of institutions, but rather out of two separate sets of interrelated institutions, including the interrelationship of the two unicentric power systems. Many cultures can exist within a unicentric system—the United States provides a vivid example; moreover, what might in other aspects be neatly regarded as a single culture may be representative of two or more states. However, it is usually reasonable to assume that the two separate but interrelated sets of institutions on which international law must draw in the process of legalization, exhibit somewhat different cultures. Therefore legalization must take place in terms of two cultures that are often vastly foreign to one another.

Obviously, the legal institutions of a bicentric and bicultural system exhibit different types of organization, different goals—different customs all round—from those of unicentric systems. More specifically, they must have different ways of disengaging the trouble situation from its matrix. Probably those ways must be more subtle precisely because the power distribution stems from two centers, and a preliminary legalization has likely been made in each. We do not as yet have adequate legal institutions for bicentric systems, nor do we have agreed ways for legalizing international law that are sufficiently subtle and consonant with multiple cultural evaluations (Jones, 1962). The problem will not be solved merely by the creation of a single "sovereign," as was supposed only a few years ago.

It is a characteristic of unicentric legal systems that they are empowered to reach and enforce decisions. It is, just so, characteristic of bicentric systems that they must reach legal compromises that are sufficiently compatible with both cultures as to be acceptable and ultimately enforceable from the two power centers. Western judges have lost and are just regaining some of their rights to compromise within the framework of the adversary procedure. Other societies, such as some of those in Africa, are only beginning to adopt a "decision" procedure in place of or in addition to a compromise procedure.

In short, it would appear that in international law—or at least in the old-fashioned view of it—there is a *treble* institutionalization: once at the level of custom, once at the level of the legal institutions of states, and again at the level of the bicentric, bicultural "international" accord.

THE DIFFERING REALMS OF JURAL ETHNOGRAPHY

It is a truism to say that if the law is to be discovered in differing realms, that legal ethnography must also be found there. But the question comes up: What should we and our students be doing? Without in any sense wanting to close any avenues, it seems possible to list several important tasks:

(1) First of all, we must study the relationship between the social institution and the legal institution in which some of its norms are (doubly or trebly) reinstitutionalized. We must know the relationships between families and family law or between received behavior and criminal law.

(2) We must get a full range of the types of institution that fulfill legal functions, and the social situations under which each is either tried or has proved successful.

(3) We must discover which customs are reinstitutionalized into law in different social, cultural, and political situations, and in accordance with what postulates. We must examine the institutions that precede and follow from such reinstitutionalization.

(4) We must seek out situations of cross-cultural conflict resolution and examine them against a set of legal qualities. (Anthropologists have been lax here.)

In short, jural ethnography, like the law itself, has no bounds. It is, on the one hand, as broad as life itself; on the other, as narrow as the recognizable reinstitutionalization in given situations of power structure and cultural field. There are three grave dangers: We may, like Barton, report all our ethnography as if it were law. We may, like Gluckman's first book, cut our insights short by defining the "legal" too rigidly before we start to write. Or we may, like my own *Justice and Judgment* (1957), stop a chapter too soon so that neither does the ethnography fit easily into the mainstream of jurisprudence nor are methods made overt that allow ready comparison among legal systems, of all the sorts discussed here.

REFERENCES

Bohannan, P.
  1957   *Justice and judgment among the Tiv.* London and New York: Oxford Univ. Press.
  1963   *Social anthropology.* New York: Holt.
Evans-Pritchard, E. E.
  1940   *The Nuer.* London and New York: Oxford Univ. Press.

Hart, H. L. A.
   1954   Definition and theory in jurisprudence. *Law Quarterly Review* **70** (1954): 37–60.
Hoebel, E. A.
   1954   *The law of primitive man: A study in comparative legal dynamics.* Cambridge: Harvard Univ. Press.
Hohfeld, W. N.
   1923   *Fundamental legal conceptions as applied in judicial reasoning and other essays.* New Haven: Yale Univ. Press.
Jones, H. W.
   1962   Law and the idea of mankind. *Columbia Law Review* **62** (1962): 752–772.
Kantorowicz, H.
   1958   *The definition of law.* London and New York: Cambridge Univ. Press.
Malinowski, B.
   1926   *Crime and custom in savage society.* London: Routledge and Kegan Paul.
   1945   *The dynamics of culture change.* New Haven: Yale Univ. Press.
Pospisil, L.
   1958   *The Kapauku Papuans and their law.* Yale University Publications in Anthropology, No. 54. New Haven: Yale Univ. Press.
Stone, J.
   1964   *Legal systems and lawyer's reasoning.* Stanford: Stanford Univ. Press.
   1965   *Social dimensions of law and justice.* Stanford: Stanford Univ. Press.
Williams, G.
   1945– Language and the law. *Law Quarterly Review* **61** (1945): 71–86, 171–195, 293–303,
   1946   384–406; **62** (1946): 387–406.

THE RULE OF LAW VERSUS THE ORDER OF CUSTOM*

Stanley Diamond

CREON:	Knowest thou the edict has forbidden this?
ANTIGONE:	I knew it well. Why not? It was proclaimed.
CREON:	But thou didst dare to violate the law?
ANTIGONE:	It was not God above who framed that law,

Nor justice, whispering from the underworld,
Nor deemed I thy decrees were of such force
As to o'er ride the sanctities of heaven;
Which are not of today or yesterday.
From whom—whence they first issued, no one knows.
I was not like to scant their holy rites
And brave the even justice of the gods
For fear of someone's edict.

Sophocles, *Antigone*

The lowest police employee of the civilized state has more "authority" than all the organs of gentilism combined. But the mightiest prince and the greatest statesman or general of civilization may look with envy on the spontaneous

---

*This article, in slightly different form, appears in *The Rule of Law*, edited by Robert Paul Wolff. New York: Simon & Schuster, 1971.

Reprinted from "The Rule of Law versus the Order of Custom" by Stanley Diamond, *Social Research*, Vol. 38 (1971): pp. 42–72. This is a slightly revised version of the original paper.

and undisputed esteem that was the privilege of the least gentile sachem. The one stands in the middle of society, the other is forced to assume a position outside and above it.

Friedrich Engels, *Origin of the
Family, Private Property and the State*

There's too much due process of law. The electric chair is a cheap crime deterrent to show these criminal elements that law and order is going to triumph.

Detective Sergeant John Heffernan,
current vice-president of the
International Conference of Police
Association and head of the
New Jersey State Police Benevolent
Association

I

W E MUST distinguish the rule of law from the authority of custom. In a recent effort to do so (which I shall critically examine because it is so typical), Paul Bohannan, under the *imprimatur* of the *International Encyclopedia of the Social Sciences* (1968), contends that laws result from "double" institutionalization. He means by this no more than the lending of a specific force, a cutting edge, to the functioning of "customary" institutions: marriage, the family, religion. But, he tells us, the laws so emerging assume a character and dynamic of their own. They form a structured, legal dimension of society; they do not merely reflect, but interact with given institutions. Therefore, Bohannan is led to maintain that laws are typically out of phase with society and it is this process which is both a symptom and cause of social change. The laws of marriage, to illustrate Bohannan's argument with the sort of concrete example his definition lacks, are not synonymous with the institution of marriage. They reinforce certain rights and obligations while neglecting others. Moreover, they subject partners defined as truant to intervention by an external, impersonal agency whose decisions are sanctioned by the power of the police.

Bohannan's sociological construction does have the virtue of denying the primacy of the legal order, and of implying that law is generic to unstable (or progressive) societies, but it is more or less typical of abstract efforts to define the eternal essence of the law and it begs the significant questions. Law has no such essence but a definable historical nature.

Thus, if we inquire into the structure of the contemporary institutions which according to Bohannan, stand in a primary relation to the law, we find that their customary content has drastically diminished. Paul Radin made the point as follows:

> A custom is, in no sense, a part of our properly functioning culture. It belongs definitely to the past. At best, it is moribund. But customs are an integral part of the life of primitive peoples. There is no compulsive submission to them. They are not followed because the weight of tradition overwhelms a man . . . a custom is obeyed there because it is intimately intertwined with a vast living network of interrelations, arranged in a meticulous and ordered manner (1953: 223).

And "What is significant in this connection," as J. G. Peristiany indicates, "is not that common values should exist, but that they should be expressed although no common political organization corresponds to them" (1956: 45).

In the words of V. C. Uchendu, writing about the Ibo:

> . . . the use of force is minimal or absent; . . . there are leaders rather than rulers, and . . . cohesion is achieved by rules rather than by laws and by consensus rather than by dictation. In general, the Igbo have not achieved any political structure which can be called a federation, a confederacy, or a state (1965: 46).*

No contemporary institution functions with the kind of autonomy that permits us to postulate a significant dialectic between law and custom. We live in a law-ridden society; law has cannibalized the institutions which it presumably reinforces or with which it interacts.

Accordingly, morality continues to be reduced to or confused with legality. In civil society we are encouraged to assume that legal behavior is the measure of moral behavior, and it is a matter of some interest that a former Chief Justice of the Supreme Court proposed, with the best of intentions, that a federal agency be established in order to advise government employees and those doing business with the government concerning the legal propriety of their behavior. Any conflict of interest not legally enjoined would thus tend to become socially or morally acceptable; morality becomes a technical question. Efforts to legislate conscience by an external political power are the antithesis of custom: customary behavior comprises precisely those aspects of social behavior which are traditional, moral, and religious, which are, in short, conventional and nonlegal. Put another way, custom *is* social morality (Simpson and Stone, 1942: Books 1 and 2). The relation between custom and law is, basically, one of contradiction, not continuity.

The customary and the legal orders are historically, not logically related. They touch coincidentally; one does not imply the other. Custom, as most

*From *The Igbo of Southeast Nigeria* by Victor C. Uchendu. Holt, Rinehart and Winston, Inc. 1965.

anthropologists agree, is characteristic of primitive society, and laws of civilization. Robert Redfield's dichotomy between the primitive "moral" order and the civilized "legal" or "technical" order remains a classic statement of the case.

William Seagle writes:

> The dispute whether primitive societies have law or custom, is not merely a dispute over words. Only confusion can result from treating them as interchangeable phenomena. If custom is spontaneous and automatic, law is the product of organized force. Reciprocity is in force in civilized communities, too, but at least nobody confuses social with formal legal relationships (1946: 35).

Parenthetically, one should note that students of primitive society who use the term "customary law" blur the issue semantically, but nonetheless recognize the distinction.

It is this overall legalization of behavior in modern society which Bohannan fails to interpret. In fascist Germany, for example, laws flourished as never before. By 1941, more edicts had been proclaimed than in all the years of the Republic and the Third Reich. At the same time, ignorance of the law inevitably increased. In a sense, the very force of the law depends upon ignorance of its specifications, which is hardly recognized as a mitigating circumstance. As Seagle states, law is not definite and certain while custom is vague and uncertain. Rather, the converse holds. Customary rules must be clearly known; they are not sanctioned by organized political force, hence serious disputes about the nature of custom would destroy the integrity of society. But laws may always be invented, and stand a good chance of being enforced: "Thus, the sanction is far more important than the rule in the legal system ... but the tendency is to minimize the sanction and to admire the rule" (Seagle, 1946: 19–20).

In fascist Germany, customs did not become laws through a process of "double institutionalization." Rather, repressive laws, conjured up in the interests of the Nazi Party and its supporters, cannibalized the institutions of German society. Even the residual customary authority of the family was assaulted: children were encouraged to become police informers, upholding the laws against their kin. "The absolute reign of law has often been synonymous with the absolute reign of lawlessness" (Seagle, 1946: 19–20).

Certainly, Germany under Hitler was a changing society, if hardly a progressive one, but it was a special case of the general process in civilization through which the organs of the state have become increasingly irresistible. It will be recalled that Bohannan takes the domination of law over custom to be symptomatic of changing societies. But the historical inadequacy of his argument lies exactly here: he does not intimate the overall direction of that change and therefore fails to clarify the actual relation between custom and law. Accordingly, the notion that social change is a function of the law, and vice versa, implies a dialectic that is out of phase with historical reality.

Plato, it deserves note, understood this well enough when he conceived the problem of civilization as primarily one of injustice, which he did not scant by legalistic definition. Whether we admire his utopia or not, *The Republic* testifies to Plato's recognition that laws follow social change and reflect prevailing social relations (the best laws would reflect the eternal order), but are the cause of neither. His remedy was the thorough restructuring of society. Curiously, this view of the relationship between law and society accords with aspects of the Marxist perspective on the history of culture. Customary societies are said to precede legal societies, an idea which, semantics aside, most students of historical jurisprudence would accept. But Marxists envision the future as being without laws as we know them, as involving a return to custom, so to speak, on a higher level, since the repressive, punitive, and profiteering functions of law will become superfluous. Conflicts of economic and political interest will be resolved through the equitable reordering of institutions. Law, for the Marxists and most classical students of historical jurisprudence, is the cutting edge of the state—but the former, insisting on both a historical and normative view of man, define the state as the instrument of the ruling class, anticipating its dissolution with the abolition of classes and the common ownership of the basic means of production. Whatever our view of the ultimate Marxist dynamic, law is clearly inseparable from the state. Sir Henry Maine equates the history of individual property with that of civilization (1889: 230):

> Nobody is at liberty to attack several property and to say at the same time that he values civilization. The history of the two cannot be disentangled. Civilization is nothing more than the name for the ... order ... dissolved but perpetually re-constituting itself under a vast variety of solvent influences, of which infinitely the most powerful have been those which have, slowly, and in some parts of the world much less perfectly than others, substituted several property for collective ownership.

In the words of Jeremy Bentham, "Property and law are born together and die together."

Law, thus, is symptomatic of the emergence of the state; the legal sanction is not simply the cutting edge of institutions at all times and in all places. The "double institutionalization" to which Bohannan refers needs redefinition. Where it does occur, it is an historical process of unusual complexity and cannot be defined as the simple passage of custom into law. It occurs, as we shall see, in several modes. Custom—spontaneous, traditional, personal, commonly known, corporate, relatively unchanging—is the modality of primitive society; law is the instrument of civilization, of political society sanctioned by organized force, presumably above society at large, and buttressing a new set of social interests. Law and custom both involve the regulation of behavior but their characters are entirely distinct; no evolutionary balance has been struck between developing law and custom, whether traditional or emergent.

II

The simple dichotomy between primitive society and civilization does not illustrate the passage from the customary to the legal order. The most critical and revealing period in the evolution of law is that of *archaic societies*, the local segments of which are the cultures most often studied by anthropologists. More precisely, the earlier phases of these societies, which I call proto-states, represent a transition from the primitive kinship-based communities to the class-structured polity. In such polities, law and custom exist side by side; this gives us the opportunity to examine their connections, distinctions, and differential relationship to the society at large. The customary behavior typical of the local groups—joint families, clans, villages—maintains most of its force; the Vietnamese, for example, still say: "The customs of the village are stronger than the law of the emperor." Simultaneously, the civil power, comprising bureaucracy and sovereign, the dominant emerging class, issues a series of edicts that have the double purpose of confiscating "surplus" goods and labor for the support of those not directly engaged in production while attempting to deflect the loyalties of the local groups to the center.

These archaic societies are the great historical watershed; it is here that Sir Henry Maine and Paul Vinogradoff located the passage from status to contract, from the kinship to the territorial principle, from extended familial controls to public law. One need not be concerned with the important distinctions among archaic societies, or with the precise language or emphases of those scholars who have recognized their centrality for our understanding of the law. The significant point is that they are transitional. Particularly in their early phase they are the agencies that transmute customary forms of order into legal sanction. Here we find a form of "double institutionalization" functioning explicitly; we can witness, so to speak, what appears to be the *emergence* of a custom, in defense of the kinship principle against the assault of the state, and the subsequent shift of the customary function into its own opposite as a legal function. The following example from the archaic proto-state of Dahomey, prior to the French conquest in 1892, will make this process clear.

Traditionally, in Dahomey each person was said to have three "best" friends, in descending order of intimacy and importance. This transitional institution, a transfiguration of kin connections, of the same species as blood brotherhood, reinforced the extended family structure, which continued to exist in the early state, but was being thrown into question as a result of the political and economic demands made by the emerging civil power. So, for example, the best friend of a joint family partriarch would serve as his testator, and, upon the latter's decease, name his successor to the assembled family. It seems that the ordinary convention of succession no longer sufficed to secure the family's integrity, since the central authority was mustering family heads as indirect rulers. In this instance, the institution of friendship was assimilated to the form and purpose of customary behavior. On the other hand, the best friend of a man charged with a civil "crime" could be seized by the king's police in his stead. However, these traditional friendships were so socially critical, so symbolically significant that the person charged, whether or not he had actually committed a civil breach, would be expected to turn himself in, rather than implicate a friend in his punishment. This may or may not have occurred conventionally, but the point is that the custom of friendship was thus given a legal edge and converted by the civil power into a means, even if only ideological, of enforcing its will. This example of "double institutionalization" has the virtue of explicitly revealing the contradiction between law and custom; but there are others in which law appears as a *reinforcement* of customary procedure.

In eleventh century Russia, for instance, Article 1 of the codified law states "If a man kills a man ... the brother is to avenge his brother; the son, his father; or the father, his son; and the son of the brother (of the murdered man) or the son of his sister, their respective uncle. If there is no avenger (the murderer) pays 40 grivna wergeld ..." (Vernadsky, 1947: 26–27).

Similarly, circa A.D. 700, the law of the Visigoths states, "Whoever shall have killed a man, whether he committed a homicide intending to or not intending to (*volens aut nolens*) ... let him be handed over into the *potestas* of the parents or next of kin of the deceased ..." (quoted in Simpson and Stone, 1942: 78). In these instances, a custom has been codified by an external agency, thus assuming legal force with *its punitive character sharpened.* Such confirmation is both the *intimation* of legal control and the antecedent of institutional change beyond the wish or conception of the family. "Whatever princes do, they seem to command," or, as Sir Henry Maine put it (1897: 383), "What the sovereign permits, he commands." Maine had specifically in mind "the Sikh despot who permitted heads of households and village elders to prescribe rules, therefore these rules became his command and true laws, which are the solvent of local and domestic usage." Simpson and Stone explain this apparent reinforcement of custom by the civil power as follows:

Turning then to the role of law in the emergent political society . . . it is true that political institutions, independent of the kin and the supernatural, had risen to power; yet these institutions were young, weak and untried. Their encroachment on the old allegiance was perforce wary and hesitating. Social cohesion still seemed based on nonpolitical elements, and these elements were therefore protected. It is this society which Pound has perceived and expressed when he says that the end of law envisaged in his period of strict law, is the maintenance of the social *status quo*. In modern terminology this means the primacy of the interest in the maintenance of antecedent social institutions (Simpson and Stone, 1942: 177).

This sort of confirmation, which betrays the structural opportunism of the early civil power, inheres in the limitations of sovereignty, and is further apparent in the sovereign's relation to the communally held clan or joint family land. In Dahomey, for example, where the king was said to "own" all property, including land, it is plain that such ownership was a legal fiction and had the effect of validating the preexistent joint-family tradition. That is, the king "permitted" the joint families, by virtue of his fictional ownership, to expand into new lands and continue transmitting their property intact, generation after generation. The civil power could not rent, alienate, or sell joint-family property, nor could any member of a joint family do so (Diamond, 1951: 109). This is borne out by A. I. Richards, who informs us that "in Northern Rhodesia (Zambia) the statement that 'all the land is mine' does not mean that the ruler has the right to take any piece of land he chooses for his own use . . . I have never heard of a case where a chief took land that had already been occupied by a commoner" (quoted in Gluckman, 1944: 14–21). The same point is made by Rattray on the Ashanti (1929) and Mair on the Baganda (1933) among others. Civil validation, then, expresses the intention but not yet the reality of state control. We might more realistically formulate Maine's epigram as: What he cannot command, the sovereign permits.

Ultimately, local groups have maintained their autonomy when their traditional economies were indispensable to the functioning of the entire society. They could be hedged around by restrictions, harassed by law, or, as we have seen, they could be "legally" confirmed in their customary usage; but, so long as the central power depended on them for support, in the absence of any alternative mode or source of production, their integrity could be substantially preserved. This certainly seems the case during the early phases of state organization in the classic nuclear areas (e.g., Egypt, Babylonia, northern India) before the introduction of large-scale irrigation and analogous public works, and it was true of pre-Colonial Africa. But in all archaic societies, whether incipient, as in sub-Saharan Africa, florescent, as in the ancient peasant societies of the Middle East or China, or in cognate contemporary societies which probably still embrace most of the world's population, the extensive kin unit was more functional, in spite of varying degrees of autonomy, than the family in commercial and industrial civilization.

As the state develops, according to Maine (1963: 140) "The individual is steadily substituted for the family as the unit of which civil laws take account." And in von Jhering's words (1866: Vol. 2, 31): "The progress of law consists in the destruction of every natural tie, in a continued process of separation and isolation." That is to say, the family increasingly becomes a reflex of society at large. Hence, one might add, the legal stipulation that spouses may not testify against each other appears as one of the last formal acknowledgments of familial integrity, and the exception that proves the historical case. Clearly, the nuclear family in contemporary urban civilization, although bound by legal obligations, has minimal autonomy; obviously, the means of education, subsistence, and self-defense are outside the family's competence. It is in this sense that, given the absence of mediating institutions having a clearly defined independent authority, the historical tendency of all state structures vis-à-vis the individual may be designated as totalitarian. Indeed, the state *creates* the disaffiliated individual whose bearings thus become bureaucratic or collective; the juridical "person," who may even be a corporation doing business, is merely the legal reflection of a social process. If "totalization" is *the* state process, totalitarianism cannot be confined to a particular political ideology but is, so to speak, *the* ideology, explicit or not, of political society.

This étatist tendency has its origins in archaic society; we can observe it with unusual clarity in the proto-states of sub-Saharan Africa. In East Africa, pastoralists, competing for land, and in West Africa, militaristic clans, catalyzed by the Arab, and, later, the European trade, notably in slaves, conquered horticulturalists, thereby providing the major occasions for the growth of civil power. Since the basic means of exploiting the environment in these polities remained substantially unchanged, and, to some extent, survived under colonialism, we can reconstruct through chronicles extending back for centuries and by means of contemporary field work, the structure of early state controls, which evolved in the absence of writing and the systematic codification of law. The absence of writing *should* relieve the scholar from that dependence on official records that has so thoroughly shaped our sense of European history; unfortunately, rubbing shoulders with the upper class in a nonliterate state creates equivalent distortions.

In such societies, Rattray tells us, referring to Ashanti, "The small state was ever confronted with the kindred organization which was always insidiously undermining its authority by placing certain persons outside its jurisdiction. It could only hold its own, therefore, by throwing out an ever-widening circle to embrace those loyalties which were lost to it owing to the workings of the old tribal organization which has survived everywhere" (1929: 80). Further, "The old family, clan and tribal organization survived in the new regime which was ever striving to make territorial considerations, and not the incidence of kindship, the basis of state control." Rattray concludes that "corporate responsibility for every act was an established principle which survived even the advent of a powerful central public authority as the administration of public justice" (p. 286). Nadel asserts, concerning the Islamized Nupe of the Nigerian Middle Belt, that what emerged from his analysis was "a much more subtle development and a deeper kind of antagonism (than interstate warfare), namely, the almost eternal antagonism of developed state versus that raw material of the community which, always and everywhere, must form the nourishing soil from which alone the state can grow" (1935: 303). And Engels refers to the "irreconcilable opposition of gentile society to the state" (1902: 133).

I have documented this conflict in detail in a study of the Dahomean proto-state. There, as elsewhere, it is apparent that the contradictory transition from customs to specified laws, "double institutionalization," if you will, *is by no means the major source of law.* Whether the law arises latently in "confirmation" of previous usage, or through the transformation of some aspect of custom, which the law itself may have, in the first instance, provoked, as in the example of the "best friend," neither circumstance brings us to the heart of the matter. For we learn by studying intermediate societies that the laws so typical of them are *unprecedented*; they do not emerge through a process of "double institutionalization," however defined. They arise in opposition to the customary order of the antecedent kin or kin-equivalent groups; they represent a new set of social goals pursued by a new and unanticipated power in society. These goals can be reduced to a single complex imperative: the imposition of the interrelated census–tax–conscription system. The territorial thrust of the early state, along with its vertical social entrenchment, demanded conscription of labor, the mustering of an army, the levying of taxes and tribute, the maintenance of a bureaucracy, and the assessment of the extent, location, and numbers of the population being subjected. *These were the major direct or indirect occasions for the development of civil law.*

The primary purpose of a census is indicative. Census figures (in nonliterate societies, pebbles, for example, would be used as counters) provided the basis on which taxes were apportioned among the conquered districts and tribute in labor exacted from the constituent kin units. The census was also essential for conscripting men into the army. This information was considered so important in Dahomey that each new king, upon his enstoolment, was escorted by his two leading ministers to a special hut in the royal compound and there admonished as he knelt: "Young man, all your life you have heard Dahomey, Dahomey, but you have never until today seen the true Dahomey, for Dahomey is its people and here they are" (Herskovitz, 1938: 73).

With this declaration, the two elders pointed to sacks of pebbles, each pebble representing a person, each sack representing a sex or age group. The young king was then told that he must never allow the contents of the sacks to diminish and that every year the pebbles would be counted to see whether their number had increased or declined. He was then given an old gun (in earlier times a hoe handle) and advised, "Fight with this. But take care that you are not vanquished" (Herskovitz, 1938: 73).

The census figures represented the potential power of the state and were carefully guarded; perhaps they were the first state secret. The act and intent of the census turned persons into ciphers, abstractions in civil perspective; people did all they could to avoid being counted. Suspicion persists; even in the United States the authorities during the period of census taking find it necessary to assert that census information will not be used to tax or otherwise penalize the individual, and, in fact, to do so is said to be against the law.

The double meanings of certain critical terms in common English use—"custom," "duty," and "court," reveal this conflict between local usage and the census–tax–conscription system of the early state. We have been speaking of custom as traditional or conventional nonlegal behavior, but custom also refers to a tax routinely payable to the state for the transportation of goods across territorial borders. All such taxes are clearly defined legal impositions, frequently honored in the breach, and they do not have the traditional command of custom. In Dahomey, the "Grand Customs" held at the unveiling of a new king, presumably in honor of his ancestors, were the occasion for the payment of taxes, the large-scale sentencing and sacrifice of criminals, and the prosecution of other state business. Camus has Caligula describe such an event in a passage that could have been extrapolated from a Dahomean chronicle:

It's only the Treasury that counts. And living is the opposite of loving . . . and I invite you to the most gorgeous of shows, a sight for gods to gloat on, a whole world called to judgment. But for that I must have a crowd—spectators, victims, criminals, hundreds and thousands of them. Let the accused come forward. I want my criminals, and they are all criminals. Bring in the condemned men. I must have my public. Judges, witnesses, accused—all sentenced to death without a hearing. Yes, Ceasonia, I'll show them something they've never seen before, the one free man in the Roman Empire (Camus, 1958: 17).*

*From *Caligula and Three Other Plays* by Albert Camus, translated by Stuart Gilbert. Copyright© 1958 by Alfred A. Knopf. Inc. Reprinted by permission of the publisher.

Along with the annual "customs," the "Grand Customs" paralleled the form of local ceremonies, but the substance had entirely changed. Fiscal or legal coercion, political imposition were not the purpose of these ancestral ceremonies which ritually reenacted reciprocal bonds. The "customs" of the sovereign were laws, the ceremonies of the kin groups were customs.

Similarly, the term "duty" implies a moral obligation on the one hand and a tax on the other. Naturally, we assume that it is the duty of citizens to pay taxes: the paradox inherent in the term becomes more obvious, as one might imagine, as we examine archaic civilizations.

The term "court" is analogously ambivalent. On the one hand, it refers to the residence or entourage of the sovereign; on the other, to a place where civil justice is dispensed, but at their root the functions fuse. The prototypical juridical institution was, in fact, the court of the sovereign where legislation was instituted, for which no precedent or formal analogue existed on the local level. Peristiany, speaking of the Kipsigis, sharpens the latter point: "One of the most significant differences between the . . . council of elders and a European judicature is to be found in the relation between officer and office. The Council elders do not hold their office from a higher authority. They are not appointed . . . (Peristiany, 1956: 42).

The contrast is well remarked by V. C. Uchendu:

Under a constitution like that of the Igbo, which does not provide for a specialized court. judicial matters are *ad hoc* affairs. The injured party takes the initiative. He may appeal to the head of the compound of the offender or to a body of arbitrators. . . . Since the arbitrators have no means of enforcing their decision, for it to be respected it must be acceptable to both parties (1965: 43).*

As Seagle, among others, indicates, the court is the first, most important, and perhaps the last legal artifact. In Montaigne's words, "France takes as its rule the rule of the court" (1965: 197). Put another way, the court is a specialized legal structure and it embraces all those particular and determinate legal bodies which are peculiar to civilization.

Clearly, the function of the court was not primarily the establishment of order. In primitive societies, as in the traditional sectors of proto-states, there already existed built-in mechanisms for the resolution of conflict. Generally speaking, as Max Gluckman, among others, has shown, in such societies conflicts generated by the ordinary functioning of social institutions were resolved as part of the customary ritual cycle integral to the institutions themselves.

With regard to more specific breaches, we recall Rattray's observation on

*See footnote on page 320.

the Ashanti: "Corporate responsibility for every act was an established principle which survived even the advent of . . . the administration of public justice." That is to say the kin unit was the juridical unit, just as it was the economic and social unit. Furthermore:

> Causes which give rise to the greater part of present 'civil' actions were practically non-existent. Inheritance, ownership of moveable and non-moveable property, status of individuals, rules of behavior and morality were matters inevitably settled by the customary law, with which everyone was familiar from childhood, and litigation regarding such matters was . . . almost inconceivable. Individual contract, moreover, from the very nature of the community with which we are concerned, was also unknown, thus removing another possible, fruitful source of litigation (Rattray, 1929: 286).

The primary purpose of the historically emerging court, the sovereign's entourage and habitation, was to govern. The distinguished British jurist Sir John Salmond has observed, "Law is secondary and unessential. . . . The administration of justice is perfectly possible without law at all" (1920: 13). And Sir William Markby writes, "Tribunals can act entirely without law" (1905: 21). The perhaps unintended point here is that justice, commonly defined, is neither deducible from the law, nor was the legislation of the court a measure of justice, but of the political thrust of the early state, and that flowed from the implementation of the census–tax–conscription system.

In the census–tax–conscription system, every conceivable occasion was utilized for the creation of law in support of bureaucracy and sovereign. We observe no abstract principle, no impartial justice, no *precedent*, only the spontaneous opportunism of a new class designing the edifice of its power. It should be reemphasized, however, that in certain instances formal analogues for civil imposition existed on the local level, but no formal or functional precedents. Civil taxation, for example, can be rationalized in the context of reciprocal gift-giving in the localities, but the latter was not confirmed by law, or specifically used by the sovereign; similarly, corvée labor is a political analogue of local cooperative work groups. But such evolutionary, and dialectical, relationships are most important for their distinctions.

Stubbs writes about the Norman kings that "it was mainly for the sake of the profits that early justice was administered at all" (Stubbs, 1890: Vol. 1, 48). Burton relates that at Whydah, in native Dahomey, in the event of a financial dispute the Yevogan, the leading bureaucrat in the district, sat in judgment. For his services, he appropriated half the merchandise involved, in the name of the king, and another quarter for various lesser officials. The remainder presumably went to the winning contestant in the judicial duel (Burton, 1964: Vol. 2, 211). Among the Ashanti, the central authority relied on the proceeds of litigation as a fruitful means for replenishing a depleted treasury. Litigation, Rattray notes, came actually to be encouraged (Rattray, 1929: 292).

Tolls were an important source of revenue. In Ashanti, the king had all the roads guarded; all traders were detained until inquiries were made about them, whereupon they were allowed to pass on payment of gold dust (Rattray, 1929: 111). W. Bosman writes that in early eighteenth century Whydah, the king's revenue "in proportion to his country is very large, of which I believe, he hath above one thousand collectors who dispose themselves throughout the whole land in all market roads and passages, in order to gather the king's toll which amounts to an incredible sum, for there is nothing so mean sold in the whole kingdom that the king hath no toll for it . . ." (1705: 362).

The punishment for the theft of property designated as the king's was summary execution by "kangaroo courts" organized on the spot by the king's agents (Norris: 1790: 201 ff.). This is echoed in the Code of Hammurabi: "If a man steals the property of a god (temple) or a palace, that man shall be put to death; and he who receives from his hands the stolen (property) shall also be put to death" (Harper transl., 1904: Section 6, 13). Where the king's property was concerned, no judicial duel was possible. In these instances, which could be endlessly multiplied, we witness the extension of the king's peace, the primary form of the civil "order," actually the invention and application of sumptuary law through the subsidiary peaces of highway and market. In Maitland's words, "The king has a peace that devours all others." If, in these proto-states, the sovereign power is not yet fully effective, it nonetheless strives to that monopoly of force which characterizes the mature state.

The purpose and abundance of laws inevitably provoked breaches. The civil authority, in fact, continually probed for breaches and frequently manufactured them. In Dahomey, for example, a certain category of the king's women were distributed to the local villages and those men who made the mistake of having intercourse with them were accused of rape, for which the punishment, following a summary trial, was conscription into the army (Le Herisse, 1911: 72). Thus, rape was invented as a *civil* crime. If rape had, in fact, occurred in the traditional joint-family villages—and such an occurrence would have been rare, as indicated by the necessity of civil definition— the wrong could have been dealt with by composition (the ritualized giving of goods to the injured party), ritual purification, ridicule, and, perhaps, for repeated transgressions, banishment; the customary machinery would have gone into effect automatically, probably on the initiative of the family of the aggressor. Such instances as this only sharpen the point that in early states crimes seem to have been invented to suit the laws; the latent purpose of the law was punishment in the service and profit of the state, not prevention or the protection of persons, not the *healing* of the breach. As Seagle indicates, "The criminal law springs into life in every great period of class conflict," and this is most obviously the case during the initial phases of state formation.

In its civil origins, then, a correlation existed between law and crime which partook of entrapment. One may even state that the substantial rationale for law developed *after* the fact of its emergence. For example, civil protection of the market place or highway was certainly not necessary to the degree implied in the archaic edicts at the time they were issued. Joint-family markets and village trails were not ordinarily dangerous places, if we are to believe the reports of the earliest chroniclers, as well as those of more contemporary observers. Moreover, if trouble had developed, the family, clan, or village was capable of dealing with it. But, in an evolving conquest state, the presence of the king's men would itself be a primary cause of disruption. Indeed, as M. Quénum, a descendant of Dahomean commoners, informs us in a remarkable work, the soldiers were referred to as bandits and predators who victimized many people. Sometimes their forays were confined to a single compound, where someone, whether man, woman, or child, resided who had spoken badly of the sovereign or whom the king suspected (Quénum, 1938: 7).[1] In common parlance, the very names of the elite army units became insults; one meant "nasty person," another "arrogant person," and one would say of a tragic event that it was worthy of yet another military cadre. It is, therefore, understandable that the peace of the highway became an issue (Quénum, 1938: 21–22).

As the integrity of the local groups declined, a process which, in the autochthonous state, must have taken generations or even centuries, conditions doubtless developed which served as an *ex post facto* rationalization for edicts already in effect. In this sense, laws became self-fulfilling prophecies. Crime and the laws which served it were, then, covariants of the evolving state.

Just as entrapment was characteristic of early civil law, the idea of protection, in the sense of a protection racket, also inheres in its origins. In Dahomey, we are told by Norris and others, prostitution was encouraged by the civil power and prostitutes were distributed through the villages, the price of their favors being set by civil decree. They were obliged to offer

[1] Quénum had a poor opinion of the ethnographers who claimed to understand and interpret his country. They failed, he believed, because of inadequate sources of information, and (or) ignorance of social customs. "Most of our ethnographers," he wrote, "have had as collaborators princes and ex-ministers of state and have believed their tales." He adds that ignorance of the native language and deficient sympathy compounded the problem. The point to note here is that Quénum is objecting to the view from the top which is a critical issue in the writing of all political history.

themselves to any man who could pay the moderate fee and once a year were convened at the "annual customs" where they were heavily taxed (1790: 257). Skertchly notes that the prostitutes were licensed by the king and placed in the charge of the Mew, the second leading bureaucrat, who was entrusted with the task of "keeping up the supply" (1874: 283). Bosman observes at Whydah that "for every affair that can be thought of, the king hath appointed a captain overseer" (Bosman, 1705: 361). *What the king permits, he commands; what he "protects," he taxes.*

The intention of the civil power is epitomized in the sanctions against homicide and suicide, typical of early polities; indeed they were among the very first civil laws. Just as the sovereign is said to own the land, intimating the mature right of eminent domain, so the individual is ultimately conceived as the chattel of the state. In Dahomey, persons were conceived as *les choses du monarque.* Eminent domain in persons and property, even where projected as a fiction, is, of course, the cardinal prerequisite of the census–tax–conscription system. We recall that Maine designated the individual the unit of which the civil law steadily takes account. Seagle stated the matter as follows: "By undermining the kinship bond, they (the early civil authorities) made it easier to deal with individuals, and the isolation of the individual is a basic precondition for the growth of law" (Seagle, 1946: 64).

Homicide, then, was regarded as an offense against the state. In Rattray's words, "The blow which struck down the dead man would thus appear to have been regarded as aimed also at the ... central authority" (Rattray, 1929: 295). In Ashanti homicide was punishable by death in its most horrible form; in Dahomey, by death or conscription into the army. There is a nuance here which should not be overlooked. By making homicide, along with the theft of the king's property, a capital offence, the sovereign power discouraged violent opposition to the imposition of the civil order.

Traditionally, murder in a joint-family village was a tort—a private, remediable wrong—which could stimulate a blood feud, not to be confused with the *lex talionis*, until redress, which did not imply equivalent injury, was achieved. But a breach was most often settled by composition. As Paul Radin put it (1953: 252): "The theory of an eye for an eye ... never really held for primitive people ... rather it was replacement for loss with damages." And this is echoed by Peristiany (1956: 43): "... they claim restitution or private damages and not social retribution." In any case, the family was fully involved. "The family was a corporation," said Rattray. "It is not easy to grasp what must have been the effect ... of untold generations of thinking and acting ... in relation to one's group. The Ashanti's idea of what we term moral responsibility for his actions must surely have been more developed than in peoples where individualism is the order of the day"

(Radin, 1953: 62). This more or less typical anthropological observation makes it clear that the law against homicide was not a "progressive" step, as if some abstract right were involved which the state, coming of age, finally understands and seeks to establish. "Anti-social conduct (is) exceptional in small kinship groups," writes Margery Perham of the Ibo (1962: 229 ff.). Crimes of violence were rare, Richard Burton (1864: 56) reported of Dahomey, and "murder virtually unknown."[2] Of course, as with other crimes defined by civil law, they may have increased as the social autonomy, economic communalism, and reciprocity of the kin units weakened. But this is much less important than Dalzel's observation that in Dahomey "many creatures have been put to death . . . without having committed any crime at all" (1793: 212), thus exemplifying the power of the sovereign literally to command the lives of his citizens. The threat and example of summary execution, especially but by no means exclusively evident at the mortuary celebrations of "Grand Customs" on the enstooling of a king, encouraged obedience to civil injunctions.

The law against suicide, a capital offense, was the apotheosis of political absurdity. The individual, it was assumed, had no right to take his own life; that was the sole prerogative, presumably, of the state, whose property he was conceived to be.

The fanatical nature of the civil legislature in claiming sole prerogative to the lives of its subjects is conclusively revealed among the Ashanti, where, if the suicide was a murderer, "the central authority refused to be cheated thus and the long arm of the law followed the suicide to the grave from which, if his kinsmen should have dared to bury him, he was dragged to stand trial" (Rattray, 1929: 299). (One recalls Antigone's defiance.) This contrasts remarkably, if logically, with the behavior of the more primitively structured Ibo, as reported by Victor Uchendu, an anthropologist who is himself an Ibo:

> Homicide is an offense against ala—the earth deity. If a villager is involved, *the murderer is expected to hang himself*, after which . . . daughters of the village perform the rite of . . . sweeping away the ashes of murder. If the murderer has fled, his extended family must also flee, and the property of all is subject to raids. When the murderer is eventually caught, he is required to hang himself to enable the daughters of the village to perform

---

[2] Acts of violence must be distinguished from *crimes* of violence. The incidence, occasions for, and character of violence in primitive, as opposed to civilized societies, is a subject of the utmost importance, which I have discussed elsewhere. But the question here has to do with crimes in which violence is used as a means for, for example, the theft of property. In contemporary societies unpremeditated acts of personal violence which have no ulterior motive, so-called crimes of passion, may not be penalized or carry minor degrees of guilt, that is, their status as legally defined crimes is ambiguous. This would certainly seem to reflect a historically profound distinction between crime and certain types of violence. In primitive societies violence tends to be personally structured, nondissociative, and, thereby, self-limiting.

their rites. It is important to realize that the village has no power to impose capital punishment. In fact, no social group or institution has this power. Everything affecting the life of the villager is regulated by custom. The life of the individual is highly respected; it is protected by the earth-goddess. The villagers can bring social pressure, but the murderer must hang himself (1965: 42–43).*

It can hardly be argued that the purpose of the civil sanction against suicide was to diminish its incidence or to propagate a superior moral consciousness. Dare we say, as with other crimes, that attempts at suicide increased as society became more thoroughly politicized? The law against suicide reveals, in the extreme, the whole meaning and intent of civil law at its origins. In the proto-state, the quintessential struggle was over the lives and labor of the people, who, still moving in a joint-family context, were nonetheless conceived to be *les choses du monarque*.

III

If revolutions are the acute, episodic signs of civilizational discontent, the rule of law, in seven millennia of political society, from Sumer or Akkad to New York or Moscow, has been the chronic symptom of the disorder of institutions. E. B. Tylor stated, "A constitutional government, whether called republic or kingdom, is an arrangement by which the nation governs itself by means of the machinery of a military despotism" (1946: Vol. 2, 156).

The generalization lacks nuance but we can accept it if we bear in mind Tylor's point of reference: "Among the lessons to be learnt from the life of rude tribes is how society can go on without the policeman to keep order" (1946: Vol. 2, 134). When he alluded to constitutional government, Tylor was not distinguishing its ultimate sanction from that of any other form of the state: all political society is based on repressive organized force. In this he was accurate. For pharaohs and presidents alike have always made a public claim to represent the common interest, indeed to incarnate the common good. Only a Plato or a Machiavelli in search of political harmony, or a Marx in search of political truth, has been able to penetrate this myth of the identity between ruler and ruled, of equality under law. The tradition of Plato and Machiavelli commends the use of the "royal" or "noble lie," while that of Marx exposes and rejects the power structure (ultimately the state) that propagates so false a political consciousness. On this issue, I follow Marx.

*See footnote on page 320.

Tylor distinguishes the civilized from the primitive order. Such a distinction has been made at every moment of crisis in the West but nowhere so pertinently as in Montaigne's contrast of a primitive society with Plato's ideally civilized republic:

> This is a nation, I should say to Plato, in which there is no sort of traffic, no knowledge of letters, no science of numbers, no name for a magistrate or for political superiority, no custom of servitude, no riches or poverty, no contracts, no successions, no partitions . . . no care for any but common kinship. How far from this perfection would he find the Republic he imagines (Montaigne, 1965: 153).[3]

The issue of law and order implicit in Montaigne's contrast between primitive and civilized societies has been a persistent underlying theme for the most reflective and acute minds of the West. The inquiry into the nature of politics probably demarcates most accurately the boundaries of our intellectual landscape. The evolution of the state toward what Max Weber called maximally politicized society, the unprecedented concentration of bureaucratic and technological power, which economically and culturally dominates the rest of the world, creates a climate in which all problems cast a political shadow. We may flee from the political dimension of our experience or we may embrace it in order to do away with it, but we are obsessed by politics. It was perhaps Plato's primary virtue that, at the very origin of the Western intellectual tradition, he understood that, in civilization, all significant human problems have a political aspect and he insisted upon the solution of the latter as a coefficient of the creative resolution of the former. *The Republic* is the first civilizational utopia, and it maintains its force both as a model of inquiry and as antithesis to all projections of the nature of primitive society. Any contrary view of the possibilities of human association must take *The Republic* into account.

The legal order, which Plato idealized, is as Tylor maintained and Marx understood, synonymous with the power of the state. Paul Vinogradoff writes:

> The state has assumed the monopoly of political co-ordination. It is the state which rules, makes laws and eventually enforces them by coercion. Such a state did not exist in ancient times. The commonwealth was not centered in one sovereign body towering immeasurably above single individuals and meting out to everyone his portion of right (1920: 93).

---

[3] In ignorance of Montaigne's contrast between primitive society and Plato's ideal republic, I published an article (Diamond, 1960), which explicates some of the points briefly noted above. For a more comprehensive model of primitive society, see Diamond (1963). In order to understand the functioning of custom in primitive society fully, one should have such a model in mind. Unfortunately, in this article I can only suggest its outlines.

And Engels, reflecting on the origins of the state, asserts: "The right of the state to existence was founded on the preservation of order in the interior and the protection against the barbarians outside, but this order was worse than the most disgusting disorder, and the barbarians against whom the state pretended to protect its citizens were hailed by them as saviors" (1902: 179). Moreover, "The state created a public power of coercion that did no longer coincide with the old self-organized and (self-) armed population" (1902: 207). Finally, in a passage that epitomizes the West's awareness of itself, Engels writes:

> The state, then, is by no means a power forced on society at a certain stage of evolution. It is the confession that this society has become hopelessly divided against itself, has estranged itself in irreconcilable contradictions which it is powerless to banish. In order that these contradictions, these classes with conflicting economic interests may not annihilate themselves and society in a useless struggle, a power becomes necessary that stands apparently above society and has the function of keeping down the conflicts and maintaining 'order.' And this power, the outgrowth of society, but assuming supremacy over it and becoming more and more divorced from it, is the state. . . ." (Engels, 1902: 206).

In a word, the state is the alienated form of society; and it is this process which has fascinated the Western intellect and which may, in fact, have led to the peculiar intensity of the reflective, analytic, and introspective consciousness in the West, to our search for origins and our inexhaustible concern with secular history. A knowledge of one's present, as Montaigne maintained, implies not only a knowledge of one's past but of one's future.

However we project, imagine, or reconstruct the past, we recognize the division, the objective correlate of the division within ourselves, between primitive and civilized society, between moral and civil order, between custom and law. Interpretation of the nature of the primitive and the civilized has, of course, not been uniform. Hobbes versus Rousseau is paradigmatic. But most theorists tend to see civilization as a kind of fall from a "natural," or at least more natural, to a legal or more repressive order. No matter how the virtues of civilization are weighed, the price exacted is inevitably noted. This is as true of Plato as of Freud or Engels. Plato, for example, notes, however inadequately, a condition of existence prior to the city-state, a type of rusticity which he views nostalgically and whose destruction he maintains was socioeconomically determined. I suspect that even the great majority of anthropologists, despite professional illusions of dissociated objectivity, sense that primitive societies are somehow closer than civilized societies to the realization of "natural" law and "natural" right. I believe this emphasis in the Western tradition to be the sounder, and it serves as the basis of my own thinking. There is, as Montaigne noted, an "amazing distance" between the primitive character and our own. In the contrast between these two sides of our historical nature, which we existentially reenact, we come to understand law as the antonym and not the synonym of order.

IV

I agree with Nadel that in the transition from primitive to political society the means of control and integration employed were, in a wider sense, "all . . . deliberately conceived and (executed); they are agencies of an assimilation conscious of itself and of the message which it carries" (1942: 144). Finally, we are led to ask, as did Nadel about the Nupe:

> What did the tax-paying, law-abiding citizen receive in return for allegiance to king and nobility? Was extortion, bribery, brutal force, the only aspect under which the state revealed itself to the populace? The people were to receive, theoretically, on the whole, one thing: security—protection against external and internal enemies, and general security for carrying out the daily work, holding markets, using the roads. We have seen what protection and security meant in reality. At their best, they represented something very unequal and very unstable. This situation must have led to much tension and change within the system and to frequent attempts to procure better safeguards for civil rights (Nadel, 1935: 287).

The struggle for civil rights, then, is a response to the imposition of civil law. With the destruction of the primitive base of society, civil rights have been defined and redefined as a reaction to drastic changes in the socioeconomic structure, the rise of caste and class systems, imperialism, modern war, technology as a means of social exploitation, maldistribution, and misuse of resources, racial hatred. The right to socially and economically fruitful work, for example, which did not come into question in a primitive society or in a traditional sector of an early state (and therefore was not conceived to be a stipulated right) becomes an issue under capitalism. The demand implies a need for profoundly changing the system and indicates that our sense of the appropriately human has very ancient roots indeed. However, we are reminded by the struggle for civil rights, that legislation alone has no force beyond the potential of the social system that generates it. From the study of proto-states we also learn that the citizen must be constantly alert to laws which seek to curb his rights in the name of protection or security. Restrictive legislation is almost always a signal of repressive institutional change, but is, of course, not the cause of it.

The major focus of the defense of the citizen as a person can only be on procedure or, as we call it in our own society, due process. Quénum reports, of the early state of Dahomey, "There was no penal code promulgated . . . punishment had no fixity . . . the Miegan (leading bureaucrat, chief judge, and executioner) would become restive if capital punishment would be too long in coming" (1938: 22). In the words of Dalzel, "There was a vast disproportion between crimes and punishments" (1793: 212). And in early states, most if not all civil breaches were what we would define as crimes, just as in primitive societies "civil crimes" were considered, where they were not unprecedented, torts or private remediable wrongs. As every intelligent lawyer knows, the substance of the law can hardly be assimilated to morality. It is clear, therefore, why von Jhering (1866: Vol. 2, 471) insisted that "form is the sworn enemy of unlimited discretion (of the sovereign power) and the twin sister of freedom." The degrees of theft or homicide, the question of double jeopardy, habeas corpus, the right to counsel, the question of legitimate witness, trial by jury and the selection of jurors, protection against summary search and seizure, the very division between civil and criminal law—these intricacies of procedure are the primary, but far from absolute, assurance of whatever justice can be obtained under the rule of law.

For example, the only way dissidents in Russia can defend themselves against summary punishment and make their cases universally understandable is by calling attention to abuses of procedure. The spirit of the laws, mummified in the excellent constitution of 1936, is irrelevant, abstract. The tribunal that discharges the intentions of the state can discard, suspend, reinterpret, and invent laws at will. The court, not the constitution, is the primary legal reality. And the politically inspired charge of insanity, which can remove dissidents from the body politic altogether, is the ultimate étatistic definition of the person—a nonbeing incapable of autonomy. And that, I should note, is foreshadowed in the consummate anti-Socratic Platonism of the Laws, the heavenly city brought to earth, wherein the ordinary citizen is "to become, by long habit, utterly incapable of doing anything at all independently."

Procedure is the individual's last line of defense in contemporary civilization, wherein all other associations to which he may belong have become subordinate to the state. The elaboration of procedure then, is a unique, if fragile, feature of more fully evolved states, in compensation, so to speak, for the radical isolation of the individual. In the proto-states, the harshness of rudimentary procedure was countered by the role of the kinship units which, as we recall, retained a significant measure of functional socioeconomic autonomy and, therefore, of local political cohesion.

But "law has its origin in the pathology of social relations and functions only when there are frequent disturbances of the social equilibrium" (Seagle, 1946: 36). Law arises in the breach of a prior customary order and increases in force with the conflicts that divide political societies internally and among themselves. Law and order is the historical illusion; law versus order is the historical reality.

In the tradition of Rousseau, Lévi-Strauss, in a moment of candor, declares,

> We must go beyond the evidence of the injustices and abuses to which the social order gives rise, and discover the unshakable basis of human society. . . . Anthropology shows that base cannot be found in our own civilization, ours is indeed perhaps the one furthest from it" (1961: 390).

The progressive reduction of society to a series of technical and legal signals, the consequent diminution of culture, that is, of reciprocal, symbolic meanings, are perhaps the primary reasons why our civilization is the one least likely to serve as a guide to "the unshakable basis of human society."

REFERENCES

Bohannan, P.
  1968   Law and legal institutions. In *International Encyclopedia of the Social Sciences*, edited by David Sills, Vol. 9, pp. 73–78. New York: Macmillan (Free Press).
Bosman, W.
  1705   *A new and accurate description of the coast of Guinea*. London: J. Knapton.
Burton, R. F.
  1864   *A mission of Gelele, a king of Dahomey*. London: Tinsley Brothers.
Camus, A.
  1958   *Caligula and three other plays*. New York: Knopf.
Dalzel, A.
  1793   *The history of Dahomey, an inland kingdom of Africa*. London: Cass.
Diamond, S.
  1951   *Dahomey, a proto-state in West Africa*. Ann Arbor: University Microfilms.
  1960   Plato and the definition of the primitive. In *Culture in history*, edited by Stanley Diamond. New York: Columbia Univ. Press.
  1963   The Search for the Primitive. In *Man's image in medicine and anthropology*, edited by I. Galdston. New York: International Universities Press.
Engels, F.
  1902   *Origin of the family, private property and the state*. Chicago: C. H. Kerr. (Orig. pub. 1884.)
Gluckman, M.
  1944   Studies in African land tenure. *African Studies* 3 (1944): 14–21.
Harper, R. F. (transl.)
  1904   *The Code of Hammurabi*. Chicago: Univ. of Chicago Press.
Herskovitz, M.
  1938   *Dahomey, an ancient West African kingdom*. New York: Augustin.
Jhering, R. von
  1866   *Geist des römischen Rechts*. Vol. 2. Leipzig: Breitkopf und Härtel.
Le Herisse, A.
  1911   *L'ancien royaume du Dahomey*. Paris: E. Larose.
Lévi-Strauss, C.
  1961   *A world on the wane*. New York: Criterion.
Maine, H.
  1889   *Village communities and miscellanies*. New York: H. Holt. (Orig. pub. 1871.)
  1897   *Lectures on the early history of institutions*. London: Murray.
  1963   *Ancient law*. Boston: Beacon. (Orig. pub. 1861.)

Mair, L. P.
  1933   Baganda land tenure. *Africa* **6** (1933): 187–205.
Markby, Sir W.
  1905   *Elements of law considered with reference to principles of general jurisprudence.*
          London and New York: Oxford Univ. Press (Clarendon).
Montaigne, M. de.
  1965   *The complete essays.* Stanford: Stanford Univ. Press.
Nadel, S. F.
  1935   Nupe state and community. *Africa* **8** (1935): 257–303.
  1942   *A black Byzantium.* London and New York: Oxford Univ. Press.
Norris, R.
  1790   *Reise nach abomey, der hofstadt des Konigs von Dahomey an von Guinea im Jahr
          1772.* Leipzig. (Publisher unknown—eds.; orig. pub. 1787 in English.)
Perham, M.
  1962   *Native administration in Nigeria.* London and New York: Oxford Univ. Press.
Peristiany, J. G.
  1956   *The institutions of primitive society.* New York: Free Press.
Quénum, M.
  1938   *Au pays des fons.* Paris. (Publisher unknown—eds.)
Radin, P.
  1953   *The world of primitive man.* New York: Schuman.
Rattray, T. S.
  1929   *Ashanti, law and constitution.* London and New York: Oxford Univ. Press.
Salmond, Sir J. W.
  1920   *Jurisprudence.* London: Stevens and Hayner.
Seagle, W.
  1946   *The history of law.* New York: Tudor Publ.
Simpson, S. P., and J. Stone
  1942   *Law and society in evolution.* St. Paul: West Publ.
Skertchly, J. A.
  1874   *Dahomey as it is.* London: Chapman and Hall.
Stubbs, W.
  1890   *The constitutional history of England.* Vol. 1. Oxford: Clarendon Press.
Tylor, E. B.
  1946   *Anthropology.* Vol. 2. London: Watts.
Uchendu, V. C.
  1965   *The Igbo of southeast Nigeria.* New York: Holt.
Vernadsky, G.
  1947   *Medieval Russian laws.* New York: Columbia Univ. Press.
Vinogradoff, P.
  1920   *Outlines of historical jurisprudence.* London and New York: Oxford Univ. Press.

Part VII

LEGAL
ORGANIZATION

THE CONTROL OF WITCHCRAFT IN RENAISSANCE EUROPE

Elliott P. Currie

THE SOCIOLOGICAL study of deviant behavior has begun to focus less on the deviant and more on society's response to him (Tannenbaum, 1938; Lemert, 1951; Goffman, 1962, 1963; Becker, 1963; Erikson, 1966; Kitsuse, 1966). One of several implications of this perspective is that a major concern of the sociology of deviance should be the identification and analysis of different kinds of systems of social control. Particularly important is the analysis of the impact of different kinds of control systems on the way deviant behavior is perceived and expressed in societies.

By playing down the importance of intrinsic differences between deviants and conventional people, and between the social situation of deviants and that of nondeviants, the focus on social response implies much more than the commonplace idea that society defines the kinds of behavior that will be considered odd, disgusting, or criminal. It implies that many elements of the behavior system of a given kind of deviance, including such things as the rate of deviance and the kinds of people who are identified as deviant, will be significantly affected by the kind of control system through which the behavior is defined and managed.

In this paper, I attempt to add to the rather small body of research on

Reprinted from "Crimes without Criminals: Witchcraft and Its Control in Renaissance Europe" by Elliott P. Currie, *Law and Society Review*, Vol. 3, No. 1 (1968): pp. 7–32.

kinds of social control systems and their impact.[1] The subject is witchcraft in Renaissance Europe, and in particular, the way in which the phenomenon of witchcraft differed in England and in continental Europe,[2] as a result of differences in their legal systems. I will show that the English and the continental legal systems during this period represented the two ends of a continuum along which different social control systems may be placed, and I will suggest some general ways in which each kind of control system affects the deviant behavior systems in which it is involved. Along the way, however, I will also suggest that the *degree* to which a social control system can influence the character of a deviant behavior system is variable and depends in part on the *kind* of behavior involved and the particular way it is socially defined.

WITCHCRAFT AS DEVIANCE

Something labeled witchcraft can be found in many societies, but the particular definition of the crime of witchcraft which emerged in Renaissance Europe was unique. It consisted of the individual's making, for whatever reason and to whatever end, a pact or covenant with the Devil, thereby gaining the power to manipulate supernatural forces for antisocial and un-Christian ends. What was critical was the pact itself; not the assumption or use of the powers which it supposedly conferred, but the willful renunciation of the Faith implied by the act of Covenant with the Devil. Thus, on the Continent, witchcraft was usually prosecuted as a form of heresy, and in England as a felony whose essence was primarily mental.[3] Witchcraft, then, came to be defined as a sort of thought-crime. It was not necessarily related to the practice of magic, which was widespread and had many legitimate forms. There were statutes forbidding witchcraft before the Renaissance, but the new conception of witchcraft involved important changes in both the nature and the seriousness of the crime. Early legislation, throughout Europe, had tended to lump witchcraft and magic in the same category, and to deal with them as minor offenses. In ninth century England, the Law of the Northumbrian Priests held that if anyone " ... in any way

---

[1] One interesting study along these lines is Schur (1962).

[2] Erikson (1966) discusses some aspects of witchcraft in America, which unfortunately cannot be discussed here without unduly lengthening the paper. For the curious, though, it should be noted that the American experience was in general much closer to the English than to the continental experience, particularly in terms of the small number of witches executed. For anyone interested in American witchcraft, Erikson's discussion and bibliography is a good place to start.

[3] Elizabeth's statute of 1563 made witchcraft punishable by death only if it resulted in the death of the bewitched; witchcraft unconnected with death was a lesser offense. However, in 1604 James I revised the statute to invoke the death penalty for witchcraft regardless of result. On this point see Davies (1947).

love witchcraft, or worship idols, if he be a king's thane, let him pay X half-marks; half to Christ, half to the king. We are all to love and worship one God, and strictly hold one Christianity, and renounce all heathenship."[4]

Similar mildness is characteristic of other early English legislation, while the Catholic Church itself, in the thirteenth century, explicitly took the position that the belief in witchcraft was an illusion.[5] In no sense were witches considered by ecclesiastical or secular authorities to be a serious problem, until the fifteenth century.

I cannot speculate here on the process through which the early conception of witchcraft as, essentially, the witch's delusion evolved to the point where the witch was believed to have actual powers. Suffice it to say that such a shift in definition did take place[6]; that during the fifteenth and sixteenth centuries a new theological and legal conception of witchcraft emerged, which amounted to an official recognition of a hitherto unknown form of deviance. In 1484, Pope Innocent IV issued a Bull recognizing the serious-ness of the crime of witchcraft, affirming its reality, and authorizing the use of the Holy Inquisition to prosecute it with full force. As an indication of the state of thinking on witchcraft at this time, this document (quoted in Davies, 1947: 4) serves admirably:

> It has recently come to our attention, not without bitter sorrow, that . . . many persons of both sexes, unmindful of their own salvation and straying from the Catholic Faith, have abandoned themselves to devils . . . and by their . . . accursed charms and crafts, enormities and horrid offenses, have slain unborn infants and the offspring of cattle, have blasted the produce of the earth . . . these wretches furthermore afflict and torment men and women . . . with terrible and piteous pains. . . . Over and above this they blasphemously renounce the Faith which is theirs by the Sacrament of Baptism, and do not shrink from committing and perpetrating the foulest abominations and filthiest excesses . . . .

---

[4] Quoted in Murray (1962): Other early legislation is also quoted by Murray, and can also be found in Ewen (1929).

[5] This position was formulated in a document known as the *Capitulum Episcopi*, apparently written in 1215, which molded Church policy for over 200 years. It reads in part as follows:

> Some wicked women . . . seduced by the illusions and phantasms of demons, believe and profess that they ride at night with Diana on certain beasts with an innumerable company of women, passing over immense distances . . . priests everywhere should preach that they know this to be false, and that such phantasms are sent by the Evil Spirit, who deludes them in dreams. . . .

Quoted in Lea (1888) and in Murray (1962).

[6] The shift, however, did not take place all at once, nor did it take place without important ideological struggles both within and beyond the Church; a number of important figures remained skeptical through-out. Interesting materials on this process can be found in Lea (1939).

A few years later, the new conception of witchcraft was given practical impetus with the publication of a manual known as the *Malleus Maleficarum* (Sprenger and Kramer, 1948), or Witch-Hammer, written by two German Inquisitors under Papal authorization, which set forth in systematic form the heretofore diffuse beliefs on the nature and habits of witches, means for their discovery, and guidelines for their trial and execution. At this point, the witch persecutions in continental Europe entered a peak phase which lasted into the eighteenth century. Estimates of the number of witches executed in Western Europe vary, but half a million is an average count (Kittredge, 1907: 59). Although there were consistently dissident voices both within and outside of the Church, the prevalence of witches was a fact widely accepted by the majority, including a number of the most powerful intellects of the time. Luther and Calvin were believers, as was Jean Bodin, who wrote an extremely influential book on witches in which he argued, among other things, that those who scoffed at the reality of witches were usually witches themselves (Davies, 1947: 5–9, 25). Witchcraft was used as an explanation for virtually everything drastic or unpleasant that occurred, leading one Jesuit critic of the persecutions to declare: "God and Nature no longer do anything; witches, everything" (quoted in Kittredge, 1907: 47). In the fifteenth century, a delayed winter in the province of Treves brought over a hundred people to the stake as witches (Lea, 1888: 549).

Once officially recognized, the crime of witchcraft presented serious problems for those systems of control through which it was to be hunted down and suppressed. The fact that no one had ever been seen making a pact with the Devil made ordinary sources of evidence rather worthless. Ordinary people, indeed, were in theory unable to see the Devil at all; as an eminent jurist, Sinistrari, phrased the problem, "There can be no witness of that crime, since the Devil, visible to the witch, escapes the sight of all beside" (quoted in Parrinder, 1958: 76). The attendant acts— flying by night, attending witches' Sabbaths, and so on—were of such nature that little reliable evidence of their occurrence could be gathered through normal procedures. The difficulty of proving that the crime had ever taken place severely taxed the competence of European legal institutions, and two different responses emerged. In England, the response to witchcraft took place within a framework of effective limitations on the suppressive power of the legal order and a relatively advanced conception of due process of law; on the Continent, the response took place within a framework of minimal limitations on the activity of the legal system, in which due process and legal restraint tended to go by the board.

CONTINENTAL EUROPE: REPRESSIVE CONTROL

In continental Europe, people accused of witchcraft were brought before the elaborate machinery of a specialized bureaucratic agency with unusual powers and what amounted to a nearly complete absence of institutional restraints on its activity. Originally, the control of witchcraft was the responsibility of the Inquisition. After the disappearance, for practical purposes, of the Inquisition in most of Western Europe in the sixteenth century, witches were tried before secular courts which retained for the most part the methods which the Inquisition had pioneered (Lea, 1939: 244). This was as true of the Protestant sectors of Europe—England excepted—as it was of those which remained Catholic (Burr, 1891: Part 3, 11). The methods were effective and extreme.

Ordinary continental criminal procedure approximated the "inquisitorial" process, in which accusation, detection, prosecution, and judgment are all in the hands of the official control system, rather than in those of private persons; and all of these functions reside basically in one individual (see Esmein, 1913: 8 et passim). The trial was not, as it was in the "accusatorial" procedure of English law, a confrontative combat between the accuser and the accused, but an attack by the judge and his staff upon the suspect, who carried with him a heavy presumption of guilt. Litigation was played down or rejected (Esmein, 1913: 8, 9):

> The system of procedure called inquisitorial is more scientific and more complex than the accusatory system. It is better adapted to the needs of social repression. Its two predominant features are the secret inquiry to discover the culprit, and the employment of torture to obtain his confession.

Above and beyond the tendencies to repressive control visible in the inquisitorial process generally, the establishment of the Holy Inquisition in the thirteenth century as a weapon against heresy ushered in a broadening of the powers of the control system vis-à-vis the accused. Ecclesiastical criminal procedure had always been willing to invoke extraordinary methods in particularly heinous crimes, especially those committed in secret (Esmein, 1913: 128). With the coming of the Inquisition a good many procedural safeguards were systematically cast aside, on the ground that the Inquisition was to be seen as "an impartial spiritual father, whose functions in the salvation of souls should be fettered by no rules" (Lea, 1958: 405). Thus, in the interest of maintaining the ideological purity of Christendom, the legal process became conceived as a tool of the moral order, whose use and limits were almost entirely contingent on the needs of that order.

Nevertheless, certain powerful safeguards existed, in theory, for the accused. Chief among these was a rigorous conception of proof, especially in the case of capital crimes. In general, continental criminal procedure, at least from the fifteenth century onward, demanded a "complete proof" as warrant for capital punishment. "Complete proof" generally implied evidence on the order of testimony of two eyewitnesses to the criminal act or, in the case of certain crimes which otherwise would be difficult to establish, like heresy or conspiracy against the Prince, written proofs bound by rigorous standards of authenticity (Esmein, 1913: 622–623). In most cases of heresy and of witchcraft generally, proof of this order was hard, if not impossible, to come by, for obvious reasons. As a result, it was necessary to form a complete proof through combining confession, which was strong but not complete evidence, with another indication, such as testimony by one witness (Esmein, 1913: 625).[7] The result was tremendous pressure for confession at all costs, as well as a pressure for the relaxation of standards for witnesses and other sources of lesser evidence. The pressure for confession put a premium on the regular and systematic use of torture. In this manner, the procedural safeguard of rigorous proof broke down in practice through the allowance of extraordinary procedures which became necessary to circumvent it (Esmein, 1913: 625).[8]

In theory, there were some restraints on the use of torture, but not many. One sixteenth century German jurist argued that it could not be used without sufficient indication of guilt, that it could not be used "immoderately," and that it should be tempered according to the strength, age, sex, and condition of the offender. German officials, when approving the use of torture, usually added the phrase *Doch Mensch-oder-Christlicher Weise*— roughly "in humane or Christian fashion" (Lea, 1939: 854–855). In theory, confessions under torture had to be reaffirmed afterward by the accused; but torture, though it could not lawfully be repeated, could be "continued" indefinitely after interruption, and few accused witches could maintain a denial of their confession after several sessions (Lea, 1939: 427–428; Esmein, 1913: 113–114).

Besides being virtually required for the death penalty, confession was

---

[7] It would still, of course, have been difficult to get even one reliable witness to an act of witchcraft; in practice, the testimony of one accused, under torture, was used for this purpose.

[8] In a study of the criminal process in China, Cohen relates, in a similar vein, that the requirements of confession for conviction in Manchu China reinforced the temptation to use torture on the accused (see Cohen, 1966). It should be noted that the employment of torture by the Inquisition was a retrograde step in continental criminal procedure. The Church explicitly condemned torture; after it had been used by the Romans, torture was not again a standard procedure in Western Europe until it was reactivated in the 1200's in the offensive against heresy (see Esmein, 1913: 9). It was early laid down as an accepted rule of Canon Law that no confession should be extracted by torment; but the elimination of trials by ordeal in the thirteenth century, coupled with the rise of powerful heretical movements, put strong pressure on the Church to modify its approach. Originally, torture was left to the secular authorities to carry out, but a Bull of Pope Alexander IV in 1256 authorized Inquisitors to absolve each other for using it directly, and to grant each other dispensation for irregularities in its use (see Lea, 1888: 421).

useful in two other important ways, which consequently increased the usefulness of torture. First, confession involved the denunciation of accomplices, which assured a steady flow of accused witches into the courts (Lea, 1939: 885). Second, confessions were publicly read at executions, and distributed to the populace at large, which reinforced the legitimacy of the trials themselves and re-created in the public mind the reality of witchcraft itself. If people *said* they flew by night to dance with the devil, then surely there was evil in the land, and the authorities were more than justified in their zeal to root it out. In extorting confessions from accused witches, the court also made use of means other than torture. Confession was usually required if the accused were to receive the last sacraments and avoid damnation, (Lea, 1888: 506) and the accused, further, were frequently promised pardon if they confessed, a promise which was rarely kept (Lea, 1888: 514, 1939: 895).[9]

In line with the tendency to relax other standards of evidence, there was a considerable weakening of safeguards regarding testimony of witnesses. Heretics could testify, which went against established ecclesiastical policy; so could excommunicates, perjurors, harlots, children, and others who ordinarily were not allowed to bear witness. Witnesses themselves were liable to torture if they equivocated or appeared unwilling to testify; and, contrary to established procedure in ordinary continental courts, names of witnesses were withheld from the accused (Esmein, 1913: 91–94; Lea, 1958: 434–437).

In general, prisoners were not provided with information on their case (Esmein, 1913:129). Most of the proceedings were held in secret (Lea, 1958: 406). The stubborn prisoner who managed to hold to a denial of guilt was almost never released from custody (p. 419) and frequently spent years in prison (p. 419). Acquittal, in witchcraft and heresy cases, was virtually impossible. Lacking enough evidence for conviction, the court could hold an accused in prison indefinitely at its discretion. In general, innocence was virtually never the verdict in such cases; the best one could hope for was "not proven" (Lea, 1958: 453).[10]

---

[9] Deception by the court in witchcraft cases was widely approved. Bodin argued that the court should use lying and deception of the accused whenever possible; the authors of the *Malleus Maleficarum* felt that it was a good idea for the courts to promise life to the accused, since the fear of execution often prevented confession.

[10] The following quote from the period shows one important motive behind the absence of outright release:

If by torture he will say nothing nor confess, and is not convicted by witnesses ... he should be released at the discretion of the judge on pain of being attainted and convicted of the matters with which he is charged and of which he is presumed guilty ... for if he be freed absolutely, *it would seem that he had been held prisoner without charge* [italics added].

Quoted in Esmein (1913: 130).

Legal counsel for the accused under the Inquisition was often prohibited, again contrary to ordinary continental procedure (Esmein, 1913: 91–94).[11] Where counsel was allowed, it was with the disturbing understanding that successful or overly eager defense laid the counsel himself open to charges of heresy or of conspiracy to aid heretics (Sprenger and Kramer, 1948:218; Lea, 1958: 444–445). Moreover, counsel was appointed by the court, was warned not to assume a defense he "knew to be unjust," and could be summoned by the court as a witness and made to turn over all his information to the court (Lea, 1958: 517–518).

Lesser indications of guilt were supplied through the court's use of impossible dilemmas. If the accused was found to be in good repute among the populace, he or she was clearly a witch, since witches invariably sought to be highly thought of; if in bad repute, then he or she was also clearly a witch, since no one approves of witches. If the accused was especially regular in worship or morals, it was argued that the worst witches made the greatest show of piety (Lea, 1939: 858). Stubborness in refusing to confess was considered a sure sign of alliance with the Devil, who was known to be taciturn (Lea, 1888: 509). Virtually the only defense available to accused witches was in disabling hostile witnesses on the grounds of violent enmity; this provision was rendered almost useless through the assumption that witches were naturally odious to everyone, so that an exceptionally great degree of enmity was required (Lea, 1888: 517).

A final and highly significant characteristic of the continental witch trial was the power of the court to confiscate the property of the accused, whether or not he was led to confess (Lea, 1939: 808–811; 1958: 529). The chief consequence of this practice was to join to a system of virtually unlimited power a powerful motive for persecution. This coincidence of power and vested interest put an indelible stamp on every aspect of witchcraft in continental Europe.

All things considered, the continental procedure in the witch trials was an enormously effective machine for the systematic and massive production of confessed deviants. As such, it approximates a type of deviance-management which may be called repressive control. Three main characteristics of such a system may be noted, all of which were present in the continental legal order's handling of the witch trials:

1. invulnerability to restraint from other social institutions;
2. systematic establishment of extraordinary powers for suppressing deviance, with a concomitant lack of internal restraints;

---

[11] This was particularly critical in continental procedure, where presumption of guilt made the defense difficult in any case; it was less critical in England, where the burden of proof was on the court. The Church well knew the vital importance of counsel in criminal trials; *free* counsel was provided, in many kinds of ordinary cases, to those unable to afford it (see Lea, 1958: 444–445).

3. a high degree of structured interest in the apprehension and processing of deviants.

The question at hand is what the effects of this type of control structure are on the rate of deviance, the kinds of people who become defined as deviant, and other aspects of the system of behavior that it is designed to control. This will be considered after a description of the English approach to the control of witchcraft, which, having a very different character, led to very different results.

ENGLAND: RESTRAINED CONTROL

There was no Inquisition in Renaissance England, and the common law tradition provided a variety of institutional restraints on the conduct of the witch trials. As a consequence, there were fewer witches in England, vastly fewer executions, and the rise of a fundamentally different set of activities around the control of witchcraft.

Witchcraft was apparently never prosecuted as a heresy in England, but after a statute of Elizabeth in 1563 it was prosecuted as a felony in secular courts.[12] The relatively monolithic ecclesiastical apparatus, so crucial in the determination of the shape of witch trials on the Continent, did not exist in England; the new definition of witchcraft came to England late and under rather different circumstances.[13] English laws making witchcraft a capital crime, however, were on the books until 1736 although executions

---

[12] The statute is 5 Eliz., c.16 (1563); see Davies (1947: 15) for a partial quote of this statute; and p. 42, for a quote from James I's 1604 statute making witchcraft *per se*, without involving the death of another person, a capital offense.

An earlier statute (33 Hen. 8, c.8 [1541]) made witchcraft a felony, but was repealed in 1547 and probably used only sporadically and for largely political purposes. Before that, too, there were occasional trials for witchcraft or sorcery, and witchcraft of a sort, as I have shown, appears in the earliest English law. But this was the older conception of witchcraft, blurring into that of magic; and it was not until Elizabeth's statute that witch trials began in earnest (see Notestein, 1911).

[13] Two of these circumstances may be mentioned. One was the general atmosphere of social and political turmoil surrounding the accession of Elizabeth to the throne; another was the return to England, with Elizabeth's crowning, of a number of exiled Protestant leaders who had been exposed to the witch trials in Geneva and elsewhere and had absorbed the continental attitudes toward witchcraft. One of these, Bishop John Jewel of Salisbury, argued before the Queen that

This kind of people (I mean witches and sorcerers) within the last few years are marvelously increased within your Grace's realm. These eyes have seen the most evident and manifest marks of their wickedness. Your Grace's subjects pine away even unto death, their color fadeth, their speech is benumbed, their senses are bereft. Wherefore your poor subject's most humble petition to your Highness is, that the laws touching such malefactors may be put in due execution (Davies, 1947: 17).

for witchcraft ceased around the end of the seventeenth century (Ewen, 1929: 43).[14] Nevertheless, the English laws were enforced in a relatively restrained fashion through a system of primarily local courts of limited power, accountable to higher courts and characterized by a high degree of internal restraint.

With a few exceptions, notably the Star Chamber, English courts operated primarily on the accusatory principle, stressing above all the separation of the functions of prosecution and judgment, trial by jury, and the presumption of the innocence of the accused (Esmein 1913: Introduction).[15] Accuser and accused assumed the role of equal combatants before the judge and jury; prosecution of offenses generally required a private accuser (Esmein, 1913: 107, 336). The English trial was confrontative and public, and the English judge did not take the initiative in investigation or prosecution of the case (Esmein, 1913: 3, 6). Again unlike the situation on the Continent, the accused witch could appeal to higher authority from a lower court, and could sue an accuser for defamation; such actions frequently took place in the Star Chamber (cf. Ewen, 1938). Reprieves were often granted (Ewen, 1929: 32). From the middle of the seventeenth century, the accused in capital cases could call witnesses in their defense (Esmein, 1913: 342). In general, the English courts managed to remain relatively autonomous and to avoid degeneration into a tool of ideological or moral interests: Voltaire was to remark, in the eighteenth century, that "in France the Criminal Code seems framed purposely for the destruction of the people; in England it is their safeguard" (quoted in Esmein, 1913: 361).

There were, nevertheless, important limitations to this picture of the English courts as defenders of the accused. Accusatory ideals were not always met in practice, and many elements of a developed adversary system were only latent. Defendants were not allowed counsel until 1836 (Esmein, 1913: 342). In general, since the defendant entered court with a presumption of innocence, the English courts did not demand such rigorous proofs for conviction as did the continental courts. Testimony of one witness was usually sufficient for conviction in felony cases; children were frequently allowed to testify (Ewen, 1929: 58). In practice, however, this worked out differently than might be expected. The lack of complex, rigid standards of proof in English courts meant that there was little pressure to subvert the series of safeguards surrounding the accused through granting the court extraordinary powers of interrogation, and it went hand-in-hand with a

[14] On the repeal of the witch laws, see Stephen (1883).
[15] See Esmein, (1913: 8 et passim). Esmein notes the similarity between the politically oriented Star Chamber and the typical continental court. A few cases of witchcraft, notably those with political overtones, were processed there; see Ewen (1938: 11).

certain care on the part of the courts for the rights of the defendant. Torture, except in highly limited circumstances as an act of Royal prerogative, was illegal in England, and was never lawfully or systematically used on accused witches in the lower courts.[16]

Given the nature of the crime of witchcraft, witnesses were not always easily found; given the illegality of torture, confessions were also relatively rare. In this difficult situation, alternative methods of obtaining evidence were required. As a consequence, a variety of external evidence emerged.

Three sources of external evidence became especially significant in English witch trials. These are pricking, swimming, and watching.[17] Pricking was based on the theory that witches invariably possessed a "Devil's Mark," which was insensitive to pain. Hence, the discovery of witches involved searching the accused for unusual marks on the skin and pricking such marks with an instrument designed for that purpose. If the accused did not feel pain, guilt was indicated. Often, pricking alone was considered sufficient evidence for conviction.

Swimming was based on the notion that the Devil's agents could not sink in water, and was related to the "ordeal by water" common in early European law (Hopkins, 1928: 38):

> The victim was stripped naked and bound with her right thumb to her right toe, and her left thumb to her right toe, and was then cast into the pond or river. If she sank, she was frequently drowned; if she swam she was declared guilty without any further evidence being required (quoted in Ewen, 1929: 68).[18]

The third source of evidence, watching, reflected the theory that the Devil provided witches with imps or familiars which performed useful services, and which the witch was charged with suckling. The familiars could therefore be expected to appear at some point during the detention of the suspected witch, who was therefore placed in a cell, usually on a stool, and watched for a number of hours or days, until the appointed watchers observed familiars in the room.

A number of other kinds of evidence were accepted in the English trials. Besides the testimony of witnesses, especially those who claimed to have

---

[16]Torture may have been used on some witches in the Star Chamber. Notestein (1911: 167, 204) suggests that it may have been used illegally in a number of cases; nevertheless, torture was not an established part of English criminal procedure, except in the limited sense noted above (see Stephen, 1883: 434; Ewen, 1929: 65). It was allowed in Scotland, where, predictably, there were more executions; several thousand witches were burned there during this period (see Black, 1938; Notestein, 1911: 95–96).

[17]This discussion is taken from Ewen (1929: 60–71), and from remarks at various places in Notestein (1911).

[18]Ewen argues, though, that swimming alone was probably not usually sufficient evidence for the death penalty.

been bewitched, these included the discovery of familiars, waxen or clay images, or other implements in the suspect's home, and of extra teats on the body, presumably used for suckling familiars (Ewen, 1929: 68).

These methods were called for by the lack of more coercive techniques of obtaining evidence within the ambit of English law. In general, the discovery and trial of English witches was an unsystematic and inefficient process, resembling the well-oiled machinery of the continental trial only remotely. The English trial tended to have an *ad hoc* aspect in which new practices, techniques, and theories were continually being evolved or sought out.

Finally, the confiscation of the property of suspected witches did not occur in England, although forfeiture for felony was part of English law until 1870.[19] As a consequence, unlike the continental authorities, the English officials had no continuous vested interest in the discovery and conviction of witches. Thus, they had neither the power nor the motive for large-scale persecution. The English control system, then, was of a "restrained" type, involving the following main characteristics:

1. Accountability to, and restraint by, other social institutions;
2. A high degree of internal restraint, precluding the assumption of extraordinary powers;
3. A low degree of structured interest in the apprehension and processing of deviants.

The English and continental systems, then, were located at nearly opposite ends of a continuum from restrained to repressive control of deviance. We may now look at the effects of these differing control systems on the character of witchcraft in the two regions.

WITCHCRAFT CONTROL AS INDUSTRY: THE CONTINENT

On the Continent, the convergence of a repressive control system with a powerful economic motive created something very much like a large-scale industry based on the mass stigmatization of witches and the confiscation of their property. This gave distinct character to the *rate* of

---

[19] Forfeiture grew out of the feudal relation between tenant and lord. A felon's lands escheated to the lord, and his property also was forfeited to the lord. A later development made the king the recipient of forfeited goods in the special case of treason; this was struck down in the Forfeiture Act of 1870 (see Pollack and Maitland, 1968: 332). This is, of course, a very different matter from the direct confiscation of property for the court treasury which was characteristic of the Continent.

witchcraft in Europe, the kinds of people who were convicted as witches, and the entire complex of activities which grew up around witchcraft.

The Inquisition, as well as the secular courts, were largely self-sustaining; each convicted witch, therefore, was a source of financial benefit through confiscation.[20] "Persecution," writes an historian of the Inquisition, "as a steady and continuous policy, rested, after all, upon confiscation. It was this which supplied the fuel to keep up the fires of zeal, and when it was lacking the business of defending the faith languished lamentably" (Lea, 1958: 529).

The witchcraft industry in continental Europe was a large and complex business which created and sustained the livelihoods of a sizable number of people. As such, it required a substantial income to keep it going at all. As a rule, prisoners were required to pay for trial expenses and even for the use of instruments of torture (Lea, 1888: 524; 1939: 1080). Watchmen, executioners, torturers, and others, as well as priests and judges, were paid high wages and generally lived well (Lea, 1939: 1080). A witch-judge in seventeenth century Germany boasted of having caused 700 executions in three years, and earning over 5000 gulden on a per capita basis (p. 1075). A partial account of costs for a single trial in Germany reads as follows (p. 1162):

	Florins	Batzen	Pfennige
For the executioner	14	7	10
For the entertainment and banquet of the judges, priests, and advocate	32	6	3
For maintenance of the convicts and watchmen	33	6	6

A total of 720,000 florins were taken from accused witches in Bamberg, Germany, in a single year (Lea, 1939: 1177–1178). Usually, the goods of suspected witches were sold after confiscation to secular and ecclesiastical officials at low prices (p. 1080). Of the prosecutions at Trier, a witness wrote that: "Notaries, copyists, and innkeepers grew rich. The executioner rode on a blooded horse, like a courtier, clad in gold and silver; his wife vied with noble dames in the richness of her array . . . not till suddenly, as in war, the money gave out, did the zeal of the Inquisitors flag" (Burr, 1891: 55). During a period of intense witch-hunting activity at Trier, secular officials were forced to issue an edict to prevent impoverishment of local subjects through the activities of the Inquisitors (Burr, 1891: 55, fn.).

Like any large enterprise, the witchcraft industry was subject to the need

---

[20] Self-sustaining control systems often view presumptive deviants as a source of profit. On a smaller scale, it has been noted that some jurisdictions in the American South have been known to make a practice of arresting Negroes en masse in order to collect fees (see Johnson, 1941).

for continual expansion in order to maintain its level of gain. A mechanism for increasing profit was built into the structure of the trials, whereby, through the use of torture to extract names of accomplices from the accused, legitimate new suspects became available.

The creation of a new kind of deviant behavior was the basis for the emergence of a profit-making industry run on bureaucratic lines, which combined nearly unlimited power with pecuniary motive and which gave distinct form to the deviant behavior system in which it was involved.

Its effect on the scope or rate of the deviance is the most striking at first glance. Several hundred thousand witches were burned in continental Europe during the main period of activity, creating a picture of the tremendous extent of witchcraft in Europe. The large number of witches frightened the population and legitimized ever more stringent suppression. Thus, a cycle developed in which rigorous control brought about the appearance of high rates of deviance, which were the basis for more extreme control, which in turn sent the rates even higher, and so on.

A second major effect was the selection of particular categories of people for accusation and conviction. A significant proportion of continental witches were men, and an even more significant proportion of men and women were people of wealth and/or property. This is not surprising, given the material advantages to the official control apparatus of attributing the crime to heads of prosperous households.

In trials of Offenburg, Germany, in 1628, witnesses noted that care was taken to select for accusation "women of property" (Lea, 1939: 1163). A document from Bamberg at about the same time lists the names and estimated wealth of twenty-two prisoners, nearly all of whom were propertied, most male, and one burgher worth 100,000 florins (Lea, 1939: 1177–1178). In early French trials, a pattern developed which began with the conviction of a group of ordinary people, and then moved into a second stage in which the wealthy were especially singled out for prosecution (Lea, 1958: 523–527). In German trials, the search for accomplices was directed against the wealthy, with names of wealthy individuals often supplied to the accused under torture (Lea, 1939: 235). At Trier, a number of burgomasters, officials, and managers of large farms were executed as witches (Burr, 1891: 29, 34). An eyewitness to the trials there in the late sixteenth century was moved to lament the fact that "[b]oth rich and poor, of every rank, age and sex, sought a share in the accursed crime" (p. 19). Apparently, resistance or dissent, or even insufficient zeal, could open powerful officials to accusation and almost certain conviction.[21]

---

[21] This fact is graphically presented in Burr's chronicle of Dietrich Flade, a powerful court official at Trier whose ultimate execution for witchcraft was apparently in part the result of his failure to zealously prosecute witches in his district.

Thus, though it was not the case that all continental witches were well-to-do or male, a substantial number were. The witch population in England, to be considered shortly, was strikingly different.

The mass nature of the witchcraft industry, the high number of witches in Europe, and the upper-income character of a sufficient proportion of them,[22] were all due to the lack of restraints on court procedure—especially, of the systematic use of torture—coupled with the legal authority to confiscate property, which added material interest to unrestrained control. That the prevalence of witches in continental Europe was a reflection of the peculiar structure of legal control is further implied by the fact that when torture and/or confiscation became from time to time unlawful, the number of witches decreased drastically or disappeared altogether. In Hesse, Phillip the Magnificent forbade torture in 1526 and, according to one witness, "nothing more was heard of witchcraft till the half-century was passed" (Lea, 1939: 1081). In Bamberg, pressure from the Holy Roman Emperor to abandon confiscation resulted in the disappearance of witchcraft arrests in 1630 (1173–1179).[23] The Spanish Inquisitor Salazar Frias issued instructions in 1614 requiring external evidence and forbidding confiscation; this move marked the virtual end of witchcraft in Spain (Parrinder, 1958: 79). It was not until criminal law reform began in earnest in the eighteenth century that witches disappeared, for official purposes, from continental Europe.

A form of deviance had been created and sustained largely through the efforts of a self-sustaining bureaucratic organization dedicated to its discovery and punishment, and granted unusual power which, when removed, dealt a final blow to that entire conception of deviant behavior. In England too, witches existed through the efforts of interested parties,[24] but the parties were of a different sort.

[22] That a greater percentage of wealthy witches did not appear is due in part to the fact that wealthy families often paid a kind of "protection" to local officials to insure that they would not be arrested (see Lea, 1939: 1080).

[23] See Lea (1939: 1173–1179). In part, also, the decrease in arrests was due to the occupation of the area by an invasion of the somewhat less zealous Swedes.

[24] It should be stressed that quite probably, a number of people, both in England and on the Continent, did in fact believe themselves to be witches, capable of doing all the things witches were supposed to be able to do. Some of them, probably, had the intent to inflict injury or unpleasantness on their fellows, and probably some of these were included in the executions. This does not alter the fact that the designation of witches proceeded independently of such beliefs, according to the interests of the control systems. Some students of witchcraft have suggested that the promotion of witch beliefs by the official control systems provided a kind of ready-made identity, or role, into which some already disturbed people could fit themselves. This is a more subtle aspect of the creation of deviance by control structures, and has, I think, applicability to certain contemporary phenomena. The images of deviance provided by newspapers and police may provide a structural pattern of behavior and an organized system of deviant attitudes which can serve as an orienting principle for the otherwise diffusely dissatisfied.

WITCHCRAFT CONTROL AS RACKET: ENGLAND

The restrained nature of the English legal system precluded the rise of the kind of mass witchcraft industry which grew up on the Continent. What the structure of that system did provide was a context in which individual entrepreneurs, acting from below, were able to profit through the discovery of witches. Hence, in England, there developed a series of rackets through which individuals manipulated the general climate of distrust, within the framework of a control structure which was frequently reluctant to approve of their activities. Because of its accusatorial character, the English court could not systematically initiate the prosecution of witches; because of its limited character generally, it could not have processed masses of presumed witches even had it had the power to initiate such prosecutions; and because of the absence of authority to confiscate witches' property, it had no interest in doing so even had it been able to. Witch prosecutions in England were initiated by private persons who stood to make a small profit in a rather precarious enterprise. As a result, there were fewer witches in England than on the Continent, and their sex and status tended to be different as well.

Given the lack of torture and the consequent need to circumvent the difficulty of obtaining confessions, a number of kinds of external evidence, some of which were noted before, became recognized. Around these sources of evidence there grew up a number of trades, in which men who claimed to be expert in the various arts of witch finding—pricking, watching, and so on—found a ready field of profit. They were paid by a credulous populace, and often credulous officials, for their expertise in ferreting out witches. In the seventeenth century, the best-known of the witch finders was one Matthew Hopkins, who became so successful that he was able to hire several assistants (Hopkins, 1928).[25] Hopkins, and many others, were generalists at the witch-finding art; others were specialists in one or another technique. Professional prickers flourished. A Scottish expert who regularly advertised his skill was called to Newcastle-upon-Tyne in 1649 to deal with the local witch problem, with payment guaranteed at twenty shillings per convicted witch. His technique of selecting potential witches was ingenious and rather efficient, and indicates how the general climate of fear and mistrust could be manipulated for profit. He sent bell ringers through the streets of Newcastle to inquire if anyone had a complaint to enter against someone they suspected of witchcraft. This provided a legitimate outlet for grievances,

---

[25] See Hopkins (1928). This is a reproduction of Matthew Hopkins' own manual for the discovery of witches.

both public and private, against the socially marginal, disapproved, or simply disliked, and was predictably successful; thirty witches were discovered, most of whom were convicted (Ewen, 1929: 62). Several devices were used by prickers to increase the probability of discovery and conviction. One was the use of pricking knives with retractable blades and hollow handles, which could be counted on to produce no pain while appearing to be embodied in the flesh—thus demonstrating the presence of an insensible "Devil's Mark" (p. 62).

Professional "watchers," too, thrived in this climate. A voucher from a Scottish trial in 1649 is indicative (quoted in Black, 1938: 59)[26]:

	Pounds	Shillings
Item: In the first, to Wm. Currie and Andrew Gray, for the watching of her the space of 30 days, each day 30 shillings	45	0
Item: More to John Kincaid for brodding (pricking) of her	6	0
More for meat and drink and wine for him and his men	4	0

An essential characteristic of all these rackets was their precariousness. To profess special knowledge of the demonic and its agents opened the entrepreneur to charges of fraud or witchcraft; money could be made, but one could also be hanged, depending on the prevailing climate of opinion. The Scottish pricker of Newcastle was hanged, and many other prickers were imprisoned (Ewen, 1929: 63); the witchfinder Hopkins continually had to defend himself against charges of wizardry and/or fraud, and may have been drowned while undergoing the "swimming" test (Hopkins, 1928: 45).[27] People who professed to be able to practice magic—often known as "cunning folk"—frequently doubled as witch finders, and were especially open to the charge of witchcraft.[28]

The peculiar and restrained character of the English control of witches led to characteristic features of the behavior system of English witchcraft. The lack of vested interest from above, coupled with the absence of torture and other extraordinary procedures, was largely responsible for the small number of witches executed in England from 1563 to 1736 (Ewen, 1929: 112; Kittredge, 1907: 54). Of those indicted for witchcraft, a relatively small percentage was actually executed—again in contrast to the inexorable

[26] This is apparently unusual for a Scottish trial, since these methods of evidence were less crucial, given the frequent use of torture.

[27] Summers, the editor of Hopkins' work, denies that Hopkins was drowned in this fashion. Hopkins' pamphlet includes a lenthy question-and-answer defense of his trade, part of which reads as follows: "Certain queries answered, which have been and are likely to be objected against Matthew Hopkins, in his way of finding out Witches. Querie 1. That hee must needs be the greatest Witch, Sorcerer, and Wizzard himselfe, else hee could not doe it. Answer: If Satan's Kingdome be divided against itselfe, how shall it stand?" (Hopkins, 1928: 49).

[28] On "cunning folk" generally, see Notestein (1911: Chapter 1).

machinery of prosecution in continental Europe. In the courts of the Home Circuit, from 1558 to 1736, only 513 indictments were brought for witchcraft; of these, only 112, or about 22 percent, resulted in execution (Ewen, 1929: 100).

Further, English witches were usually women and usually lower class. Again, this was a consequence of the nature of the control structure. English courts did not have the power or the motive to systematically stigmatize the wealthy and propertied; the accusations came from below, specifically from the lower and more credulous strata or those who manipulated them, and were directed against socially marginal and undesirable individuals who were powerless to defend themselves. The process through which the witch was brought to justice involved the often reluctant capitulation of the courts to popular sentiment fueled by the activities of the witch finders; the witches were usually borderline deviants already in disfavor with their neighbors. Household servants, poor tenants, and others of lower status predominated. Women who worked as midwives were especially singled out, particularly when it became necessary to explain stillbirths. Women who lived by the practice of magic—cunning women—were extremely susceptible to accusation. Not infrequently, the accused witch was a "cunning woman" whose accusation was the combined work of a witch finder and a rival "cunning woman." In the prevailing atmosphere, there was little defense against such internecine combat, and the "cunning" trade developed a heavy turnover (Notestein, 1911: 82). In general, of convicted witches in the Home Circuit from 1564–1663, only 16 of a total of 204 were men (Ewen, 1929: 255–270),[29] and there is no indication that any of these were wealthy or solid citizens.

The decline of witchcraft in England, too, was the result of a different process from that on the Continent, where the decline of witchcraft was closely related to the imposition of restraints on court procedure. In England, the decline was related to a general shift of opinion, in which the belief in witchcraft itself waned, particularly in the upper strata, as a result of which the courts began to treat witchcraft as illusory or at best unprovable. English judges began refusing to execute witches well before the witch laws were repealed in 1736; and although there were occasional popular lynchings of witches into the eighteenth century, the legal system had effectively relinquished the attempt to control witchcraft (Davies, 1947: 182–203). With this shift of opinion, the entire structure of witchcraft collapsed, for all practical purposes, at the end of the seventeenth century.[30]

---

[29] Also, compare the list of English witches in Murray (1962: 255–270).

[30] An incident supposedly involving the anatomist, William Harvey, is indicative of this change of opinion. Harvey, on hearing that a local woman was reputed to be a witch, took it upon himself to dissect one of her familiars, which took the shape of a toad; he found it to be exactly like any other toad, and a minor blow was struck for the Enlightenment (see Notestein, 1911: 111).

CONCLUSION

If one broad conclusion emerges from this discussion, it is that the phenomenon of witchcraft in Renaissance Europe strongly reinforces on one level the argument that deviance is what officials say it is, and deviants are those so designated by officials. Where the deviant act is nonexistent, it is necessarily true that the criteria for designating people as deviant do not lie in the deviant act itself, but in the interests, needs, and capacities of the relevant official and unofficial agencies of control, and their relation to extraneous characteristics of the presumptive deviant. Witchcraft was invented in continental Europe, and it was sustained there through the vigorous efforts of a system of repressive control; in England it was sustained, far less effectively, through the semiofficial efforts of relatively small-time entrepreneurs. In both cases, witchcraft as a deviant behavior system took its character directly from the nature of the respective systems of legal control. On the Continent, the system found itself both capable of and interested in defining large numbers of people, many of whom were well-to-do, as witches; therefore, there *were* many witches on the Continent and many of these were wealthy and/or powerful. In England, the control system had little interest in defining anyone as a witch, and consequently the English witches were those few individuals who were powerless to fend off the definition supplied by witchfinders on a base of popular credulity. Witches were, then, what the control system defined them to be, and variation in the behavior system of witchcraft in the two regions may be traced directly to the different legal systems through which that definition was implemented.

Witchcraft, however, is an extreme case. It is made extreme by virtue of the extent to which it is an *invented* form of deviance, whose definition lacks roots in concrete behavior. While it could be argued that all definitions of deviance, referring to whatever kinds of acts, contain a degree, however slight, of this element of invention, it is certainly true that the degree to which it is present is highly variable. There may be a large element of invention in current American definitions of mental illness, and perhaps drug addiction[31]; there is less in the definition of murder or battery. This means that variations in the behavior system of mental illness or drug addiction are more likely to result from differences in the control system through which they are managed than are variations in the behavior system of murder or battery. This is not to say that the definitions of the latter kinds of deviance are somehow fixed or inherent in the acts to which they refer, rather than

---

[31] On mental illness, see the various works of, among others, Thomas Szaz. In the case of drugs it may be argued that the discrepancy between the legal and medical definitions of marijuana use bespeaks the existence of a sizable element of official invention.

being socially derived. Eskimos define murder differently from Englishmen, and present-day Englishmen define it differently from medieval Englishmen.[32] But the fact that the definition of murder is closely connected to a tangible, concrete, and potentially highly visible act[33] means that its social derivation has minimal consequences, especially for variation in the behavior system of murder under different systems of legal control. Systems of control create the character of the deviance which they define and manage only to the extent that a gap between deviant definition and deviant act gives them the latitude to do so. Anyone could be called a witch in Renaissance Europe, given the fact that witchery could be neither proved nor disproved; and witches were therefore created according to the capacity of the relevant control systems to create them, and were created in the image of the interests of these systems. It is more difficult, however, to create murderers, and especially difficult to create more murderers than there are victims. Hence, the element of potential creativity of the control system and thus of variation in the deviant behavior system under different control systems is reduced.

This has more than academic relevance, for it speaks directly to the problem of the abuse of the function of social control by the officials and institutions charged with it. To the extent that the element of invention enters into a society's definition of deviance, there is an open invitation to potentially abusive creativity on the part of systems of control or, particularly in the case of societies with limited systems of control, on the part of individuals or groups peripheral to the control system.[34] The case of witchcraft in England shows that virtually no amount of limitation on the power of a control system can consistently and effectively protect individuals against such abuse, once an invented definition of deviance has become officially established. Beyond this, invented deviance undermines the ability of control agencies to maintain procedural integrity. The inevitable inability of both continental and English legal systems to deal with witchcraft without

[32] Stricly speaking, this discussion would have to be backed up by data throwing light on the treatment of murder under different control systems; it is therefore to be considered speculative. Common sense, though, suggests that there is something peculiar about crimes like witchcraft which probably makes for a profound impact on the character of social control.

[33] By visibility I refer to consequences primarily, rather than commission. Proof of homicide generally requires a body, which is a highly visible thing. Offenses which, unlike witchcraft, have reference to an act which is real but of low visibility—such as heresy or thought—crimes generally, and some of the "victimless" crimes—create many of the same consequences for control systems as do invented offenses. Again, this is largely because their commission is so difficult to establish through ordinary means that extraordinary means may need to be invoked, and if that is done, not only does the character of the control system change, but the offense now becomes virtually impossible to *disprove*. As a consequence, the official incidence of the offense can vary greatly depending on the interests of the control system.

[34] The remarks above apply here as well. This, of course, is an important factor in the rejection of legal control of mental acts by democratically inclined people.

straining normal standards of procedure illustrates this. It could be argued that a number of such definitions—or definitions which contain at least a large element of invention—currently exist in this country, with the consequence of severely straining standards of due process of law in the institutions charged with controlling them.[35] It would be profitable to study some of these with an eye to establishing relations between degree of "invention" and degree of strain on established standards of legal procedure.

Different kinds of deviance, then, vary in the degree to which they can be creatively imputed to people, and hence in the degree of variability in their behavior systems which may occur across different control systems. Keeping this in mind, some generalizations can be suggested about the effects of the two kinds of control systems—repressive and restrained—which have already been defined.

Repressive control systems, by virtue of their superior power to accuse, convict, and certify deviants, tend to create a higher official incidence of a given kind of deviance than do systems of restrained control.[36] This is reflected both in a higher rate of accusation or stigmatization and in a higher ratio of conviction to accusation. A system of repressive control will uncover and successfully prosecute an exceptionally high amount of deviance; further, it may do so more or less independently of the actual incidence of the deviance—through, among other things, its ability to systematically produce confessions from, if necessary, the innocent. A system of restrained control, on the other hand, produces a relatively low rate of official deviance and is restricted in its ability to create deviance independently of its actual incidence. Restrained systems may, and generally do, process *less* deviance than actually exists; rarely, however, can they successfully or consistently process *more*.

Systems of repressive control, in the nature of things, tend to develop a greater vested interest in the successful prosecution of deviants than do restrained systems. This tends to increase the effect of creating an exceptionally large deviant population under systems of repressive control. Repressive systems combine the power to prosecute successfully masses of deviants with a structured motive for doing so, both of which are lacking in the restrained system. The ability of continental witch courts to confiscate the property of witches is but one example of this kind of vested interest. Similarly, vested interests in deviance may be political, religious, or psychic,

---

[35] As indicated above, I believe this may be at least partially true of definitions of mental illness and of drug addiction. It is also perhaps relevant to certain kinds of political offenses built on the notion of "subversion," and on certain peculiar categories of juvenile justice, such as the notion of "incorrigibility," among others.

[36] Under the system of expanded control during the politically harsh years 1949–1953 in Communist China, approximately 800,000 political deviants—"counterrevolutionaries," "class enemies," and so on—were liquidated (see Cohen, 1966: 477–478).

rather than economic; in any case, even lacking such specific interests, systems of repressive control tend to foster the growth of an "industry" geared to the official creation of deviance, with a complex organizational structure which strains toward self-perpetuation.[37] They support a division of labor whose personnel depend for their livelihood on the continued supply of confirmed deviants. Even at best, therefore, there is a degree of tension between organizational interests and the security of individuals which is not found in the restrained system, and a powerful strain toward arbitrariness and the relaxation of procedural standards.

Restrained systems, on the other hand, may be vulnerable to abuse from below. This is particularly true where the community generates definitions of deviance which include a large amount of invention, putting a strain on the ability of the system to handle deviance while keeping its procedural standards intact. Under these circumstances especially, restrained systems tend to foster the development of a system of "rackets" around the deviant activity, involving officials, deviants themselves, and private or semiofficial entrepreneurs operating on the precarious borderline between licit and illicit behavior.

Because of their combination of power and interest, repressive control systems tend to concentrate most heavily on stigmatizing people whose successful prosecution will be most useful in terms of the system's own needs and goals. This is true whether the goal is economic profit or the elimination of sources of moral or political dissent, or a combination of these. Consequently, the deviant population under a system of repressive control will contain an unusually large number of relatively wealthy and/or powerful people, and of solid citizens generally. Under a restrained control system, on the other hand, the typical deviant will be lower class; the deviant population will be most heavily represented by the relatively powerless, who lack the resources necessary to make successful use of those safeguards which the restrained system provides, and who are particularly vulnerable to abuse.

ACKNOWLEDGMENTS

The research on which this paper is based was partially supported by a grant from the Ford Foundation, administered by the Center for the Study of Law and Society. I thank Howard S. Becker, Egon Bittner, Fred Dubow, David Matza, Sheldon L. Messinger, and Philip Selznick for their comments on earlier versions of this paper, though they are not to be held responsible for the outcome.

[37] Special agencies of enforcement or prosecution within the context of a generally restrained system may, of course, develop vested interests of this kind, but their effect is limited by the nature of the larger system. For an example of this, see the discussion of the enforcement of marijuana laws in Becker (1963: 121–146).

REFERENCES

Becker, H. S.
   1963   *Outsiders: Studies in the sociology of deviance.* New York: Free Press.
Black, G. F.
   1938   *A calendar of cases of witchcraft in Scotland, 1510–1727.* New York: New York Public Library.
Burr, G. L.
   1891   The fate of Dietrich Flade. *Papers of the American Historical Association* **5**, Part 3 (July): 3–57.
Cohen, J. A.
   1966   The criminal process in the People's Republic of China: An introduction. *Harvard Law Review* **79** (1966): 469–533.
Davies, R. T.
   1947   *Four centuries of witch beliefs.* London: Methuen.
Erikson, K. T.
   1966   *Wayward Puritans.* New York: Wiley.
Esmein, A.
   1913   *A history of continental criminal procedure.* Boston: Little, Brown.
Ewen, C. l'E.
   1929   *Witch hunting and witch trials.* London: K. Paul, Trench, Trubner.
   1938   *Witchcraft in the star chamber.* London: published by the author.
Goffman, E.
   1962   *Asylums: Essays on the social situation of mental patients and other inmates.* Garden City, New York: Anchor Books.
   1963   *Stigma: Notes on the management of spoiled identity.* Englewood Cliffs: Prentice-Hall.
Hopkins, M.
   1928   *The discovery of witches.* London: Cayme Press.
Johnson, G. B.
   1941   The Negro and crime. *The Annals of the American Academy of Political and Social Sciences* **271** (September): 93–104.
Kitsuse, J. I.
   1966   Societal response to deviance: Some problems of theory and method. *Social Problems* **9** (Winter): 247–256.
Kittredge, G. L.
   1907   *Notes on witchcraft.* Worcester, Massachusetts: Davis Press.
Lea, H. C.
   1888   *A history of the inquisition in the Middle Ages.* New York: Harper.
   1939   *Materials toward a history of witchcraft.* Philadelphia: Univ. of Pennsylvania Press.
   1958   *A history of the inquisition in the Middle Ages.* New York: Russell and Russell.
Lemert, E. M.
   1951   *Social pathology.* New York: McGraw-Hill.
Murray, M. A.
   1962   *The witch-cult in Western Europe.* London and New York: Oxford Univ. Press (Clarendon).
Notestein, W.
   1911   *A history of witchcraft in England.* (Publisher unknown—eds.)
Parrinder, G.
   1958   *Witchcraft: European and African.* Middlesex, England: Penguin.

Pollack, F., and F. W. Maitland
  1968   *A history of English law: Before the time of Edward I*. Vol. 1. London and New York: Cambridge Univ. Press. (Orig. pub. 1895.)
Schur, E. M.
  1962   *Narcotic addiction in Britain and America: The impact of public policy*. Bloomington: Indiana Univ. Press.
Sprenger, J., and H. Kramer
  1948   *Malleus maleficarum*. London: Puskin Press. (Orig. issued 1496.)
Stephen, Sir J. F.
  1883   *History of the criminal law in England*. London: Macmillan.
Tannenbaum, F.
  1938   *Crime and the community*. New York: Ginn.

TWO FORMS OF DISPUTE SETTLEMENT AMONG THE KPELLE OF WEST AFRICA

James L. Gibbs, Jr.

AFRICA AS a major culture area has been characterized by many writers as being marked by a high development of law and legal procedures. In the past few years research on African law has produced a series of highly competent monographs such as those on law among the Tiv (Bohannan, 1957), the Barotse (Gluckman, 1955), and the Nuer (Howell, 1954). These and related shorter studies have focused primarily on formal processes for the settlement of disputes, such as those which take place in a courtroom, or those which are, in some other way, set apart from simpler measures of social control. However, many African societies have informal, quasi-legal, dispute-settlement procedures, supplemental to formal ones, which have not been as well studied or—in most cases—adequately analyzed.

In this paper I present a description and analysis of one such institution for the informal settlement of disputes, as it is found among the Kpelle of Liberia; it is the moot, the *bɛrɛi mu meni saa* or "house palaver." Hearings in the Kpelle moot contrast with those in a court in that they differ in tone and effectiveness. The genius of the moot lies in the fact that it is based on a covert application of the principles of psychoanalytic theory which underlie psychotherapy.

Reprinted by permission of the International African Institute from "The Kpelle Moot: A Therapeutic Model for the Informal Settlement of Disputes" by James L. Gibbs, Jr., *Africa*, Vol. 33 (1963): pp. 1–10.

The Kpelle are a Mande-speaking, patrilineal group of some 175,000 rice cultivators who live in Central Liberia and the adjoining regions of Guinea. This paper is based on data gathered in a field study which I carried out in 1957 and 1958 among the Liberian Kpelle of Panta Chiefdom in northeast Central Province.

Strong corporate patrilineages are absent among the Kpelle. The most important kinship group is the virilocal polygynous family which sometimes becomes an extended family, almost always of the patrilineal variety. Several of these families form the core of a residential group, known as a village quarter, more technically, a clan-barrio (Murdock, 1949: 74). This is headed by a quarter elder who is related to most of the household heads by real or putative patrilineal ties.

Kpelle political organization is centralized although there is no single king or paramount chief, but a series of chiefs of the same level of authority, each of whom is superordinate over district chiefs and town chiefs. Some political functions are also vested in the tribal fraternity, the Poro, which still functions vigorously. The form of political organization found in the area can thus best be termed the polycephalous associational state.

The structure of the Kpelle court system parallels that of the political organization. In Liberia the highest court of a tribal authority and the highest tribal court chartered by the Government is that of a paramount chief. A district chief's court is also an official court. Disputes may be settled in these official courts or in unofficial courts, such as those of town chiefs or quarter elders. In addition to this, grievances are settled informally in moots, and sometimes by associational groupings such as church councils or cooperative work groups.

In my field research I studied both the formal and informal methods of dispute settlement. The method used was to collect case material in as complete a form as possible. Accordingly, immediately after a hearing, my interpreter and I would prepare verbatim transcripts of each case that we heard. These transcripts were supplemented with accounts—obtained from respondents—of past cases or cases which I did not hear litigated. Transcripts from each type of hearing were analyzed phrase by phrase in terms of a frame of reference derived from jurisprudence and ethno-law. The results of the analysis indicate two things: first, that courtroom hearings and moots are quite different in their procedures and tone, and second, why they show this contrast.

Kpelle courtroom hearings are basically coercive and arbitrary in tone. In another paper (Gibbs, 1962) I have shown that this is partly the result of the intrusion of the authoritarian values of the Poro into the courtroom. As a result, the court is limited in the manner in which it can handle some types of disputes. The court is particularly effective in settling cases such as assault, possession of illegal charms, or theft where the litigants are not linked in a relationship which must continue after the trial. However, most of the cases brought before a Kpelle court are cases involving disputed rights over women, including matrimonial matters which are usually cast in the form of suits for divorce. The court is particularly inept at settling these numerous matrimonial disputes because its harsh tone tends to drive spouses farther apart rather than to reconcile them. The moot, in contrast, is more effective in handling such cases. The following analysis indicates the reasons for this.

The Kpelle *bɛrɛi mu meni saa*, or house palaver, is an informal airing of a dispute which takes place before an assembled group which includes kinsmen of the litigants and neighbors from the quarter where the case is being heard. It is a completely *ad hoc* group, varying greatly in composition from case to case. The matter to be settled is usually a domestic problem: alleged mistreatment or neglect by a spouse, an attempt to collect money paid to a kinsman for a job which was not completed, or a quarrel among brothers over the inheritance of their father's wives.

In the procedural description which follows I shall use illustrative data from the Case of the Ousted Wife:

> Wama Nya, the complainant, had one wife, Yua. His older brother died and he inherited the widow, Yokpo, who moved into his house. The two women were classificatory sisters. After Yokpo moved in, there was strife in the household. The husband accused her of staying out late at night, of harvesting rice without his knowledge, and of denying him food. He also accused Yokpo of having lovers and admitted having had a physical struggle with her, after which he took a basin of water and "washed his hands of her."
>
> Yokpo countered by denying the allegations about having lovers, saying that she was accused falsely, although she had in the past confessed the name of one lover. She further complained that Wama Nya had assaulted her and, in the act, had committed the indignity of removing her headtie, and had expelled her from the house after the ritual hand-washing. Finally, she alleged that she had been thus cast out of the house at the instigation of the other wife who, she asserted, had great influence over their husband.
>
> Kɔb Waa, the Town Chief and quarter elder, and the brother of Yokpo, was the mediator of the moot, which decided that the husband was mainly at fault, although Yua and Yokpo's children were also in the wrong. Those at fault had to apologize to Yokpo and bring gifts of apology as well as local rum [cane juice] for the disputants and participants in the moot.

The moot is most often held on a Sunday—a day of rest for Christians and non-Christians alike—at the home of the complainant, the person who calls the moot. The mediator will have been selected by the complainant. He is a kinsman who also holds an office such as town chief or quarter elder, and therefore has some skill in dispute settlement. It is said that he is chosen to preside by virtue of his kin tie, rather than because of his office.

The proceedings begin with the pronouncing of blessings by one of the oldest men of the group. In the Case of the Ousted Wife, Gbenai Zua, the elder who pronounced the blessings, took a rice stirrer in his hand and, striding back and forth, said:

> This man has called us to fix the matter between him and his wife. May ðala [the supreme, creator deity] change his heart and let his household be in a good condition. May ðala bless the family and make them fruitful. May He bless them so they can have food this year. May He bless the children and the rest of the family so they may always be healthy. May He bless them to have good luck. When Wama Nya takes a gun and goes in the bush, may he kill big animals. May ðala bless us to enjoy the meat. May He bless us to enjoy life and always have luck. May ðala bless all those who come to discuss this matter.

The man who pronounces the blessings always carries a stick or a whisk (*kpung*), which he waves for effect as he paces up and down chanting his injunctions. Participation of spectators is demanded, for the blessings are chanted by the elder (*kpung namu* or "*kpung* owner") as a series of imperatives, some of which he repeats. Each phrase is responded to by the spectators who answer in unison with a formal response, either *e ka ti* (so be it), or a low, drawn-out *eeee*. The *kpung namu* delivers his blessings faster and faster, building up a rhythmic interaction pattern with the other participants. The effect is to unite those attending in common action before the hearing begins. The blessing focuses attention on the concern with maintaining harmony and the well-being of the group as a whole.

Everyone attending the moot wears his next-to-best clothes or, if it is not Sunday, everyday clothes. Elders, litigants, and spectators sit in mixed fashion, pressed closely upon each other, often overflowing onto a veranda. This is in contrast to the vertical spatial separation between litigants and adjudicators in the courtroom. The mediator, even though he is a chief, does not wear his robes. He and the oldest men will be given chairs as they would on any other occasion.

The complainant speaks first and may be interrupted by the mediator or anyone else present. After he has been thoroughly quizzed, the accused will answer and will also be questioned by those present. The two parties will question each other directly and question others in the room also. Both the testimony and the questioning are lively and uninhibited. Where there are witnesses to some of the actions described by the parties, they may also speak and be questioned. Although the proceedings are spirited, they remain orderly. The mediator may fine anyone who speaks out of turn by requiring him to bring some rum for the group to drink.

The mediator and the others present will point out the various faults committed by both the parties. After everyone has been heard, the mediator expresses the consensus of the group. For example, in the Case of the Ousted Wife, he said to Yua: "The words you used towards your sister were not good, so come and beg her pardon."

The person held to be mainly at fault will then formally apologize to the other person. This apology takes the form of the giving of token gifts to the wronged person by the guilty party. These may be an item of clothing, a few coins, clean hulled rice, or a combination of all three. It is also customary for the winning party in accepting the gifts of apology to give, in return, a smaller token such as a twenty-five-cent piece[1] to show his "white heart" or good will. The losing party is also lightly "fined"; he must present rum or beer to the mediator and the others who heard the case. This is consumed by all in attendance. The old man then pronounces blessings again and offers thanks for the restoration of harmony within the group, and asks that all continue to act with good grace and unity.

An initial analysis of the procedural steps of the moot isolates the descriptive attributes of the moot and shows that they contrast with those of the courtroom hearing. While the airing of grievances is incomplete in courtroom hearings, it is more complete in the moot. This fuller airing of the issues results, in many marital cases, in a more harmonious solution. Several specific features of the house palaver facilitate this wider airing of grievances. First, the hearing takes place soon after a breach has occurred, before the grievances have hardened. There is no delay until the complainant has time to go to the paramount chief's or district chief's headquarters to institute suit. Second, the hearing takes place in the familiar surroundings of a home. The robes, writs, messengers, and other symbols of power which subtly intimidate and inhibit the parties in the courtroom, by reminding them of the physical force which underlies the procedures, are absent. Third, in the courtroom the conduct of the hearing is firmly in the hands of the judge, but in the moot the investigatory initiative rests much more with the parties themselves. Jurisprudence suggests that, in such a case, more of the grievances lodged between the parties are likely to be aired and adjusted. Finally, the range of relevance applied to matters which are brought out is extremely broad. Hardly anything mentioned is held to be irrelevant. This too leads to a more thorough ventilation of the issues.

There is a second surface difference between court and moot. In a courtroom hearing, the solution is, by and large, one which is imposed by the adjudicator. In the moot the solution is more consensual. It is, therefore, more likely to be accepted by both parties and hence more durable. Several features of the moot contribute to the consensual solution: first, there is no unilateral ascription of blame, but an attribution of fault to both parties.

---

[1] American currency is the official currency of Liberia and is used throughout the country.

Second, the mediator, unlike the chief in the courtroom, is not backed by political authority and the physical force which underlies it. He cannot jail parties, nor can he levy a heavy fine. Third, the sanctions which are imposed are not so burdensome as to cause hardship to the losing party or to give him or her grounds for a new grudge against the other party. The gifts for the winning party and the potables for the spectators are not as expensive as the fines and the court costs in a paramount chief's court. Last, the ritualized apology of the moot symbolizes very concretely the consensual nature of the solution. The public offering and acceptance of the tokens of apology indicate that each party has no further grievances and that the settlement is satisfactory and mutually acceptable. The parties and spectators drink together to symbolize the restored solidarity of the group and the rehabilitation of the offending party.

This type of analysis describes the courtroom hearing and the moot, using a frame of reference derived from jurisprudence and ethno-law which is explicitly comparative and evaluative. Only by using this type of comparative approach can the researcher select features of the hearings which are not only unique to each of them, but theoretically significant in that their contribution to the social control functions of the proceedings can be hypothesized. At the same time, it enables the researcher to pinpoint in procedures the cause for what he feels intuitively: that the two hearings contrast in tone, even though they are similar in some ways.

However, one can approach the transcripts of the trouble cases with a second analytical framework and emerge with a deeper understanding of the implications of the contrasting descriptive attributes of the court and the house palaver. Remember that the coercive tone of the courtroom hearing limits the court's effectiveness in dealing with matrimonial disputes, especially in effecting reconciliations. The moot, on the other hand, is particularly effective in bringing about reconciliations between spouses. This is because the moot is not only conciliatory, but *therapeutic*. Moot procedures are therapeutic in that, like psychotherapy, they reeducate the parties through a type of social learning brought about in a specially structured interpersonal setting.

Talcott Parsons (1951: 314–319) has written that therapy involves four elements: support, permissiveness, denial of reciprocity, and manipulation of rewards. Writers such as Frank (1955: 524–525), Klapman (1959), and Opler (1959: 296–298) have pointed out that the same elements characterize not only individual psychotherapy, but group psychotherapy as well. All four elements are writ large in the Kpelle moot.

The patient in therapy will not continue treatment very long if he does not feel support from the therapist or from the group. In the moot the parties are encouraged in the expression of their complaints and feelings because they sense group support. The very presence of one's kinsmen and neighbors demonstrates their concern. It indicates to the parties that they have a real problem and that the others are willing to help them to help themselves in solving it. In a parallel vein, Frank, speaking of group psychotherapy, notes that "even anger may be supportive if it implies to a patient that others take him seriously enough to get angry at him, especially if the object of the anger feels it to be directed toward his neurotic behavior rather than himself as a person" (1955: 531). In the moot the feeling of support also grows out of the pronouncement of the blessings which stress the unity of the group and its harmonious goal, and it is also undoubtedly increased by the absence of the publicity and expressive symbols of political power which are found in the courtroom.

Permissiveness is the second element in therapy. It indicates to the patient that everyday restrictions on making antisocial statements or acting out antisocial impulses are lessened. Thus, in the Case of the Ousted Wife, Yua felt free enough to turn to her ousted co-wife (who had been married leviratically) and say:

> You don't respect me. You don't rely on me any more. When your husband was living, and I was with my husband, we slept on the farm. Did I ever refuse to send you what you asked me for when you sent a message? Didn't I always send you some of the meat my husband killed? Did I refuse to send you anything you wanted? When your husband died and we became co-wives, did I disrespect you? Why do you always make me ashamed? The things you have done to me make me sad.

Permissiveness in the therapeutic setting (and in the moot) results in catharsis, in a high degree of stimulation of feelings in the participants, and an equally high tendency to verbalize these feelings. Frank notes that "neurotic responses must be expressed in the therapeutic situation if they are to be changed by it" (1955: 531). In the same way, if the solution to a dispute reached in a house palaver is to be stable, it is important that there should be nothing left to embitter and undermine the decision. In a familiar setting, with familiar people, the parties to the moot feel at ease and free to say *all* that is on their minds. Yokpo, judged to be the wronged party in the Case of the Ousted Wife, in accepting an apology, gave expression to this when she said:

> I agree to everything that my people said, and I accept the things they have given me—I don't have *anything else* about them on my mind. (*My italics.*)

As we shall note later, this thorough airing of complaints also facilitates the gaining of insight into and the unlearning of idiosyncratic behavior which is socially disruptive. Permissiveness is rooted in the lack of publicity and the lack of symbols of power. But it stems, too, from the immediacy of the hearing, the locus of investigatory initiative with the parties, and the wide range of relevance.

Permissiveness in therapy is impossible without the denial of reciprocity. This refers to the fact that the therapist will not respond in kind when the patient acts in a hostile manner or with inappropriate affection. It is a type of privileged indulgence which comes with being a patient. In the moot, the parties are treated in the same way and are allowed to hurl recriminations that, in the courtroom, might bring a few hours in jail as punishment for the equivalent of contempt of court. Even though inappropriate views are not responded to in kind, neither are they simply ignored. There is denial of *congruent* response, not denial of *any* response whatsoever. In the *bɛrɛi mu meni saa*, as in group psychotherapy, "private ideation and conceptualization are brought out into the open and all their facets or many of their facets exposed. The individual gets a 'reading' from different bearings on the compass, so to speak, and perceptual patterns ... are joggled out of their fixed positions. . . ." (Klapman, 1959: 39).

Thus, Yua's outburst against Yokpo quoted above was not responded to with matching hostility, but its inappropriateness was clearly pointed out to her by the group. Some of them called her aside in a huddle and said to her:

> You are not right. If you don't like the woman, or she doesn't like you, don't be the first to say anything. Let her start and then say what you have to say. By speaking, if she heeds some of your words, the wives will scatter, and the blame will be on you. Then your husband will cry for your name that you have scattered his property.

In effect, Yua was being told that, in view of the previous testimony, her jealousy of her co-wife was not justified. In reality testing, she discovered that her view of the situation was not shared by the others and, hence, was inappropriate. Noting how the others responded, she could see why her treatment of her co-wife had caused so much dissension. Her interpretation of her new co-wife's actions and resulting premises were not shared by the co-wife, nor by the others hearing a description of what had happened. Like psychotherapy, the moot is gently corrective of behavior rooted in such misunderstandings.

Similarly, Wama Nya, the husband, learned that others did not view as reasonable his accusing his wife of having a lover and urging her to go off and drink with the suspected paramour when he passed their house and wished them all a good evening. Reality testing for him taught him that the group did not view this type of mildly paranoid sarcasm as conducive to stable marital relationships.

The reaction of the moot to Yua's outburst indicates that permissiveness in this case was certainly not complete, but only relative, being much greater than that in the courtroom. But without this moderated immunity the airing of grievances would be limited, and the chance for social relearning lessened. Permissiveness in the moot is incomplete because, even there, prudence is not thrown to the winds. Note that Yua was not told not to express her feelings at all, but to express them only after the co-wife had spoken so that, if the moot failed, she would not be in an untenable position. In court there would be objection to her blunt speaking out. In the moot the objection was, in effect, to her speaking *out of turn*. In other cases the moot sometimes fails, foundering on this very point, because the parties are *too* prudent, all waiting for the others to make the first move in admitting fault.

The manipulation of rewards is the last dimension of therapy treated by Parsons. In this final phase of therapy the patient is coaxed to conformity by the granting of rewards. In the moot one of the most important rewards is the group approval which goes to the wronged person who accepts an apology and to the person who is magnanimous enough to make one.

In the Case of the Ousted Wife, Kɔlɔ Waa, the mediator, and the others attending decided that the husband and the co-wife, Yua, had wronged Yokpo. Kɔlɔ Waa said to the husband:

> From now on, we don't want to hear of your fighting. You should live in peace with these women. If your wife accepts the things which the people have brought, you should pay four chickens and ten bottles of rum as your contribution.

The husband's brother and sister also brought gifts of apology, although the moot did not explicitly hold them at fault.

By giving these prestations, the wrongdoer is restored to good grace and is once again acting like an "upright Kpelle" (although, if he wishes, he may refuse to accept the decision of the moot). He is eased into this position by being grouped with others to whom blame is also allocated, for, typically, he is not singled out and isolated in being labeled deviant. Thus, in the Case of the Ousted Wife the children of Yokpo were held to be at fault in "being mean" to their stepfather, so that blame was not only shared by one "side," but ascribed to the other also.

Moreover, the prestations which the losing party is asked to hand over are not expensive. They are significant enough to touch the pocketbook a little; for the Kpelle say that if an apology does not cost something other than words, the wrongdoer is more likely to repeat the offending action. At the same time, as we noted, the tokens are not so costly as to give the loser additional reason for anger directed at the other party which can undermine the decision.

All in all, the rewards for conformity to group expectations and for following out a new behavior pattern are kept within the deviant's sight. These rewards are positive, in contrast to the negative sanctions of the court-room. Besides the institutionalized apology, praise and acts of concern and affection replace fines and jail sentences. The mediator, speaking to Yokpo as the wronged party, said:

> You have found the best of the dispute. Your husband has wronged you. All the people have wronged you. You are the only one who can take care of them because you are the oldest. Accept the things they have given to you.

The moot in its procedural features and procedural sequences is, then, strongly analogous to psychotherapy. It is analogous to therapy in the structuring of the role of the mediator also. Parsons has indicated that, to do his job well, the therapist must be a member of two social systems: one containing himself and his patient; and the other, society at large (1951: 314). He must not be seduced into thinking that he belongs only to the therapeutic dyad, but must gradually pull the deviant back into a relationship with the wider group. It is significant, then, that the mediator of a moot is a kinsman who is also a chief of some sort. He thus represents both the group involved in the dispute and the wider community. His task is to utilize his position as kinsman as a lever to manipulate the parties into living up to the normative requirements of the wider society, which, as chief, he upholds. His major orientation must be to the wider collectivity, not to the particular goals of his kinsmen.

When successful, the moot stops the process of alienation which drives two spouses so far apart that they are immune to ordinary social control measures such as a smile, a frown, or a pointed aside. A moot is not always successful, however. Both parties must have a genuine willingness to cooperate and a real concern about their discord. Each party must be willing to list his grievances, to admit his guilt, and make an open apology. The moot, like psychotherapy, is impotent without well-motivated clients.

The fact that the Kpelle court is basically coercive and the moot therapeutic does not imply that one is dysfunctional while the other is eufunctional. The court and informal dispute settlement procedures have separate but complementary functions. In marital disputes the moot is oriented to a couple as a dyadic social system and serves to reconcile them wherever possible. This is eufunctional from the point of view of the couple, to whom divorce would be dysfunctional. Kpelle courts customarily treat matrimonial matters by granting a divorce. While this may be dysfunctional from the point of view of the couple, because it ends their marriage, it may be eufunctional from the point of view of society. Some marriages, if forced to continue, would result in adultery or physical violence at best, and improper socialization of children at worst. It is clear that the Kpelle moot is to the Kpelle court as the domestic and family relations courts (or commercial and labor arbitration boards) are to ordinary courts in our own society. The essential point is that both formal and informal dispute-settlement procedures serve significant functions in Kpelle society and neither can be fully understood if studied alone.

REFERENCES

Bohannan, P.
   1957   *Justice and judgment among the Tiv*. London and New York: Oxford Univ. Press.
Frank, J. D.
   1955   Group methods in psychotherapy. *Mental health and mental disorder: A sociological approach*, edited by A. Rose, pp. 524–535. New York: Norton.
Gibbs, J. L., Jr.
   1962   Poro values and courtroom precedures in a Kpelle chiefdom. *Southwestern Journal of Anthropology* **18** (1962): 341–350.
Gluckman, M.
   1955   *The judicial process among the Barotse of Northern Rhodesia*. Manchester, England: Manchester Univ. Press.
Howell, P. P.
   1954   *A handbook of Nuer law*. London and New York: Oxford Univ. Press.
Klapman, J. W.
   1959   *Group psychotherapy: Theory and practice*. New York: Grune & Stratton.
Murdock, G. P.
   1949   *Social structure*. New York: Macmillan.
Opler, M. K.
   1959   Values in group psychotherapy. *International Journal of Social Psychiatry* **4** (Spring): 296–298.
Parsons, T.
   1951   *The social system*. New York: Free Press.

LEGAL EVOLUTION AND SOCIETAL COMPLEXITY

Richard D. Schwartz
James C. Miller

T HE STUDY of legal evolution has traditionally com-
mended itself to scholars in a variety of fields. To mention only a few, it has
been a concern in sociology of Weber (1954)[1] and Durkheim (1947); in jurisprudence of Dicey (1905), Holmes (1881),[2] Pound (1917, 1930, 1943), and
Llewellyn (1960); in anthropology of Maine (1917) and Hoebel (1954); in
legal history of Savigny (1931) and Vinogradoff (1920–1922).

[1] For a discussion and development of Weber's thinking on legal evolution, see Talcott Parsons
(1964: 350–353).

[2] Holmes's discussion of the place and limitations of historical analysis provides an appropriate
background for the present study:

> The law embodies the story of a nation's development through many centuries, and it cannot be
> dealt with as if it contained only the axioms and corollaries of a book of mathematics. In order
> to know what it is, we must know what is has been, and what it tends to become. But the most
> difficult labor will be to understand the combination of the two into new products at every stage.
> The substance of the law at any given time pretty nearly corresponds, so far as it goes, with what
> is then understood to be convenient; but its form and machinery, and the degree to which it is able
> to work out desired results depend very much on its past (1881:1–2).

In stressing history as providing an explanation for procedure rather than substance, Holmes points
to those aspects of legal development that—in the present study at least—appear to follow highly uniform
sequences of change.

Reprinted from "Legal Evolution and Societal Complexity" by Richard D. Schwartz and James C. Miller,
American Journal of Sociology, Vol. 20 (1964): pp. 159–169. © 1964 by the University of Chicago. All
rights reserved.

There are theoretical and practical reasons for this interest. Legal evolution[3] provides an opportunity to investigate the relations between law and other major aspects and institutions of society. Thus Maine explained the rise of contract in terms of the declining role of kinship as an exclusive basis of social organization. Durkheim saw restitutive sanctions replacing repressive ones as a result of the growth of the division of labor and the corresponding shift from mechanical to organic solidarity. Dicey traced the growth of statutory lawmaking in terms of the increasing articulateness and power of public opinion. Weber viewed the development of formal legal rationality as an expression of, and precondition for, the growth of modern capitalism.

For the most part, these writers were interested in the development of legal norms and not in the evolution of legal organization. The latter subject warrants attention for several reasons. As the mechanism through which substantive law is formulated, invoked, and administered, legal organization is of primary importance for understanding the process by which legal norms are evolved and implemented. Moreover, legal organization seems to develop with a degree of regularity that in itself invites attention and explanation. The present study suggests that elements of legal organization emerge in a sequence, such that each constitutes a necessary condition for the next. A second type of regularity appears in the relationship between changes in legal organization and other aspects of social organization, notably the division of labor.

By exploring such regularities intensively, it may be possible to learn more about the dynamics of institutional differentiation. Legal organization is a particularly promising subject from this point of view. It tends toward a unified, easily identifiable structure in any given society. Its form and procedures are likely to be explicitly stated. Its central function, legitimation, promotes cross-culturally recurrent instances of conflict with, and adaptation to, other institutional systems such as religion, polity, economy, and family. Before these relationships can be adequately explored, however, certain gross regularities of development should be noted and it is with these that the present paper is primarily concerned.

This article reports preliminary findings from cross-cultural research that show a rather startling consistency in the pattern of legal evolution. In a sample of 51 societies, compensatory damages and mediation of disputes

---

[3]The term "evolution" is used here in the minimal sense of a regular sequence of changes over time in a given type of unit, in this case, societies. This usage neither implies nor precludes causal links among the items in the sequence. For a discussion of diverse uses of, and reactions to, the term "evolution," see Tax (1960).

were found in every society having specialized legal counsel. In addition, a large majority (85%) of societies that develop specialized police also employ damages and mediation. These findings suggest a variety of explanations. It may be necessary, for instance, for a society to accept the principles of mediation and compensation before formalized agencies of adjudication and control can be evolved. Alternatively or concurrently, nonlegal changes may explain the results. A formalized means of exchange, some degree of specialization, and writing appear almost universally to follow certain of these legal developments and to precede others. If such sequences are inevitable, they suggest theoretically interesting causative relationships and provide a possible basis for assigning priorities in stimulating the evolution of complex legal institutions in the contemporary world.

METHOD

This research employed a method used by Freeman and Winch in their analysis of societal complexity (1957). Studying a sample of 48 societies, they noted a Guttman-scale relationship among six items associated with the folk–urban continuum. The following items were found to fall in a single dimension ranging, the authors suggest, from simple to complex: a symbolic medium of exchange; punishment of crimes through government action; religious, educational, and government specialization; and writing.[4]

To permit the location of legal characteristics on the Freeman–Winch scale, substantially the same sample was used in this study. Three societies were dropped because of uncertainty as to date and source of description[5] or because of inadequate material on legal characteristics.[6] Six societies were

---

[4]This ordering has not been reproduced in other studies that followed similar procedures. Freeman repeated the study on another sample and included four of the six items used in the first study. They scaled in a markedly different order, from simple to complex: government specialization, religious specialization, symbolic medium of exchange, writing. The marked change in position of the first and third items appears attributable to changes in definition for these terms (Freeman, 1957:45, 49–50, 80–83). Young and Young studied all six items in a cross-cultural sample of communities, changing only the definition of punishment. Their ordering is somewhat closer to, but not identical with, that found by Freeman and Winch (1957). From simple to complex, the items were ordered as follows: punishment, symbolic medium of exchange, governmental specialization, religious specialization, writing, educational specialization (Young and Young, 1962: 378–379).

In the present study, we will rely on the Freeman–Winch ratings and orderings, since the samples overlap so heavily. The reader should bear in mind, however, that the order is tentative and contingent upon the specific definitions used in that study.

[5]Southeastern American Negroes and ancient Hebrews.

[6]Sanpoil.

added, three to cover the legally developed societies more adequately[7] and three to permit the inclusion of certain well-described control systems.[8]

Several characteristics of a fully developed legal system were isolated for purposes of study. These included counsel, mediation, and police. These three characteristics, which will constitute the focus of the present paper,[9] are defined as follows:

counsel: regular use of specialized nonkin advocates in the settlement of disputes,

mediation: regular use of nonkin third party intervention in dispute settlement,

police: specialized armed force used partially or wholly for norm enforcement.

These three items, all referring to specialized roles relevant to dispute resolution, were found to fall in a near-perfect Guttman scale. Before the central findings are described and discussed, several methodological limitations should be noted.

First, despite efforts by Murdock (1957) and others, no wholly satisfactory method has been devised for obtaining a representative sample of the world's societies. Since the universe of separate societies has not been adequately defined, much less enumerated, the representativeness of the sample cannot be ascertained. Nevertheless, an effort has been made to include societies drawn from the major culture areas and from diverse stages of technological development.

---

[7] Three societies—Cambodian, Indonesian, and Syrian—were selected from the Human Relations Area Files to increase the number of societies with counsel. The procedure for selection consisted of a random ordering of the societies in the Human Relations Area Files until three with counsel were located in geographically separate regions. These were then examined to determine the presence or absence of other legal characteristics. The random search eliminated the possibility of a bias in favor of societies conforming to the scale type.

The three societies were quota sampled by region to represent a randomly determined three of the following six regions: Asia, Africa, the Middle East, North America, South America, and Oceania. Purposely omitted from the sample were Europe and Russia because they were already represented in the "counsel" type in the Freeman–Winch sample. Selection from different regions was designed to avoid the problem, first noted by Francis Galton, that cross-cultural regularities might be due to diffusion rather than to functional interrelationships. For a discussion of the problem and evidence of the importance of geographical separateness in sampling, see Naroll (1961, 1964), and Naroll and D'Andrade (1963).

[8] These three—Cheyenne, Comanche, and Trobrianders—were selected by James C. Miller before the hypothesis was known to him. Selection of both the Comanche and Cheyenne is subject to some criticism on the grounds that they were prone to diffusion, but this hardly seems a serious difficulty in view of the difference in their scale positions. At all events, the coefficients of reproducibility and scalability would not be seriously lowered by eliminating one of the two.

[9] The original study also included damages, imprisonment, and execution. These were dropped from the present analysis, even though this unfortunately limited the scale to three items, to permit focus on statuses rather than sanction. Data on damages will be introduced, however, where relevant to the discussion of restitution.

Second, societies have been selected in terms of the availability of adequate ethnographic reports. As a result, a bias may have entered the sample through the selection of societies that were particularly accessible—and hospitable—to anthropological observers. Such societies may differ in their patterns of development from societies that have been less well studied.

Third, despite the selection of relatively well-studied societies, the quality of reports varies widely. Like the preceding limitations, this problem is common to all cross-cultural comparisons. The difficulty is mitigated, however, by the fact that the results of this study are positive. The effect of poor reporting should generally be to randomize the apparent occurrence of the variables studied. Where systematic patterns of relationship emerge, as they do in the present research, it would seem to indicate considerable accuracy in the original reports (see Campbell, 1961: 347).[10]

Fourth, this study deals with characteristics whose presence or absence can be determined with relative accuracy. In so doing, it may neglect elements of fundamental importance to the basic inquiry. Thus no effort is made to observe the presence of such important phenomena as respect for law, the use of generalized norms, and the pervasiveness of deviance-induced disturbance. Although all of these should be included in a comprehensive theory of legal evolution, they are omitted here in the interest of observational reliability.[11]

Fifth, the Guttman scale is here pressed into service beyond that for which

---

[10]This inference should be treated with caution, however, in light of Raoul Naroll's observation that systematic observer bias can lead to spurious correlations (1962).

[11]Determination of the presence of a characteristic was made after a detailed search by Miller of the materials on each society in the Human Relations Area Files. His search began with a thorough reading for all societies of the material filed under category 18 "total culture." [All categories used are described in detail in Murdock *et al.* (1961).] This was followed by a search of the annotated bibliography (category 111) to locate any works specifically dealing with legal or dispute-settling processes. When found, works of this kind were examined in detail. In addition, materials filed under the following categories were read: community structure (621), headmen (622), councils (623), police (625), informal in-group justice (627), intercommunity relations (628), territorial hierarchy (631), legal norms (671), liability (672), offenses and sanctions (68), litigation (691), judicial authority (692), legal and judicial personnel (693), initiation of judicial proceedings (694), trial procedure (695), execution of justice (696), prisons and jails (697), and special courts (698). If this search did not reveal the presence of the practice or status under investigation, it was assumed absent. The principal sources relied on for these determinations are given in a mimeographed bibliography which will be supplied by the authors on request.

A reliability check on Miller's judgments was provided by Robert C. Scholl, to whom the writers are indebted. Working independently and without knowledge of the hypotheses, Scholl examined a randomly selected third of the total sample. His judgments agreed with those of Miller 88%, disagreed 4%, and he was unable to reach conclusions on 8% of the items. If the inconclusive judgments are excluded, the reliability reaches the remarkable level of 96%.

The use of a single person to check reliability falls short of the desired standard. In a more detailed and extensive projected study of the relationships reported here, we plan to use a set of three independent naïve judges. For discussion of the problems involved in judging cross-cultural materials see Whiting and Child (1953: 39–62), and Swanson (1960: 32–54).

it was developed. Originally conceived as a technique for the isolation of uni-dimensional attitudes, it has also been used as a means of studying the inter-relationship of behavior patterns. It should be particularly valuable, however, in testing hypotheses concerning developmental sequences, whether in individuals or in societies.[12] Thus, if we hypothesize that A must precede B, supporting data should show three scale types: neither A nor B, A but not B, and A and B. All instances of B occurring without A represent errors which lower the reproducibility of the scale and, by the same token, throw doubt in measurable degree on the developmental hypothesis.[13] Although the occur-rence of developmental sequences ultimately requires verification by the observation of historic changes in given units, substantiating evidence can be derived from the comparative study of units at varying stages of develop-ment. The Guttman scale seems an appropriate quantitative instrument for this purpose.

FINDINGS

In the 51 societies studied, as indicated in Table 1 (pages 386–387), four scale types emerged. Eleven societies showed none of the three characteristics; 18 had only mediation; 11 had only mediation and police; and 7 had mediation, police, and specialized counsel. Two societies departed from these patterns: the Crow and the Thonga had police, but showed no evidence of mediation. While these deviant cases merit detailed study, they reduce the reproducibility of the scale by less than 2%, leaving the coefficient

---

[12] The use of the Guttman scale is extensively treated by Robert L. Carneiro (1962). In a sophisticated critique of the Carneiro paper, Ward L. Goodenough (1963) suggests that quasi-scales may be needed for charting general evolutionary trends and for treating the traits that develop and then fail to persist because they are superseded by functional equivalents. While the quasi-scale is a desirable instrument for analyzing supersedence, Goodenough appears unduly pessimistic about the possible occurrence of approxi-mately perfect scales (p. 246). Studies that obtained such scales, in addition to the one reported here, include Freeman and Winch (1957); Udy (1958); Young and Young (1962); Carneiro and Tobias (1963).

The suggestion that Guttman scales could be used for discovering and testing temporal sequences was made earlier by Háwkins and Jackson (1957). Their proposal referred, however, to individuals rather than societies.

[13] The developmental inference does not preclude the possibility of reversal of the usual sequence. It merely indicates which item will be added if any is acquired. Cf. Eisenstadt (1964: 378–381). The finding of a scale also does not rule out the possibility that two items may sometimes occur simultaneously, although the existence of all possible scale types indicates that no two items invariably occur simultaneously and that when they occur separately one regularly precedes the other.

at the extraordinarily high level of better than .98.[14] Each characteristic of legal organization may now be discussed in terms of the sociolegal conditions in which it is found.

MEDIATION

Societies that lack mediation, constituting less than a third of the entire sample, appear to be the simplest societies. None of them has writing or any substantial degree of specialization.[15] Only three of the thirteen (Yurok, Kababish, and Thonga) use money, whereas almost three-fourths of the societies with mediation have a symbolic means of exchange. We can only speculate at present on the reasons why mediation is absent in these societies. Data on size, using Naroll's definition of the social unit, indicate that the maximum community size of societies without mediation is substantially smaller than that of societies with mediation.[16] Because of their small size, mediationless societies may have fewer disputes and thus have less opportunity to evolve regularized patterns of dispute settlement. Moreover, smaller societies may be better able to develop mores and informal controls which tend to prevent the occurrence of disputes. Also, the usually desperate struggle for existence of such societies may strengthen the common goal of survival and thus produce a lessening of intragroup hostility.

The lack of money and substantial property may also help to explain the absence of mediation in these societies. There is much evidence to support the hypothesis that property provides something to quarrel about. In addi-

---

[14]This coefficient of reproducibility far exceeds the .90 level suggested by Guttman as an "efficient approximation . . . of perfect scales" (Stouffer, 1950: 77). The coefficient of scalability, designed by Menzel to take account of extremeness in the distribution of items and individuals, far exceeds the .65 level that he generated from a scalability analysis of Guttman's American Soldier data (Menzel, 1953: 276). The problem of determining goodness of fit for the Guttman scale has still not been satisfactorily resolved (see Torgerson, 1958:324). A method utilizing χ^2 to test the hypothesis that observed scale frequencies deviate from a rectangular distribution no more than would be expected by chance is suggested by Schuessler (1961). Applied to these data, Schuessler's Test II permits the rejection of the chance hypothesis at the .001 level. $\chi^2 = 60.985$ (7 df).

[15]Statements of this type are based on the ratings in the Freeman–Winch study, as noted in footnote 4. For societies that did not appear in their sample, we have made our own ratings on the basis of their definitions.

[16]Data were obtained for thirty-nine of the fifty-one societies in the sample on the size of their largest settlement. Societies with mediation have a median largest settlement size of 1000, while those without mediation have a median of 346. Even eliminating the societies with developed cities, the median largest settlement size remains above 500 for societies with mediation.

TABLE 1
SCALE OF LEGAL CHARACTERISTICS

Society	Counsel	Police	Mediation	Errors	Legal scale type	Freeman— Winch scale type
Cambodians	×	×	×		3	*
Czechs	×	×	×		3	6
Elizabethan English	×	×	×		3	6
Imperial Romans	×	×	×		3	6
Indonesians	×	×	×		3	*
Syrians	×	×	×		3	*
Ukrainians	×	×	×		3	6
Ashanti		×	×		2	5
Cheyenne		×	×		2	*
Creek		×	×		2	5
Cuna		×	×		2	4
Crow		×		1	2	0
Hopi		×	×		2	5
Iranians		×	×		2	6
Koreans		×	×		2	6
Lapps		×	×		2	6
Maori		×	×		2	4
Riffians		×	×		2	6
Thonga		×		1	2	2
Vietnamese		×	×		2	6
Andamanese			×		1	0
Azande			×		1	0
Balinese			×		1	4
Cayapa			×		1	2
Chagga			×		1	4
Formosan aborigines			×		1	0
Hottentot			×		1	0
Ifugao			×		1	0
Lakher			×		1	2
Lepcha			×		1	3
Menomini			×		1	0
Mbundu			×		1	3
Navaho			×		1	5
Ossett			×		1	1
Siwans			×		1	1
Trobrianders			×		1	*
Tupinamba			×		1	0
Venda			×		1	5
Woleaians			×		1	0
Yakut			×		1	1
Aranda					0	0
Buka					0	0
Chukchee					0	0
Comanche					0	*

TABLE 1 (continued)

Society	Counsel	Police	Mediation	Errors	Legal scale type	Freeman–Winch scale type
Copper Eskimo					0	0
Jivaro					0	0
Kababish					0	1
Kazak					0	0
Siriono					0	0
Yaruro					0	0
Yurok					0	1

*Not included in Freeman–Winch sample.

Coefficient of reproducibility = $1 - 2/153$ = .987; coefficient of scalability = $1 - 2/(153 - 120)$ = .94; Kendall's tau = $+.68$.

tion, it seems to provide something to mediate with as well. Where private property is extremely limited, one would be less likely to find a concept of damages, that is, property payments in lieu of other sanctions. The development of a concept of damages should greatly increase the range of alternative settlements. This in turn might be expected to create a place for the mediator as a person charged with locating a settlement point satisfactory to the parties and the society.

This hypothesis derives support from the data in Table 2. The concept of damages occurs in all but 4 of the 38 societies that have mediation and thus appears to be virtually a precondition for mediation. It should be noted, however, that damages are also found in several (seven of thirteen) of the societies that lack mediation. The relationship that emerges is one of damages as a necessary but not sufficient condition for mediation. At present it is impossible to ascertain whether the absence of mediation in societies having the damage concept results from a simple time lag or whether some other factor, not considered in this study, distinguishes these societies from those that have developed mediation.

TABLE 2

DAMAGES IN RELATION TO LEGAL FUNCTIONARIES

	No mediation	Mediation only	Mediation and police	Mediation, police, and counsel	Total
Damages	7	17	10	7	41
No damages	6*	3	1	0	10
Total	13	20	11	7	51

*Includes Thonga, who have neither mediation nor damages, but have police.

POLICE

Twenty societies in the sample had police—that is, a specialized armed force available for norm enforcement. As noted, all of these but the Crow and Thonga had the concept of damages and some kind of mediation as well. Nevertheless, the occurrence of twenty societies with mediation but without police makes it clear that mediation is not inevitably accompanied by the systematic enforcement of decisions. The separability of these two characteristics is graphically illustrated in ethnographic reports. A striking instance is found among the Albanian tribesmen whose elaborately developed code for settling disputes, *Lek's Kanun*, was used for centuries as a basis for mediation. But in the absence of mutual agreements by the disputants, feuds often began immediately after adjudication and continued unhampered by any constituted police (Hasluck, 1954).

From the data it is possible to determine some of the characteristics of societies that develop police. Eighteen of the twenty in our sample are economically advanced enough to use money. They also have a substantial degree of specialization, with full-time priests and teachers found in all but three (Cheyenne, Thonga, and Crow), and full-time governmental officials, not mere relatives of the chief, present in all but four (Cuna, Maori, Thonga, and Crow).

Superficially at least, these findings seem directly contradictory to Durkheim's major thesis in *The Division of Labor in Society*. He hypothesized that penal law—the effort of the organized society to punish offenses against itself—occurs in societies with the simplest division of labor. As indicated, however, our data show that police are found only in association with a substantial degree of division of labor. Even the practice of governmental punishment for wrongs against the society (as noted by Freeman and Winch, 1957) does not appear in simpler societies. By contrast, restitutive sanctions—damages and mediation—which Durkheim believed to be associated with an increasing division of labor, are found in many societies that lack even rudimentary specialization. Thus Durkheim's hypothesis seems the reverse of the empirical situation in the range of societies studied here.[17]

[17] A basic difficulty in testing Durkheim's thesis arises from his manner of formulating it. His principal interest, as we understand it, was to show the relationship between division of labor and type of sanction (using type of solidarity as the intervening variable). However, in distinguishing systems of law, he added the criterion of organization. The difficulty is that he was very broad in his criterion of organization required for penal law but quite narrow in describing the kind of organization needed for nonpenal law. For the former the "assembly of the whole people" sufficed (Durkheim, 1947: 76); for the latter, on the other hand, he suggested the following criteria: "restitutive law creates organs which are more and more specialized: consular tribunals, councils of arbitration, administrative tribunals of every sort. Even in its most general part, that which pertains to civil law, it is exercised only through particular functionaries: magistrates, lawyers, etc., who have become apt in this role because of very special training" (p. 113). In thus suggesting

COUNSEL

Seven societies in the sample employ specialized advocates in the settlement of disputes. As noted, all of these societies also use mediation. There are, however, another thirty-one societies that have mediation but do not employ specialized counsel. It is a striking feature of the data that damages and mediation are characteristic of the simplest (as well as the most complex) societies, while legal counsel are found only in the most complex. The societies with counsel also have, without exception, not only damages, mediation, and police but, in addition, all of the complexity characteristics identified by Freeman and Winch.

It is not surprising that mediation is not universally associated with counsel. In many mediation systems the parties are expected to speak for themselves. The mediator tends to perform a variety of functions, questioning disputants as well as deciding on the facts and interpreting the law. Such a system is found even in complex societies, such as Imperial China. There the prefect acted as counsel, judge, and jury, using a whip to wring the truth from the parties who were assumed *a priori* to be lying (van der Sprenkel, 1962; T'ung-tsu, 1961). To serve as counsel in that setting would have been painful as well as superfluous. Even where specialized counsel emerge, their role tends to be ambiguous. In ancient Greece, for instance, counsel acted principally as advisors on strategy. Upon appearance in court they sought to conceal the fact that they were specialists in legal matters, presenting themselves merely as friends of the parties or even on occasion assuming the identity of the parties themselves (Chroust, 1954).

At all events, lawyers are here found only in quite urbanized societies, all of which are based upon fully developed agricultural economies. The data suggest at least two possible explanations. First, all of the sample societies with counsel have a substantial division of labor, including priests, teachers, police, and government officials. This implies an economic base strong enough to support a variety of secondary and tertiary occupations as well as an understanding of the advantages of specialization. Eleven societies in the sample, however, have all of these specialized statuses but lack specialized

---

Footnote 17 *continued*

that restitutive law exists only with highly complex organizational forms, Durkheim virtually insured that his thesis would be proven—that restitutive law would be found only in complex societies.

Such a "proof," however, would miss the major point of his argument. In testing the main hypothesis it would seem preferable, therefore, to specify a common and minimal organizational criterion, such as public support. Then the key question might be phrased: Is there a tendency toward restitutive rather than repressive sanctions which develops as an increasing function of the division of labor? Although our present data are not conclusive, the finding of damages and mediation in societies with minimal division of labor implies a negative answer. This suggests that the restitutive principle is not contingent on social heterogeneity or that heterogeneity is not contingent on the division of labor.

counsel. What distinguishes the societies that develop counsel? Literacy would seem to be an important factor. Only five of the twelve literate societies in the sample do not have counsel. Writing, of course, makes possible the formulation of a legal code with its advantages of forewarning the violator and promoting uniformity in judicial administration. The need to interpret a legal code provides a niche for specialized counsel, especially where a substantial segment of the population is illiterate.[18]

CONCLUSIONS

These data, taken as a whole, lend support to the belief that an evolutionary sequence occurs in the development of legal institutions. Alternative interpretations are, to be sure, not precluded. The scale analysis might fail to discern short-lived occurrences of items. For instance, counsel might regularly develop as a variation in simple societies even before police, only to drop out rapidly enough so that the sample picks up no such instances. Even though this is a possibility in principle, no cases of this kind have come to the authors' attention.

Another and more realistic possibility is that the sequence noted in this sample does not occur in societies in a state of rapid transition. Developing societies undergoing intensive cultural contact might provide an economic and social basis for specialized lawyers, even in the absence of police or dispute mediation. Until such societies are included in the sample, these

[18]Throughout the discussion, two sets of explanatory factors have been utilized. The observed pattern could be due to an internal process inherent in legal control systems, or it could be dependent upon the emergence of urban characteristics. It does seem clear, however, that the legal developments coincide to a considerable extent with increased "urbanism" as measured by Freeman and Winch. Evidence for this assertion is to be found in the correlation between the Freeman–Winch data and the legal scale types discerned. For the 45 societies appearing in both samples, the rank correlation coefficient (Kendall's tau) between positions on the legal and urbanism scales is + .68. While this coefficient suggests a close relationship between the two processes, it does not justify the assertion that legal evolution is wholly determined by increasing urbanism. A scatter diagram of the interrelationship reveals that legal characteristics tend to straddle the regression line for five of the seven folk-urban scale positions, omitting only scale types 2 (punishment) and 3 (religious specialization). This suggests that some other factor might emerge upon further analysis that would explain why roughly half of the societies at each stage of urbanism appear to have gone on to the next stage of legal evolution while the others lag behind. A promising candidate for such a factor is the one located by Gouldner and Peterson in their cross-cultural factor analysis of Simmons' data and described by them as "Apollonianism" or "Norm-sending" (Gouldner and Peterson, 1962: 30–53).

To test whether the legal sequence has a "dynamic of its own," it would seem necessary to examine the growth of legal systems independent of folk-urban changes, as in subsystems or in societies where the process of urbanization has already occurred. The data covered here do not permit such a test.

findings must be limited to relatively isolated, slowly changing societies.

The study also raises but does not answer questions concerning the evolution of an international legal order. It would be foolhardy to generalize from the primitive world directly to the international scene and to assume that the same sequences must occur here as there. There is no certainty that sub-tribal units can be analogized to nations, because the latter tend to be so much more powerful, independent, and relatively deficient in common culture and interests. In other ways, the individual nations are farther along the path of legal development than subtribal units because all of them have their own domestic systems of mediation, police, and counsel. This state of affairs might well provide a basis for short-circuiting an evolutionary tendency operative in primitive societies. Then too, the emergent world order appears to lack the incentive of common interest against a hostile environment that gave primitive societies a motive for legal control. Even though the survival value of a legal system may be fully as great in today's world as for primitive societies the existence of multiple units in the latter case permitted selection for survival of those societies that had developed the adaptive characteristic. The same principle cannot be expected to operate where the existence of "one world" permits no opportunity for variation and consequent selection.

Nonetheless, it is worth speculation that some of the same forces may operate in both situations.[19] We have seen that damages and mediation almost always precede police in the primitive world. The sequence could result from the need to build certain cultural foundations in the community before a central regime of control, as reflected in a police force, can develop. Hypothetically, this cultural foundation might include a determination to avoid disputes, an appreciation of the value of third-party intervention, and the development of a set of norms both for preventive purposes and as a basis for allocating blame and punishment when disputes arise. Compensation by damages and the use of mediators might well contribute to the development of such a cultural foundation, as well as reflecting its growth. If so, their occurrence prior to specialized police would be understandable. This raises the question as to whether the same kind of cultural foundation is not a necessary condition for the establishment of an effective world police force and whether, in the interest of that objective, it might not be appropriate to stress the principles of compensatory damages and mediation as pre-conditions for the growth of a world rule of law.

[19] For an interesting attempt to develop a general theory of legal control, applicable both to discrete societies and to the international order, see Carlston (1962).

ACKNOWLEDGMENTS

The authors are indebted to Arnold S. Feldman, Raoul Naroll, Terrence Tatje, and Robert F. Winch for their helpful comments on this paper. A grant from the Graduate School of Northwestern University aided in the completion of the work.

REFERENCES

Campbell, D. T.
  1961   The mutual methodological relevance of anthropology and psychology. In *Psychological anthropology*, edited by F. L. K. Hsu, pp. 333–352. Homewood, Illinois: Dorsey Press.
Carlston, K. S.
  1962   *Law and organization in world society*. Urbana: Univ. of Illinois Press.
Carneiro, R. L.
  1962   Scale analysis as an instrument for the study of cultural evolution. *Southwestern Journal of Anthropology* 18 (1962): 149–169.
Carneiro, R. L., and S. L. Tobias
  1963   The application of scale analysis to the study of cultural evolution. *Transactions of the New York Academy of Science, Series 2*, 26 (1963): 196–207.
Chroust, A. H.
  1954   The legal profession in ancient Athens. *Notre Dame Law Review* 29 (Spring): 339–389.
Dicey, A. V.
  1905   *Lectures on the relation between law and public opinion in England during the nineteenth century*. London: Macmillan.
Durkheim, E.
  1947   *The division of labor in society*. New York: Free Press. (Orig. pub. 1893.)
Eisenstadt, S. N.
  1964   Social change, differentiation and evolution. *American Sociological Review* 29 (June): 378–381.
Freeman, L. C.
  1957   An empirical test of folk-urbanism. Unpublished Ph. D. Dissertation, Department of Sociology, Northwestern University.
Freeman, L. C., and R. F. Winch
  1957   Societal complexity: An empirical test of a typology of societies. *American Journal of Sociology* 62 (March): 461–466.
Goodenough, W. L.
  1963   Some applications of Guttman scale analysis to ethnography and culture theory. *Southwestern Journal of Anthropology* 19 (Autumn): 235–250.
Gouldner, A. W., and R. A. Peterson
  1962   *Technology and the moral order*. Indianapolis: Bobbs-Merrill.
Hasluck, M.
  1954   *The unwritten law in Albania*. London and New York: Cambridge Univ. Press.
Hawkins, N. G., and J. K. Jackson
  1957   Scale analysis and the prediction of life processes. *American Sociological Review* 22 (1957): 579–581.
Hoebel, E. A.
  1954   *The law of primitive man: A study in comparative legal dynamics*. Cambridge: Harvard Univ. Press.

Holmes, O. W., Jr.
1881 *The common law.* Boston: Little, Brown.
Llewellyn, K. N.
1960 *The common law tradition: Deciding appeals.* Boston: Little, Brown.
Maine, H. S.
1917 *Ancient law.* London: Dent. (Orig. pub. 1861).
Menzel, H. A.
1953 A new coefficient for scalogram analysis. *Public Opinion Quarterly* **17** (Summer): 268–280.
Murdock, G. P.
1957 World ethnographic sample. *American Anthropologist* **59** (August): 664–687.
Murdock, G. P., *et al.*
1961 *Outline of cultural materials.* (4th ed.) New Haven: Human Relations Area Files.
Naroll, R.
1961 Two solutions to Galton's problem. *Philosophy of Science* **28** (1961): 15–39.
1962 *Data quality control: A new research technique.* New York. Free Press.
1964 A fifth solution to Galton's problem. *American Anthropologist* **64** (1964): 863–867.
Naroll, R., and R. G. D'Andrade
1963 Two further solutions to Galton's problem. *American Anthropologist* **65** (October): 1053–1067.
Parsons, T.
1964 Evolutionary universals in society. *American Sociological Review* **29** (June): 339–357.
Pound, R.
1917 Limits of effective legal action. *International Journal of Ethics* **27** (1917): 150–165.
1930 *Interpretations of legal history.* London: Macmillan.
1943 *Outlines of lectures on jurisprudence.* (5th ed.) Cambridge: Harvard Univ. Press.
Savigny, F. von
1831 *Of the vocation of our age for legislation and jurisprudence.* London: Littlewood.
Schuessler, K. F.
1961 A note on statistical significance of scalogram. *Sociometry* **24** (September): 312–318.
Stouffer, S., *et al.*
1950 *Measurement and prediction.* Princeton: Princeton Univ. Press.
Swanson, G. E.
1960 *The birth of the gods.* Ann Arbor: Univ. of Michigan Press.
Tax, S. (Ed.).
1960 *Issues in evolution.* Chicago: Univ. of Chicago Press.
Torgerson, W. S.
1958 *Theory and methods of scaling.* New York: J. Wiley.
T'ung-tsu, C.
1961 *Law and society in traditional China.* Vancouver, B. C.: Institute of Pacific Relations.
Udy, S. H.
1958 Bureaucratic elements in organizations: some research findings. *American Sociological Review* **22** (1958): 415–420.
van der Sprenkel, S.
1962 *Legal institutions in Manchu China.* London: Athlone Press.
Vinogradoff, P.
1920–1922 *Outlines of historical jurisprudence,* Vol. 1 and 2. London and New York: Oxford Univ. Press.
Weber, M.
1954 *Law in economy and society.* Cambridge: Harvard Univ. Press. (Orig. pub. 1922.)

Whiting, J. W. M., and I. L. Child.
  1953   *Child training and personality.* New Haven: Yale Univ. Press.
Young, F. W., and R. C. Young
  1962   The sequence and direction of community growth: A cross-cultural generalization. *Rural Sociology* **27** (December): 374–386.

AUTHOR INDEX

Numbers in italics refer to the pages on which the complete references are listed.

SUBJECT INDEX